D1525576

CAMBRIDGE SOUTH ASIAN STUDIES

THE STATE AND
PEASANT POLITICS
IN SRI LANKA

A list of the books in the series will be found at the end of the volume.

THE STATE AND PEASANT POLITICS IN SRI LANKA

MICK MOORE

*Fellow, Institute of Development Studies
at the University of Sussex*

The right of the
University of Cambridge
to print and sell
all manner of books
was granted by
Henry VIII in 1534.
The University has printed
and published continuously
since 1584.

CAMBRIDGE UNIVERSITY PRESS

CAMBRIDGE

LONDON   NEW YORK   NEW ROCHELLE

MELBOURNE   SYDNEY

Published by the Press Syndicate of the University of Cambridge
The Pitt Building, Trumpington Street, Cambridge CB2 1RP
32 East 57th Street, New York, NY 10022, USA
10 Stamford Road, Oakleigh, Melbourne 3166, Australia

First published 1985

Printed in Great Britain
at the University Press, Cambridge

Library of Congress catalogue card number: 84–29210

British Library cataloguing in publication data
Moore, Mick
The state and peasant politics in Sri Lanka.–
(Cambridge South Asian studies)
1. Peasantry–Sri Lanka   2. Agriculture and
state–Sri Lanka
I. Title
323.3'2   HD1537.S6

ISBN 0 521 26550 9

This book is dedicated to
the memory of
Arthur Charles Moore

CONTENTS

MAPS

TABLES

Tables

ACKNOWLEDGMENTS

I have accumulated such piles of professional debts in the course of producing this book that it is not possible to survey them from a commanding position and assign them orders of magnitude. They are, in an order which is approximately chronological: to the Agrarian Research and Training Institute, Colombo and to the Institute of Development Studies, Sussex, for institutional support; to U. A. Hemachandra, W. M. Wijepala and P. M. Wimalasiri for their extremely willing and loyal assistance in formal field research; to countless Sri Lankans with whom the author has spoken in many different contexts over the past decade; to many academic colleagues from several countries for fruitful discussions over the years; to several Sri Lankan academics, notably Michael Roberts, Vijaya Samaraweera and Ranjit Seneratne, from whose work a great deal of inspiration and historical evidence was drawn; to Ron Dore, Bruce Graham, John Harriss, Michael Lipton, Barrie Morrison and two anonymous referees for comments on earlier drafts, including the doctoral thesis on which this book is based; and to Michael Roberts in particular for giving me the benefit of his detailed knowledge of Sri Lankan history and many useful suggestions after reading an earlier draft.

The essential physical and social infrastructure was provided by: my family (tolerance and vacations foregone); Christine Annells and Katie King (typing); and the Dissanayakes (a home in Colombo).

Mick Moore

May 1984

GLOSSARY OF SRI LANKAN TERMS

ande	Sharecropping tenancy
asweddumise	To undertake the clearing, levelling and bund construction required to convert land into paddy fields
ayurvedic	Homeopathic medical system widely used in Sri Lanka
Berava	A low caste, traditionally drum beaters at ceremonies
bhikkhu	A Buddhist priest
boutique	A small shop
bushel of paddy	The most common measure of yield. It weighs on average about 46 lb and converts after milling to about 31 lb of rice
chena	Shifting cultivation
devalagam	Lands belonging to non-Buddhist temples
Goigama	The highest caste in the Sinhalese caste hierarchy, accounting for about half of the Sinhalese population
Grama Seveka	An appointed public officer, replacing the village headman
JVP	The party which organised the 1971 Insurrection and has since 1978 been contesting elections
Karava	A caste concentrated mainly along the southwestern coast and traditionally associated with fishing
kurakkan	Millet
LSSP	Lanka Sama Samaj Party, until recently the largest of the Marxist parties
Maha	The main cultivating season, beginning around September
Malayali	A person from Kerala State in South India
MEP	1. The SLFP-dominated coalition which won the 1956 general election
	2. A small Marxist/Sinhalese nationalist party set up by Philip Gunawardena in 1959

mudalali	A trader or shopkeeper
nindagam	Lands held under feudal tenure by the Kandyan aristocracy
Perahera	A ceremonial procession
Radala	The Kandyan aristocracy
Raja Rata	'The land of the kings' – the North Central Province, the locale of the historic Sinhalese Dry Zone kingdoms
Salagama	A small caste living mainly along the southwest coast, traditionally associated with cinnamon peeling
Sangha	The collective term for the Buddhist priestly orders
SLFP	Sri Lanka Freedom Party. The more left-wing of the two main Sinhalese parties
TULF	Tamil United Liberation Front. This emerged as the dominant political party among the Sri Lanka Tamils at the 1977 general election
UNP	The more right-wing of the two main Sinhalese parties
Vahumpura	A numerous low-caste group
Vel Vidane	Irrigation headman
viharagam	Land belonging to Buddhist temples
Yala	The second and minor cultivating season, beginning in March or April

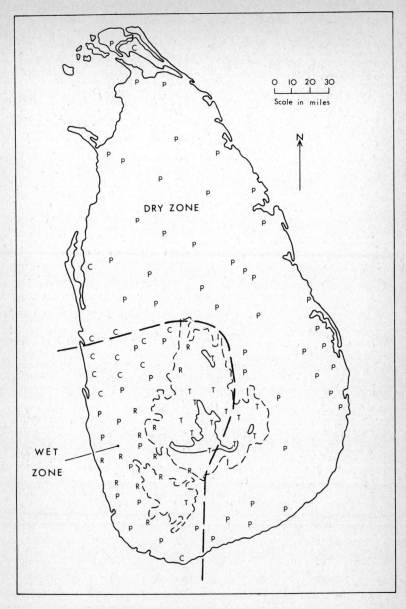

_____ 5,000 ft contour

- - - - 1,000 ft contour (heights in feet above sea level)

━ ━ ━ Boundary between Wet and Dry Zones

Main crops: T = Tea   C = Coconuts
              P = Paddy   R = Rubber

Map 1.   Sri Lanka: elevation, climate and main crops (adapted from Peiris, 1977a: 7, 15; and *Ceylon Land Utilisation*, map published by the Survey Department, Colombo, 1972)

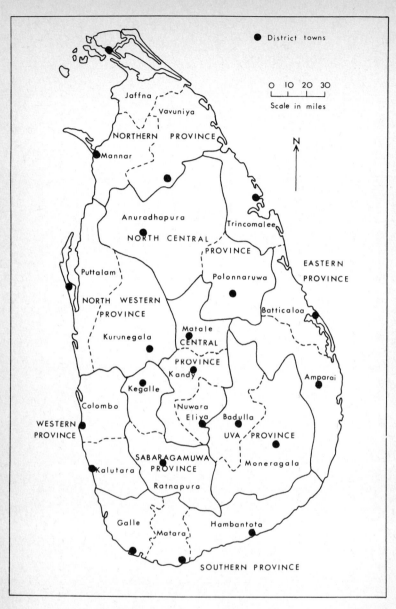

Map 2. Sri Lanka: provincial and district boundaries, 1977 (Peiris, 1977a: 2)

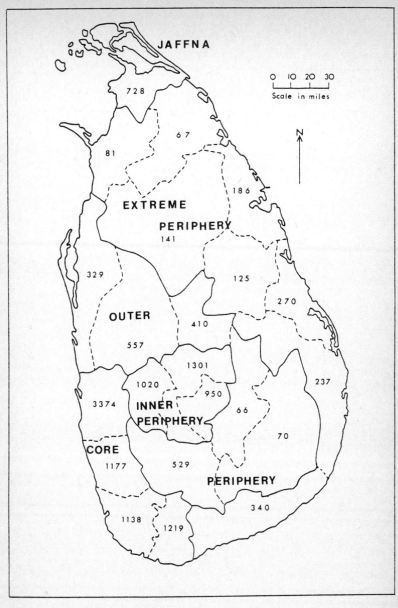

JAFFNA

728

67

81

186

EXTREME

PERIPHERY
141

329

125

270

OUTER

557

410

1301

1020

950

3374

INNER
PERIPHERY

66

237

70

CORE

1177

529

PERIPHERY

1138

1219

340

N

Scale in miles
0   10   20   30

————— Regional boundaries

- - - - - District boundaries

728   Population density: persons per square mile, 1971

Map 3.   Sri Lanka: district population densities (1971) and regional categories (Peiris, 1977a: 2, and *Census of Population 1971, Volume 2, Part 1*: Table 1). For regional classification, see text

XV

1

Puzzles and agendas

It is appropriate to conclude by placing the Sri Lankan case in the broader Indian context. Its distinctive features are the weakness of the caste system, the strength of communal identities, the early and advanced politicisation of rural society, the importance of the plantation economy, and *the absence of agrarian movements*.[1]

Introduction: the problem

This book had small beginnings in the early 1970s, when I first became acquainted with Sri Lanka. At that time the current of left-wing radicalism which had long been prominent in Sri Lankan politics had reached a peak. The rural-oriented United Front coalition of the Sri Lanka Freedom Party, the Communist Party and the (Trotskyist) Lanka Sama Samaj Party, headed by Mrs Sirimavo Bandaranaike, had won the 1970 general election on a radical-socialist-statist programme of economic reform. The state sector was expanding rapidly at the expense of the private market economy. The personnel of the ruling parties were cashing in, and many others, including poorer people, were pushing in the queue for a share in the material benefits of political power. The new government had already been seriously challenged from the left by the Insurgency of April 1971. Although the JVP movement, which led the Insurgency, had been vigorously repressed, the government's broader response was a series of attempts to validate its own radical credentials. Much of the privately owned plantation sector had been nationalised in 1972, and preparations were being made to nationalise all corporately owned estates in 1975. Many government supporters had been granted access to a share in the fruits of plantation production. Even within the relatively conservative Sri Lanka Freedom Party, the numerically predominant component of the ruling coalition, the radical so-called 'China wing' was well entrenched at the highest levels. In public at least, politics was dominated by the language, symbols and credos of the Marxian and populist left.

In this atmosphere of political ferment rural dwellers, as always, exhibited very little reluctance to complain about their situation in life,

I

criticise government policies, and make suggestions for change. Yet, curiously, farmers rarely seemed to include inadequate farm product prices in their lists of complaints and demands. Many other things were wrong, including the inefficiency or corruption of public agencies, the inadequacy of subsidies from government, and the high prices of commodities, including farm inputs like fertilisers and tractors. Later experience was to confirm and strengthen this impression: farmers rarely seemed to view farm output prices as a major political issue, and the subject had scarcely featured in the agenda of national politics. This in itself was enough to raise questions. It formed a marked contrast to the situation in other Asian countries, notably India and Malaysia, which in different ways each had a great deal in common with Sri Lanka, and where farm product prices had featured so prominently on the national political agenda. And in Sri Lanka the prices of most agricultural inputs and outputs had to a large degree been determined by government since World War Two. The institutional mechanisms through which governments could have responded to farmers' pressure for higher output prices had long been in place.

Here then was something of a paradox: a highly politicised rural electorate had regularly played a major role in replacing governments at successive general elections, but had apparently not used its electoral power to even place on the national political agenda an issue which directly and deeply influenced its material welfare. In fact, in the absence of any mobilisation of the rural electorate around issues of agricultural output pricing, successive Sri Lankan governments had pursued policies of a kind familiar in the Third World and often ascribed to 'urban bias':[2] the manipulation of price ratios to transfer material resources from farmers to the state and to food purchasers.

A deeper acquaintance with recent Sri Lankan political history began to suggest that the absence of the output-pricing issue from the political agenda should not be seen as an isolated phenomenon. It was rather an aspect of a broader pattern: the general failure of the farming population to define the major rural policy issues in terms of its own class or occupational interests. There were indeed important public programmes to transfer resources to rural people, which in a quantitative sense in large degree offset the 'urban bias' in price policy. But in origin these owed very little to grassroots rural pressures or demands. Major land reform legislation had been conceived and initiated by members of Sri Lanka's political elite in the context of intra-elite competition, but without generating any obvious electoral dividends. The ideas had not come from below, and had not been major issues at general elections. This legislation was often framed in such a way that the advantages to the potential beneficiaries were very limited. Since 1931 state land had been alienated on a large scale to the rural poor, not by outright grant or sale, but on restrictive and irksome long-term lease. The first legislation to control paddy land leasing arrangements in the interests of the tenant had involved a major misunderstanding of agrarian social relations in the districts to which it applied. Later and more ambitious legislation had caused a political crisis. But many tenants, the nominal beneficiaries, had been evicted, and neither then nor since had any major political party even advocated a simple 'land to the tiller' reform of the kind familiar and often successful in other Asian countries.

This lack of an effective representation of the class or occupational interests of smallholders in the political process seemed to be associated with a tutelary, custodial or paternalistic attitude towards the 'peasantry' on the part of the political and administrative elite. Newspaper reports of political speeches, the records of parliamentary debates, and official documents all conveyed the same impression: a sense of obligation on the part of the elite to use state power on behalf of the 'peasantry', which was combined with a reluctance to trust 'peasants' to manage effectively their own personal and household affairs. In their own best interests 'peasants' were expected to submit to public programmes to uplift their morals; restrict their freedom to transfer land to prevent their being cheated by speculators or 'capitalists'; enforce correct cultivation practices; and prevent the dissipation of harvest earnings on alcohol. The symbolic primacy of the 'peasantry' in national and nationalist myth coexisted with an implicit or explicit derogation of 'peasant' culture, lifestyles and personal capacities. Admittedly, the policies stemming from these custodial attitudes were widely evaded on the ground. But the fact that the elite continued to express such attitudes publicly seemed further evidence of the failure of the smallholding population to set the terms and tone of political debate over rural policy.

The problem which this book seeks to explore emerged easily, if slowly, from a mass of impressions. Why should a politicised and electorally powerful rural farming population not have sought to impose on the agenda of national politics the issues which derived from its position as a distinct occupational interest group? The problem is not that the Sri Lankan farming population is particularly disadvantaged or exploited through public policy. The state both appropriates substantial material resources from farmers through price policy and transfers resources to rural people through a range of development and welfare programmes. The puzzle is that farmers do not make the

3

political demands that one would expect given their occupational position: demands for higher farm output prices, better performance from public agencies providing agricultural services, and land policies more directly beneficial to smallholders. Unlike in, for example, India, Malaysia, Japan, North America and most of Western Europe, there is no distinct 'agrarian interest' in Sri Lankan politics. In the political sphere farmers do not act as members of a farming occupational category, but as members of broader or different interest groups, e.g. consumers of purchased commodities, adherents of particular political parties, potential beneficiaries of state programmes to redistribute material resources to broad population categories, members of particular social strata not primarily defined in occupational terms, or members of particular socio-cultural categories.

Resolving the problem

The problem set out above is tackled here by focusing on the relationships between 'interests' and 'demands'. How is it that certain interests are translated into demands and thus placed on the political agenda?

The starting point is the truism that any individual or group has a wide range of potential identities or interests in politics, e.g. locality, region, socio-cultural category, social stratum, gender, occupation, or ties of personal obligation. At the individual level some of these interests may directly compete with one another. For example, a farmer may have a choice between supporting a politician or party which is tender to farmers' concerns, and supporting someone who, if in power, is likely to generate public investment in his locality or steer public resources, such as public-sector jobs or subsidies, to the farmer's own family. At the level of the political system all potential interests and identities are in conflict with one another. No political system can cope with the mobilisation of all issues. The range of issues dealt with must be limited. If socio-cultural group conflicts are to be articulated successfully, then the scope for simultaneously mobilising support on the basis of, for example, occupation or social stratum may be very restricted – depending of course on how far membership of socio-cultural groups, occupational groups and social strata overlap and are perceived to overlap.

Insofar as particular groups are able to influence which identities or interests are mobilised into political competition, they also help determine which are excluded. They influence the political agenda and thus exercise considerable power even before they begin to influence

4

the outcome of issues which are overtly contested: 'The final test of power is not *who* decides but what is decided – and not decided.'[3] The exclusion from the public agenda of Sri Lankan politics of the issue of farm output prices is an important dimension of our broader argument about the absence of mobilisation among farmers around an occupational identity.

It is argued here that smallholders in Sri Lanka have mainly been inducted into electoral participation on the basis of identities other than that of agricultural producer. And insofar as the agricultural producer identity has been important, the dimension which has been most salient has been that of recipient of agricultural and household inputs provided by the state: fertiliser, tractors, land on irrigated settlement schemes, and homestead plots, etc. Smallholders have been far more concerned to use politics to receive favourable public allocations of these resources on an individual or small-group basis than to demand national-level policies in the sphere of agricultural output prices, agricultural service delivery, or land policy which would benefit smallholders as an occupational category. By competing as individuals or as small and localised groups for a greater share in the large volume of material resources allocated by the state, Sri Lankan smallholders have implicitly rejected a class or occupational identity in national politics which would bring them into conflict with other broad classes, e.g. food consumers or the urban population generally. They have failed to become a 'class for itself'.

A summary of the reasons why Sri Lankan smallholders have not realised a class identity in national politics can be oriented around three broad questions.

Smallholder interests

The first question is: what are smallholders' material interests? What policies would in fact have benefited the smallholder population as a whole or large categories thereof? Is there in fact an objective basis for the class demands whose absence is taken as problematic here?

An important dimension of this question is introduced in Chapter Two, where it is explained that a substantial proportion of the smallholder population also depends to a large extent on non-agricultural sources of income, and therefore has potentially conflicting interests even in occupational terms. This issue is dealt with in detail in Chapter Seven. The potential base for the political mobilisation of smallholder interests is both smaller and, perhaps more importantly, more fragmented than is implied by the observation that smallholders are the largest single population category, accounting for perhaps 50% of rural households in 1962. The smallholding population is internally differentiated by crops grown, especially between producers of export cash crops (tea and rubber) and producers of food crops for the domestic market (paddy and other food crops). (Coconut producers appear in both categories.) Large numbers of people in each category tend to benefit from policies which adversely affect the other: food crop producers from the public subsidies financed by heavy taxation of agricultural exports; many consumers of coconuts from policies which depress the prices received by those who produce a surplus of coconuts; and export crop producers from policies which depress the market prices of cereals. At the same time, the practice of dealing with the separate crops through separate public institutions and separate policy packages encourages farmers to define their interests in crop-specific rather than broader occupational terms. Public policy, as well as agrarian structure, influences what individuals' interests are and how they are perceived.

Yet these divergences and conflicts of interest between rural producers do not explain all. In the first place, smallholders have common interests in matters such as land policy which might partially override differences of interest over economic policy. In the second place, in relation to economic policy there is in principle scope for the various cultivating groups to ally and bargain to their mutual benefit and to the cost of non-farmers generally. In the third place, there is a marked spatial dimension to this pattern of interest differentiation in relation to economic policy. Producers of export cash crops and coconuts, and paddy farmers who produce so little grain that they need to purchase cereals to meet family consumption requirements, are heavily concentrated in the southwestern corner of the Island – the Wet Zone, or, in terms of the regional categories introduced in Chapter Six, the core and inner periphery regions. By contrast the economy of most of the Dry Zone, especially the extreme periphery region, is characterised by a high degree of dependence on market sales of surpluses of paddy and other food crops. The Dry Zone population thus has an apparent clear interest in high market prices for food crops.

There is then a question of why producer interests in relation to economic policy have not been articulated on a regional basis. For the reasons why this has not happened in the Wet Zone one must look mainly to the largely hidden mechanisms through which export crop producers are taxed, and to the failure of the owners of large plantations to take a lead in challenging this appropriation. To explain why the surplus-food producers of the Dry Zone periphery have not given birth to a strongly 'ruralist' regional political movement is to take us into the

6

issues raised by our two other broad orienting questions: how the identities, beliefs and relationships 'existing' (and produced and reproduced) in the spheres of society and polity respectively (rather than the economy in the narrow sense), have affected the terms under which the peasantry have been inducted into competitive electoral politics.

Society and politics

We deal first with the influence on smallholder political action of existing identities and relationships generated from within society rather than from within the contemporary state or polity.

It is argued in Chapter Eight that collective identities (of religion, ethnicity, caste, etc.), rather than purely 'objective' occupation-based commonalities of interest, have been important vehicles for the political mobilisation of rural populations in Sri Lanka and other Asian countries. In India and Malaysia these collective identities have often coincided sufficiently with farming as an occupation to provide strong ideological and material stimuli to agrarian political movements. This has not been the case in Sri Lanka. In contrast to India, a sense of 'peasantness' – of difference and antagonism between the rural people on the one hand, and, on the other, a relatively homogeneous population identified with towns, government and commerce – is largely absent from Sinhalese political culture. Also in contrast to India, caste identity is not a potential base for agrarianism in Sri Lanka. Finally, intra-rural class conflicts – between tenants and landlords, small and large farmers, or farmers and labourers – have not been clearly articulated in Sri Lanka, and have similarly 'failed' to provide a stimulus for the political mobilisation of large sections of the cultivating population.

However, ethnic identity – notably the conflict between Sinhalese and non-Sinhalese, especially Tamils – has been salient in Sri Lankan politics over the past half century. It is explained in Chapter Nine that, historically, this conflict owes more to competition between urban-based populations over control of the state and of the consequent benefits, than to conflicts of interest between Sinhalese and Tamil or Muslim farmers. But the result has been the political fragmentation of the Dry Zone surplus-food producers into antagonistic ethnic groups. In particular, the larger surplus-farmers, the potential leadership of any movement oriented to higher output prices for Dry Zone farmers, are disproportionately Tamils and Muslims. The Dry Zone Sinhalese have 'lost' the political leadership they might have obtained from within the farming community itself. In the same chapter an account is given of the character of the local political leadership of the Dry Zone Sinhalese. These leaders are to a large extent traders and former public servants from the Low Country Sinhalese community, while most of the farmers are Kandyan Sinhalese. This has probably helped impede the development among the Dry Zone Sinhalese of autonomous farmers' politics oriented to farmers' occupational interests.

Polity and politics

The arguments summarised in the two preceding subsections exhibit a close affinity to a broad perspective which has tended to dominate the explanations of politics and policy – especially, but not only, democratic politics – offered by social scientists of very different ideological orientations: the attribution of policy outcomes to the results of competition between different interest or class groups formed and existing within 'civil society'. Within this perspective the state, polity or government does not play a determining role, but exists largely as an arena within which interests or groups (pluralist theory) or classes (mainstream conventional Marxism) compete to advance their interests. And these interests in turn are shaped mainly by relationships within the spheres of the economy and society.[4] There is, however, an additional dimension to the argument of this book, and one whose broader theoretical implications are discussed in the concluding chapter. This is that the political action of Sri Lankan smallholders has been partly shaped by various aspects of the Sri Lankan polity itself. The polity both reproduces itself and helps shape its own evolution, and thus to some extent has exhibited a degree of historical autonomy from civil society. Indeed, although this is not a prominent theme of this book, the polity and politics can be seen to have played an important role in the evolution of civil society – in the structuring of relationships between different social groups.

Politics and policy have helped shape the political actions of Sri Lankan smallholders in two main ways. In the first place, over the past half century or so since the smallholding population began to participate in electoral politics, successive governments have influenced the development of smallholder political consciousness through the policies they have either pursued or failed to pursue.

Let us take the omissions first. It is argued in Chapters Three, Five and Eight that, in comparison with India in particular, rural policy in Sri Lanka has been remarkable by virtue of the fact that on no occasion has it involved the imposition on farmers of any particular burden which could be viewed as violating the legitimate expectations of the farming population and thus stimulate them to mobilise in opposition.

8

In India attempts to produce foodgrain quotas from surplus-food producers at less than market prices and attempts to impose landownership ceilings which threatened the landholdings of the rural political leadership played precisely this role. They have helped give birth to farmers' political parties and movements which have, in contrast to Sri Lanka, been articulate and militant at various points over recent decades. By contrast the Sri Lankan state, capitalising on its large bank of state land and a large financial surplus taxed from plantation crop exporters, has *de facto* and *de jure* accepted large-scale encroachments on state lands; left the smallholding population free of all land and income taxes and irrigation water charges; met the perceived need for additional land for redistribution by nationalising plantations and leaving alone the bulk of the larger holdings in the smallholder sector; and shrunk from imposing food delivery quotas on rice farmers even at the height of the 1974–5 food crisis.

More positively, successive Sri Lankan governments have in effect, if not by intention, helped thwart the creation of smallholder political class consciousness by instituting, at an early stage in the process of the induction of smallholders into competitive electoral politics, public programmes which diverted the attentions and political energies of smallholders in other directions. Here land policy has been particularly important. Sri Lanka is a relatively densely populated country, which experienced relatively rapid rates of population growth in the 1950s and 1960s. In addition, in the colonial era a large proportion of land in the Wet Zone, where most of the Sinhalese population was concentrated, was appropriated for large-scale plantation production. Smallholder demands for access to additional land have thus always been latent. And should they not have been satisfied, the issue could easily have mobilised the smallholding population on a national scale. Instead, mechanism for the large-scale redistribution of a large reserve of state land to the rural poor almost without charge were instituted in the early 1930s. The existence and scale of this programme has helped politicise the rural population. It has been possible for a large proportion of the rural poor, including those already owning some land, to see themselves as having a good chance of obtaining a land allocation if they could only make the right political connections. And the continual exchange of governmental power between different party blocs since 1956 has intermittently provided a large proportion of people with the right political connection. State land allocation has been a major political issue, but mainly at the *local* level. The contested issue has not been the aggregate level of state land redistribution, but who should receive a particular piece of land in a given locality. The

9

contest has thus not been between the state and potential beneficiaries as a class, but between individuals and small groups at the local level – between clients of opposed local patrons, or supporters of different parties.

The particular policies pursued or not pursued by the state over the past half century have thus helped shape the political consciousness and action of the smallholding population. But there is a second and perhaps more important dimension to the argument about the influence of polity on smallholder politics. This is that smallholders in general, and the food surplus producers of the Dry Zone in particular, have been relatively late entrants into competitive electoral politics. In becoming active and conscious participants they have had to adjust to and fit into an already well-developed and stable pattern of national party competition. The practical possibilities for making smallholder occupational concerns prominent on the national political agenda have thus been limited. This already established system of national party competition has deep roots in the Wet Zone, especially the areas closest to and historically most intimately connected to Colombo; is very much oriented to the issues and political conflicts of the Colombo region; and has been in large part created and continually reshaped by the Colombo-based political elite, which still exerts a major influence.

Compared for example to India, where Independence was associated with rather more change in society and polity, the contemporary Sri Lankan polity is more the product of slow historical evolution.

Chapter Ten takes the discussion beyond rural and agricultural issues to look at the effect on rural politics of the national political system. It is argued that the absence of any clearly agrarian party or programme is in part the consequence of the continued political dominance of an elite little involved in food production; the relative weakness of social and economic associations and organisations outside the sphere of the state; the stability of a left–right spectrum of party competition originating in the capital–labour conflicts of the Colombo- and Wet Zone-based plantation economy; and the orientation of day-to-day political competition to the question of access to the large volume of resources, especially land and financial surpluses appropriated from export agriculture, available to the state as a legacy from the plantation period.

Organisation

Following on the more detailed elaboration in Chapter Two of why the political action of Sri Lankan smallholders should be considered puzzling, the remainder of the book falls loosely into two main sections. Chapters Three to Five, dealing with land and agricultural policies, are intended mainly to substantiate the case that Sri Lankan smallholders have not been mobilised politically to pursue their occupational interests. After the introduction in Chapter Six of the concept of the core–periphery continuum as an analytical tool for later use, Chapters Seven to Ten are devoted to the resolution of the puzzle along the lines sketched out above.

Because of the need to weave a great deal of factual information into the argument, and to avoid fragmenting discussion of particular events or issues across separate chapters, the distinction between the two main sets of chapter is not complete. Aspects of the argument about why smallholders have not become a 'political class' are located in the first group of chapters where this seems convenient. For the same reasons, there is not in the second part of the book a complete one-to-one correspondence between individual chapters and the three main aspects of the argument treated separately in the section above. The need for the chronicler to present coherent historical accounts of particular events and processes to some degree comes into conflict with the desire of the social scientist to permit the analysis to determine the arrangement of the material. The conflict is, however, hopefully not too serious, and the compromises made clearly signposted.

2

Methods, scope and elaborations

Introduction

The main argument has been sketched out briefly in Chapter One. The present chapter is devoted to certain preliminary exercises which have to be conducted before the argument itself can be allowed to flow. The first issue dealt with is method. On methods used for data collection little need be said in the main text:[1] the dominant eclecticism will soon become evident. Rather more needs to be said on the concept of 'objective interests', which is a contested issue within social science, and central to the argument here. That is followed by an elaboration on various aspects of the main thesis propounded here. After the scope and historical scale of the argument are defined, the chapter concludes with an introduction to Sri Lankan politics intended to justify the claim that the smallholder population wield great electoral power and have available an unexploited moral basis for making claims for government policies more oriented to small-farmer interests.

'Objective interests'

In defining the analytic problem to be the explanation of an aspect of the political agenda – the dearth of cultivators' occupational demands despite the substantial electoral influence of the cultivating population – I have adopted a particular stance in the wider debate on the nature and extent of political power.[2] This stance is broadly that of radical theorists.[3] Concerned about the narrow and biased definition of the scope of political power implicit in the behavioural view that it can only be studied by examining overt political decisions, these radical critics argue that power both can and should be viewed as extending to the shaping of the political agenda. For a common and, almost by definition, conservative, use of power involves the suppression of potential 'issues' and their exclusion from the political agenda.

The conservative response to the radical critique is that any attempt to attribute to particular populations 'objective interests' other than those revealed through expressed preferences is to enter on a very slippery slope. There are no safeguards against the attribution of any 'interest' one wants to a population. One would be wiser and less open to error to stick to the narrower conception of interest as revealed preference. The debate reveals clearly that the concept of power is 'essentially contested', i.e. any apparently 'operational' definition has very overt ideological implications.

The ideological implications of my declared affinity with the radical theorists are, however, relatively uncontentious. For it is not claimed either that the absence of cultivator demands results mainly from any identifiable exercise of power on the part of conservative interests or, more broadly, that the clash of class interests in a conventional sense is central to the determination of the Sri Lankan political agenda. Explanation is found rather in a range of contingent and historical factors. The perspective shared with the radical theorists is conceptual and methodological: the belief that, despite the pitfalls and problems,[4] the notion of 'latent' or 'unexpressed' objective interests can be used in a fruitful and empirically verifiable way. It is argued that some cultivators would clearly stand to benefit from certain kinds of policy and that, insofar as they are politically active yet not concerned to demand such policies, there is clearly a problem which needs to be explained. Adoption of the narrow approach of equating interest with revealed preference would not have permitted this question to be asked at all.

Elaborations

The nature of 'this question' may still at this stage appear to require some elaboration. It can hopefully be clarified by making a few related points about the argument presented here.

The first point is that the goal is to explain aspects of the agenda for political action in relation to agriculture, *not* to account for policy. As is explained below, especially in Chapters Three to Five, electoral and other grassroots demands are but some of the factors shaping policy intentions and outcomes. The nature and consequences of rural policy are discussed at various points below, but in the context of explaining demands, rather than vice versa.

The second point is that the term 'peasantry' is here used as the equivalent of the smallholding population, i.e. members of households cultivating their own or rented land within the smallholder sector rather than the estate sector. The differences between the smallholder and estate sectors of the rural economy are discussed in Chapter Four, where it is demonstrated that, despite inconvenient overlaps at the margin, the two are very distinct. In the interim, the phrase 'smallholder sector' may be taken to denote mainly small farms, relatively few of which are of more than five acres, which produce mainly food crops, especially rice and coconuts, but also in some areas export crops, mainly tea and rubber. The estate sector comprises large-scale units employing a regular labour force to produce mainly tea, rubber and coconuts.

The third point follows closely: the alleged absence of certain categories of political demands is in no way the result of sleight of hand in defining 'smallholder'. One would normally expect demands for higher output prices in particular to be articulated more strongly and effectively by larger farmers. Large-scale producers of export crops are by definition in the estate sector and out of the direct purview of this book. Policy has in fact defined their interests to be very distinct from those of most smallholders. Large-scale producers of non-estate crops, few of whom are large landowners by Asian or even Sri Lankan estate standards,[5] are included in the 'smallholder' category. The term 'smallholder' includes all small farmers, all producers of food crops, and thus all the large farmers whose political action is relevant to the present topic.

Points four and five are also about definitions of the problem. Point four is that no attempt has been made to define 'farmer demands' in an exclusive fashion. In South Asia farmer demands are likely to be expressed in an 'impure' form, i.e. fused in origin and expression with the demands of particular socio-cultural rather than purely occupational or economic categories, e.g. castes, or religious, ethnic or linguistic communities. Part of the explanation offered for the weakness of farmer demands in Sri Lanka is the absence of an appropriate vehicle, in the form of a politically mobilised caste, or ethnic, linguistic, regional or religious population category, into whose programme farmer demands might be integrated.

The fifth point is that the search for the missing farmer demands has covered the full range of potential channels of expression: political parties; pressure groups; patterns of electoral behaviour – programmes, voting and parliamentary activity – not tied to particular parties; extra-parliamentary social movements; or networks of privileged contact between cultivator interests and public servants. Failure to unearth them is not due to constraints on the search.

The sixth point is that we are here concerned with the political demands of farm operators, and not in any important sense with those of non-cultivating agricultural strata, such as labourers or landlords. However, there has been very little class mobilisation of these latter categories in Sri Lanka. Insofar as the reasons relate to the central problem of cultivator demands, they are discussed in Chapter Eight.

The seventh point is that the book is concerned to explain mainly the process through which needs, demands or grievances are aggregated and articulated at regional or national level, and thus find a place on the national political agenda. There is inadequate material, either from my own research or from other sources, for detailed analysis of political attitudes and conceptualisations at the local level.

The eighth and final point is that the claim that certain categories of farmer demand have been weak or absent is inherently difficult to validate. The possibility of the unexamined instance is always there. I try to cope with this problem in what appears to be the only acceptable way: examining in as much detail as possible certain apparently important policies and processes. It would accord with the logical structure of the book to present the results of this examination at this point. That would, however, be an ungainly procedure, both because of the large amount of space required and because the examination of policy generates positive information relevant to the arguments of later chapters about what factors did influence policy. The politics of rural policy are discussed in a group of chapters (Chapters Three to Five) devoted to the provision of information relevant to both the statement of the problem and the attempt to explain it. In the meantime the reader is asked to take on trust the claim that smallholder interests have been weakly articulated.

Coverage – Sri Lankan and Sinhalese

Sri Lanka is characterised by a high degree of socio-cultural pluralism. The distribution of the population according to religious affiliation was as follows in 1971: Buddhists – 67%; Hindus – 18%; Christians – 8%; and Muslims – 7%.[6] The classification by socio-cultural category, officially termed 'ethnic' or 'racial' categories, was as follows: Low Country Sinhalese – 43%; Kandyan Sinhalese – 29%; Sri Lanka Tamils – 11%; Indian Tamils – 9%; Sri Lanka Moors – 7%; and 'Others', mainly Burghers (Eurasians), Malays and Indian Moors – 1%.[7] Most Sinhalese are Buddhists and most Tamils are Hindus. Most Christians are Catholic Sinhalese living along the western coast. There are, however, small but powerful minorities of Protestant Christians among both the Sinhalese and Sri Lanka Tamil upper classes. The very small ethnic minorities include both Christians (Burghers), Muslims (Malays, Indian Moors, Borahs) and Parsis. Sinhala is the main language of the Sinhalese, and Tamil the language of the two Tamil categories. The Sri Lanka Moors speak Tamil as their first language, but are generally also conversant with Sinhala. English is widely spoken among the superior socio-economic strata in all categories, and is especially common among the Sri Lanka Tamil, Burgher and Malay minorities.

Although this is a study of Sri Lanka as a national polity, it is at the same time, and without contradiction, primarily a study of the Sinhalese, amongst whom the differences between the Low Country and the Kandyan categories are relatively minor. For not only do the Sinhalese dominate numerically, but they also dominate politically whilst remaining divided among themselves. The main political and electoral competition is between Sinhalese groups and parties. The politics of the minorities are derived from the politics of the Sinhalese in two senses.[8]

Firstly, access to governmental power is achieved by alliance with Sinhalese parties, and to a large extent the two-bloc electoral system among the Sinhalese has been reproduced among the separate political systems of the three numerically significant minority categories – the Sri Lanka Tamils, the Indian Tamils, and the Muslims (including Sri Lanka Moors, Indian Moors and Malays).

Secondly, the salience of ethnic or communal themes in contemporary politics is largely a reaction to the use by the Sinhalese of electoral democracy to attack the 'privileges' – income, status, education, employment, assets, and power – which all categories except the Sinhalese Buddhists appeared, at the time of Independence, to have acquired in generous degree during the colonial era. Politically the minorities, especially the Sri Lanka and Indian Tamils, have mainly been on the defensive, and reacting to events in the Sinhalese-dominated national sphere. This book therefore focuses interest on the Sinhalese. Issues relating to interethnic conflict are treated only insofar as they impinge on the main topic.

Because of the political significance of ethnicity and language the term 'Sri Lankan', which has national application, must be clearly distinguished from 'Sinhalese', which refers to the main socio-cultural category, whose language is Sinhala.

Coverage – time scale

An issue about the scope of the book which cannot be disposed of quite so neatly concerns time scale. There is an ever-present threat, to put it no more strongly, of disjuncture between the overt argument of the book on the one hand and, on the other, the methods used to justify that argument. The argument is explicitly historical. That is to say, the main foci of concern – smallholder political consciousness, organisation and demands – are viewed as products of particular historical circumstances, and are in the process of continual change. The objective is to explain the weakness of smallholder class demands since the introduction of universal suffrage in 1931. Although it is explicitly argued that the situation is currently undergoing change, the method of argument may not always convey the same sense of historical dynamic. The material is not structured chronologically and, because of the greater availability of information, most of the case material relates to the post-Independence period. Generally speaking, the 1970s receive the greatest attention and the past fades away. The chronological points of reference of individual elements of the argument are, however, very much determined by the availability of suitable statistics.

This relatively static presentation of dynamic phenomena is justified by the relatively slow rate of change of many of the contextual variables, above all perhaps the persistence between World War Two and the present day of a politico-economic structure characterised by Sinhalese electoral dominance; heavy taxation of estate exports; and the redistribution of this estate surplus in the form of mass welfare programmes.

The choice of 1931 as our point of departure requires justification, and that in turn requires some discussion of the historiography of contemporary Sri Lanka. All attempts to use secondary historical sources must be informed by a critical awareness of the biases they embody. On certain occasions, when the ideological and emotive factors favouring particular interpretations of history are especially strong, such awareness becomes all the more important and often, at the same time, particularly difficult to sustain. The colonial and post-colonial histories of former colonies provide many such occasions. Powerful sentiments and interests channel historians and history along a course which commences at 'The Foreign Impact', continues along 'The Road to Independence', leaps the hurdle of 'Independence' itself, and ends up at some point determined by a dialectic between a direction set by colonial traditions and a new path mapped out by new rulers. Historians may differ in their interpretations of the observations they make along the road, but the possibilities of disagreement are constrained by the fact that most observations are made from the same perspective. History is written around the foreign role–liberation sequence. The greater the depth of popular political awareness and nationalistic sentiment, the more likely it is that recent history moulded in this perspective will be a popular as well as a scholarly product.[9]

Partly because Sri Lanka did not experience a protracted, mobilising and unifying nationalist movement on Indian lines, and partly because of the more prominent Marxian and 'anti-establishment' currents in Sri Lankan historiography,[10] it has not generated the same contrast between established nationalist and recent revisionist history as one now finds in Indian historiography.[11] Perspectives are more diverse. Few Sri Lankan intellectuals are, however, totally free of the influence of the colonial experience:

The colonial era produced deep, dark stains in the psyche of the Ceylonese intelligentsia. These stains have flowed on into the era of political decolonisation, albeit with dilutions, embellishments and other transformations. They have left their imprint on the focus and the nature of historical scholarship. One manifestation has been a powerful interest in the nature of the 'British impact' and the variety of local responses to the penetration of British power.[12]

To understand the way in which consciousness of colonialism has influenced Sri Lankan historiography, it is first essential to appreciate that the Sinhalese, unlike most colonial peoples, and in contrast to the non-Sinhalese Sri Lankans, are heirs to an ancient and deeply rooted consciousness of nationhood – an identity as a distinct people associated with a national state, the Buddhist religion, and with the island of Lanka.[13] Within modern nationalism 'the ideological fusion between the venerable indigenous concepts and the foreign concept of a nation state developed into a dominant force'.[14]

The historical scenario which has entered most deeply into popular consciousness and on which there is the greatest consensus is that of the historical greatness of ancient Sinhalese civilisation and its subsequent collapse – followed by a long 'dark age' – under the impact of the physical, economic and cultural assaults of Tamil, Portuguese, Dutch, British, Muslim and various other alien elements. As ideology this theme is of some importance to this book. As an account of history it is in large part too remote for its accuracy to concern us, except insofar as the nature of and the consequences for the plantation economy are concerned. The veracity of this account matters here. With the aid of some revisionist scholarship, an attempt is made in Chapter Four to provide a more balanced view than that of the Sinhalese nationalist version.

As there is a considerable diversity of views about the last few decades of Sri Lankan history, the perils facing the user of secondary sources are relatively less acute. They do, however, exist, and their nature can be illustrated by the problems which implicitly arise from the decision to take 1931 as our starting point. In what sense is this particular periodisation justified? It does not appear to coincide with any periodisation prominent in published or verbal history.

To explain the choice of 1931 it is useful, first, to examine the historical literature for the messages it proclaims or implies about 'turning points' or 'watersheds' in recent Sri Lankan history. There appear to be three main views, all of them oriented to the process of attaining independence. It would not constitute undue violation of the facts to associate each with a particular partisan and party viewpoint.

1948, the year of Independence, is naturally widely viewed as a significant watershed. Independence was negotiated by politicians of the United National Party (UNP – formed out of the Ceylon National Congress in 1946). The view that Independence marks the most significant watershed in recent Sri Lankan history is therefore especially characteristic of the UNP.

A completely opposed view is presented by those Marxian observers who emphasise the dependent nature of Sri Lanka's capitalist plantation economy. Belittling formal independence as a facade behind which lies continuing dependent underdevelopment, they tend to emphasise the essential conservatism of the nationalist/UNP leadership and its vested interests in plantation production and dependent capitalist development generally.[15] There is characteristically an emphasis on the fact, not in itself seriously in doubt, that Sri Lankan independence was largely a by-product of the success of Indian nationalism. The main area of dispute is about the extent to which this is true. Roberts[16] suggests that radical scholars have been too emphatic. Their case has been supported by the fact that universal suffrage was introduced in 1931 *against* the advice of the 'nationalist' leadership, who argued for a narrower franchise, and at the insistence of a British member of the Donoughmore Constitutional Commission.[17] One might, however, conclude that this is evidence not of the absence of desire for independence, but of an attempt to maintain control in the hands of a Sri Lankan oligarchy: to ride on the historical current of nationalism while reining in the current of democracy.

'Sri Lanka Freedom Party history' shares with the Marxists the view that in 1948 the UNP perpetuated a false and incomplete independence.[18] The emphasis is, however, less on economic structures than on cultural, linguistic and religious factors on the one hand, and foreign policy on the other, notably the close Cold War identification of Sri Lanka with the West, defence treaties with Britain, and British military bases in Sri Lanka. Genuine independence was ushered in in 1956 when the Sri Lanka Freedom Party-led government set about remedying these problems and ushered in the 'Era of the Common Man'.[19]

Illustration of the practice which both emanates from and supports contrary 'party historiographies' is provided in official ceremonial. UNP governments celebrate Independence Day as the main state and national occasion of the year, while Sri Lanka Freedom Party (SLFP) governments choose Bandaranaike Memorial Day.

An extension or amendment to the 'SLFP line' is that the 1956 government did not fulfil the declared intention of the party's founder, S. W. R. D. Bandaranaike, to achieve republican status for Sri Lanka (then Ceylon). This was effected only in 1972 in the 'Republican Constitution' introduced by the United Front government (SLFP, Lanka Sama Samaj Party and Communist Party).[20] That the abolition of the largely nominal right of the British Privy Council to interfere in Sri Lankan affairs should have evoked such pride on the part of both the SLFP and the Lanka Sama Samaj Party (LSSP) – one of whose leaders, Colvin R. de Silva, was Minister for Constitutional Affairs and architect of the 1972 constitution – illustrates both the continuing potency of Sinhalese nationalist sentiment and the extent to which the nominally Trotskyist LSSP had in fact strayed from a revolutionary programme.[21]

I find little merit in suggestions that either 1948 (Independence) or 1972 (Republican Constitution) represents a significant watershed in Sri Lankan history in anything other than a symbolic and emotive sense.[22] 1956 is a more attractive candidate, but subject to the limitation that high levels of electoral participation long predate 1956. The broadly Marxian arguments about essential structural continuity from colonial to neocolonial status seem to have little application to the political sphere unless one is prepared to view this as a reflection of systemic determinants in the economic sphere.

My own view on periodisation is that the major transformation this century occurred approximately in the two decades between 1925 and 1945. Major changes occurred from an older set of political, social and economic structures to the set which have broadly characterised Sri Lanka since. The dominant aspects of the transition are the introduction of universal suffrage and a substantial degree of internal self-government in 1931;[23] the introduction of organised mass political parties and inter-party competition for governmental power with the establishment of the LSSP in 1935;[24] the cessation of the growth in area of the plantation sector in the 1930s and the relative expansion, beginning in the 1920s and continuing to the present day, of the smallholders' share of export production;[25] the associated tailing off of new immigration of estate labour from South India and the exodus of those already present, leading to a decline of the Indian Tamil proportion of the population from the peak of 15% reached in 1931;[26] the acceleration in the early 1930s of the proportion of Sri Lankans (i.e. those not classified as Indian Tamils) in the estate labour force;[27] the introduction in the 1930s of a substantial state-financed welfare programme, and its rapid expansion during World War Two such that, by the end of the war, social services – mainly education, health and food subsidies – absorbed over half of government revenue;[28] the introduction in 1942 of a system of subsidised food rations which persists today; the commencement in the early 1930s of what has since become a major programme for the alienation of state land in small lots to the rural poor and landless; and the simultaneous inception of what rapidly became the dominant programme for smallholder develop-ment – large-scale colonisation-cum-irrigation projects in the Dry Zone undertaken by state agencies and legitimated in terms of historic Sinhalese themes.

Most of these transitions have their roots in the first one listed: the introduction of universal franchise and the consequent orientation of political activity to the electoral preferences of the mainly poor and rural, but also relatively politically conscious Sinhalese majority. More broadly, and somewhat crudely, this marked a transition from a polity oriented mainly to securing and expanding profits from plantation production to one oriented to perpetuating an elite-dominated elec-toral system through the provision of 'welfare' for the broad mass of the population. It is therefore convenient and appropriate to nominate 1931 as the starting point for the present work, although the emphasis on the more recent period drains this choice of much of its potential significance. It is convenient if for no other reason than as a declaration of dissent from periodisations which I believe represent partisan and unhelpful interpretations of recent Sri Lankan political history.

The electoral power of the peasantry

The remainder of this chapter is occupied with an explanation of why the absence of certain smallholder class demands from the Sri Lankan polity should be considered a problem worthy of explanation. There is a substantial intellectual tradition in which the political powerlessness of peasantries is considered almost axiomatic. If one were to accept that perspective, the focus of this book would have to be inverted. The problem would be to explain why the peasantry exercises any political power at all. Two very different propositions are put forward here. In this section it is argued that the Sri Lankan peasantry is dominant electorally. In the succeeding section it is claimed that certain features of the economic and political situation provide a potential practical, symbolic and moral stimulus to and justification for demands for pro-smallholder economic policies.

The electoral process is but a part of the political process. Other ways in which interests are represented are discussed at various points below and in later chapters. However, the electoral process is arguably of greater salience in Sri Lanka than in many other democracies and is especially likely to be the prime channel for the expression of peasant demands. It is therefore on the electoral role of the peasantry that the present section is focused. It is argued that the Sri Lankan smallholding population is numerous, that it occupies a particularly strategic electoral position, and that it is politicised to a very high degree.

Peasant numbers

As countless introductions to Sri Lanka relate, it is mainly a rural and agricultural country. The rural proportion of the population, standing at 78% in 1971, has scarcely changed since Independence in 1948.[29] This experience in itself, so radically different from the rapid urbanisation experienced by most developing countries in recent decades, illustrates the degree to which material resources have been successfully channelled to the rural population. The proportion of the work force engaged mainly in agriculture has only declined slowly: 53% in 1953, 50% in 1971, and 46% in 1980–1.[30]

The agriculture category, however, includes the large estate population producing rubber, coconuts and, above all, tea. The problems of drawing a precise boundary between the estate sector and the smallholder sector have already been mentioned. An adequate indication of the size of the smallholder labour force may be obtained by subtracting from the total agricultural labour force those primarily occupied as hired labourers in the production of tea, rubber and coconuts. This indicates that the smallholder sector occupied 24% of the total national labour force in 1953, and 31% in 1971.[31] The reasons for this relative increase in the smallholder work force are discussed in Chapter Five: the decline in production of export crops as a consequence of falling real world prices and heavy taxation, and the promotion of smallholder agriculture through state action.

Employment statistics, then, indicate that the smallholder sector occupies a significant but minority fraction of the labour force – in 1971, 31% of the national labour force and 36% of the rural labour force.[32] Landholding statistics, however, indicate that the great majority of rural households either own or rent in agricultural holdings, and therefore imply that the smallholder sector is considerably more important than employment statistics suggest. The landholding statistics pose a number of problems of interpretation and reliability. Some of the most reliable data, derived from the 1962 Census of Agriculture,[33] indicate that at that stage about three-quarters of rural households, including estate households, operated agricultural holdings.[34]

The reason for this apparent divergence between employment statistics and landholding statistics is the small size of many holdings and the high incidence of part-time farming among cultivating households. For example, at the 1962 Census of Agriculture, in which an 'agricultural holding' was defined as constituting at least an eighth of an acre of cultivated land, 36% of all enumerated holdings amounted to less than an acre in extent.[35] Of all land operators 29% declared non-agricultural activities to be their main source of income, and a further 16% admitted to supplementary earnings from non-agriculture.[36] Part-time farming is not confined to very small landholders. For example, in 1962, 27% of operators of holdings of between one and five acres, many of them no doubt relatively well-endowed with land and wealthy by village standards, admitted to non-agricultural income sources.[37] And experience and commonsense suggest that such non-agricultural income sources are likely to be understated.

The extent and significance of this high incidence of part-time farming are discussed again in Chapters Six and Seven. The point of immediate relevance is that a substantial proportion of rural households potentially hold divided allegiances insofar as the interests of agriculture and non-agriculture are concerned. Any estimate of the size of the smallholder electorate must be qualified by this consideration.

As they stand, the statistics quoted above suggest that in 1962 own cultivation was the main source of income of 53% of rural households.[38] Correction for the likely understatement of non-agricultural incomes would reduce this figure. On the other hand, the figure can be considered to be unrealistically deflated by the inclusion in the base population of the entire estate sector, including the mainly landless Indian Tamil estate workers. Since they have been disenfranchised since 1948, and are peripheral to the essentially Sinhalese political system with which this book is concerned, they may be excluded from any calculation. In 1971 Indian Tamils or, what amounts to almost the same thing, resident non-citizens, constituted just over 9% of the total population, almost all of them located in the Up Country estate areas.[39]

If the uncertainties of the landholding data and the year-to-year changes induced by the very considerable instability of an export economy are allowed for, it appears that the best estimate is that around the early 1960s approximately one-half of Sri Lankan-citizen rural households obtained the greater part of their income from own cultivation. Another substantial fraction obtained some income from this source (see also Table 7.7).

Electoral representation

The potential electoral influence of the smallholding population is greater than its number alone suggest. For this there are two reasons. The first is the marked overrepresentation in Parliament[40] of the regions where the smallholding population is concentrated. The second is that the same areas have constituted the main electoral battlefield between the two main Sinhalese political parties, the United National Party (UNP) and the Sri Lanka Freedom Party (SLFP), which alternated in power after each of the seven general elections between 1952 and 1977. (The record of electoral 'see-sawing' was broken in 1982 when the UNP, already in power, won both the presidential elections – an innovation under the 1978 constitution – and a subsequent referendum to approve an extension of the life of the existing Parliament for a further six years.)

To explain these points necessitates a brief preview of the regional categories presented in Chapter Six, and of the interregional differences in the rural economy discussed in Chapter Seven. Generally speaking, the southwestern coastal districts around Colombo are densely populated and their inhabitants, both urban and rural, are relatively heavily engaged in non-agricultural occupations. Peasant landholdings are small. Part-time farming is especially common. Rice, the main locally grown staple, is produced in large part for subsistence rather than for sale. The area produces only a fraction of its own food requirements. As one moves away from this region, around or across the central Kandyan hills (see Maps One and Three), one comes to areas which are less densely populated and more dependent on agriculture and on the sale of food surpluses. The smallholder interest is thus especially strong in the Dry Zone areas remote from Colombo.

All parliamentary general elections held under universal franchise, i.e. since 1931, have been held under electoral demarcations which, by giving weight to territorial area as well as population numbers, significantly overrepresented these lightly populated areas where the smallholder interest is concentrated.[41] A further bias was created immediately after Independence, when the Indian Tamil population was disenfranchised but continued to be enumerated for purposes of electoral delimitation.[42] This did not benefit the Dry Zone, but rather the Kandyan hills where the tea estates, and most of the Indian Tamils, are located. These Kandyan areas stand mid-way between the Dry Zone and the southwestern coastal plain in the extent of the commitment of village populations to smallholder agriculture and the production of food surpluses. Their overrepresentation tends to benefit smallholders, although not the areas where the smallholder interest is most heavily concentrated.

The combined effect of these two electoral biases has been to overrepresent the smallholding areas. Defined generously as the entire country except the four southwestern coastal districts of Colombo, Kalutara, Galle and Matara, in 1977 the smallholding areas contained 51% of registered electors and returned 67% of all MPs. In Colombo district there were 51,000 registered voters per MP, while in Badulla district there were only 24,000, and in Nuwara Eliya and Vavuniya districts only 27,000.[43]

At the time that these electoral biases were created the dominant electoral cleavage among the Sinhalese was between, on the right, the nationalist leadership organised first into the Ceylon National Congress and, since 1946, in the UNP; and, on the left, the Marxist parties.[44] Shortly after Independence one of the most outstanding members of the nationalist elite, S. W. R. D. Bandaranaike, left the UNP and formed the SLFP. Although faring only moderately at the 1952 general election,[45] the SLFP-dominated Mahajana Eksath Peramuna (People's United Front) coalition swept the polls in 1956. Since then, and until 1982, the UNP and the SLFP have alternated in power, one of them winning an outright majority of seats on almost every occasion, and neither absolutely dependent on the governmental coalitions into which they have from time to time entered with minor parties[46] (see Appendix One).

In all general elections since 1956 the UNP has generally been relatively secure in most urban seats while the Marxist parties, although a declining electoral force, have continued at least until 1977 to form the main opposition to the UNP in much of the densely populated southwestern coast. Sri Lanka Tamil electorates almost invariably return members of separate Tamil parties. Thus the question of which of the major (Sinhalese) parties should take power has mainly been decided in the Kandyan and Dry Zone Sinhalese electorates.[47] These areas, already overrepresented, are where the smallholder interest is especially strong.

Politicisation

Whether or not the peasantry exploits its numerical and strategic potential in the electoral system depends upon politicisation: on voting turnout; on involvement in other forms of political action; and on awareness of the means of influencing policy and administrative action. In each of these respects Sri Lankans, especially the Sinhalese, and rural dwellers as much as urban ones, probably rank as one of the most highly politicised people in the world. The main points are simply stated here and references given. There are a number of interesting questions about the nature and origins of this high level of politicisation, but these are not centrally relevant here and are deferred until Chapter Ten.

Sri Lankans are remarkably assiduous in turning out to vote, all the more so considering the relatively high levels of voter registration.[48] In the first democratic general election in 1931, for the State Council, 80% of the seats were contested and, in those electorates, 55% of registered voters polled.[49] Voter turnout has increased more or less continuously to reach 87% in the 1977 general election.[50] A slightly lower turnout in the 1970 general election was said to have 'marked a greater participation than in almost any competitive democracy with voluntary voting . . . In the Kandyan areas . . . turnout reaches the maximum found possible in other voluntary systems . . . What is particularly remarkable about Ceylonese voters is that they vote in equally large proportions in municipal contests and at by-elections. They are not simply swept away by the national campaign, as in many Western nations.'[51]

Participation in political organisations is also very high, and has been so particularly since 1956, when the election of the SLFP-led coalition, on a wave of Sinhalese religious, linguistic, and cultural fervour, marked the introduction of a new and more popularistic and participatory style of politics.[52] The party system, already relatively strong, has since developed to such an extent that the independent politician is now very rare in national-level Sinhalese politics, and the exception in Tamil and Muslim politics.[53] Even excluding trade union affiliates, the 'enrolled membership of the parties compares well with European proportions in terms of member–voter ratios . . . Since 1956 . . . there has been a positive explosion in formal membership of trade unions, co-operative societies, political parties, youth leagues and many other groups.'[54] Almost all trade unions have very close party connections, many of them having been created by political parties.[55]

26

Less susceptible to statistical demonstration than formal political participation, but perhaps more evident to the first-hand observer, is the obsessive interest of the ordinary Sinhalese in politics and the inevitability of their high level of personal involvement because of the importance of overtly political channels for the distribution of important resources. The latter point will become clearer in later chapters. The first is indicated by Jupp as follows: 'Mass sports or entertainments are unknown in the villages and politics remains the consuming passion.'[56] The implication that the high level of interest in politics arises from the lack of alternative diversions is questionable; the fact of this obsessive interest is beyond doubt.

Peasant numbers, the geography of electoral competition and high levels of mass politicisation thus combine to explain why the peasantry is sometimes thought of as the tail which wags the dog of Sri Lankan politics.[57] Insofar as the peasantry lacks power, this does not arise from inadequate participation in the electoral arena.

The moral basis for smallholder demands

It is here taken as axiomatic that all political demands emanating from a social category, however narrowly and directly self-interested they may be, require moral legitimation in the eyes of their exponents.[58] It therefore appears constructive to ask whether the absence of cultivator demands might not owe something to exceptional problems in making a morally acceptable case for them. Investigation reveals that, far from this being so, there are in fact two strong potential moral bases for smallholder demands: the needs of the national economy and the image of the Sinhalese villager/farmer in conventional political ideology and discourse.

The background to the point about the needs of the national economy is commonplace to almost all observers of contemporary Sri Lanka. The colonial export economy was both in quantitative and institutional senses heavily geared to the export of plantation products and the import of consumer goods, especially food.[59] In the early post-Independence years almost two-thirds of cereals consumed were imported.[60] Progress towards self-sufficiency has been halting and is very far from complete. At the same time, the balance of payments has been in almost perpetual deficit since 1951, a major concern of all governments, and a serious obstacle to economic progress and to the pursuit of autonomous national economic policies.[61]

Arguments for policies to stimulate domestic food production to substitute for imports of rice and wheat flour have a powerful appeal in any long-term view of economic policy, all the more so as these imports are in fact heavily subsidised and thus constitute a major drain on the exchequer. Policies to stimulate domestic food production have continually been urged on Sri Lanka by economists and international institutions. They have not been entirely ignored but neither have they been vigorously pursued. Reliance on food imports and entanglement in foreign exchange scarcities, leading to considerable subservience to the policies advocated by the World Bank and the International Monetary Fund, are continuing features of the economic situation. The potential they offer for pro-smallholder demands couched in terms of nationalist pride and national economic efficiency has not been exploited by any section of the electorate.

An agricultural self-sufficiency programme based on the stimulation of smallholder production would also be able to draw strong support from the 'sectional nationalism'[62] of the Sinhalese, as opposed to Sri Lankans as a whole. For the notion of the Sinhalese – rather than, or, indeed, in contrast to, the various socio-cultural minorities – as having a peculiar affinity with peasant agriculture, village life, and rice production is prevalent in political discourse and imagery. In part this has a valid statistical base. For in the colonial period all the various minorities, except the estate-bound Indian Tamils, were relatively concentrated in both urban and commercial activities, while the Sinhalese remained relatively tied to smallholder agriculture. Urbanism, capitalism and commerce are conceived to be the peculiar province of Sri Lanka Tamils, Sri Lanka Moors, Indian Moors, Burghers, Malays, and the various trading and commercial groups identified as being of Indian origin – Chetties, Borahs, Parsis, etc.[63]

This is not a convenient point at which to explore in detail the Sinhalese nationalist self-image or its relationship to the facts. But three aspects of it are of immediate relevance. One is that it is endowed with a major historical dimension through the identification of the ancient Dry Zone kingdoms, whose ruined cities, sculptures and irrigation systems so impress contemporary observers, as the high point of Sinhalese civilisation. The downfall of this civilisation is seen as an aspect of a long cultural 'dark age' when the Sinhalese, especially the Sinhalese Buddhists, were subject to, and maltreated by, others – Tamils, Portuguese, Dutch, British, Muslim traders. Correspondingly, the repopulation of the Dry Zone through the settlement of Sinhalese in irrigation colonies, mostly based on the restoration of ancient irrigation sites, is seen, along with Independence, as an aspect of the resurgence of the Sinhalese nation.

The second point is that rice is identified as a 'Sinhalese' crop. This arises from its association with ancient Dry Zone irrigation schemes, its cultural significance in village life, and because the most troublesome domestic competitor to Sinhalese political and cultural ascendancy, the Sri Lanka Tamils, are, in their homeland in the Jaffna peninsula, specialists in cash crops such as bananas, tobacco, fruit, vegetables and chillies, and dependent on outside supplies of rice.

The third point is that, since the election of the SLFP-led coalition government in 1956 on a wave of Sinhalese Buddhist cultural and religious fervour, Sri Lanka has in effect become a Sinhalese Buddhist polity and state. Both SLFP and UNP governments have, at least until very recent years,[64] pursued policies which have been designed for, and have largely succeeded in, establishing the symbolic supremacy of the Sinhalese and Buddhism; enforcing the use of Sinhala as the official language; and stripping the various minorities of their privileged positions in public-sector employment, commerce and higher education.[65]

The use of state power for the benefit of the ordinary Sinhalese has been, and remains, the primary legitimation, implicit or explicit, of all governments elected since 1956 at least, and arguably, since 1931. And smallholder agriculture is identified as a uniquely Sinhalese and worthy occupation. The considerable investments which have been made in smallholder agriculture, especially rice production, have to a large extent been justified in terms of the historic and Sinhalese themes identified above. The benefits to smallholders are, however, much less than they are made to appear. The thematic seams of national economic efficiency, food self-sufficiency, national pride, rice production, and the Sinhalese historic identity have been mined for political purposes when required. The miners, however, have rarely been the cultivators themselves, and there remains a great store of ideological ore which could be exploited by politicians strongly identifying themselves with the economic interests of Sinhalese smallholders.

Numbers, location and political activism explain why the Sri Lankan peasantry are widely held to be the arbiters of politics. Economic circumstances and the ideological correlates of the Sinhalese identity could provide a strong moral justification for the vigorous assertion of smallholder interest. Circumstances internal to Sri Lanka thus provide ample justification for treating as problematic the weak articulation of smallholder demands. External comparisons strengthen the point. I have demonstrated elsewhere that there are several good reasons for predicting similarities between the politics of Sri Lanka and those of India and Malaysia. And smallholder demands have been prominently voiced in both of these latter countries since Independence.[66]

3

Crown lands

Introduction

This and the two succeeding chapters are very closely connected and are jointly intended to serve three broad purposes: to justify the claim that Sri Lankan smallholders have not been active in promoting their class interests in politics – they have failed to voice class demands and have been passive recipients of some of the major policy measures affecting their interests; to illustrate the nature of the demands with which smallholders have been associated; and to explain some of the other important factors shaping rural policy.

No attempt is made to provide a comprehensive chronological or thematic account of rural policy. The latter, at least in a relatively descriptive form, is already available elsewhere,[1] and the information required to update it is easily obtained. The method used here is to select a few policy instances – events, processes or issues – for detailed analysis. Their treatment is necessarily shaped by the availability of information, but in no case have potential candidates been ignored for lack of information. The justification for the choices made should become evident from the text.

The subject of the present chapter is the process by which the state has acquired, protected and alienated very large extents of Crown land, and the consequences of this for political culture and political action in the contemporary period. While there has been considerable debate on these issues among historians,[2] I believe that the full political and sociological[3] implications of this process have not been realised. By international standards Sri Lanka is almost unique in the extent to which, over the past half century and more, vast areas of land have been transferred to large numbers of smallholders on a continuing basis through the mediation of the state and within a relatively elaborate and planned legal and institutional framework. Any attempt to come to grips with rural politics in Sri Lanka could do worse than begin here. This chapter focuses on three main issues: the reasons why initiatives were taken to alienate state lands to the rural population; the ideologies through which this policy was justified; and the consequences of this land redistribution for political culture and action.

The origin of Crown land

The quantitative importance of Crown lands derives from the Crown Lands Encroachment Ordinance No. 12 of 1840, commonly known as the Waste Lands Ordinance. Aimed at facilitating the acquisition of land by capitalists for plantation development, the Ordinance forcefully cut through the ambiguities surrounding land rights by declaring to be Crown property all land not *permanently* cultivated or demonstrably under private ownership. The balance of procedural advantage in validating claims lay with the Crown.[4] 'At a stroke the Crown became the largest landholder in the country.'[5] There has been considerable dispute, little informed by historical research, on the extent to which this and succeeding ordinances were implemented in such a way as to deprive village populations of land which was actually used for cultivating, grazing or other productive purposes. It is, however, clear that there was much more competition between peasant and state land claims in Sri Lanka than in, for example, Malaysia. Because of the relative abundance of uncultivated land in Malaysia[6] the plantation sector was able to expand without infringing on Malay land rights.[7]

I have been unable to locate comprehensive statistics on the total acreage ever under Crown control in Sri Lanka, partly perhaps because the process of settling title, the responsibility of the Land Settlement Department, is still incomplete.[8] It is, however, possible to estimate closely the magnitudes involved.

The total land area of the Island is almost exactly sixteen million acres. In the period 1833–1930 two and a half million acres of Crown land were sold to private individuals.[9] Between 1935 – the date of the Land Development Ordinance embodying the recommendations of the Land Commission – and 1946 a further 100,000 acres were alienated to smallholders.[10] Yet at Independence in 1947 the state still owned three and a quarter million acres of land, a fifth of the entire land area.[11] These figures imply that almost six million acres, more than a third of the land area, have been at some time in Crown possession. The state has been the dominant source of new land during the entire century and a half since plantation development was initiated.

The plantation period

The consequences for the peasantry of the Crown's holding this large land bank have varied over time. The issue is best approached chronologically. This section treats the 'plantation period', i.e. the period up to about 1920 or 1930 when plantation interests dominated state policy.

The main initial impact of the 1840 Waste Lands Ordinance was that the rural population were denied, legally and/or physically, access to land which they had previously used, especially as grazing land and for shifting cultivation. The extent of this deprivation is a matter of considerable disagreement. Further comment may be postponed until Chapter Four, where the broader issue of the impact of plantation development on village society is discussed.

A second and related impact was that a restrictive policy was pursued, at least at the level of intention, over access to Crown land for purposes of shifting cultivation. It followed from the provisions of the Waste Lands Ordinance that almost all land suitable for shifting cultivation – *chena* in Anglo-Sri Lankan terminology – became part of the Crown's estate. *Chena* was officially disliked for fear of adverse consequences on the natural environment. An annual licensing system was the device chosen to control and restrict the practice. The main beneficiaries were probably the village headmen who controlled the granting of licences.[12] Otherwise the issue remained a perpetual irritant to both the public bureaucracy and the peasantry, and has only been 'solved' in recent years by the almost complete abandonment of any attempt at control.[13] The relative significance of the restrictions for the peasantry had, however, already declined to very low levels in many areas because the growing density of population had made shifting cultivation physically impossible. An issue of greater recent contention has been the encroachment onto Crown lands by villagers for the purposes of permanent settlement and cultivation.

By appropriating to itself all 'unused' land in 1840 the Crown guaranteed that, if peasant numbers were to expand substantially, the peasant population would be obliged to turn to the state for new land, either formally or by encroachment.[14] That was, however, an issue for the future. The farmers and implementers of the Waste Lands Ordinance intended above all to facilitate the alienation of large blocks of land for plantation development. The procedures for alienation served this end admirably. The prospective purchaser was obliged to initiate and nudge along the administrative processes of earmarking land for alienation, surveying it, and holding an auction. The system was weighted heavily in favour of those with money and connections.[15] It was not, however, racially discriminatory, and indeed proved to be a major mechanism for the development of the plantation-owning wing of the indigenous Sri Lankan capitalist class. Between 1868 and 1906 one million acres of Crown land were alienated. Only in the tea-planting areas – Central and Uva Provinces – did European purchasers predominate.[16] Elsewhere Sri Lankans faced little competition, and purchased almost three-quarters of those million acres.[17]

The prevalence of Sri Lankan purchasers is related to the fact that, despite the original intention to assist plantation development, the *average* size of the alienated lots soon fell to low levels. After 1861, taking five-yearly periods, the average never exceeded ten acres. By the end of the century it was down below five acres. Sales of lots of less than an acre were frequent.[18] Further, the peasantry appear to have been well able to circumvent formal restrictions intended to prevent the sale of very small lots.[19]

Although the system of alienating Crown land was rather more flexible in meeting the needs of the small purchaser than was widely alleged, it was to come under increasing political pressure in the early decades of this century. As both population and the estate acreage increased, village and estate were more and more bound to come into direct conflict. The rate of population increase accelerated almost continuously after the first national census of 1871.[20] The estate area also continued to grow rapidly, expanding by about 60% in the last two decades of the nineteenth century, and by a further 55% in the first two decades of the twentieth century.[21] Estate jobs were, however, mainly occupied by immigrants from South India, and offered only limited prospects for the Sinhalese rural poor, although the plantations were located almost entirely in Sinhalese areas. By the early part of this century, 'evidence was forthcoming from the plantation regions of villages being hemmed in by estates of tea, rubber and coconut without room for expansion'.[22] The concerns to which this gave rise were to lead to a sea-change in the formal purposes and procedures of Crown land alienation – away from responsiveness to the requests of capitalists and in favour of the planned alienation in small lots for the rural landless. However, before looking at this policy change we shall turn our attention to a chronologically prior attempt to escape from the increasing pressure of population on land in the Wet Zone/plantation areas – the promotion of colonisation in the sparsely populated Dry Zone.

Early attempts to develop the Dry Zone

The sparsely populated Dry Zone covers most of the country except the densely populated southwestern quadrant, the Wet Zone, where the plantations and the capital city are located (see Maps One and Three).

In the latter half of the nineteenth century the government had put substantial administrative effort into the repair and rehabilitation of small Dry Zone 'tanks', i.e. irrigation reservoirs. The financial backing for the enterprise had, however, been but modest,[23] reflecting the lack of urgency over the matter of food supply. Sri Lanka had been partly dependent on imports of rice, the staple foodgrain, even before the Portuguese conquest of some of the coastal areas in the sixteenth century.[24] Imports had increased steadily with the expansion of the estate sector, and by the inter-war period accounted for about two-thirds of total supply.[25] The economy could generate ample foreign exchange surpluses to pay for imports of food and other consumer goods.[26] There was some official concern about the danger of the physical interruption of food supplies,[27] but the dominant plantation and urban interests required cheap food,[28] and there was little support for any idea of stimulating local production by offering higher prices.

Local rice production was unremunerative, and had been recognised to be so from the 1860s if not before: 'It is evident that in relative terms wet paddy cultivation in nineteenth-century Ceylon was simply not profitable.'[29] The buoyancy of estate production on the one hand attracted labour and enterprise into urban, commercial and plantation activities and, on the other, financed the food imports which depressed local producer prices. In relation to paddy production Roberts records:

Particularly within the wet zone, during the nineteenth century a rural capitalist had a wide range of more profitable alternatives: a trading, money-lending, or contracting venture; a graphite or a gem pit or mine; the taking up of paddy, arrack or toll rents; developing a cash crop smallholding or even a small plantation.[30]

The unprofitability of local food production was reflected in occupational distribution. In 1921 smallholding agriculture occupied only 33% of the total labour force; plantations directly occupied 28%, and other sectors 39%.[31]

Although the country was heavily dependent on rice imports and the Dry Zone had abundant unused land, attempts to transfer population there were unsuccessful. In the latter part of the nineteenth century and the early twentieth century a number of unsuccessful initiatives were taken. Concerned individual public-service officers promoted small-scale peasant settlement; companies tried large-scale capital-intensive projects; and efforts were made to attract Indian immigrants, who were generally held, on the basis of comparing Sinhalese with Indian estate labour,[32] to be superior in enterprise and endurance. The failure of all these schemes was generally attributed to the difficulties of life in the Dry Zone, especially the poor communications, unpleasant climate, water supply problems, and malaria.[33] The rice farmers themselves appeared to be well aware that low prices provided no incentive for enterprise and effort.[34] Their 'champions', members of the administrative and political elites, appear, however, to have viewed the problem in terms of physical, cultural and institutional deficiencies, and thus conceived of solutions in terms of physical, legal and institutional, rather than economic policy interventions.[35]

The attempt to develop smallholder agriculture through legal, institutional and infrastructural, rather than economic policy measures, evident early this century and the dominant mode of state action to the present day, involves a remarkable continuity from the period of colonial plantation development. Contrary to a common stereotype, the colonial state was in the economic sphere far removed from the 'nightwatchman state'.It was heavily engaged in legal and institutional measures to facilitate land acquisition, in the supervision of the supply and conditions of immigrant plantation labour,[36] and in the provision of a transport and communications infrastructure for the estate areas.[37] At the aggregate level the government sector played a major role in the economy.[38] Attempts to manipulate input prices or output prices did not, however, feature in the array of weapons for promoting plantation development; the state practised *laissez-faire* in this direction.[39] May there not have been some direct carryover to the 'smallholder era' of the habits and expectations about state action developed in the 'plantation era'?

The politics of land policy in the 1920s

The paternalistic concern for the peasantry which had shaped early Dry Zone colonisation efforts was even more evident in the vigorous debate on land policy in the 1920s, the deliberations of the 1928 Land Commission, and the new land policy which emerged. The historian of these events has remarked that it 'was perhaps during this period of time that the peasant found his most effective champions'.[40] 'Champions' is a very appropriate term, for the issues were contended very much on behalf of the peasantry rather than by the peasantry. 'Self-appointed' might be added. Who were these champions?

The first group were to be found in the higher-level public service, especially the elite Ceylon Civil Service which, as the core of the system of territorial administration, was officially recognised as the legitimate spokesman for the peasant interest.[41] One can remain sceptical of colonial administrative ideology, illustrated for example in the claim that 'relations between the government agent and the headmen and villagers were happy',[42] without doubting the authenticity of the concern of the public service for the lot of the poor and landless peasantry.[43] In the first place there was even by the early part of this century a substantial Sri Lankan contingent in the upper ranks of both the public service in general and the Ceylon Civil Service in particular.[44] Secondly, and probably more importantly, the public service was in background, ethos and interest very distinct from, and even on occasion opposed to, the British plantation interest. There can be little doubt that, at least until the 1920s or 1930s, the prime rationale of the colonial state was the promotion of plantation interests.[45] That interest was, however, not unchallenged. The bureaucratisation of plantation management under the aegis of large vertically integrated and London-based companies introduced a substantial transient element into the British 'planter' population.[46] In consequence, the British plantation interest did not develop the local roots, power and tenacity of settler populations like British farmers in Kenya and Rhodesia or French *colons* in Algeria. The public service was able and willing to articulate a public interest demonstrably broader than the immediate concerns of plantation production.

The peasantry's other champion, more significant from our point of view, was the Sri Lankan capitalist plantation elite, which by the early part of the century was developing the independent organisation and consciousness which were later to earn it the title of 'the nationalist movement'. Previously represented in government through nomination, from 1909 this elite began to compete in elections for places on the Legislative Council, albeit on a very restricted franchise.[47]

Why should this plantation-owning elite, which itself had such a large stake in the existing system for alienating Crown lands, take a lead in introducing a new system to benefit the rural landless? There are several possible (and partial) answers to this question.

One is that the Sri Lankan elite had already made its fortune, both inside and outside plantation enterprise, and in large part through the purchase of Crown lands.[48] It could afford to be generous with what remained. In addition, the depressed economic conditions of the 1920s dampened appetites for further plantation expansion and probably increased willingness to give the peasantry access to Crown land.[49] One might speculate that those near the middle of the socio-economic order, the 'village elite', might have been less eager to deprive themselves of opportunities for land accumulation by reserving Crown land for the landless. This was not the last time that the national elite, out of honest conviction, the quest for votes, or some other reason, was to pass legislation intended to benefit the poor at the expense of the rural 'middle class'.

These are merely possible reasons why the elite should have failed to resist a reorientation of land policy. To explain why it took a lead one needs to seek more positive motivations.

One was no doubt a concern, common to both the administration and the elite, that landlessness posed a threat to the political order.[50] One might, however, note that the concern about landlessness long predated the 1930s, when the world economic depression and a malaria epidemic affected the Wet Zone Sinhalese peasantry very adversely, especially those resident in the rubber plantation areas and employed in part on the plantations.[51]

It is more plausible that the elite's championing of the peasantry over the Crown land issue was motivated less by fear of political disorder than by the more positive goal of sustaining claims to political power. This has recently been argued by Vijaya Samaraweera, the leading historian of these events.[52] The precise form of his argument is very important for the thesis of this book. He expresses doubts that 'in championing the cause of the peasantry these men [the elite] thought of them in terms of a potential clientele for the future, for they were yet to be committed to either mass-based agitational politics or a full democratisation of the system of government'.[53] Democracy was eventually to be imposed from outside and over the heads of the political leaders of this same elite. Samaraweera prefers to locate this championing of peasant land 'rights' in the context of a struggle between the elite and the colonial authorities for control of the state. The elite, aware of the vulnerability of its claims to national leadership because of the immense economic and cultural gulf between itself and the mass of the rural population, needed to demonstrate its responsiveness to and responsibility for the same masses in the face of the competing claims of the Ceylon Civil Service and thus of the colonial order. For the Ceylon Civil Service had often found itself, and certainly liked to see itself, as the guardian of peasant land rights against the encroachments of plantation interests, including the Sri Lankan elite itself.

Samaraweera goes on to discuss an issue which we shall postpone until the next chapter: the way in which the elite created and very successfully popularised an interpretation of the plantation impact which validated the right of the Sinhalese peasantry to Crown lands by virtue of their suffering at the hands of the plantation system, while at the same time obfuscating its own (the elite's) major role in that plantation development. For the present, one might note how neatly Samaraweera's analysis chimes in with recent developments in the theory of the political role of ideology. Both Skocpol[54] and Abercrombie *et al.*[55] have argued, in implicit or explicit opposition to Gramscian and other emphases on the role of ideology in ensuring the quiescence of politically subordinate populations, that ideology plays a major role in providing political elites, or would-be elites, with morally acceptable interpretations of their own position and actions and a common frame of reference to overcome barriers to working together, arising from differences in social, economic and cultural backgrounds. The latter 'need' may not have been very pressing in the present case, for the Sri Lankan elite was already, or was becoming, relatively homogeneous in these respects. However, the most authoritative and plausible interpretations of the elite's articulation of concern about land policy certainly fits the overall emphasis on the self-validating aspects of ideology. As we shall now see, the details of the resultant new policy provisions also support the general argument advanced here that land policy was not primarily a response to grassroots demands.

The 1928 Land Commission

The Land Commission moved with the tide. In 1925 severe restrictions had been placed on the alienation of Crown land for estate development.[56] Although appointed four years before the introduction of democratic self-government in 1931, the Commission was staffed mainly by the Sri Lankan nationalist elite, a reflection of its increasing challenge for state power. The most prominent European member, C. V. Brayne, had been personally heavily involved in colonisation projects.[57] Whatever the hidden conflicts about the right to speak on behalf of the peasantry, the nationalists and the public servants on the Commission found themselves in close agreement on practical steps. The Commission's recommendations caused little dispute among the members, and in large part arose from practical experience in colonisation projects.[58]

At the heart of the Commission's deliberations and recommendations there lay a view of the peasant land problem which may for simplicity be reduced to three elements.[59] The first was a belief in the importance of preserving the 'peasantry' as a class. Small-scale family farming was highly valued. Landlessness, explained in terms of descent from some earlier and better social order when land had been available for all, was undesirable for welfare, moral and political reasons. Secondly, landlessness was blamed on the activities of 'capitalists', a term loosely and inconsistently used to refer to either plantation capitalists or smaller-scale operators, including moneylenders, who were alleged to obtain land, either from the peasantry or the Crown, by dubious means. The apparent paradox of a very wealthy and very capitalist elite reproving the activities of 'capitalists' is commented upon below. Thirdly, it was felt that the nefarious activities of the 'capitalist' and the moneylender, combined with the peasant's weakness for drink and gambling or his general fecklessness, meant that the peasant could not be trusted with the freehold of land. He required protection and supervision.

The Commission's recommendations were in fact put into effect by the Sinhalese-dominated government democratically elected in 1931 even before they were finally codified in the 1935 Land Development Ordinance. The major element was provision for the planned alienation of land *en bloc* to groups of landless households, but under restrictive conditions, including controls on land fragmentation, the grant only of a long-term lease rather than freehold, and the liability of the allottees to small annual payments. There thus arose, in the shape of the new Land Commissioner's Department, a large bureaucracy concerned not only to alienate Crown land but to collect payments on that already alienated and thus keep a watchful eye on the allottees.[60] The peasantry were thus invested with a new category of land which, however welcome, could never be valued as much as freehold land because it could not be freely mortgaged or passed on to heirs and did not truly belong to them.[61] They were also faced with a new bureaucracy which had to be appeased, tolerated or circumvented. Only in 1981 did the government pass legislation which enabled it to embark on a *Bhoomidari* (land gift) programme for granting full ownership rights to recipients of state land. And even that was very much a personal initiative, and not even hinted at, for example, in the governing UNP's previous election manifesto.[62]

Land alienation after 1928

The formal outcome of the 1935 Land Development Ordinance in respect of Crown land alienation, summarised in Table 3.1, is somewhat different from that foreseen by the Commission. This is firstly because Dry Zone settlements – especially the Major Colonisation Schemes – have become more important than the previous adverse experience with experimental Dry Zone projects had led the Commission to expect. It had envisaged the problem of landlessness being solved mainly in the Wet Zone itself.[63] Secondly and more importantly, as we have seen above, the Commission's vision was very much occupied with the small family farm. Yet in fact the Land Development Ordinance has, in terms of the number of persons affected, served mainly as a source of new homestead plots for *residential* purposes, not as a device for converting the landless into respectable, loyal and law-abiding small *farmers*.

Table 3.1. *Crown land alienated under the Land Development Ordinance, 1935–70*

Type of scheme	Area alienated (thousand acres)	Number of allottees	Average size of allotment (acres)
Village Expansion Schemes	777	580,104	1.3
Alienation of Acquired Estates	34	55,063	0.6
Major Colonisation Schemes:			
Paddy land	211 }	74,265	} 4.4
Highland	116 }		
Highland Colonisation Schemes	32	8,755	3.7
Special Leases	39	208	187.9
Alienation of Marginal Lands	26	1,108	23.4
Middle-Class Schemes	153	11,627	13.1
Youth Settlement Schemes	10	2,281	4.6
Total	1,398	733,411	1.9

Note: The sources suggest, but do not explicitly confirm, that all regularisations of illegal encroachments on Crown land are included in one of the above categories.
Source: Land Commissioner's Department, *Administration Report of the Land Commissioner for 1969–1970*: 30–1, 41, 73, 81, 83, 87–8, 92, 229.

The strength of the grassroots demand for residential land derives from the strong Sri Lankan preference for scattered settlement, and for a homestead which includes a compound, coconut and other trees and a home garden as well as a house. The first four types of land alienation schemes listed in Table 3.1 all have a major residential element.[64] Almost all the land allotted from acquired estates is used for residential purposes. The plots are too small for anything else. According to available statistics, only between a quarter and a third of the land alienated under Village Expansion Schemes was under cultivation in 1970. Most of this was in a few Dry Zone districts on projects combining settlement with the rehabilitation of minor irrigation tanks.[65] At the same time, only about half the land alienated under Highland Colonisation Schemes was under cultivation.[66] The two primarily residential schemes, Village Expansion and Alienation of Acquired Estates, together accounted for 87% of all land recipients, and 60% of all land alienated.

There is less of a dichotomous pattern than one might expect between the granting of small residential allotments in the Wet Zone and larger agricultural allotments in the Dry Zone. Major Colonisation Schemes and programmes for Alienation of Land from Acquired Estates are by their natures confined to the Dry Zone and the Wet Zone respectively.[67] The greater availability of land in the Dry Zone has made Village Expansion Schemes much more common there than in the Wet Zone.[68] The average allotment alienated in the Dry Zone, measuring only 1.5 acres, is, however, not a great deal larger than the average of 1.24 acres for the rest of the Island,[69] and has a major residential component. In the eight main agricultural districts of the Dry Zone, the acreage alienated under Village Expansion Schemes is greater than the entire area alienated for both residential and agricultural purposes under all Major Colonisation Schemes in the Island, and has benefited almost three and a half times as many allottees.[70] Even in the Dry Zone, state land has in large part been alienated for residential rather than purely agricultural purposes. In some places, probably the Wet Zone in particular, large blocks of land have been alienated in quarter-acre plots. Cultivation has been physically impossible.

'Cultivation' is in Sri Lanka an extremely ill-defined activity. Every household would like to have at least a few coconut trees or some other useful plants. Any attempt to draw a clear dividing line between this and 'cultivation' proper can only be arbitrary, for small-scale highland cultivation – of coconut and a wide range of other tree food crops, of tea, rubber, cinnamon, spices, nutmeg, citronella and other cash crops, and of various kinds of vegetables – comprises a major element in the rural economy, although one which is far too diverse and fragmented to appear frequently or adequately in official statistics. It was mentioned in Chapter Two that the framers of the 1962 Census of Agriculture were prepared to accept a cultivated area of an eighth of an acre as an 'agricultural holding' in an attempt to cope with this problem. It follows that even small allotments of Crown land may support agriculture of some kind. It is equally certain that many do not. Highland allotments both on Major Colonisation Schemes and Village Expansion Schemes are notoriously underutilised.[71] It seems likely that, of all the land alienated under the Land Development Ordinance, more than half is not used for agricultural purposes.[72]

The political consequences of Crown land alienation

To point out the relative insignificance of cultivation – rather than residential plots – in allotments alienated under the Land Development Ordinance is not, however, to deny the enormous impact of Crown land distribution in other respects, especially in the socio-political sphere.

The quantitative impact

Crown land alienation has maintained at very low levels the incidence of total landlessness in rural Sri Lanka, i.e. non-possession of even a household plot. Precise statistics are lacking. However, if those households owning homestead land but not qualifying for enumeration as 'agricultural operators' are left aside, then in 1962 about three-quarters of rural households, almost all of them owners of at least some land,[73] were recorded as operating agricultural holdings. Since 'rural' here includes estates, where many of the Indian Tamil labourers are genuinely landless,[74] it follows that the incidence of total landlessness in the villages is very low. This, in relative Asian terms, is no mean achievement for a densely populated country. Apart from the distinctive estate labour force, there is a substantial village labouring population living mainly by selling its labour to other villagers. Its lack of consciousness and organisation, and political invisibility, must owe something to the fact that almost every household maintains at least a toe-hold in the landowning class.

A very large fraction of households, rural and urban, have received state land, almost on a gift basis, over the past few decades. Detailed statistics are once again lacking. I have, however, estimated that more than a quarter of the nation's households currently reside on allotments obtained under Village Expansion Schemes alone. In the Dry Zone the figure is far higher. Depending on the (unknown) proportion of recipients taking up residence on allotted land, it is possible that 70%–90% of households live on plots officially ceded them or their recent predecessors by the Crown.[75] The statistics on official land allocations do not, however, reveal the full extent of public enjoyment of former Crown land. For encroachment is extremely common, and indeed is the origin of a large but unknown proportion of those land grants later officially recorded under 'Village Expansion Schemes' or one of the other categories in Table 3.1.[76] Evictions of encroachers are rare, 'and most genuine land seekers are finally regularised'.[77] The main exception affects 'non-citizens', i.e. Indian Tamils, who appear to be treated much more harshly.[78] The normal processes for both tracing and regularising encroachments are, however, slow, and the extent of encroachment seriously underestimated. A special survey conducted in 1978 revealed that almost a million acres of Crown land were being illegally occupied by over half a million persons/households.[79] It is intended to legalise the encroachments of the 'genuinely landless' up to a total of three acres[80] and thus, presumably, to bid farewell to much of what formally remains of the Crown's previously large estate.

The political consequences of land alienation procedures

Apart from the political consequences of the sheer volume of Crown land alienated, there are three points to be made about the consequences of the alienation procedures themselves.

The first point is that the process of distributing this benefit has involved extreme discretion on the part of the public officials and politicians concerned, and has thus been both very political and a stimulus to politicisation. 'Landlessness' is a term in practice open to a variety of interpretations, while, especially in relation to the choice of settlers for Dry Zone irrigation schemes, a variety of other criteria have also been introduced, formally or informally. The scope for political intervention has been very wide.[81] The same is true of the legalisation of encroachments.

The second point is that the state has in practice been 'soft' in relation to Crown land. Encroachment has generally been accepted, and formal criteria for land allocation not rigidly applied. One consequence has probably been that the less poor village populations, in principle disadvantaged by the reservation of land for the landless, have been able to obtain land if adequately determined, and have thus had no cause for dissatisfaction.[82]

A further aspect of the 'softness' of the state is that firm supervisory control over the use of alienated land, which is implicit in the paternalist and custodial nature of official discussion, legislation and institutional provision, has not in fact been practised. In Dry Zone irrigation schemes the state has almost ceased to attempt to control illegal fragmentation, sales, mortgages and leasing of allotments. These practices are widespread.[83] Attempts to enforce the cultivation of crops other than paddy on these schemes have failed. The small annual payments due to the state from all holders of land alienated under the 1935 Land Development Ordinance are very much in arrears.[84]

The final point, arising from those above, is that Crown lands have never seemed likely to become a major electoral issue, i.e. to give rise to a grievance around which a broad national or even regional political demand or movement could crystallise. The early percipience of the nationalist elite in making Crown land widely and very cheaply available largely pre-empted the possibility of any politician finding support by demanding more liberal allocations. Once the mechanism for generous allocation was instituted, demands became focused not on land in the abstract, but on particular pieces of land – an estate, an uncultivated hillside – in particular locations. Because of this and the wide discretion possible, demands became highly localised and individualised. To some extent the interests of potential beneficiaries are in conflict at the local level. Demands are thus expressed at the level of the individual or the small group. There is no rationale or mechanism for aggregating them up to regional or national political arenas as the demands of particular class or occupational categories.[85]

The more general point, which recurs again in later chapters, is that the introduction, at early stages of the development of representative politics, of comprehensive 'welfare' programmes delivered as *individual* services seems to militate against the formation of political solidarities among class or occupational categories.

Ideology and land policy

The previous section dealt with relatively concrete and observable impacts of the Crown land alienation process on the Sri Lankan political system. There is, however, a broader ideological dimension to the same process: the way it has both helped sustain, and in turn drawn sustenance from, certain interpretations of Sri Lankan history and society. These interpretations certainly confirm, and arguably contribute to, a tendency to accept the political elite as the custodian of the smallholder population, and thus as the legitimate spokesman for smallholder interests. Insofar as this ideology plays any independent role it tends to militate against the assertion of autonomous political demands by the smallholders themselves. If the exercise of ideological hegemony over the peasant population by the elite does play any role in explaining patterns of peasant political action, then it is to the ideologies discussed below that we must mainly look.

The ideology of Dry Zone colonisation

The 1928 Land Commission had envisaged finding Crown land to solve the problem of Wet Zone landlessness mainly in the Wet Zone itself. However, beginning with the government democratically elected immediately after the Commission reported, successive administrations have in practice used the Crown land alienation procedures to distribute land in the Dry Zone under combined irrigation-cum-colonisation projects, and, in some degree, to transfer population from the Wet Zone. Various aspects of the colonisation process impinge on the arguments of later chapters. Our present concern is with the ideological interpretation of this process, an interpretation which has become very widely accepted throughout Sinhalese society.

This programme became a major component, at both practical and symbolic levels, of the nationalists' policy towards the peasant sector from the very inception of responsible democratic self-government in 1931. A leading role was played by D. S. Senanayake, leader of the nationalist movement, chairman of the Agriculture and Lands Executive Committee under the collegial Donoughmore Constitution of 1931, and the first Prime Minister of independent Sri Lanka. His zeal in promoting colonisation and irrigation development in the Dry Zone is almost legendary. The term 'legend' is, however, appropriate in more than one sense. For until 1927 Senanayake, a member of one of the wealthiest Sri Lankan plantation-owning families, had been a partisan of alienating estate land for *plantation* development. It was in response to the conflict with the colonial bureaucracy over guardianship of the peasant interest that he suddenly changed tack.[86] More than anyone else, D. S. Senanayake was responsible for infusing Sinhalese nationalism with the vision that the colonisation of the Dry Zone was a return to the heartland of the ancient irrigation civilisation of the Sinhalese. His son Dudley, who was to succeed him as Prime Minister, followed in his footsteps.[87] The place of Dry Zone colonisation in Sinhalese political culture and ideology seems assured. The archaeological sites of the Dry Zone – Polonnaruwa, Mihintale, and, above all, the sacred city of Anuradhapura – have been of increasing importance as places of pilgrimage and national ceremonial. They evoke a combination of the sentiments of Buddhist religiosity, Sinhalese nationalism and historical pride, in which rurality, rice and irrigation works also feature prominently.[88]

The Senanayakes' attempt to imprint their own identity onto this panorama by demonstrating descent from the ancient Dry Zone rulers[89] may not have been very successful. The Senanayakes have, however, been successful in ensuring that the historical significance of Dry Zone irrigation development is firmly entrenched in the political culture. The UNP government elected in 1977 was led by a man, J. R. Jayawardena, who is generally eager to display his distance from the 'family-bandyism' of the Senanayake clique, which had deprived him of the UNP leadership for decades. Yet he inaugurated a rapid acceleration of the enormous complex of Dry Zone power and irrigation schemes collectively known as the Mahaweli Programme, continued to legitimate this in historical terms,[90] and made a great occasion in October 1977 of the '*Vap Magula*' ceremony, held in the historic Dry Zone site of Panduwasnuwara, in which he played the historic role of the Sinhalese kings by entering the paddy field behind a team of buffaloes to cut the first furrow. This has since become an annual event. That this imagery does indeed chime well with grassroots

Sinhalese communalist sentiment is illustrated, for example, in the concluding words of one such communalist in a letter to the press in the aftermath of the communal violence of 1983: 'In the end it is the Sinhala peasant and the new civilisation he will build on the banks of the Mahaweli which will determine the future of Sri Lanka.'[91]

At the level of symbolism and of state action, Dry Zone development represents an attempt to re-create a society of small family farmers, each cultivating a few acres, mainly of paddy. It has concentrated on symbolically powerful irrigated rice at the expense of other crops; and it has simply ignored the phenomenon of the heavy use of hired labour in even small-scale agriculture. Provision is made to settle only family farmers, and the hired labourers they use must consequently either encroach on state lands in order to establish themselves locally[92] or accept the risks and weak bargaining position involved in seasonal migration to the Dry Zone from the Wet Zone. To recognise officially the very evident need for a hired labour force, even in settlement schemes where individual allotments measure only three acres,[93] would implicitly undermine the myth that relates Dry Zone settlement to the glories of ancient Sinhalese society and to the re-creation of a Sinhalese peasant society. And here the term 'Sinhalese' has been used very intentionally. For not only have large-scale irrigation schemes intruded Sinhalese settlers into areas formerly occupied mainly by Tamil speakers – Sri Lanka Tamils or Muslims – but this has been the conscious and admitted intention. There is thus a territorial dimension to what has been termed, in relation to Sinhalese political and cultural resurgence, 'The Myth of Reconquest'.[94] Land policy, and the ideologies which support it, have in general focused much more on the control of land than on the cultivation or use of land.

The 'peasantry' in political discourse

The language of politics is not a neutral medium that conveys ideas independently formed; it is an institutionalised structure of meanings that channels political thought and action in certain directions. Those who simply use established concepts to get to the facts of political life, those who act unreflectively within the confines of established concepts, actually have the perceptions and models of conduct available to them limited in subtle and undetected ways.[95]

This quotation serves as an introduction to and a justification for the attention given here to the analysis of Sri Lankan political discourse – the terms, concepts, and language used, and the incidence of particular kinds of discussion. This attention is predicated on the belief that the study of discourse in this broad sense is an extremely effective, perhaps indispensable, means for an outsider to obtain some understanding of a political culture.

In the text above, the term 'peasantry' has been used as a neutral descriptive term. It is, however, much more than that. The fact that it was the standard term used by the Anglophone elite to discuss land problems in the early part of this century – and remains widely used today – is a phenomenon which requires explanation. And that explanation in turn reveals a great deal about the nature of elite 'championing' of peasant rights.

The significance of the use of the term 'peasantry' is made very pointed by the fact there is no equivalent in 'traditional' Sinhala, i.e. the language oriented to the circumstances of pre-colonial Sinhalese feudalism. Sinhalese feudalism had no large servile farming population, and thus no term connoting 'peasantry'. The Sinhala term for 'farmers', *govi*, conveys no hint of social inferiority or subordination. Insofar as it is etymologically and ideologically identified with *Goigama*, the largest and highest caste in the Sinhalese hierarchy, it carries the implication of 'free citizenship' in contrast to the semi-servile status of smaller caste groups obliged to provide specialist labour services to the feudal state.[96] It is an honorific rather than a derogatory term. A neologism, *grameeya prajawa*, has, however, been coined so that it is possible to talk in Sinhala of 'the peasantry'.[97]

This neologism is rather closer to the common English usage of the term 'peasantry', implying a relatively homogeneous category oriented to small-scale farming, and containing clear, although not blatantly insulting connotations of 'earthiness', limited socio-cultural horizons and inferiority. Such usage was especially widespread among the English middle and upper classes in the late nineteenth and early twentieth centuries,[98] and this is no doubt the source of its use among the Sri Lankan upper classes.

One significance of the use of 'peasantry' is that it indicates the great cultural distance between the political elite and the people they were 'championing'. Another is that it provides a means of referring to the smallholder population as a whole while ignoring, and thus in effect disguising, the marked socio-economic stratification which exists within it. Above all it avoids recognition of the existence of an agricultural proletariat *within* village society. Agricultural labourers are categorised as 'landless peasants', and thus identified as essentially part of the landed class, but unfortunately stricken with the (temporary?) misfortune not to have land.

At the same time that it helps soften the internal divisions within the smallholding population, 'peasantry' helps draw some politically convenient categorical distinctions between smallholders and others. And here it is useful to introduce some of the terms used to label the 'others'. 'Capitalist' is one such term.[99] It was noted above that there was considerable irony in the Land Commission, dominated by wealthy Sri Lankan capitalists, blaming 'capitalists' for the peasants' land problems. In Sri Lanka 'capitalist' is not generally used, except by the more intellectual Marxists, in the formal social scientific sense. It is rather the popular English usage, implying the exploitative sharp commercial operator, that is in common use. In the context of rural policy 'capitalists' (bad) are counterposed to 'peasants' (good). In the broader political arena the 'peasants' are coupled with the 'workers' by many Marxists, and with both the 'workers' and the 'middle classes' by politicians of almost all persuasions.

The broad 'populism' of Sinhalese politics demands that no potentially antagonistic class or category distinctions be admitted among the Sinhalese. The 'peasants, workers and middle classes' formula encompasses the Sinhalese as a whole, and 'peasants' the symbolically important rural element.[100] The term 'capitalists' provides a scapegoat for the adverse experiences of individuals or groups in commercial transactions. It is all the more useful because local commerce – trade, moneylending and retailing – has traditionally been dominated by 'other' socio-cultural categories. In relation to the Sinhalese as a whole, Tamils and, even more, Muslims, have been major sources of commercial services,[101] while the Low Country Sinhalese have performed the same role *vis-à-vis* the Kandyan Sinhalese in the plantation areas. The fears of nineteenth-century British public servants that 'their' simple Kandyan peasants were being spoiled by the loud, sharp, uncouth and vicious Low Country traders and contractors and Indian Tamil labourers[102] provide an early illustration of the way in which the terms 'peasants' and 'capitalists' have been used dichotomously and with overt racial overtones. The terms may be used to convey messages the speaker would not wish to make explicit.

Conclusion

The alienation of state land to villagers has been conducted on a very large scale since the Sri Lankan elite became an effective challenger for state power in the 1920s. The programme has been conducted in the name of the peasantry, but owes little in origin or in detail to political pressure from the villages. Instead, the elite seized upon and articulated what appeared to be a potential or actual grievance in such a way as to give moral and ideological support to its own claims to rule. The issue of Crown lands was placed within an interpretation of Sri Lankan history and society which served both to boost the elite's claims to leadership and obfuscate its own responsibility, via plantation enterprise, for some of the alleged ills of that society. The notion of a homogeneous peasantry played, and continues to play, an important part in this interpretation.

The sheer scale and impact of the Crown lands alienation process has helped to politicise the village population by encouraging it to make plausible and relatively easily achievable claims on state lands. The village population has, however, never been obliged to unite to fight for the principle of access to state land. The possibility of obtaining access for the individual or small group has always been there, even, to some degree, before the 1928 Land Commission. The means of access have been individual and localised. The politicisation associated with the disposal of the Crown's estate has not generated any broad horizontal political linkages between different rural localities.

4

Land reform

Introduction

In the late colonial era there were four main categories of larger landowners in Sri Lanka: the state; the plantations; owners of paddy lands leased out in small lots on a sharecropping basis; and, mainly among the Tamil and Muslim populations of the Eastern and Northern Provinces (see Map Two), large rice farmers making extensive use of hired labour. Each of these categories of landowner has been attacked through different policies and in the name of the Sinhalese peasantry. The alienation of Crown lands was the politically least contentious of these assaults because it did not pose any challenge, practical or ideological, to the interests of any major Sri Lankan class or group. In the post-Independence era two sets of land reform legislation have, with varying success, threatened the interests of the last three categories of landowner listed above, and thus the interests of powerful Sri Lankan groups. This legislation has necessarily been politically contentious. Yet the major conclusions of Chapter Three can be shown to continue to hold true. The initiative for this legislation has lain in political conflicts between elements of the political elite, and has owed little to villagers' demands. And the issues have been debated in the context of an accepted interpretation of Sri Lankan history and society which serves to legitimate the concept of an essential unity of Sinhalese interests and to represent the rural core of those interests as a homogeneous 'peasantry'.

The two sets of land reform legislation, treated chronologically below, are attempts, beginning in the early 1950s, to regulate the sharecropping relationship on paddy land; and the imposition in the 1970s of ceilings on all landholdings, including the total nationalisation of foreign-owned estates.

The regulation of sharecropping

The sharecropping of paddy land (*ande*) is widespread in rural Sri Lanka, especially in the Sinhalese areas. Statistics relating to 1946, collected before any threat of land reform existed to encourage misreporting, indicate that, in the mainly Sinhalese areas (i.e. excluding the Northern and Eastern Provinces), at least 30% of paddy land was held under *ande* tenure.[1] Other kinds of tenancy arrangement are rare in Sinhalese areas, although common among Tamils and Muslims.[2] The declared intention of a series of laws to reduce and restrict rents and give *ande* tenants security of tenure therefore represents a major and uncharacteristic attempt to intervene in socio-economic relationships within the peasant sector. It appears to stand in marked contrast to the tendency, recorded in Chapter Three, to avoid making, let alone acting on the basis of, distinctions in socio-economic category within the peasant sector.

There is clearly something to explain here, although the problem this form of argument poses is very different from, and in many ways a complete contrast to, the problematic set by most commentators on this tenurial legislation. Focusing on the 1958 Paddy Lands Act, the first piece of legislation with teeth, most commentators have emphasised its widespread evasion: the mass eviction of tenants, the loopholes in the legislation, and the continuing prevalence of tenant insecurity and of rents of 50% of the crop, double the legal maximum. Their problematic is why the legislation 'failed' and how it could be made more effective.[3] While sharing their belief in the need to protect tenants, I adopt a different analytic perspective. The question is why tenancy legislation was ever introduced at all.

Since we are here dealing with origins rather than consequences, the account must begin not with the 1958 Paddy Lands Act but with its immediate predecessor, labelled 'The Forgotten 1953 Paddy Lands Act' by its historian.[4]

The 1953 Paddy Lands Act

The 1953 Paddy Lands Act was 'forgotten' because its direct impact on the landlord–tenant relationship was almost zero. It only applied to the two districts of Hambantota and Batticaloa where the tenure situation was judged most in need of regulation. It made modest provision for the limitation of rents and extremely weak provision for giving the tenant some security of tenure. Since it applied only to registered tenancies, and included no mechanism or sanction for ensuring registration, it proved totally ineffective.[5]

Why did the 1953 Act see the light of day at all? It was conceived and established by a property-conscious UNP government, and, while not materially implemented, it did represent a moral attack on the prerogatives of property.

One might start by eliminating certain potential backers. In the first place, there appear to have been no pressures or demands whatever from the tenantry. In the second place, there had been little concern about *ande* tenure from the ranks of UNP or independent politicians, and even the Marxists had been but lukewarm on the issue. In the longstanding debates about land problems which preceded the Act it was mainly public servants who had expressed concern about the consequences of *ande* tenure. Politicians, by contrast, had rarely seen *ande* tenure as problematic, but had engaged themselves in issues of landlessness, joint landholding and land fragmentation, none of which raised issues of class conflict within village society.[6]

Part of the stimulus behind the Act lay in unrealised fears that the Marxist parties, still the main opposition to the UNP, were poised to penetrate the countryside through the tenantry. The other main motivation lay in the deteriorating economic situation and the high cost of rice imports occasioned by the Korean war.[7] The unproven but widespread assumption that sharecropping was associated with insecurity, low incentives and low productivity[8] justified tenure reform in the interests of national economic efficiency.[9]

That there were particular reasons for bringing in the legislation does not, however, seem an adequate response to the question of why a conservative government representing the propertied classes should have felt obliged to expose paddy landlordship to such public and official criticism. The situation appears less puzzling if one recalls the 'distance' of the nationalist elite from paddy land cultivation in two senses. Firstly, the elite was but little dependent on paddy land for its own income, and so was endangering not its own interests but those of the rural middle classes. The UNP MP for Horowupotana was exaggerating when, in the course of the parliamentary debate over the later 1958 Paddy Lands Bill, he claimed that 'the schoolmaster, the ayurvedic physician, the registrar, the retired government servant, the pensioner; these are the people who own ninety-five per cent of the paddy land in the country today, especially in the Kandyan areas'. As a spokesman for a paddy-growing area, he was, however, drawing attention to the relatively humble status of those who stood to lose from this elite-inspired measure. To quote him again: 'Can anyone truthfully say that a single person in this country has become a capitalist from paddy cultivation alone?'[10]

Secondly, and perhaps more importantly, communications between the elite and the rural areas, especially the main paddy-growing areas, seem to have been poor. Organised party politics had still not penetrated the rural areas[11] and most of the elite depended on personal political linkages, which were especially strong in the localities in which they owned estates. One consequence was relative ignorance of the village economy and society, especially in the paddy-growing districts, i.e. in the Dry Zone. This is evidenced for example in the uncritical acceptance of the unproven and probably false claim that sharecropping results in poor agricultural performance and, even more, in the gross misunderstanding of the nature of rural production relations, upon which the 1953 Act was predicated.

This misunderstanding existed at two levels. Firstly, and most concretely, the Act was based on the false belief that sharecropping was actually widespread in the two districts of Hambantota and Batticaloa to which it applied. In fact sharecropping in the usual sense was virtually unknown in Batticaloa. The dominant tenurial system was fixed-rent leasing. In Batticaloa the use of hired labour in rice cultivation was (and is) far more common than in any other part of the Island. It is true that many of these labourers worked on what were effectively sharecropping terms, but they were outside the scope of the Act. Even if 'implementation problems' could magically have been whisked away, there would have been very little to implement in Batticaloa.[12]

The second level of misunderstanding relates more broadly to how rural social relationships are conceived. The more radical supporters of both the 1953 and the 1958 Acts not only viewed the landlord–tenant relationship as a class relationship, but saw it as the keystone to the whole arch of 'feudal relationships' still prevailing in the countryside. The elite and articulate Marxists who dominated the parliamentary debate on the 1958 Paddy Lands Bill spoke continually to the need to remove the 'last remnants of feudalism' or of 'liquidating these feudal remnants in our land tenure system'.[13] The breaking of the landlord–tenant nexus was thus the strategic key to the ending of feudalism. Leaving aside serious doubts about the usefulness of the term 'feudalism' in relation to contemporary Sri Lanka, this characterisation implied at least two empirical errors. In the first place, it ignored the fact that in many areas landlord and tenant have close personal or kinship links and are of similar social standing.[14] The large landlord renting out numerous small parcels of land to a retinue of sharecropping clients has never been a common feature of the rural scene in Sri Lanka. Secondly, it ignored the fact that, in Hambantota and Batticaloa in particular, tenants are often relatively wealthy farmers employing large numbers of labourers, and not in the least in need of protection against their absentee landlords.[15]

The tendency for Sri Lanka's Marxists to reduce the 'agrarian problem' to land tenure, and to view tenure in highly stereotyped terms reflects their more general failure to establish a rural base outside the plantation areas.[16] They too have continued to talk in terms of a relatively homogeneous 'peasantry', in this case juxtaposing them to a small 'landlord' class. In this they are not alone, for Indian and Pakistani Marxists have also lent their efforts and rhetoric to similar ends, supporting less poor tenants while ignoring the existence of much more exploited and desperate agricultural proletariats.[17] It would, however, be wrong to see the Marxist leaders, themselves generally from extremely elite landed backgrounds,[18] as untypical of the Sri Lankan political elite generally. For in their ignorance of rural social organisation, their eagerness to impose their own ideas for reform on the peasantry, and their insensitiveness to villagers' attachment to property, the Marxists had much in common with other elements of the elite. S. W. R. D. Bandaranaike, who was in 1956 to lead the MEP coalition to victory as the champion of Sinhalese Buddhist village society, had only a few years previously publicly called for the nationalisation of all paddy land as part of a programme to stimulate rice production and develop the national economy.[19] He was to recall this unapologetically in Parliament when his government passed the 1958 Paddy Lands Act.[20]

In relation to its stated objectives the 1953 Paddy Lands Act was in many ways absurd. This absurdity was probably not the result of some clever conspiracy to persuade tenants that the UNP was on their side while passing an Act never 'really' meant to be implemented. This would anyway have been very poor politics, far more likely to stir up the tenantry than pacify them. Certainly the Act was never taken very seriously, but its provisions reveal a close continuity with the tone and content of the longstanding elite debate on the 'peasant problem', which was characterised by ignorance of rural conditions and a cavalier disregard for what the peasants felt about their land. The 1953 Act did not stir up wrath in the rural areas because it was so ineffective; the story in 1958 was somewhat different, although the initiative once again came entirely from within the political elite.

The 1958 Paddy Lands Act

The question of why it was ever introduced at all is as apposite to the 1958 as it is to the 1953 Paddy Lands Act. A part of the answer for 1958 is that the 1953 Act had passed into law and had been shown to be totally ineffective. This provided stimulus and justification for more effective measures, and generated more interest in *ande* tenure, especially among the Marxist parties.[21] And the 1958 Act was very much the brainchild of the leading Marxist politicians, above all of Philip Gunawardena, the Minister of Agriculture in the Cabinet formed after the 1956 general election.[22] Gunawardena, a member of a wealthy Low Country landed family,[23] is widely hailed as the 'Father of Sri Lankan Marxism'. He had left, partly because of personal animosities, the largest Marxist party, the LSSP, and taken his own Revolutionary Marxist Party into the MEP coalition which won the 1956 election. His party was, however, a tiny minority within the coalition, which was dominated by the SLFP and included also the Bhasha Peramuna (Language Front).[24] Gunawardena was to symbolise and to some extent effect the electoral and ideological rapprochement between the rural cultural, linguistic and religious radicalism of the early SLFP and the urban and organised working-class radicalism of the pre-existing Marxist parties.[25] His total estrangement from the LSSP and the Communist Party was, however, a thing of the future. The parliamentary debate on his Paddy Lands Bill was dominated by the approbation of other leading Marxists, and their support helped the measure to pass, at the Second Reading, by sixty-one votes to seven.[26]

Gunawardena's Revolutionary LSSP, however, commanded only five parliamentary votes, and the LSSP and the Communist Party only thirteen between them. The Paddy Lands Bill was passed predominantly by SLFP votes, the only recorded opposition coming from four Tamil and three UNP MPs.[27] And it is precisely this SLFP support which raises questions. For the SLFP victory in 1956 is almost universally characterised as an upsurge of the 'rural middle classes',[28] precisely those characters whom the MP for Horowupotana had depicted as the owners of 'ninety-five per cent of the paddy land' – 'the schoolmaster, the ayurvedic physician, the registrar, the retired government servant, the pensioner'. It matters little for our purposes whether one believes this 'rural middle class' to have been suddenly catapulted into politics by the linguistic and religious revivalism of the 1956 election campaign or whether one accepts the more plausible view that the SLFP received much of its *élan* from local elites who were tired of playing second fiddle to the Westernised national elite represented by the UNP, and were seeking their own 'place in the sun'.[29] The point is that Gunawardena's proposals – to register *ande* tenancies, grant security of tenure, limit rents to a small fraction of the crop[30] and, above all, to establish special institutions to enforce these measures – posed a direct threat to the interests of the class most strongly identified with the governing majority. The usual rent payable by *ande* tenants was one-half of the crop, and the control of paddy land tenancies was an important mechanism of economic, social and political dominance in the rural areas, especially the densely populated Kandyan areas where social relationships remained relatively traditional, and opportunities for non-agricultural work were relatively few.

In fact the SLFP did not take at all happily to the Paddy Lands Bill. As paddy landlords were organising and mobilising in opposition outside Parliament, the SLFP MPs provided major opposition within it.[31] The Bill precipitated a major crisis within the governing coalition. The opposition tended to cluster around the regional group most directly threatened, the 'Kandyan aristocracy', as represented in particular by the family of the Prime Minister's wife, Mrs Sirimavo Bandaranaike. Not only did the 'Kandyan aristocracy' have a direct interest in smallholder rents, in contrast to the plantation and commercial economic base of the dominant Low Country wing of the national elite, but it was also closely interested, through personal and institutional connections, with the substantial landholdings of the Kandyan temples, which were also seriously threatened.

Gunawardena and his supporters had to compromise all along the line. The Act was a much watered-down version of the proposals he at various times put forward. Perhaps the most remarkable thing is that it was passed at all. It owed almost everything to Gunawardena and a small group of supporters, yet Gunawardena himself was 'only a last minute inclusion in the 1956 Cabinet'.[32] The authority of the Prime Minister pushed the Act comfortably through Parliament,[33] but it passed the Senate by only fourteen votes to thirteen.[34] The episode exacerbated distrust within the SLFP of Gunawardena's ambitions and policies, and in the year after the Act was passed S. W. R. D. Bandaranaike was obliged to force Gunawardena and his followers out of the government.[35] The Paddy Lands Act did indeed have a very precarious birth.

In the short term the main consequences of the Act were adverse: large numbers of tenants were evicted. Due to a large number of apparently unforeseen loopholes in the wording of the Act, and to the *de facto* collaboration of the police and the judiciary with landlords,[36] tenants obtained little benefit. The long-run outlook was not so bleak. Before, however, we conclude that this measure, so clearly 'handed down to the peasantry by an intellectual elite',[37] was made, if not *by* the peasantry, then at least *for* the peasantry, the provisions of the Act need to be examined in more detail.

The provisions of the 1958 Paddy Lands Act

An Act to provide security of tenure to tenant cultivators of paddy lands; to specify the rent payable by tenant cultivators to landlords; to enable the wages of agricultural labourers to be fixed by Cultivation Committees and agricultural labourers to be appointed as tenant cultivators and collective farmers; to provide for the consolidation of holdings of paddy lands, the establishment of collective farms for paddy cultivation, and the regulation of the interest on loans to paddy cultivators and the charges made for the hire by paddy cultivators of implements and buffaloes; to make provision for the establishment of Cultivation Committees; to specify the powers and duties of such Committees; to confer and impose certain powers and duties on the Commissioner of Agrarian Services; to abolish the liability of proprietors within the meaning of the Irrigation Ordinance, No. 32 of 1946, to pay remuneration to irrigation headmen; to control the alienation of paddy lands to persons who are not citizens of Ceylon; to repeal the Paddy Lands Act, No. 1 of 1953; and to provide for matters connected with or incidental to the matters aforesaid.[38]

As the preamble to the 1958 Paddy Lands Act indicates, it was concerned with much more than the regulation of sharecropping. It was in fact the first of a series of general agrarian laws covering the smallholder sector. Nominally extended in 1972 by the Agricultural Productivity Law, and superseded in 1973 by the Agricultural Lands Law and in 1979 by the Agrarian Services Act,[39] it still largely survives in shape and spirit. There are major overlaps between the 1958 Act and the 1979 Agrarian Services Act.[40]

The omnibus nature of the 1958 Act is in itself significant, reflecting as it did the view that the regulation of sharecropping was an integral part of a wider set of measures to promote smallholder agriculture, especially rice production. It seems most fruitful to present the melange of specific provisions of the 1958 Act as reflecting three overlapping but nevertheless distinct programmes for smallholder development, here called 'national economic efficiency', 'nationalist populism', and 'class struggle'.[41] These are, however, observer, not actor categories. Not only did the actors not see them in this way, but in the Marxist rhetoric which characterised so much of the support for the Bill they were very clearly conflated – not to say fudged – into an overarching framework that spoke of 'abolishing the feudal remnants'. In his characteristically outspoken fashion Gunawardena talked of using the Act to 'clean the soil of all feudal rubbish'.[42]

It is not difficult to see in the Marxists' usage of 'feudal' a synonym for anything they considered 'non-modern' in relation to agriculture. For example, *thattumaru* paddy land tenure, a unique and complex but distinctly egalitarian and non-exploitative form of rotational tenure, common in one part of Sri Lanka, was included in lists of 'feudal remnants' by two leading Marxists in the parliamentary debate on the 1958 Act.[43]

57

National economic efficiency

An account has already been given of the way in which, without much evidence, the granting of security and low rents to paddy tenants was expected to stimulate production. A supporter of Gunawardena might well have retorted, however, that the question of whether or not the sharecropper produced more than the owner–cultivator next door was barely relevant, and that the issue was one of the total and simultaneous transformation of both economic and social relationships in the countryside. Sharecropping was at the heart of feudalism, and feudalism was outmoded and inefficient as a system. To break the social relations of sharecropping was thus a major step on the road to a more efficient economic system. Both the conservative concerned with the national economy and the Marxist aiming at social transformation could, and did, agree on the need for tenure reforms.[44]

Gunawardena and his supporters envisaged the path out of feudal agriculture to lead to large-scale collective production. They believed very firmly in the absolute superiority of large-scale cultivation, and indeed generated major opposition on just this issue alone.[45] Provision 'for the establishment of collective farms for paddy cultivation' was made in the Act, and juxtaposed in the preamble to provision for 'the consolidation of holdings of paddy lands'[46] because the two were seen to be part of the same process of overcoming the problem of fragmentation and smallness of scale inherent in peasant production.

Collectivisation was, however, not immediately on the cards, and, for the interim, a number of provisions were made to promote peasant production. One is of special interest here. The 1958 Act incorporated and extended a provision of the 1953 Act not so far mentioned: the *legal* obligation of the paddy cultivator to make effective use of his land, and the threat of requisition if he failed to do so. In 1953 the concern was simply to prevent land lying uncultivated.[47] The 1958 Act repeated the injunction to cultivate, forbade the cultivation of crops other than paddy on paddy land without express permission, and gave the Department of Agrarian Services and Cultivation Committees authority to determine cultivation practices on privately operated land.[48] These obligations, restrictions and powers were reiterated and extended in the later agrarian laws.[49] The 1979 Agrarian Services Act places cultivators of all crops under an obligation to cultivate 'efficiently' in a rather elaborate sense, to the extent that every cultivator in the country could probably be found guilty of inefficient husbandry if the law were to be rigorously enforced.

In fact these provisions have apparently never been invoked.[50] Threats to use them may have been used locally in partisan political conflict, and indeed it is difficult to believe that this was not part of the latent intention behind the comprehensive specification of 'efficiency' in the 1972 and 1979 measures. The public threat of administrative action against inefficient farmers is, however, a recurrent instrument of rural policy, and the existence of these laws an indication of the moral and symbolic subordination of the small farmer to the spokesmen for the 'national interest'. A belief that the peasantry needs and will tolerate brow-beating unites diverse elements of the political and administrative elite: the authors of the 1958 Act who hoped 'to unleash a force which might jerk the paddy cultivators out of the rut which it has [*sic*] fallen';[51] the Secretary to the Ministry of Agriculture, who in 1979 publicly threatened cultivators with confiscation of their land unless they used it efficiently;[52] and the UNP MP for Colombo Central, who asked that the 1958 Bill include a clause to make the 'lazy' villagers work hard at cultivation.[53]

Nationalist populism

Behind the phrase in the preamble which reads: 'to abolish the liability of proprietors within the meaning of the Irrigation Ordinance, No. 32 of 1946, to pay remuneration to irrigation headmen', lies what was probably one of the least contentious elements in the 1958 Act: the abolition of the *Vel Vidanes*, or irrigation headmen.

Along with the ordinary headmen, the irrigation headmen formed part of the colonial politico-administrative system.[54] Broadly speaking, the ordinary village headmen performed general administrative duties and the *Vel Vidanes* were concerned with cultivation matters. However, the two spheres were not always distinct,[55] and the two offices were certainly very much part of the same structure. Both were filled by appointed members of locally dominant families who were almost always from the highest *Goigama* caste, even in areas where the *Goigama* formed only a small minority.[56] Apart from their almost inevitable exploitation of their positions for personal ends, headmen were widely alleged to be corrupt and especially disliked by non-*Goigama* castes for their role in perpetuating *Goigama* social dominance.[57] The abolition of the 'Headman system', long a Marxist demand, also became part of the programme of the SLFP.[58]

The government elected in 1956 replaced village headmen by a new cadre of appointed public servants called *Grama Sevekas*. The abolition under the Paddy Lands Act of the associated post of *Vel*

Vidane was thus a part of a broader popular programme not directly concerned with agriculture at all, although one that fitted neatly into the programme of 'abolishing feudal remnants'.

Class struggle

In addition to conforming conceptually to the Marxist programme, the abolition of the *Vel Vidanes* fitted in a more practical way. For this left a vacuum at village level in the supervision and management of irrigation and agriculture in general, and helped justify the elected village-level Cultivation Committees which appear to have been the centrepiece of Gunawardena's personal programme for smallholder agriculture. He talked openly of these Cultivation Committees as the cutting edge of the struggle of the peasantry against the feudal classes.[59] How far he was carried away by his own rhetoric is not clear. His opponents certainly took him seriously, although they interpreted his intentions slightly differently. Fear that Gunawardena aimed to use the Cultivation Committees to establish his personal political machine throughout the rural areas was one of the biggest single causes of opposition to the 1958 Act.[60] A major theme in intra-governmental disputes over the Act was the rivalry between Gunawardena and C. P. de Silva, the Minister of Lands. The latter, whose stamping grounds were the new cultivation schemes of the North Central Province, controlled the alienation of Crown lands. The dispute between the two acquired overtones of disagreement on development strategy: whether to 'unleash the productive forces' on existing land (Gunawardena) or rely on expansion into the Dry Zone land frontier (de Silva).[61] De Silva was to acquire the agriculture portfolio after Gunawardena's downfall.

The rural class struggle which Gunawardena had promised never took place, either inside or outside the Cultivation Committees. He had been forced to compromise and permit non-cultivating landlords to sit on the Committees, and, fairly predictably, they appear to have exercised great influence.[62] The poor performance of the Committees could initially be blamed on landlord sabotage,[63] although this ceased to be a valid excuse after the landlords were excluded in 1964. The Committees continued to perform poorly,[64] and this appears due to deep-seated features of the Sri Lankan polity rather than to any easily corrected problem of dishonesty, poor management, or sabotage.

To even begin to talk of the details of Cultivation Committee organisation and activities as possible causes for the non-appearance of the rural class war between peasantry and landlords is, however, to take one step too many towards accepting the myth propounded by Gunawardena, S. W. R. D. Bandaranaike, and many other eminent supporters of the Paddy Lands Act: that there is some essential overlap between the peasantry and the tenantry, and that the landlord class stands distinct from the two. It has already been recorded that the belief that tenants and landlords constituted distinct classes or strata was generally false. The proponents of the Act compounded error by talking interchangeably of 'peasants' and 'tenants' as if they were a single category and class.[65] The Act was presented as a measure of benefit to the peasantry as a whole. In his speech to Parliament in support of the Bill, S. W. R. D. Bandaranaike articulated in an extreme form the ideology of the peasantry already discussed above. He first informed the House that the 'vast majority' of the population were peasants,[66] a claim which sits oddly beside the finding of the 1953 census that only 23%, even including hired labourers, of the economically active population were engaged in the production of crops other than tea, rubber and coconuts.[67] He went on to identify paddy cultivation as the main and characteristic activity of the rural population.[68] And we might in this context note that the 1958 Act related only to paddy lands, despite the fact that it contained provisions relating to credit, draft power, land collectivisation and a range of other things not intrinsically associated with any particular crop. Only in 1973 were its provisions to be generalised to non-paddy crops.[69]

There was in fact no 'peasantry' to fight the kind of anti-feudal, anti-landlord class war of which Gunawardena talked. If there had been, it seems extremely unlikely that it would have danced to his tune, if only for the simple reason that Gunawardena was offering very little immediate benefit. Despite his rhetoric he was not offering a 'land to the tiller' programme. He was promising only rent reduction and security of tenure. This was not even envisaged as a step on the road to 'land to the tiller', but as a step towards collectivisation. In Gunawardena's own words, he was 'not a believer in peasant proprietorship',[70] and did not wish to give the land to the tenants if that meant, as it almost certainly would, that they would then resist handing it over to the collective. In the context of the sharecropping issue, Gunawardena's attempt to use an imaginary 'peasantry' to pursue his own ends resulted in very moderate legal provisions acceptable even to conservative interests.[71]

In his refusal to contemplate a 'land to the tiller' programme of a kind which is relatively common in the Third World, Gunawardena was no more conservative than the Sri Lankan Marxist movement as a whole. Individual Marxists have been attracted to the 'land to the tiller' ideal,[72] but it has not found a place in party programmes. At the 1977 general election the Marxist parties of United Left Front,[73] freed of electoral alliance with the SLFP for the first time in thirteen years, simply repeated in their manifesto the call, which they made before the SLFP alliance, for the full implementation of the tenancy provisions of the 1958 Act.[74] No suggestion was made for a more radical attack on landlordism.

The Paddy Lands Act and agricultural labour

If there was one rural class that might legitimately have expected the unambiguous approval and support of Marxist-inspired legislation, then that was agricultural labour. In the words of the LSSP's leading theoretician: 'Why is there a fear of the growth of agricultural labour in the countryside? That is the way to the future.'[75] Theory and programme were, however, not to meet. Although having a firm base among the Sinhalese estate proletariat, the Marxist parties were never to make a bid for the support of labour in the smallholder sector.

The Paddy Lands Act did in fact classify labourers as 'qualified cultivators', thus making them eligible for election to the Cultivation Committees. This was, however, an afterthought. They had not been included in the original draft.[76] That the poor and low-status landless could at best play only a marginal role in the Cultivation Committees should have been evident. That these same Committees should be empowered by the Act to determine wage rates can only have been either the result of ignorance of rural social structure or part of a conscious policy of refusing to recognise conflicts of interest among the peasantry. It was not an oversight. The idiosyncrasy of authorising committees of employers to set wage rates had been pointed out in the parliamentary debate, not by a Marxist, but by a radically minded Independent who was soon to join the UNP.[77]

Labourers, along with non-cultivating landlords, were excluded from the Cultivation Committees under the 1964 amendment. This was passed by an SLFP government dependent on the parliamentary support of the LSSP.[78] A zealous supporter of Gunawardena's and an implementer of the Act was later to describe this as a rectification of 'anomalies', and say, of agricultural labourers: 'in most paddy producing districts they were migratory and had no permanent interest in the land'.[79] Herring's comments on the conceptual status of the agricultural labourer seem to approach nearer to the heart of the matter: 'in the traditional cultural setting, he is an anomaly and an embarrassment, a peasant without land; this was the chief worry for the British, and they were forever formulating schemes to protect existing peasants and create more from the pool of landless'; and 'in the Marxist vision the agricultural labourer has an honoured place, but the vision remains largely restricted to the speeches and writings of wealthy men who live in cities'.[80]

In practical politics the Marxist parties have been no less willing than the UNP or the SLFP to suppress recognition of conflicts of interest within the smallholder sector in obeisance to the myth of a homogeneous peasantry assailed by various external forces – capitalists, landlords, estates, landlessness.[81] The irony is that the peasantry have not been prepared to reciprocate by awarding the Marxists their votes.

Tenurial legislation after 1958

Mention has already been made of the extension of the 1958 Paddy Lands Act by means of the Agricultural Productivity Law of 1972, the Agricultural Lands Law of 1973, and the Agrarian Services Act of 1979. In the interim, it was amended in 1961, 1964, and 1970.[82] To discuss this legislation in detail would take us mainly into issues of local farmers' organisations barely relevant here. One question is, however, very pressing. Why, despite the unpropitious circumstances in which the 1958 Act emerged, were its tenancy provisions five times strengthened and extended by both SLFP and UNP governments? (The exception is the 1979 Agrarian Services Act, which weakened them.)

For the last two decades or so the Act has in fact been of some beneficial consequence in granting security of tenure. The legal maximum of a quarter of the crop as rent, although widely flouted in the Kandyan areas, is generally observed in the more politicised and radicalised areas of the Low Country.[83]

Strangely enough, although the details of the amendments have been chronicled by commentators on the 1958 Act, they rarely appear to have thought of asking why they came about.[84] The amendments are accepted as the result of some 'natural' desire to see the Act working more effectively. Fortunately these sources indicate an answer to the question, or at least several partial answers. Firstly, the relative conservatism of the tenure provisions has probably meant that, once the wider threat of Gunawardena's personal power was removed, the law ceased to appear very threatening to property. Secondly, and probably more importantly, a certain 'equilibrium' between landlord and tenant appears to have been established after the mass evictions of the early days. Drafting weaknesses, the attitude of the police and judiciary, and the delayed and staggered implementation of the Act[85] probably permitted landlords to evict all potentially 'troublesome' tenants. Thirdly, and most importantly, the Department of Agrarian

Services, established to administer the 1958 Act, became a powerful and committed spokesman for the tenant interest within the government: 'it was left to the Agrarian Services Department to voice the views of the peasantry'.[86]

The commitment of the Agrarian Services Department to the interests of the tenant and the small farmer derives from the fact that many of its original staff were handpicked by Gunawardena and his close associates.[87] Originally intended to support the peasantry and tenants through supervision of the Cultivation Committees, the Department very quickly found itself playing a leading rather than a supporting role. For the Cultivation Committees never established themselves as vigorous and independent local organisations. Failing to fulfil the conflictual role envisaged by Gunawardena, they fairly soon became defined as development bodies: they were loaded with a wide range of duties and powers over the whole field of smallholder development, and became but an arm of the state.[88] It was not, however, a very strong arm. Inertia, and even failure to fulfil the elementary conditions for formal recognition, have been persistent and widespread problems. The Department of Agrarian Services found itself substituting more or less completely for local-level organisations, and indeed formally undertook this role in 1979 when Cultivation Committees were abolished.[89]

It was thus the very weakness of farmer organisations which, for a couple of decades or so, supported the Agrarian Services Department in the belief in its own mission: 'as the Act passed through a number of successive governments, it was the bureaucracy that stood amidst change to implement the law'.[90] The various measures taken to strengthen the Act were the result of the badgering of sometimes reluctant governments by the Department.[91] The importance of the Department's role is illustrated in the events following the removal in 1977 of the last of its directors personally connected with and committed to its radical origins.[92] The Department then drafted the Agrarian Services Act of 1979, a comprehensive revision of agrarian law. This incorporated a substantial, if extremely covert, weakening of the legal and procedural protection previously granted the paddy land tenant, thus reversing for the first time the trends set in motion in 1953. Not only was the direct resumption of tenanted land by the owner facilitated, but, more importantly perhaps, major procedural barriers were raised against the passing on of tenancies through inheritance.[93] Yet in the parliamentary debates on the Bill only the first of these legal reversals – the facilitation of resumption by the owner – was even identified by Opposition MPs.[94] The Bill was otherwise presented and passed into law as a measure to strengthen tenants' rights. No longer represented departmentally, tenants' interests were protected mainly by a reluctance on the part of the government to be seen to be reversing the achievements of 1958. The tenants themselves played no part in these achievements, and are unlikely to be stirred by this covert and underhand attack on their rights. For it is heavily disguised in the minutiae of the wording of the legislation, and none of the radical parties has seen fit to make an issue of it.[95]

Land reform in the estate sector

The legislative process concerned with the regulation of paddy land tenure has been protracted, yet only marginally effective. By contrast, action on the estate sector was sudden and decisive. Under the Land Reform Law, No. 1 of 1972, all privately held land above an individual ownership ceiling of twenty-five acres of paddy land and fifty acres of other land was acquired by the state.[96] Three years later, under the Land Reform (Amendment) Law, No. 39 of 1975, all land held by public companies was nationalised.[97] These two measures resulted in the acquisition by the state of 563,000 and 418,000 acres of land respectively. Out of the total of 981,000 acres thus acquired, 801,000 acres were cultivated. This equalled 18% of the cultivated area of the country and included over 60% of the tea acreage, 30% of the rubber acreage, and 10% of the coconut acreage.[98]

This legislation barely touched paddy land, and thus in large part dealt with a different population and affected different regions than the legislation discussed immediately above. The company-owned sector nationalised in 1975 included scarcely any paddy land, and the twenty-five-acre ceiling on paddy land ownership imposed in 1972 brought in only 18,000 acres, just over 1% of the total paddy acreage in the Island. Almost all the land acquired was located in the Wet Zone, the site of the plantation sector, where about 40% of the cultivated acreage underwent a change of ownership.[99]

Although implemented rapidly and uncompromisingly once it was taken, the decision to nationalise the plantation sector was no great surprise. Action of this kind had long been advocated by the Marxist parties.[100] The British plantation companies had run down their investments in anticipation, and in the end were far less upset by the reform than the Sri Lankan government seemed to have expected.[101] For one of the main reasons for the reluctance to grasp the nettle had been the fear that the British plantation companies, who also dominated tea marketing, would impose heavy costs on an economy heavily

65

dependent on plantation exports in general and tea in particular.[102] The other main interest threatened by plantation sector reform was the political elite itself. Apart from the fact that much of the plantation area had originated in Sri Lankan enterprise, political independence had also seen a transfer of capital of all kinds from British to Sri Lankan hands, often with financial support from the state.[103] 'Between 1948 and 1972, the percentage extent held by the companies registered in the United Kingdom and by non-Ceylonese fell from 69 to 30 per cent of the total acreage of tea, 38 to 13 per cent of rubber and 11 to 4 per cent of coconut.'[104] In consequence both the foreign and the company elements in landownership were by 1972 in a minority even in the tea industry. The dominant categories of owner were Sri Lankan companies and individuals owning holdings of more than ten acres (see Table 4.1).

Two apparently powerful interests thus stood to lose from land reform in the estate sector. Ranged against them were powerful political demands for land, very strongly bolstered at the ideological level by a particular interpretation of the history of the plantation episode. For reasons which will become evident, this interpretation of history, here called the 'Sinhalese myth of the plantation impact', will be examined before reverting to the details of the reform.

The Sinhalese myth of the plantation impact
Many of the empirical claims associated with this particular interpretation of history are contentious. The term 'myth' is *not* used to indicate that they are necessarily false – although they are certainly exaggerated – but rather to describe an account of events which is widely accepted and transmitted without regard for or enquiry into its veracity.[105] It is termed a Sinhalese rather than a Sri Lankan myth because plantations were established almost exclusively in the Sinhalese area – the Wet Zone – and because the myth has played an important role in the development of the distinctive Sinhalese 'nationalism' which stands in awkward but generally antagonistic relationship to the corresponding 'nationalisms' or 'patriotisms' of the minorities, especially the Sri Lanka Tamils.

It is in the nature of myths that there is no authorised version. Some accounts of the one we are interested in are committed to paper,[106] sometimes in the guise of social science,[107] although most of my own encounters have been with verbal presentations. The central components found in the more elaborated versions appear to be as follows:

(i)   Above all, a dichotomy between the foreign – British-owned and Indian Tamil-worked – plantation and the neighbouring Sinhalese village.

66

Table 4.1. *Ownership of land area under export crops, 1972, prior to land reform (percentages)*

Form of ownership[a]	Tea	Rubber	Coconut	Total
Sterling companies[b]	24	11	neg.	9
Rupee companies[c]	25	13	neg.	10
Non-Sri Lankan individuals	2	2	—	1
Sri Lankan individuals	26	42	49	42
Public-sector agencies	5	1	neg.	1
Cooperative farms	neg.	neg.	neg.	neg.
Smallholdings	18	31	50	37
Total	100	100	100	100

[a] All holdings are of estates except for smallholdings, which are defined as being of less than ten acres.
[b] i.e. incorporated in the UK.
[c] i.e. incorporated in Sri Lanka.
Source: Peiris, 1978: 615.

(ii)   The use of force and fraud in the original process of plantation land acquisition.
(iii) The occupation by plantations of land either used by villagers at the time of acquisition or currently required for village agriculture.
(iv) The damaging effect of plantations on the local ecology and the village economy through such mechanisms as the appropriation of land required for grazing cattle and buffaloes, and the deforestation of hillsides for plantation crops, which leads to the drying-up of small streams used to irrigate village paddy fields in the valley bottoms.
(v)   The absence of benefits to the village population from plantation enterprise.
(vi) The general disintegration of village society and culture as a result of the monetisation and commercialism associated with plantations, and the uncouthness and viciousness of the immigrants attracted to them.
(vii) Somewhat paradoxically in view of the last point, the total insulation from one another of the plantation and village spheres.[108]

The contradiction between these two last emphases is perhaps not quite as total as it first appears, for point (vi) seems to refer mainly to history and point (vii) to the contemporary situation. This should not, however, be allowed to obscure the fact that, like so many myths, this one does contain contradictory elements.

Parts of two of the more influential written versions of the myth are reproduced in Appendix Two, and the interested reader may look there for details. Apart from the points listed above, the following features of one of them, the 1951 Report of the Kandyan Peasantry Commission, merit comment: a belief in the harmony, unity and self-sufficiency of the pre-colonial village, i.e. a reiteration of the myth, widespread in South Asia in particular, of a golden village-based past; the identification of Buddhism as the central socio-cultural theme of this village community; the conviction that autonomous and quasi-democratic village self-government was replaced by a bureaucratic administrative structure as part of the general process of decay associated with colonialism and plantation development; the identification of rice cultivation as the material focus of village life; a concern with the moral deterioration of the peasantry; the advocacy of remedial state action in the areas of marriage, divorce[109] and child labour; and a stress on the importance of protecting the peasantry from the 'grave danger' of persons of non-peasant character, for they encouraged 'gambling, drink and immorality'.[110]

The Sinhalese myth of the plantation impact links closely with other prominent themes in Sinhalese political culture. It forms a major component in the nationalist interpretation of Sinhalese history, and provides an instance of the way in which the contemporary village population is represented as a 'peasantry' subject to the blows of (non-Sinhalese) forces from outside village society.

The plantation impact: myth and reality
The veracity of the myth discussed above concerns us here not for its own sake but because the structure of the rural economy, especially the usefulness of the plantation–smallholder dichotomy, has major implications for the present work. The dichotomy is an aspect of the representation of the Sinhalese as essentially village-level paddy cultivators, and this in turn has in a variety of ways provided ideological and moral support for policies contrary to the interests of many smallholders.

In a discussion of the myth's veracity it is useful to separate out two issues: the circumstances of the origin of plantations, and the place of plantations in contemporary social and economic relationships. To make this distinction is not to fail to recognise that the element in the myth dealing with the original 'land-grabbing' for plantation development invests it with much of its contemporary moral force.

The issue of the historical accuracy of the myth need detain us only briefly, if only because it is the subject of relatively little research and much contention. One might simply point out a few of the revisions suggested by recent work. On the basis of his research on the Kegalle district, Meyer suggests that estate land was acquired through processes which, if morally dubious, were formally and legally correct, and also brought benefits to the local headmen and land agents who acted as intermediaries.[111] He and others have also found that the Sinhalese component of the permanent resident estate labour force in the nineteenth century was larger than is generally believed;[112] that the use of local Sinhalese village labour for casual work has long been widespread; and that there has probably been some cultural assimilation of the Sinhalese into the Indian Tamil estate labour force.[113] Roberts has shown that there is little empirical basis for claims that the land scarcity consequent upon plantation development generated a retrogression in Kandyan paddy cultivation technologies.[114] Sri Lankan-owned plantations were mainly built up by the purchase of small lots of Crown land. Meyer has made the very interesting suggestion that the rancour incurred by the estates was mainly the result of a political clash between estate and village, a conflict of territorial jurisdictions, rather than the result of any adverse effects of estate development on the village economy and society.[115]

The contemporary relevance of the myth of the deleterious plantation impact can best be assessed through the information given in Table 4.2. It is evident that the notion of estate–village isolation most nearly approaches descriptive accuracy in the case of tea production. Here one has large foreign-owned units employing large numbers of immigrant, non-Sinhalese labour resident on the estate; factory-like production processes involving continuity, expensive processing plants, extensive division of labour, and the dense spatial concentration of labourers; the extensive use of female labour; and a crop little grown in surrounding villages.[116] Through a variety of mechanisms all ultimately rooted in the degree to which the production process was spatially concentrated and factory-like in nature, coconut production contrasts on every one of these dimensions, while rubber production is intermediate. Coconut estates were often owned by absentees, but they were Sri Lankans, who often took a major interest in the locality and employed village labour. The crop was grown by the villagers and was familiar to them. The technical nature of the work differed little from what they undertook on their own plots.

Whether or not the isolation of village from estate has at any particular time been characteristic of rural Sri Lanka is not a question which can be answered unambiguously. In the first place, there are important and significant regional variations (see Table 4.2 and Map One; and, for some of the consequences, Chapter Six). In the second place, the question may be tackled from different perspectives, each useful, and each yielding different answers. This point may be illustrated by juxtaposing two contrasting approaches, here called 'the

Table 4.2. *Characteristics of the production of the three export crops in the 1940s*

	Tea	Rubber	Coconut
Total acreage (1946)	580,000	668,000	1,071,000
Main location	In Up Country areas with sparse Sinhalese village populations	In Mid Country areas with relatively dense Sinhalese village populations	In the coastal plain with dense Sinhalese village populations
Frequency of main kinds of work	Necessarily continuous	Continuous most of year but partially flexible	Continuous but flexible
Organisation of processing	Continuous, rapid and timely tea-making in on-site tea factories; specialist division of labour	Continuous making of latex locally, on a small scale, with little division of labour	Coconuts typically sold before off-site processing
Number of labourers required per acre	1.00	0.25	0.10
Main type of labour	Permanent Indian Tamil	Indian Tamil and Sinhalese, some of them local villagers	Local Sinhalese villagers, often casual
Place of residence of labour	Estate 'lines'	'Lines' and villages	Villages
Relative size of average estate	Large	Large	Small
Proportion of cropped area owned by smallholders (1946)	11%	23%	60%

Main type of ownership (1940s)	British companies	British and Sri Lankan companies and Sri Lankan individuals/families	Sri Lankan individuals/families
Number of persons employed (1946)	468,000	204,000	70,000
Proportion of females in labour force (1946)	47%	32%	19%

Sources: Snodgrass, 1966: Chapter 2, especially Table 2.10; Roberts and Wickremeratne, 1973; Wickremeratne, 1973b; Peiris, 1977b; *Census of Population 1946, Volume 1, Part 2*: Tables 48 and 53; and Meyer, 1978.

contemporary macro-economic perspective' and 'the historical socio-logical perspective'. The issues which they raise are very similar to those arising in discussions of the usefulness of 'dual economy' models. Indeed in Sri Lanka the two debates are often closely intertwined, for they relate to virtually the same set of empirical observations.

The first perspective[117] focuses on the *current* flows of *economic resources*, and identifies two quasi-autonomous circuits or networks. One network involves the production, transport and export of estate crops and the use of the consequent surpluses to import food and consumer goods for the populations involved in urban, plantation, mercantile and transport activities. The other network, located mainly in the traditional sector, is centred on the production of food for local consumption at the village level. The juxtaposition of these two networks suggests the usefulness of the 'dual economy' concept at the national level and of the notion of estate–village isolation at the local level. Estates produce crops for export and profits for foreign/urban owners, and use 'foreign' labour, which purchases imported food and consumer goods. It is admitted that there are 'leakages' or interactions between the two sectors. These are, however, least evident in the case of tea production, and, because tea so dominates the economy in value terms, the kinds of exception provided, for example, by the coconut industry, can be dismissed as peripheral phenomena.[118]

The 'historical sociological perspective'[119] is concerned with the *longer-term interaction* of the two sectors, and with the impact on *social relations* rather than with the enumeration of the monetary value of resource flows. It does not give the experiences associated with tea production the same priority. For the very concentration of tea estates in the Up Country Kandyan areas,[120] where village populations were sparse, meant that they did not figure prominently in the consciousness of daily experience of the bulk of the village population. Far more typical, in this sense, were the estates in the more densely populated Mid and Low Country, which produced mainly rubber and coconuts, and interacted more substantially with the local village populations (see Table 4.2). In the 'coconut triangle' to the north of Colombo and in the tea- and rubber-producing areas of the Low Country one can find extensive estate–village integration: ownership of estates by persons with roots in the locality; recruitment of all labour from local villages; substantial local purchases of supplies and services by estates; and, in the case of tea production, purchase of green leaf from village smallholders for processing in estate tea factories and sales of tea seedlings between estate and villagers.[121] From this experience of estate–village integration stem several important features of recent Sri

Lankan political history, including the entrepreneurial and plantation base of the national elite and a rural Sinhalese proletarian base for the Marxist parties.

The final point to note on these contrasting perspectives on the estate–village relationship is that over the past half century or more the trends have been firmly in the direction of integration. The transfer of estates from British to Sri Lankan hands has already been noted above. At the same time the average size of estates has been declining and the relative and absolute importance of the smallholder element in export crop production has increased.[122] The Sinhalese proportion of the estate labour force appears to have been steadily increasing over the past century,[123] and the number of Indian Tamils in the population, in relative decline since 1931, has been in absolute decline since 1963.[124] More broadly, the relative contribution of export crop production to the national economy has been falling, and the smallholder food-producing sector expanding. The number of people engaged in producing estate crops was almost the same in 1971 as in 1946, declining from 28% to 16% of the work force.[125] Estates have declined in distinctiveness and importance, and continue to do so.

Ideologies of estate and village: the 'Kandyan connection'

To delineate the outlines of the Sinhalese interpretation of the estate impact is an important step towards understanding contemporary Sri Lankan politics. The next step is to explain the origins and persistence of this ideology. For this purpose we may hearken back to the discussion in Chapter Three of the interests served by the representation of the Sinhalese as a rural peasantry, victimised by a colonial land policy which benefits 'alien' and plantation interests, and meriting, under proper supervision and control, a reversal of this policy, aimed at restoring their rights. It was pointed out that this programme helped give legitimacy to the political aspirations of the elite, although only if the blame for the existing state of affairs could be pinned on alien (non-Sinhalese) planters, estate labourers and capitalists, and the (capitalist) plantation elite itself omitted from the ranks of demons. Sinhalese political assertiveness, the ruptured traditional village community, land-grabbing, the assaults of aliens and capitalists, the homogeneity of the peasantry and the isolation of village from estate are all of a piece in terms of the logic of ideology. Accepting that these related elements of a total interpretation of history have served, and continue to serve, the political interests of both elite groups and the general 'Sinhaleseness' of the contemporary political order, it still seems reasonable to question how an ideology so substantially at variance with the villagers'

experience can continue to receive so much support. Part of the answer
– the part which concerns us here – is that the myth neither originates in
nor relates to the estate area as a whole, but to only a part of it: the
Kandyan districts in general – Kandy, Kegalle, Matale, Ratnapura,
Nuwara Eliya and Badulla – and Kandy district in particular. It is
descriptively most accurate in relation to these areas, is articulated
most vocally there, and is especially significant in the context of their
politics.[126]

The particular historical experience of the Kandyan areas are
outlined in more detail in Chapter Six. A few important elements may
be sketched in here: the existence of an independent Kandyan state in
the seventeenth and eighteenth centuries when the Low Country – the
southwestern littoral – was under European rule; the greater
'traditionality' of Kandyan society; the contemporary identification of
Kandyan culture as authentic Sinhalese culture; the relatively limited
access of the Kandyan population to non-agricultural employment; the
very limited involvement of the Kandyan aristocracy, compared to the
Low Country elite, in plantation capitalism; the fact that plantations in
the Kandyan areas were mainly large and British-owned, while those in
the Low Country were smaller and Sri Lankan-owned; and the
relatively limited engagement of Kandyan villagers in plantation
employment, at least on a permanent basis. In addition, large tea
estates were concentrated in the higher-altitude Kandyan areas, and it
was thus there that the relatively stark village–estate dichotomy and
opposition described above was to be found.

For a number of reasons these experiences have combined with other
factors to make hostility to estates an especially prominent ideological
and political theme in rural Kandy. Although population densities are
no greater in the Kandyan areas than in the Low Country,[127] the lack of
access to non-agricultural or even estate employment has meant that
the consequences of rural population growth have been especially
acute in the Kandyan areas. The estates, located on the hills, seem to be
more visibly hemming in and pressing down upon the villages, which
are generally in the valley bottoms where paddy fields are found. The
demand for land, agricultural and residential, is especially acute in
rural Kandy.[128] Wage rates in smallholder agriculture are noticeably
lower than elsewhere in the Island,[129] while the rents paid by *ande*
tenants have remained high there after the Paddy Lands Acts, although
they have tended to come down elsewhere.[130] Land hunger seems to
have been one factor in the relative persistence in the Kandyan areas of
'traditional' or 'feudal' social relations, i.e. relations of social and
political dependence expressed through and arising from control of

access to land.[131] Land hunger is especially acute in Kandy district itself, where a particularly dense rural population coexists with a proportionately large estate sector.[132]

Politically the rural Kandyan population have long been relatively radicalised. They have turned out to vote in higher numbers than elsewhere in the Island, indeed in numbers almost unheard of under voluntary electoral systems.[133] Yet this radicalism has not been channelled through the Marxist parties. Probably mainly because in the 1930s and 1940s the Marxists were politically very close to the organisations representing Indian Tamil estate labour, whom the Kandyan poor identify as one of their main enemies and oppressors, the Marxists have garnered very few votes in the Kandyan districts, and those mainly from the estate populations.[134]

The main channel for mobilising the grievances of the Kandyan poor has been the SLFP.[135] This might seem somewhat paradoxical in view of the fact that, since S. W. R. D. Bandaranaike's assassination in 1959, the SLFP has been reorganised by his widow, Mrs Sirimavo Bandaranaike, around a leadership nucleus in which members of the Kandyan aristocracy, many of them connected to her by family links, have been prominent.[136] The relationship has not always been easy.[137] But it is precisely in providing an ideological and programmatic bridge between the 'aristocratic' or 'feudal' leadership of the SLFP and the Kandyan poor that the Sinhalese myth of the plantation impact has had its greatest significance. Apart from articulating the undoubted resentments of the Kandyan poor against both the estates and their Indian Tamil work force, it has the great advantage of distracting the attention of the rural poor away from the persistence of 'feudal' dominance. The Kandyan aristocracy, although benefiting indirectly from plantation enterprise, was not itself much involved in plantation ownership. It has thus found the Sinhalese myth of the plantation impact extremely useful. Unlike the longer-established Low Country capitalist class, the Kandyan aristocracy, a relatively *arriviste* component of the *national* political elite, has found compelling reasons to articulate anti-plantation sentiments into a consistent ideology and has also been relatively free to do so without running into direct contradiction with its own background and interests.

It is scarcely surprising that these sentiments should be most loudly and effectively articulated in Kandy district itself, which is an area of especially acute rural overcrowding; is, as the nucleus of the old Kandyan kingdom, the main bearer of Kandyan traditions; and has the political advantage of containing a large population centre, while the villages of the more remote Kandyan districts are characterised by relative inaccessibility.[138] Leading Kandyan politicians represent electorates in and around Kandy town.

With this background information on the 'Kandyan connection' the course of the 1970s land reforms can be interpreted more clearly. However, before we come on to that issue, it will be useful to look briefly at two earlier programmes for relieving the landlessness and poverty of the Kandyan poor.

Programmes for the Kandyan poor

Some decades before the estates were nationalised it had been felt expedient to make provision for acquiring blocks of estate land for redistribution among the landless.[139] This had never been a major programme in comparison with the Crown lands alienation programme (see Table 3.1), but ended up as being of especial benefit to the poor of the three Kandyan districts of Kandy, Kegalle and Matale, where the topography is relatively mild, access to Kandy and Colombo relatively easy, and where Sinhalese villagers are in a majority, yet live alongside substantial plantation sectors. These districts contained 28% of the plantation area in 1962, yet by 1970 had accounted for 44% of the land acquired and redistributed under the Acquired Estates Programme. This was granted in homestead-size lots averaging two-thirds of an acre.[140]

The other programme which concerns us is, unlike the acquisition of estate lands, rooted in the Kandyan districts by explicit intention and by statute. Until the inauguration in the late 1970s of a number of integrated rural development programmes specific to particular districts, the Department for Kandyan Peasantry Rehabilitation was operating the only rural programme expressly confined to a particular part of the Island. The Department has its origins in the work of the Kandyan Peasantry Commission, which was appointed immediately after Independence, was staffed mainly by prominent Kandyan MPs, and reported in 1951.[141]

Appendix Two contains an extensive quotation from the Commission's diagnosis of the causes of poverty and landlessness in the Kandyan areas. This diagnosis is radical in the sense that it pins much of the blame on basic features of the socio-economic system, above all the very existence of the plantation sector. The report represents one of the most authoritative channels for the articulation of the Sinhalese myth of the plantation impact. As was noted above, it locates the causes of poverty very firmly outside the boundaries of village society. For example, the *ande* (sharecropping) system, especially widespread in the Kandyan districts,[142] is treated with no more than a mild rebuke. The system is said to be essentially unobjectionable, but to be encumbered with a number of unfortunate 'incidental features', including high 'preliminary payments' (known as *madaran*), the tenants' obligation to provide free services to landlords, and insecurity of tenure. Legislation to control these practices is recommended.[143]

In contrast to the radicalism of the Commission's verbal attack on the plantation system, the outcome of its report has been mild and not oriented to structural reform. The Kandyan Peasantry Rehabilitation Department has been engaged almost entirely on topping up public expenditure on social infrastructure – mainly roads, schools, medical facilities and water supplies – in the two Kandyan provinces, Central Province and Uva Province.[144] The ideological connotations of the terms 'peasantry' and 'rehabilitation' require little comment. The latter is not explicitly defined, but clearly bears some relation to the censorious attitude of the Commission to various aspects of the behaviour and morality of the rural population (see Appendix Two), and connotes the repair of moral and social damage caused by the plantation system.[145]

The report itself is an important landmark in the process by which the rural Kandyan areas were officially recognised as having special needs, and a special claim on public resources.

The 1970s reforms

The 'Kandyan connection' is important not so much in explaining that estates were nationalised in the 1970s, but in explaining the way the land so acquired was distributed. A key figure in this was the late Mr Hector Kobbekaduwa, Minister of Agriculture and Lands in the United Front government of 1970–7, a relative of Mrs Bandaranaike, a Kandyan 'aristocrat' and MP for the Yatinuwara electorate, a very densely populated rural area close to Kandy town. Kobbekaduwa was a relatively prominent member of the Cabinet, was generally identified as a radical, yet, unlike some other leading SLFPers, had no close contacts with or background in the Marxist parties.[146] His Deputy Minister, H. M. Navaratne, also represented a Kandyan seat, Minipe.

The 1970 United Front represented the most stable SLFP–Marxist alliance that Sri Lanka has experienced. Since 1956 the SLFP had shifted somewhat from its religious, cultural and linguistic focus and developed a firmer orientation to economic radicalism. The Marxist parties had also learned to mute their orthodox cosmopolitan and working-class 'line' and style in order to operate within a polity dominated by the language and symbols of Sinhalese Buddhist nationalism.[147]

Despite the firmness of the radical alliance, land reform had not featured in the United Front's common electoral programme. Hector Kobbekaduwa had been toying with the idea of a land reform since coming to power, but had mainly been concerned to meet the demands of the Kandyan poor for homestead plots.[148] His plans were, however, overwhelmed in the atmosphere of political crisis following the Insurgency of April 1971.

The JVP youth movement had a very profound impact both because its insurgency came so near to initial military success and because the resort of so many young people to arms seemed to constitute a devastating criticism of the alleged radicalism of the recently elected government. The JVP had worked for a United Front electoral victory, was linked to the establishment Marxist parties by a common Marxist idiom and ideology, and to the SLFP through a social base in much the same rural 'petit bourgeoisie' who had played a prominent role in the SLFP electoral upsurge in 1956, a generation before.[149]

The JVP had no clear agrarian programme and one main objective: state power.[150] The decision of the government to respond with a massive programme of estate nationalisation appears to have been determined by the need to both establish its credentials for radical action and contribute to solving the problem of youth unemployment, which had contributed so much to the JVP's support.[151]

The decision to nationalise the estates was certainly taken and implemented decisively. In comparative perspective the most notable aspect of both the 1972 and the 1975 measures is that the land acquisition process was implemented very rigorously. Contrary to the typical Asian experience, there appears to have been very little evasion. Indeed, it could be argued that the reform was 'overimplemented': tales of UNP supporters having lost their best lands and being left with fifty acres of poor or even barren land were common at the time, and seem to account for most of the land restitutions which have taken place since the change of government in 1977.[152] There was also scope for some administrative discretion over the amount of land to be retained, and this too appears to have been used against political opponents of the regime.[153] Further, the use for compensation purposes of the land values declared to the income tax authorities was clearly confiscatory in intent,[154] and has been the subject of amending legislation by the subsequent government.

Although supporters of the United Front government were on occasion granted temporary continued access to the fruits of their expropriated land through their political connections and positions in 'cooperative' organisations,[155] there have to the author's knowledge

78

been few credible allegations that such persons were able to retain more land than could be justified legally.[156] The reform was thus relatively very complete. The Prime Minister lost 1,300 acres of land under the reform, and the then leader of the Opposition, currently the President, J. R. Jayawardena, lost 600 acres.[157]

Personal and class interests were sacrificed to perceived electoral imperatives. These imperatives could, however, be said to have arisen from peasant class demands only to a small degree. The demands of the Kandyan rural dwellers for homestead plots, articulated by Kobbekaduwa, played only a small role in the decision to nationalise estates, which was taken very much in haste and on high. As is recounted below, haste (and inefficiency) also describes the way in which the land acquired was distributed.

The distribution and use of the acquired land[158]

The pattern of distribution of acquired land by formal institutional categories is given in Table 4.3. For our purposes it is, however, useful to use three somewhat broader categories relating more squarely to the politics of the operation. The first is 'acquisitive nationalisation', indicating the transfer of ownership to a public corporation operated very much in traditional plantation style. The second is 'redistributive nationalisation', a term which covers a variety of institutional arrangements united by the fact that they permitted MPs and other politicians of the ruling alliance a large degree of direct control, especially of labour hiring. The third is redistribution to individual villagers. These three political categories relate mainly to the first six institutional categories in Table 4.3. The other categories are of minor quantitative and political significance and will not be discussed here.

The main recipients of land were the two large public-sector corporations, the State Plantations Corporation and the Janawasama (Janatha Estates Development Board). As they fell under the jurisdiction of the Ministry of Plantation Industries, these two corporations were run very much along established lines, especially at the estate level itself, where no concession was made to principles of 'socialism' or 'participation'. Until the expulsion of the LSSP from the governing coalition in 1975, the Ministry of Plantation Industries was run on strong 'productionist' lines by the LSSP Minister, Colvin R. de Silva and his LSSP Secretary, Doric de Souza.[159] There were perpetual clashes between the Ministry and those politicians who were more concerned to redistribute estate land to villagers or obtain jobs on the estates for their supporters.[160] The strongly 'productionist' stance of the LSSP, fully consistent with the fact that its leaders have in the past

Table 4.3. *Recipients of land under the land reform programme*
(thousand acres)

Recipient	Mid-1976	1978
State Plantation Corporation	197	344
Janawasama[a]	230	335
Usawasama[b]	68	—
Electoral cooperatives	185	—
Janawasa Commission	50	31
Individual villagers	52	109
Estate Management Service Scheme	—	35
Land Commissioner's Department	71	30
District Land Reform Authority	29	24
Livestock Development Board	8	19
Revenue Department	30	9
District development projects	1	8
Tea, Rubber and Coconut Research Institutes	12	5
Multipurpose Cooperative Societies	3	3
Sri Lanka Sugar Corporation	3	3
Conservator of Forests	1	3
Sri Lanka Cashew Corporation	neg.	1
Coconut Cultivation Board	2	1
Agricultural Productivity Committees	4	—
Special cooperative organisations	2	—
Others	31	20
Total	981	981

Note: In this table and subsequent tables neg. stands for a negligible amount and — for none.
[a] Peoples Estates Development Board.
[b] Up Country Cooperative Estates Development Board.
Source: Wanigaratne *et al.*, 1980: Appendix 6; and Central Bank of Ceylon, *Review of the Economy*, 1978: 41.

prided themselves on the efficiency with which their personal estates were run,[161] reflects in part the fact that the LSSP leadership tends to share with the leadership of the UNP, but far less so with the SLFP, a concern for efficiency and good management associated with the value system of the 'colonial' pre-1956 social and political order.

The Usawasama (Up Country Cooperative Estates Development Board) was also a public-sector corporation. It was, however, under the control of the Ministry of Agriculture and Lands and, as its name implies, managed land located in the Kandyan areas. Its cooperative principles were soon abandoned.[162] It became widely known for poor management; sacrifice of output for immediate benefits to local villagers in the form of jobs, especially non-productive jobs as 'watchers' or 'supervisors', rights to pluck estate tea, or allotments; and inconsiderate treatment of Indian Tamil employees.[163] Electoral cooperatives, which were effectively under the control of local MPs or politicians of the ruling coalition, were generally run in much the same way as Usawasama estates.[164] *Janawasas* were distinctive in that they were claimed to be production cooperatives run collectively by the work force. Their existence was the outcome of the strength of radical elements both in the SLFP and in the governing coalition in general in the early 1970s. The *Janawasa* Commission was headed by the Prime Minister's daughter who, jointly with her then husband, Kumar Rupasinghe,[165] formed the main focus of radical elements in the SLFP. Effective control of *Janawasas* may, however, not have been in their hands.[166] The *Janawasas* certainly never lived up to their collective principles.[167]

For a few years estates managed under these various forms of 'redistributive nationalisation' generated extra jobs for those with the appropriate political connections, and so ensured them a certain income, sometimes in return for little work. The benefits did not, however, last long. The return of the UNP government in 1977 brought the wholesale replacement of 'political' employees by those with UNP connections. The estates managed by the Usawasama, the electoral cooperatives and the *Janawasa* Commission were transferred to one or other of the public plantation corporations, and thus brought under 'regular' management (see Table 4.3).

Land for the peasantry?

The estate land reform was conducted in the name of the peasantry,[168] yet the actual benefits, mainly short-term, took the form of estate jobs for those with the appropriate political connections. The total amount alienated to villagers was small (see Table 4.3), and that mainly low-value, uncultivated land.[169] Allotments were very small.[170] The pattern of distribution of land among individual villagers very much reflects the personal influence of the Minister of Agriculture and Lands. As of mid-1976 a quarter of all land distributed among individuals had been alienated in one district out of the total of twenty-two – Kandy.[171] Elsewhere little effort seems to have been made, despite the approach of the general election and the obvious electoral benefits to be obtained. As a result, in its first year in office the UNP government elected in 1977 was able to distribute to individuals a further 39,000 acres, increasing the former total by 56%.[172] This was followed by special legislation, the Land Grants (Special) Provision Act, No. 43 of 1979, under which it was planned to grant free to the landless, and under full ownership rather than under permit, 190,000 acres of land under the control of the Land Reform Commission.[173] The process of alienation had been so casual and arbitrary that some allotments were inconveniently located and not claimed or used. This facilitated their repossession and redistribution by the new government.[174]

Even in Kandy district the redistribution to villagers was not a great success. For basic facts of topography often make it difficult for villagers' resentments against estates and Indian Tamil labour to be translated into stable and productive tenure reforms. Villages are generally located in valley bottoms, and estates up in the hills. If given individual blocks of tea land, villagers are reluctant to move house there and, as well as suffering from unfamiliarity with tea production, face a long daily climb if they are to cultivate efficiently. Many plots seem simply to have been plucked while they continued to yield and then abandoned. Estate employment is similarly viewed warily. Unproductive and undemanding jobs as 'watchers' are welcome. Labouring jobs impose the threat of a loss of status as they are associated with Indian Tamils. Residence on the estate is even less welcome, and likely to result in a total loss of economic and social mobility prospects for children due to poor access to education and the loss of social and political connections.[175]

A final point about the absence of a peasant interest in the land distribution procedure concerns those paddy farmers who found themselves, as a result of the reform, tenants of the Land Reform Commission or of the various other institutions listed in Table 4.3. They were not given title to their lands, and continued to pay rent to their institutional landlord.[176] It was the UNP government elected in 1977, perhaps concerned as much as anything with the administrative inconvenience of this arrangement, which decided to vest them with ownership rights.

Land reform and class interest

The nationalisation of the estates was, very much like the 1958 Paddy Lands Act, an elite-inspired measure owing little to popular demands or pressures. One difference was that in 1972 there was a fairly well-articulated demand – the demand of the Kandyan poor for estate land – which was ready to exploit the legislation. In the general disorganisation which reigned, the Sinhalese villagers of Kandy district in particular were allocated a substantial amount of land and obtained many places on estate payrolls. There was a degree of truth in at least the latter part of the claim, contained in the SLFP's 1977 election manifesto, that 'The Kandyan peasants who had been driven out of their homelands were given back land acquired from the

82

plantations.'[177] The emphasis should perhaps be on the 'given', for policy and programme, even in the context of Kandy district, showed clear marks of elite leadership.

In the first place, the enormous practical problems of translating anti-estate resentments into programmes bringing permanent benefit to the villagers suggest that these resentments may have been encouraged and channelled to serve the interests of the elite.

Secondly, and more concretely, the 1972 reform deliberately excluded the one category of land which would have been unreservedly welcome to the Kandyan poor: the paddy land owned by the rural middle classes and the temples.[178] The extremely high ceiling of twenty-five acres of paddy land was clearly set to exclude the first almost completely, while the total exemption from both the 1972 and the 1975 measures of religious and charitable foundations left even the larger temple holdings untouched.[179]

The issue of temple lands was important to the Kandyan aristocracy, for their own interests – personal and class, material and political – were closely bound up with the wealth, status and landholdings of the Kandyan temples. The ambiguity of the SLFP alliance of Kandyan aristocracy and poor is illustrated by Hector Kobbekaduwa's dilemma over a bill to abolish *rajakariya*, the obligation of tenants on certain temple lands, almost all Kandyan, to provide ceremonial and other services to the temple. The interests of the poor and of local elites were starkly opposed, and the SLFP had obligations to both. Kobbekaduwa delayed the bill, and finally introduced it, too late for action, in the closing stages of the 1970–7 Parliament. One might note in contrast that, in the 1958 Paddy Lands Bill, Philip Gunawardena had tackled temple lands frontally, and with some success, to the extent that attempts to have them excluded from its provisions met with no success.[180]

The exemption of the rural middle classes from the 1977 reform of the land is an indication of the way in which the political system had changed since 1958. The increasing significance of party organisation and the declining role of 'notables' operating outside the party system were associated with a more stable and deeply rooted set of political linkages from Colombo down to the villages, and a more effective pattern of articulation of demands. Unlike in 1958, the elite could not risk upsetting the rural middle classes in a flush of enthusiasm for doing something about the condition of the peasantry. Instead, a section of the elite turned upon its own class. It seems to have been 'insufficiently prepared for the inevitable demands which would be made by local politicians on the government side',[181] and was obliged to acquiesce in the short-term plunder of many of the acquired estates for the purpose of creating rather short-lived jobs for party supporters.[182] Party interests dominated over the potential claims of the smallholder class. At no stage was serious consideration given to the possibility of alienating large areas of land in smallholdings to the rural population.

Conclusion

The policy instances discussed in this and the preceding chapter run through a period of more than half a century which has witnessed considerable changes in the Sri Lankan polity. At the beginning both the administration and the national political elite had considerable freedom to decide on the measures they would pursue for the good of the peasantry. The more effective articulation of interests through the party system has considerably reduced this freedom to manoeuvre and, in the more recent period, a section of the elite has reacted to what it perceived as urgent electoral imperatives by attacking the plantation base of its own class. There has, however, been very considerable continuity in the broader dimensions of the politics of land policy: the origin of major policy initiatives in the imperatives of political competition between elite groups (including, in the early period, the colonial administration); the attribution, sometimes incorrectly, of needs and demands to the peasantry by their political masters; the near absence of clearly articulated demands from the grassroots; the presentation and justification of land policy within the framework of the Sinhalese nationalist interpretation of history; the avoidance of any effective major attack on the landholdings of the rural middle classes, the source of the local cadres of all political parties; the representation of the village population as a peasantry not fundamentally divided by internal conflicts of interest over land or any other issue; the adoption of land redistribution procedures which helped stifle the emergence of any class-like, horizontal political linkages between categories of the rural poor; and the effective exclusion of the Indian Tamil population from any share in this process through which large extents of land have been redistributed to the rural Sinhalese population.[183]

5

Pricing and agricultural services

Introduction

The previous two chapters have been concerned with land policy, and thus with the 'land control' aspects of agricultural production. The relatively extended treatment is justified by the emotive and political salience of land questions in contemporary Sri Lankan politics and by the convenience – from the scholarly point of view – of the form in which these issues have surfaced politically. For land policy has been punctuated by a few major breaks in policy, each associated with new legislation. The politics involved can be relatively easily grasped through an analysis of the events and debates surrounding each policy change. This is not the case with the policies treated in this chapter: attempts by the government to affect the ways in which smallholders use their land. Here we are much nearer the realm of 'normal politics': continual incremental policy changes; the more visible influence of established practice; the continual replication in debate of similar diagnoses and prescriptions; and the persistent influence on policy towards smallholders of the imperatives, pressures and constraints which affect policy, especially economic policy, more broadly. The latter point is especially salient in an economy such as Sri Lanka's which has been under the pressure of rapid population growth, almost continually declining terms of trade, and only mediocre aggregate growth performance. It follows that it is not always easy to discover the 'real' politics behind the policy issues discussed in this chapter. One must rely in part on inference of various kinds.

The chapter is divided into six main sections. The first deals with the crop composition of the smallholder economy; the second with the nature and content of the main policy measures designed to promote smallholder production; the third with agricultural pricing policy; the fourth with the politics of agricultural prices; the fifth with inter-party differences in agricultural policy; and the sixth with the ideology and discourse which suffuses discussion of policy towards smallholders.

The chapter is intended to demonstrate five main sets of conclusions. The first is that policy has been, to an unusual degree, focused on, and supportive of, only one crop of a wide range grown by smallholders – paddy.

The second is that the support given to paddy production has mainly taken the form of generous financial allocations in the form of subsidy rather than remunerative producer prices or any major effort to ensure the efficient delivery of subsidised services. The net subsidy from the state to paddy producers is: (a) lower than is widely believed; (b) highly concentrated on a relatively small number of recipients; (c) partly outweighed by the transfer of income from rice producers to consumers through government policies which depress rice producer prices: and (d) massively outweighed by a large transfer of resources out of the smallholder sector as a whole, achieved by the direct and indirect taxation of smallholder producers of export crops, especially coconut producers. The appropriation of a large surplus from the export crop sector has generally permitted the state to subsidise both domestic rice producers and food consumers. However, when the interests of local food producers and consumers have come into direct conflict, the latter have generally prevailed.

The third conclusion is that, as in the case of land policy, state assistance to smallholders has mainly taken the form of individual subsidies over whose allocation enormous political and administrative discretion can be exercised.

The fourth conclusion is that there has been very little articulation of any demand for higher output prices for smallholder crops, despite the high level of institutional capacity to meet such a demand.

The fifth conclusion is that debate on smallholder policy is suffused with concepts, terms and assumptions which express and perhaps support the continued political subordination of the peasantry and, more specifically, justify the policy of giving financial subsidies rather than providing price incentives.

Rice and the smallholder economy

In his speech to Parliament in support of the 1958 Paddy Lands Bill the then Prime Minister, S. W. R. D. Bandaranaike, made the grossly exaggerated claim that the 'vast majority' of the population were 'peasants'. He followed this with another exaggeration, which is less gross and more excusable, although at the same time less grammatical:

Whatever may be his status, whether he is a tenant under the *ande* system or in what other method it may be, paddy cultivation appears to be offering the vast bulk of our rural population that chief occupation such as it is.[1]

86

Table 5.1. *Estimated value of smallholder production according to crop (1970–9 average)*[a]

Crop	Percentage of the crop attributable to smallholders by:		Average annual value of smallholder production (1970–9)	
	Acreage	Value	Total (Rs million)	As percentage of smallholder production
Tea	18	10	73	1
Rubber	31	20	82	1
Coconuts	50	50	517	10
Paddy	100	100	1,534	29
Other crops	100	100	3,118	59
Total			5,324	100

[a] The smallholder acreage is defined, according to the only statistics available, as (a) that in holdings of fewer than ten acres of *each* crop in the case of tea, rubber and coconuts, and (b) as the entire acreage of paddy and other crops. For warnings about the reliability of these data and information on the assumptions used in calculations, see Moore, 1981d: 184–5.

Source: The figures on the total value of output by crop are obtained from the Central Bank of Ceylon, *Review of the Economy*, 1979: Table 2; and those on the division of the plantation crop acreage between smallholdings and estates from Peiris, 1978: 615.

The view that the Sri Lankan/Sinhalese smallholder population live – and have traditionally lived – mainly from paddy production is very widespread. It is a view which has entered almost as dogma into official and academic literature, and is one which in the past I have helped perpetuate.[2] It is also false in a material sense, as is simply illustrated by the information in the final two columns of Table 5.1. In the 1970s, after a long period of rapid growth of paddy production under state sponsorship (see Table 7.3), paddy accounted for only about a third of smallholder production by value. The evidence indicates that rice has become *more important* as a crop and a food relative to other staples such as millet, maize and root crops, since the plantation crop boom in the late nineteenth century made it possible for the economy to support more rice imports.

Why then should Bandaranaike, and so many others, falsely equate Sri Lankan/Sinhalese smallholder agriculture with paddy production? There are a number of reasons why one can be genuinely misled in this direction. One is that paddy is by far the most important single smallholder crop. The 'other crops' category in Table 5.1 is extremely diverse. It includes a fairly discrete subcategory of so-called 'minor export crops' (cocoa, cinnamon, citronella, nutmeg, cloves, pepper,

Table 5.2. *Distribution of cultivated area according to holding size and crop category, 1962*

Size class of holding (acres)	Percentage of cropped area under:				Percentage of holdings in the size class
	Paddy[a]	Plantation crops[b]	Other crops	All crops	
Less than 0.25	8	56	36	100	8
0.25–0.49	10	54	36	100	12
0.50–0.99	21	49	30	100	16
1.00–2.49	31	44	25	100	30
2.50–4.99	44	37	19	100	19
5.00–9.99	50	34	16	100	11
10.00–24.99	39	51	10	100	3
25.00–49.99	22	73	5	100	1
50.00–99.99	9	88	3	100	1
100.00 +	3	91	6	100	
All holdings	28	58	14	100	100

Note: A very similar cropping pattern by holding size is found at the level of individual districts.
[a] Asweddumised acreage.
[b] Tea, rubber and coconuts, plus very small acreages of cinnamon and cocao.
Source: Census of Agriculture 1962, Volume 2: Table 2.

papain, kapok, arecanuts and tobacco), chillies, vegetables of many kinds, potatoes, manioc, sweet potato and other starchy root crops, soya beans, gingelly and other oil seeds, cotton, coffee, onions, groundnuts, maize, millet, sorghum, cowpea, dhal and other pulses, sugarcane, fruits of many kinds, animal products and – probably not registered in the official statistics – cannabis.

The second reason is revealed by a comparison of the figures in the final column of Table 5.1 with those in the final row of Table 5.2. The per-acre value of production is much lower for paddy than for 'other crops'. The landscape implies paddy is of greater economic significance than it actually is.

The third reason is that paddy is indeed of particular cultural significance in Sri Lankan, especially Sinhalese, villages, and this leads villagers themselves to accord it undue importance. One aspect of this is that cultivation-related magico-religious practices relate almost entirely to paddy fields and the paddy crop.[3] Another is that the honorific value attached to the status of paddy producer leads villagers to vastly exaggerate the material importance of producing paddy in response, for example, to census questions about sources of livelihood.[4] The honorific status attached to paddy rather than other crops is probably also related to social status in a broader sense. While cultivation has never been the monopoly of any caste group, and, unlike in India, all Sri Lankan castes have traditionally held and cultivated land, paddy land ownership is particularly associated with the *Goigama* caste, the highest ranking group.

It would, however, be inconsistent with the perspective of this book to leave the matter here. Let us ask instead what interests are served by this tendency to reduce, mentally, smallholder production to paddy cultivation. There are two. Firstly, this conceptual reductionism may be seen as an aspect of that broader set of images[5] which are being pieced together in this book, and which add up to a consistent ideology which represents the rural population as a homogeneous traditional peasantry both entitled to and needing the protection and tutelage of the state and of the political elite which controls the state. Secondly, the reduction of 'smallholder' to 'paddy farmer', and the associated tendency for policy to focus mainly and beneficially on the paddy sector, actually benefits some strata of rural society more than others. The point is easily illustrated through the data in Table 5.2. In terms of crops, large landowners mainly concentrate on tea, rubber and coconuts, owners of very small holdings on 'other crops', and owners of medium holdings, especially those in the two- to ten-acre range, on paddy. 'Paddy bias' tends to benefit the rural middle classes, the source of most political cadres, rather than the poor and near landless. The latter cultivate mainly in the form of home gardens. 'It is a serious mistake to believe that paddy incomes accrue mainly to the poor.'[6]

The paddy bias of ideology and policy is also reflected in statistics and in research. There is much more that one can say about paddy than other smallholder crops. Insofar as this book exhibits the same bias, that is mainly conscious and intentional. For paddy, as the major smallholder crop, and the only one grown Island-wide, is *the* potential political rallying point for Sinhalese/Sri Lankan smallholders' economic policy demands. If we are to explain why these smallholders have been backward in articulating certain kinds of political demands, then the paddy sector does merit special attention.

State provision of farmer services

Smallholder cultivation in Sri Lanka is supported by an impressive array of state-provided services: extension advice; supply of fertilisers, pesticides and other chemicals; tractor services; marketing; small- and large-scale irrigation development; subsidies for tree crops, both for replanting and new planting; agricultural research; a crop insurance

scheme; provision of sprayers and other items of agricultural equip-
ment; production and duplication of certified seed; price support
schemes; credit; land colonisation; milk collection schemes; and supply
of planting material or pedigree animals. No attempt is made here to
give further details of most of the schemes[7] and only a small number are
selected for detailed discussion below. Three particular points are
worth making about the evolution of this very comprehensive pattern
of state-provided services.

The first point is that many services are long-established, especially
in comparison with other former European colonies. Although unwill-
ing to grant the smallholder remunerative crop prices – partly perhaps
because of the belief that he would not respond to price incentives –
colonial governments were sufficiently concerned about the 'peasant
sector' to establish special institutions to promote its development,
notably the Department of Agriculture in 1912.[8] The first steps to
encourage rural cooperative credit were taken in 1911. A crop
insurance scheme has been in operation since 1958. State purchasing of
paddy at a fixed guaranteed price, generally competitive with or not
very far below private market rates, dates from 1948. Major state
initiatives to settle the peasantry in Dry Zone irrigation colonies date
from the 1930s. Paddy fertilisers have been subsidised since 1950.[9]

The second point is that war-induced food scarcities have been
important in both underlining the disadvantage of dependence on food
imports and, in the case of the Second World War in particular, in
creating the outlines of the food policy which has been pursued more or
less continually since.[10] The Japanese conquest of Burma in 1942
brought a food crisis: the introduction of wheat flour as an alternative
to rice in the popular diet; food rationing; a state monopoly of food
importing; state purchasing of paddy from farmers on a large scale.[11]

The third point is that the main agency for serving the smallholder,
the Department of Agriculture, has, from the time of its establishment,
been accused of an undue paddy bias. The accusation has been
repeated continually since, and remains valid.[12] Part of the explanation
is that the Department has been very much oriented to the development of agriculture in the irrigation-cum-settlement schemes in the
Dry Zone,[13] and that paddy is the major crop in these schemes. That is,
however, not in itself a completely satisfactory explanation. In the first
place, why should irrigated agriculture receive such an emphasis that,
for example, a promising research programme on dry-land crops at the
main research station, Maha Illupallama, was in the late 1960s swept
aside in favour of paddy research in the context of the expansion of the
irrigation-cum-settlement programme in the shape of the Mahaweli

scheme?[14] In the second place, it has been a continual source of complaint that this irrigation investment is underutilised partly for lack of adequate research and partly because government has paid little attention to the promotion of non-paddy crops to be grown in the water-scarce dry season. It is difficult to believe that paddy bias has not been accentuated by emotive and ideological considerations.

Chemical fertilisers

The mechanisms and magnitudes of the subsidy on paddy fertilisers have changed frequently since the practice began in 1950, and only in the early 1970s was the policy changed in favour of a general subsidy on all chemical fertilisers.[15] One set of figures suggests that in the early 1970s the value of the paddy fertiliser subsidy amounted to almost a half of the net subsidy from the state to rice producers.[16] The other major component of the subsidy was irrigation development. The latter, however, benefits relatively few farmers. The fertiliser subsidy has thus been the form of state bounty most widespread among paddy producers, and indeed farmers generally.

Not surprisingly, the evidence suggests that, both at local and regional levels, farmers located within easy access of the distribution points and road transport, use more fertiliser than other farmers. The benefits of the subsidy are unequally located over space, and also between socio-economic categories.[17] This does not, however, alter the fact that the price of fertiliser constitutes an important theme in the relationship between governments and the smallholder population. Cultivators are prone to bemoan the cost of fertiliser, and politicians to quote fertiliser subsidies as examples of their beneficence to the rural population. Further, the recurrent physical shortages of what is generally a much sought-after good create many occasions for political intervention and the use of administrative discretion in channelling supplies.

These physical shortages of fertiliser are especially interesting. In 1977 the Central Bank was moved to record officially that 'Delays in fertiliser supplies have been a recurrent experience in the major paddy growing areas.'[18] One widespread and conventional response has been to blame cultivators for ordering too late from the cooperatives.[19] This is clearly disingenuous. For if the formal procedures for obtaining fertiliser from the Fertiliser Corporation continually result in late delivery, then the procedures themselves require changing. The problem seems to lie in the distribution system, not with farmers. The procedures used by the local multipurpose cooperatives are conducive to a great deal of delay and disorder.[20] Perhaps more importantly, there have been major deficiencies in the logistics of the fertiliser supply operation at national level. These include the absence of regional warehouses between Colombo port and the local cooperatives, making difficult any flexible response to local needs; and the existence of an unnecessarily large and confusing number of different fertiliser mixes.[21] Efficient delivery has not been a major consideration in the management of public fertiliser supply.

Administrative efficiency is an extremely broad concept, and not an issue which I have been able to investigate in any detail for different sectors of the Sri Lankan government machine. Neither can the causes of high or low levels of efficiency in relation to smallholder services be easily explained. The existence of causal connections between administrative performance and politics can then at best be inferred only tentatively and indirectly. The pattern is, however, suggestive.

The Sri Lankan state machinery still retains some of its earlier reputation for relative effectiveness. Despite the wholesale politicisation discussed in Chapter Two, it has in several instances performed both continuing and *ad hoc* operations with commendable efficiency.[22] Yet performance in the distribution of smallholder services has generally been poor. At the same time, finance for smallholder programmes has been relatively lavish and the programmes themselves have multiplied. This pattern is at least consistent with the broader argument of this book. Financial generosity reflects some of the political and economic policy imperatives discussed in this and the previous chapter, but poor administrative performance reflects the inability of smallholder interests to enforce consideration of their occupational interests on the state machinery on a day-to-day basis.

One possible reaction to the above argument might be to suggest that 'administrative inefficiency' is not necessarily an unwelcome or an unintended phenomenon: that the shortages and opportunities for the use of influence which it creates are not only of positive benefit to certain categories of political actors, but the intended result of their actions. No evidence to support such a view is available. Clearly inefficiency does provide opportunities for political mediation. If it were in any degree the result of the specific intentions of these mediators then this would strengthen the argument about the weakness of smallholder class interests. Inefficiency does *not* appear to benefit those classes whose interests lie in a high rate of extraction of cheap food from the countryside. The regional pattern of paddy fertiliser use suggests that the distribution system is biased *against* the producers of marketable surpluses, who happen to be located furthest from Colombo. Inefficiency reduces the marketed food surplus. The most plausible explanation of poor delivery systems seems to lie in the political weakness of smallholders, who would generally benefit from a better system. At present politicians (and administrators) benefit from demands for mediation. It is impossible to say whether they consciously seek to increase such opportunities by causing shortages, either by commission or omission.

Agricultural credit

The experience in agricultural credit is similar to that in fertilisers: financial generosity combined with an inefficiency and arbitrariness which have seriously undermined the value of credit to smallholders *qua* smallholders, i.e. as cultivators requiring credit for the development of their agricultural activities. The subject has generated a very considerable literature[23] but the main points of present concern can be conveyed briefly from the data in Table 5.3.

Rates of default are high. They have been a problem ever since official cooperative credit was introduced.[24] They are not related to crop failure and thus the ability to repay.[25] Indeed, there appears, in the case of paddy, to be a coincidental association between good harvests and reduced rates of repayment. Most big increases in paddy production (1969/70, 1973/4, 1976/7, and 1977/8) have coincided with a big fall in the repayment rate (see Table 5.3). Apart from the apparent secular decline in repayment rates, two main factors affect the aggregate volume of advances and repayments.

One is what has been described as 'an unfortunate rural credit sequence'[26] of aggregate individual defaults leading to default on the part of the local cooperative union, the suspension of credit and then the commencement of a new cycle of lending and default. 'While at any one time the country as a whole is located at some point on this cycle . . . individual unions and branches show considerable variation.'[27]

The other factor determining the volume of credit and repayment is how and how far governments choose to use for partisan political purposes the volume of credit outlays and the degree of pressure for repayment which is applied to recipients. Repayment rates tend to fall before general elections. After the 1977 election, for example, the government offered what can only be described as a credit 'bonanza' to those rural people able to obtain a loan. Quite predictably, this was widely viewed as a reward for supporters of the government party. For the complicated procedures for obtaining credit, the subject of so much complaint from farmers, may be used in a discretionary manner to

93

Table 5.3. *Advances and repayments of official agricultural credit,*
1967–81

Year	Paddy			Other crops	
	Advances (Rs m.)	Percentage repaid	Paddy production (million bushels)	Advances (Rs m.)	Percentage repaid
1967–8	73	86	65	5	83
1968–9	56	66	66	6	83
1969–70	52	57	77	8	76
1970–1	29	61	67	5	82
1971–2	31	67	63	9	75
1972–3	28	66	63	10	76
1973–4	111	54	76	26	61
1974–5	86	53	55	28	58
1975–6	76	59	60	39	47
1976–7	102	47	80	79	29
1977–8	448	26	89	133	32
1978–9	60	78	92	17	79
1979–80	60	81	102	21	75
1980–1	97	81	107	30	72
1981–2	128	59	103	23	50

Source: Central Bank of Ceylon, *Annual Review of the Economy*, various years; and data on paddy production supplied by the Department of Economics and Statistics.

exclude some applicants and include others with the proper recommendations or political and personal connections.[28]

It is evident from Table 5.3 that credit for crops other than paddy is a relatively recent innovation. Further, the figures for credit to 'other crops' include no allocation for smallholder producers of tea, rubber and coconut, or indeed for producers of the 'minor export crops' such as cinnamon, cloves, cardamon, citronella, cocoa, coffee and black pepper. There is no credit scheme for any of these export crops,[29] a fact which seems to stem historically from their identification with the plantation sector. The main beneficiaries of agricultural credit have been paddy farmers, and in their case there has been a large gift element. It is reported that in parts of the North Central Province the disbursement of credit is referred to as 'cultivation pay day'.[30] There has not, however, been any reliable credit system such as would be required to support an expanding commercial farming sector. And, indeed, the absence of any pressure from farmers as an occupational group over credit allocation is reflected in the absence in Sri Lanka, unlike in India, of any obligation on official credit agencies to reserve a proportion of their funds for rural lending.

Crop insurance[31]

A similar degree of cynicism might be justified in relation to Sri Lanka's Agricultural Insurance Scheme. The mechanics of such schemes are especially complex and few countries have actually operated them. The Sri Lankan scheme, introduced in 1958 and relating only to paddy land, has been characterised by the extreme unwillingness of farmers to pay premia and their insistence on receiving indemnities in the event of alleged crop failure. Premia collected have typically amounted only to a fraction of those due, despite attempts to tie payments to the receipt of official credit. At the same time, indemnities paid have in most years exceeded the value of premia collected, and the scheme has operated at a small but regular cash loss, even when administration costs are excluded.[32] One device used has been to pay indemnities when claimed, subtracting unpaid premia on the spot.[33]

In many ways the experience with the Agricultural Insurance Scheme epitomises policy towards the smallholder more generally. The scheme has been of net financial benefit to some paddy cultivators, albeit only on a very small scale. The 'softness' with which it has been operated has turned what was intended to be a self-financing operation into a net subsidy, and one providing considerable opportunities for administrative discretion. At the same time, the harassment associated with officials' attempts to collect premia has made the scheme unpopular with cultivators in some areas at least.[34] The scheme has come to resemble an extremely elaborate and selective form of 'disaster relief'.

Irrigation and land development

The settlement of peasant cultivators in Dry Zone irrigation schemes has been a major element in rural policy in both symbolic and financial terms. Capital expenditure on irrigation and land development in the Dry Zone has absorbed a large proportion of public expenditure. For example, in 1976 and 1977, before the rapid expansion of irrigation investment resulting from the decision to accelerate the Mahaweli irrigation-cum-power project, capital expenditure on agriculture, irrigation and land development, most of it concentrated on new Dry Zone schemes, accounted for 22% of government capital expenditure. At this time the production of crops other than tea, rubber and coconuts was estimated to account for 19% of gross national product.[35] These figures suggest that Sri Lanka provides a significant exception to the situation found in most developing countries of a bias in public-sector investment against the smallholder sector.[36] It is, however, both more and less of an exception than these aggregate figures suggest. For this large public-sector investment is in fact concentrated very heavily on one part of non-export agriculture – paddy growers in Dry Zone settlement schemes – to the exclusion of others.

Plans to develop production of non-paddy crops under these schemes have so far had little success. It remains true that, of the subsidies to irrigation development, 'the great majority . . . are correctly attributed to rice'.[37] Rice is, however, grown Island-wide, and public-sector agricultural investment since the 1930s has been concentrated on new Dry Zone schemes. A guesstimate for around 1970 suggests that no more than about a fifth of all rice-farming households were cultivating land brought into production as a result of this investment.[38] The great majority of rice cultivators were thus not beneficiaries of the major element in the net subsidy to rice production.

Economic evaluations of the experience with large-scale settlement schemes have yielded relatively depressing conclusions. The cost per family settled has been high, and aggregate returns to projects low or even negative.[39] In part this may be attributed to the 'normal' processes by which the expected benefits of large-scale projects are inflated in the planning stage. There are, however, several ways in which this particular outcome in Sri Lanka can be seen to be related to specific features of the policy and of politics.

The first is the fact that Dry Zone development has been explicitly viewed as a means of increasing the Sinhalese population in the historic heartland of Sinhalese civilisation. Between 1946 and 1971 the proportion of the Island's population recorded as Sinhalese increased from 69% to 72%, mainly as a result of the repatriation to India of estate labourers.[40] A much larger increase in the Sinhalese population, however, occurred in the 'frontier' zone of the Dry Zone development between the Sinhalese area of the southwest and the Tamil and Muslim areas of the north and east. Between 1946 and 1971 the Sinhalese proportion of the population of the five 'frontier' districts – Amparai, Batticaloa, Polonnaruwa, Trincomalee and Anuradhapura (see Map Two) – increased from 33% to 51%.[41] The main cause was the migration of Sinhalese settlers to new irrigation schemes.[42] This 'intrusion' is particularly evident in certain localities, for example the Gal Oya and Padaviya irrigation schemes, which brought mainly Sinhalese settlers into what were previously almost exclusively Tamil-speaking areas.[43]

A second way in which the colonisation process conforms to broader aspects of Sri Lankan politics is that the beneficiaries have been treated generously and not been asked to contribute to the cost. There are effectively no charges for the land and irrigation water provided.[44] Early practice was to provide ready-made houses and a substantial social and communications infrastructure. Costs have been pared down over the years,[45] but the gift element is still substantial, as is the general insistence on planning and constructing the physical environment in very great detail. For example, unlike in many Asian irrigation development projects, the whole network of irrigation channels, including field channels, is constructed by the government, leaving nothing to the initiative of the allottees.

Although the high cost per settler and the low rate of creation of new jobs have prompted continual decreases in allotment sizes from eight acres (five acres of paddy and three acres of highland) down to the current norm of less than three acres,[46] the general principle of comprehensive preparation for the individual settler has been pursued at least at the level of intention, planning and financial allocation. This conforms to the general custodial style characterising elite discussion of, and institutional provision for, development programmes for the peasant sector. One might note that even on Village Expansion Schemes and similar programmes for the allocation of housing lots there is institutional provision for the construction of a package of free facilities including wells, roads, houses and latrines.[47] As in most rural programmes, there is little expectation of a provision for self-help on the part of recipients.

A third political aspect of the Dry Zone development programme is that, in direct analogy to the cases of fertilisers and credit discussed above, there has been a marked contrast between generous funding for the construction of irrigation facilities and the poor quality of the irrigation services provided by state agencies. To draw clear conclusions about the reasons is difficult, partly because relatively poor water management is characteristic of most canal irrigation systems, especially those in the tropics. Performance in Sri Lanka is, however, especially poor, and part of the cause appears to lie in the relationship between the cultivators and the government agencies responsible for water issues, especially in the Irrigation Department. Some aspects of this relationship relating to poor water management include the lack of strong local farmers' organisations able to challenge the definition of problems and the behaviour of the irrigation staff; the consequent prevalence of diagnoses of the problem in which blame is heaped on farmers despite manifest deficiencies at other levels; and the failure to develop on new large-scale schemes more appropriate and effective means for representing farmers' views and interests than the practice of seasonal 'water meetings', which were transferred from small-scale schemes.[48]

Agricultural pricing policies

We are not here concerned with levels and changes of prices *per se*, but with the effect of state action on prices, and with the motives and intentions behind that action. Direct information on intentions and motives is, however, available only in a fragmentary fashion. Considerable reliance must be placed on inference from actions, and inference in turn requires some background on the context of decisions and the range of options open. Some of that background is provided in the two succeeding sections. The first sets out the institutional and physical context of state action on prices, and the second provides a brief sketch of the general pattern of changes in agricultural product prices in the post-Independence period. Specific pricing policies are then discussed in relation to three crop categories: plantation crops, paddy, and other food crops.

The state and price determination

The points to be made here are brief: that the state has the institutional and physical means to intervene heavily in the determination of prices on a very wide range of goods and services, especially those directly related to agriculture; and that it has intervened heavily.

The origin of this intervention lies in the structure of the colonial economy: heavy dependence on the export of plantation crops to generate national income, and on the import of food to feed the population. For physical and institutional reasons the state was easily drawn to intervene in the disposal of export crops and the distribution of imported food. Both commodities passed physically through a small number of ports, in fact nearly all through Colombo, and were handled and accounted for by a few large-scale commercial organisations. One might note in particular the existence since the nineteenth century of commercial distribution systems supplying imported rice to a large fraction of the rural population *outside* the estate areas.[49] To supplant, regulate or tax the activities of trading firms was a relatively easy task from the physical and institutional point of view, and so political and economic pressures to do so have been correspondingly difficult to resist.

Plantation exports have been heavily taxed, while the preponderance of plantation crops in exports and the importance of the state-controlled cereals trade in imports have provided a solid base from which the state has been able to assert further controls, sometimes almost total, on all foreign trade and currency transactions.[50] The export of coconuts, both a source of foreign exchange and a major item in the national diet, has been controlled and on occasion forbidden. The state monopoly of the import of rice, wheat and sugar, imposed to deal with the 1942 food crisis, has been in operation ever since.[51] The rice ration scheme arose at the same time. Between 1950 and the drastic curtailment of the scope of the scheme in 1978 and 1979, it delivered annually between one-third and two-thirds of the total consumption of the two basic staples, rice and wheat flour.[52] The very elaborate and dense network of cooperative retail branches,[53] which was built up to deliver the rice ration, has also been used to deliver a variety of other food and consumer items, including extra-ration issues of subsidised rice intended to force down open-market rice prices. Further, the need to provide the rice ration and the availability of this cooperative network have respectively encouraged and facilitated the deep involvement of state agencies in the procurement of locally grown paddy. Relying heavily on cooperatives as procurement agents, the state paddy-purchasing arrangement, known as the GPS (Guaranteed Price Scheme), has annually handled between a fifth and two-thirds of domestic rice production since it became well-established in the mid-1950s.[54] Although originally intended to serve as a price support scheme for paddy producers, the GPS has always threatened to become an arm of the Food Commissioner oriented to procuring as much rice as cheaply as possible to feed the ration scheme.[55] A study conducted in 1958 suggested that the degree of state involvement in the food system was higher in Sri Lanka than in each of the other nine comparable Asian nations.[56]

It has already been recorded in Chapter Two that both the needs of the national economy and the symbolic connotations of the Sinhalese historic identity provide powerful support for a policy of national food self-sufficiency, and protection and encouragement for local food production. The state also has the physical and institutional means to manipulate prices to this end. However, it has not in practice, as opposed to rhetoric, been prepared to incur the inevitable costs of giving this target effective priority.

Food and agricultural price trends since Independence

The absence of any reliable domestic price index for Sri Lanka before 1974,[57] and especially for consumers, is a real obstacle to even a satisfactory, purely descriptive account of real price trends for agricultural producers and food consumers. The best one can do is to compare trends in the prices of various commodities against one another. The purpose in doing so is not to explain price trends, but to indicate those which might have a bearing on the broader arguments of this book.

The periods before and after 1970 are best treated separately. For while the former was characterised by relative stability in both the Sri Lankan and the world economies, the interpretation of the indices relating to the 1970s is complicated by general inflation, fuelled especially by international oil-price increases dating from 1973 and, at the very end of the period, by the ambitious capital investment programme of the UNP government elected in 1977; increases in farm costs, especially fertiliser and tractor-operating costs consequent upon the rise in the cost of oil; increases in food prices in 1973–4 as a result of the difficulties faced in paying for imports, and simultaneous poor domestic paddy harvests; other food-price increases arising from the programme, initiated in 1969, of curtailing imports of subsidised food crops; and the large devaluation of the rupee and the wholesale liberalisation of foreign trade and payments in late 1977, together with the related change in the basis of the taxation of plantation exports.

For the period 1948–70 the important trends[58] are the relative decline in real terms of tea and rubber producer-prices, which is associated with the relative decline of the plantation sector compared to the (mainly smallholder) food production sector, and results directly from the international market situation; the steady rise in the cash price of paddy received by producers (whether the real price increased one cannot say); and the relatively low rate of growth of consumer food prices, including price-controlled coconuts, and, above all, wheat flour, which was imported in ever larger quantities at subsidised prices and became a major item in the diet.

In the 1970s the effects of the long decline in coconut production, in part the result of continual restrictions on prices,[59] could no longer be repressed by administrative regulation. Consumer prices went up sharply. Once an important export product, coconuts may soon, it is widely feared, appear in the import statistics. That the consumer prices of rice and wheat flour have continued to rise only relatively slowly in the 1970s, except during the crisis period of 1974, is partly the result of the ready resort to imports. Only in 1978 were major steps taken to reduce the very heavy subsidy on imported wheat flour,[60] although the effect was in large part countered by the rise in import prices.

Surplus-paddy farmers, having experienced a windfall in the form of high output prices in 1974 before the increase in fertiliser and fuel prices worked through to them, have since seen paddy prices fall in real terms and their 'costs of production' increase 'quite dramatically . . . leading to a significant reduction in the producer margin'.[61]

Policies affecting the prices of plantation crops

The pricing of plantation crops affects smallholders in two main ways. In the first place a significant fraction of smallholder incomes are obtained from plantation crops, and in the second place smallholders *qua* consumers and *qua* producers of paddy are the recipients of some of the substantial economic surplus from plantation crop production which is acquired and redistributed by the state.

As was recorded in Table 4.1, the proportion of export crops produced by smallholders is highest in the case of coconuts and lowest in the case of tea. If one accepts the definition of 'smallholding' used in Table 5.1, then it appears that in the 1970s the value of smallholder production of tea and rubber collectively amounted to only about a tenth of the value of paddy production, while coconuts amounted to a third. Figures on the number of cultivators suggest a far greater relative importance of smallholder plantation crop production *vis-à-vis* paddy. For example, treating holdings of less than ten acres as smallholdings, the 1962 Census of Agriculture enumerated 870,000 smallholders cultivating plantation crops (on 786,000 acres), and only 532,000 paddy producers (cultivating 851,000 acres of paddy).[62] The reason for this apparent divergence between these two sets of figures is the prevalence among smallholder plantation crop producers of coconut growers, whose output and rates of labour use per acre are relatively very low. Of those 870,000 smallholders enumerated as growing plantation crops in 1962, two-thirds were coconut growers.[63]

For most of the period since Independence export crop producers have been the milch cows of the economy. They have been heavily taxed and provided a large proportion of government revenue. Details are available elsewhere,[64] and only illustrative statistics will be provided here. During 1978 and 1979, when taxation of plantation exports was direct rather than indirect, and via the overvaluation of the rupee on foreign exchange markets, export levies alone accounted for an average of 44% of export earnings in the case of tea, 50% in the case of rubber, and 23% in the case of coconuts. Additional amounts were raised from sales taxes on tea and coconuts, and taxes on turnover and income on privately owned estates. (The recently nationalised estates were running at a post-tax loss.)[65] One of a number of similar estimates suggests that in 1966 duties on sales and exports served, together with profit taxes, to expropriate 86% of the gross surplus from tea production.[66] In 1978 and 1979 export levies and sales taxes on plantation products alone accounted for 40% of government revenue.[67]

In addition to these heavy tributes to the state, coconut producers have had to pay additional tribute to local consumers, extracted through retail price controls on nuts and, probably more importantly, through restrictions on export volumes. 'For quite some time, exports of coconuts have been tightly regulated with a view to keeping domestic prices low as coconuts form an important part of indigenous diets.'[68] A large gap has existed between the export price and the domestic price for most coconut products.[69]

The above quotation from the Central Bank's annual *Review of the Economy* reflects the fact that the government elected in 1977 has expressed great concern about the plight of the coconut industry and, to coordinate a range of measures to improve it, created a special Ministry of Coconut Industries. Yet the consumer pressures resulting from substantial retail price increases had by the end of 1979 generated major new restrictions on coconut exports and the public threat of forcible requisitions from producers to keep the market supplied at 'reasonable' prices.[70] Export bans have been periodically imposed and lifted since.

The relative importance of coconuts to the smallholder and the severity of these administrative price control measures mean that a very substantial volume of economic resources has thus regularly been transferred out of the smallholder sector by state action. My calculations relating to 1971–3 suggest that at that time the net income lost to smallholder coconut producers was around twice the net transfer of income to paddy producers, and the total net income transfer from smallholder producers of export crops was around three times the net subsidy to paddy production.[71]

This pattern of milking the export crop sector while giving a small subsidy to paddy producers has been directly contrary to the immediate material interests of many of the political elite, especially as this elite had major investments in coconut plantations. Not only do we find here a direct parallel with the nationalisation of these estates discussed in Chapter Four, but also some partial explanation for it. For the relative unprofitability of estate production probably helped mitigate opposition to the nationalisation measures.

Policies affecting the price of paddy

Although rarely appearing as an issue on the public agenda in Sri Lankan politics,[72] the dependence of the polity and public revenues on the heavy taxation of the export crop sector is widely appreciated, and the mechanisms of surplus extraction understood. The situation with regard to paddy production is very different and rather more complicated. At the political and official levels at least, the conventional view is that the paddy farmer is a net recipient of subsidies, not only in the form of credit, fertiliser subsidies and irrigation development, but also through the operation of the Guaranteed Price Scheme (GPS).

To some extent the prevalence of such views reflects a lag of perception behind changes in economic magnitudes. For when the GPS was introduced in 1948, the cash price paid to the farmer for his rice was substantially above both the price paid by the Food Commissioner for rice imports and local open-market prices. Tea was still relatively dear on international markets in comparison with later years, the Sri Lankan rupee correspondingly strong in international exchange markets, and imports, including rice and wheat flour, relatively cheap compared to the production costs of locally grown rice. The 'colonial economy' of cheap food imports persisted. In consequence, a failure of the local paddy crop was good news for the Treasury.[73] The gaps between local and world market prices have, however, been steadily narrowing. Local open-market prices have generally exceeded the GPS price since the late 1960s, and GPS purchases became cheaper than imports at various points in the 1970s.[74]

However, it is not *market* prices which are appropriate either to the estimation of the real costs and benefits of particular policies from the point of view of the Sri Lankan economy or, more directly relevant here, to the calculation of whether or not local food producers are being subsidised or economically exploited by the state. For market prices themselves are in large part determined by state action, and do not reflect the relative scarcities of different resources to the national economy. It is more appropriate to use world market prices as a base for calculation, not because they are in any normative or policy sense 'correct', but because they are indicators of the price levels which would pertain if state intervention in the economy were 'intersectorally neutral', i.e. did not effect any redistribution of resources among sectors. It then becomes evident that domestic food producers, including paddy producers, are in some ways the victims rather than the beneficiaries of public policy. Three different sets of policies separately serve to depress the output prices received by domestic food producers, and thus to set market prices for food well below its true scarcity value to the local economy. An attempt has been made elsewhere to estimate the magnitude involved for rice producers.[75] The mechanisms will simply be outlined here.

The first and most important mechanism for depressing rice prices is the maintenance of the overvaluation of the rupee in the foreign currency markets. This dates from 1961, when the extended and continuing processes of deteriorating terms of trade and maintenance of high consumption levels first led to the imposition of foreign exchange controls.[76] The overvaluation of the rupee meant that imports were artificially cheap to those individuals or institutions able to obtain foreign currency quotas for imports, while exporters (i.e. mainly plantation crop producers) were subsidising imports at the cost of their own incomes.

Between 1968 and 1977 exchange control was elaborated and extended with a dual foreign exchange rate system. The Food Commissioner, always a priority recipient of foreign currency for importing, was, along with licensed importers of medicines, fertiliser, books, and a few other miscellaneous items, privileged to receive foreign currency at the official rate. All other importers were obliged not only to obtain a licence but to pay a premium to purchase foreign currency at the so-called FEEC rate (Foreign Exchange Entitlement Certificate), which stood at 65% in excess of the official rate for most of the duration of the scheme. Exporters were similarly divided into two categories. Exporters of so-called 'traditional exports', i.e. tea, rubber and coconuts, received rupees for their sales only at the official rate, while all other exporters received a bonus at the FEEC rate (i.e. generally 65%). The government obtained a substantial proportion of its revenue from operating the FEEC system.[77]

Thus between 1961 and late 1977, when foreign trade and payments were almost completely liberalised, the Food Commissioner was able to purchase imported food at an artificially low price which did not reflect the true scarcity of foreign currency. Had he been obliged to pay the FEEC rate, itself not sufficiently high to reflect the true scarcity of foreign exchange, the Food Commissioner would have found locally produced rice cheaper than imports almost every year since 1968 at least.[78] A substantial part of the potential market for domestically produced rice was thus pre-empted by imports (see Table 5.4), and demand pressures on the market price for local rice were artificially bridled.

The second mechanism for depressing local prices is the import of (mainly American) wheat flour by the Food Commissioner at concessionary rates. 'Between 1968 and 1972, more than half of wheat imports were made on concessionary terms.'[79] Between 1948 and 1970 the retail price of wheat flour increased much less than the prices of the other two main staples, rice and coconuts.[80] Wheat flour imports have increased steadily, such that the much vaunted target of 'self-

Table 5.4. *Average annual domestic rice production and cereal imports, 1961–82 (thousand metric tons)*

Year	Domestic rice production	Imports		Cereal self-sufficiency ratio (%)
		Rice	Wheat flour	
1961–3	653	421	160	53
1964–6	617	353	252	44
1967–9	863	339	445	52
1970–2	965	352	346	58
1973–5	908	362	410	54
1976–8	1,076	362	501	56
1979–82	1,476	176	539	67

Source: Central Bank of Ceylon, *Review of the Economy*, various years, and information on paddy production provided by the Department of Economics and Statistics.

sufficiency in rice' has begun to appear somewhat spurious, and progress towards self-sufficiency in cereals is only slow and halting (see Table 5.4).

The third mechanism for depressing local rice prices is the distribution of imported rice and wheat flour to consumers at a price even lower than the (artificially low) cost to the Food Commissioner. In the case of rice, one is talking mainly of the ration scheme and of the entire period since 1942. There have in addition, however, been occasions when advantage has been taken of the excellence of the cooperative retail system to force down open-market rice prices, either by selling or threatening to sell subsidised rice through cooperatives, in addition to the subsidised ration.[81] In the case of wheat, open-market sales at controlled prices[82] have resulted in a cash loss to the Food Commissioner only since 1972; in earlier years they generated a profit.[83]

Resource transfers

Overall, during the 1960s and 1970s the net annual cost to the government of the Food Commissioner's operations, mainly in rice and wheat flour, but also in sugar and a range of other minor foods, amounted variously to between 9% and 13% of total public expenditure,[84] and thus constituted a very significant resource transfer. Most of this loss was incurred in handling cereals; sugar was a source of substantial net profits until the early 1970s.

An attempt to estimate the economic – as opposed to the financial – magnitudes involved, faces particular conceptual and empirical problems when a ration is involved; for the extent to which a ration actually substitutes for, or encourages the expenditure of, other income on food is variable. The only study made of the Sri Lankan rice ration, however, concludes that a large proportion of the ration actually substitutes for private food expenditure, thus reducing demand pressures on the market for local rice and disadvantaging domestic surplus-food producers.[85] I have elsewhere[86] attempted to calculate, for the years 1971–3, the net impact on various categories of agricultural producers of all public interventions in the prices of agricultural inputs and products, including subsidies on such items as credit, replanting of export crops, and irrigation. That smallholder producers of tea, rubber and coconuts have been victims of public policy is already well-known. The results for rice producers do, however, tend to challenge the widely held view that they are heavily subsidised. It is true that in aggregate they *are* subsidised. But most of these subsidies are heavily concentrated on a relatively small number of rice producers in the Dry Zone irrigated settlement schemes, and their subsidies mainly take the form of cheap irrigated rice land developed by government and cheap tractors.[87] Other rice producers are net victims of public economic policy. The aggregate loss to all rice producers in 1971–3 of policies depressing the open-market price of rice actually exceeded the bounty offered to all rice producers in the form of subsidised credit and fertilisers.

Policies affecting the prices of 'other crops'

For reasons given above the present discussion of the pricing of other crops will be relatively brief. On the 'minor export crops',[88] which are grown on smallholdings and small estates, one might simply note that their producers have been penalised less than growers of the traditional estate crops. Exports of these minor crops have not been taxed and, although producers have been adversely affected by the overvaluation of the rupee in foreign exchange markets, they, unlike producers of tea, rubber and coconuts, did not incur the penalty of especially unfavourable treatment under the dual exchange rate scheme.

Of more significance is policy towards the so-called 'subsidiary (or 'minor') food crops', a category which overlaps closely with the list of 'other crops', given above. The relative insignificance of these crops in the colonial period appears to have been partly due to the strength of the rupee and the cheapness of rice imports. It seems that in the nineteenth and early twentieth centuries, because of the availability of cheap imports, rice came to dominate totally as a staple at the expense of other grains and root crops.[89] Rice was thus confirmed in its status as the traditional crop and foodgrain. India became a major source of locally consumed subsidiary food crops.[90] Domestic sugarcane production, for example, appears to have been almost entirely destroyed by import competition.

The Guaranteed Price Scheme introduced in 1948 was formally intended to apply to all smallholder crops. However, low guaranteed prices and the unwillingness of cooperatives to handle small quantities of often perishable products have, until recently, meant that the GPS has been confined almost entirely to paddy.[91] For most of the post-Independence period, public policy has affected producers of subsidiary food crops mainly by subsidising competing rice and wheat flour imports. However, an import substitution programme was initiated by the UNP government in 1967 with restrictions on imports of potatoes, chillies and onions.[92] Potato imports were halted completely in 1968. Although the United Front government elected in 1970 partially reversed this, it more than compensated in respect of other crops. Imports of onions were terminated in 1971, and chillies in 1973. Sugar imports were never cut off entirely, but in 1974–6 they were cut to a fraction of their former levels.[93] The result was high market prices and big increases in domestic production.[94]

Producers of minor food crops enjoyed a brief period of almost legendary prosperity. The election of the UNP government in 1977, however, brought a complete change of policy. As a part of the liberalisation of the economy almost all import controls were removed. Despite the devaluation of the rupee, the levels of food imports were sufficient to bring tumbling down the local producer prices for chillies, onions and sugar. Local production of minor food crops fell sharply.[95]

The new government has frequently promised to ensure producers of minor food crops a reasonable market price through the mechanism of a buffer stock operated by the Food Commissioner's Department. This is represented as aiming at price stability and a balancing of producer and consumer interests.[96] Yet there are signs that producer interests are not being very seriously regarded. The Central Bank has recently suggested that the operations of the buffer stock scheme, along with consumer subsidies on wheat and flour, are among the main causes of the continuing decline in the production of minor crops.[97] It has also been claimed that the scheme barely operates at all in purchasing locally grown crops, and has not procured even 1% of production.[98]

One might simply note in closing that there is a clear, established trend towards increasing the relative emphasis in smallholder production on certain minor food crops, and that it is one which is sufficiently resilient to survive radical changes in government policy. Production of maize, millet, manioc and sweet potatoes, considered very inferior staples, peaked in 1974 because of the food crisis which had been building up during 1973. Production has since fallen continuously and steeply. As is recorded above, prices and production of chillies, onions and sugarcane fell due to the ending of import controls. Yet the production of other minor crops, above all potatoes, and a clutch of pulses and oilseeds (green gram, soya beans, gingelly, cowpea and black gram), has continued to rise steadily throughout the 1970s, despite the vicissitudes of the general economic situation. In 1979, after the immediate consequences of import liberalisation had taken effect, the acreage of the sixteen listed minor food crops (excluding manioc, sweet potatoes and sugarcane) was one-third greater than its 1973 level.[99] Sri Lanka is clearly on the way to a more diversified and commercialised smallholder sector. The political implications are discussed below.

The politics of agricultural product prices

The pricing of minor food crops
The import liberalisation of 1977 was a substantial blow to that section of the economy dependent on the production of minor food crops. In the long run, however, it may prove to be of greater political than economic significance. For there are signs that it has helped set in train the growth of a conscious and organised producer interest or, rather, a number of such interests. For they are fragmented by crop and locality, and in no sense begin to resemble an organised national or even regional movement.

The geographical background to this development is the specialisation of a number of areas in a small range of crops. For reasons of climate and geology the Jaffna peninsula has always concentrated on the intensive production of a range of minor crops, including bananas, tobacco, vegetables, potatoes, onions, chillies and fruit.[100] It is the only Dry Zone district which fails to produce at least its own requirements of rice (see Table 7.1). Hence one understands the motivation behind the demand made in Parliament in 1964 by the MP for Nallur (Jaffna peninsula) that higher guaranteed prices be offered to producers of minor food crops and that this be financed by a reduction in paddy prices.[101]

This speech suggests that the farming population of the Jaffna peninsula have for some time been well aware of their objective interest. They have continued to express demands from time to time, but probably more so since the 1977 import liberalisation knocked the bottom out of the market prices for minor food crops. In early 1978 Jaffna chillie farmers were reported to be complaining about this policy, and later in the year the Jaffna District Agricultural Producers Association was formed to press for more remunerative output prices, especially for chillies and onions. A few months later it was announced that, as a result of protests from Jaffna and Anuradhapura districts, the newly created National Prices Commission was to investigate the adequacy of producer prices for chillies.[102] The fortnightly English-language journal *Tribune*, which is edited by a Tamil and pays particular attention to Tamil affairs, has been a regular and vociferous critic of liberalised imports of subsidiary food crops.[103] In the 1982 presidential election this issue played an important role in the Jaffna district.[104] The ability of Jaffna farmers to obtain any response to their demands is, however, very constrained by the marginality of the Sri Lanka Tamils to the electoral system as a whole.

Apart from the Jaffna peninsula, two other areas appear to contain potential farm lobbies concerned with the pricing of subsidiary food crops. One is the Up Country districts of Nuwara Eliya and Badulla which, along with Jaffna, account for virtually all of the expanding potato-growing industry.[105] In Badulla and Nuwara Eliya potatoes are grown along with so-called 'Up Country' or 'European' vegetables, e.g. cabbages and leeks. The expression of demands for protection against imports may be constrained by the social heterogeneity of the industry, which includes both Sinhalese villagers and Indian Tamil estate labourers, and appears to be to a large extent organised around a relatively small number of wealthy traders who advance credit against the very high costs of land preparation and seed purchase.[106] Because of the substantial dependence on imported seed potatoes and packeted vegetable seeds, the main demands of the industry appear to date to have focused on the price of seed rather than output prices.[107]

It is my impression that the most outspoken farm lobby to have emerged as a result of policy changes relating to imports is that of sugarcane producers. They are concentrated on the drier eastern slopes of the Kandyan hills, mainly in Uva Province (Badulla and Moneragala districts). The vociferousness of their demands appears to owe a great deal to the fact that it is a capital-intensive industry run by relatively wealthy villagers and outsiders. The substantial fixed investment in the original land clearance, in standing cane, in tractors for the transport of cane, and in crushing-mills means that it is difficult for investors to withdraw after a price collapse. There is every stimulus to political action if output prices can be seen to be directly related to public policy.

The consequences for the sugar industry of the 1977 import liberalisation have been aired publicly, and a sympathetic attitude has been taken by the government.[108] A recent decision to encourage direct private foreign investment in agriculture on a 'free trade zone' basis, which appears in practice to benefit mainly those proposing to develop sugarcane production and processing, was taken on the initiative of the MP for Uva-Paranagama, a sugarcane-growing area in Badulla district.[109] The fact that by 1983 the government had succumbed to the temptation of importing sugar cheaply suggests the continuing relative impotence of the producer interest. But the issue of sugar imports and their effect on domestic producers at least appears to be established on the national political agenda.[110]

Paddy prices and the political agenda

These public demands for more remunerative prices for minor food crops are significant because they are recent and because they have no equivalent in the case of paddy and estate crops: demands for higher prices for producers of paddy and estate crops barely appear in the agenda of electoral politics.

How can this proposition be verified? The general answer is: with great difficulty. For the absence of an abstract negative phenomenon is always hard to prove. The best evidence, and that on which I primarily rely, comes from 'fieldwork' of various kinds: in the fact that, in a highly politicised environment where various aspects of rural policy are widely discussed, the level of producer prices is an issue rarely raised spontaneously by farmers, politicians or administrators. Agreement with this view has been expressed to me by people closely involved in the economic policy-making process.[111] It is, however, difficult to convince an outsider on the strength of such evidence. One must search for written sources.

The academic literature on Sri Lankan politics deals with the issue of agriculture price policies and politics barely at all. This might be taken as indirect evidence of the absence of the theme from the political agenda. The value of such evidence is, however, somewhat vitiated by the fact that this literature has generally dealt very inadequately with the broad issue of interest representation in politics, focusing instead on the formal institutions.[112] Another source is parliamentary speeches. I can only use the official reports of parliamentary proceedings in a fragmentary way. *Hansard* is printed in the language in which the speech was delivered, and this is very often Sinhala, especially in

more recent years and in debates concerning agriculture. The English-
language press, supplemented by some translations of *Hansard*, has
been used to help fill the gaps. The following examples can, however, be
no more than illustrative.

It was mentioned above that in 1964 the MP for Nallur suggested in
Parliament that, in order to allow an increase in the producer prices of
minor food crops, the paddy price, which was too high, be reduced.
This generated not a single protest on behalf of paddy producers.[113]

In the 1973 debate on the financial votes of the Ministry of
Agriculture and Lands the (Tamil) MP for Vavuniya drew attention to
the rising cost of paddy production. However, rather than using this as
a basis for a demand for an increase in the GPS price, he went on to
attribute it to the excessive use of tractors, and to advocate measures to
promote the use of animal draft power in their place.[114]

In the corresponding 1976 debate the Independent MP for
Nikaweratiya, a Dry Zone paddy area, similarly bewailed the high costs
of paddy production and, equally similarly, went on to ask for measures
to cut production costs rather than to question the adequacy of the
output price. The government MP from the neighbouring electorate of
Galigamuwa, also a paddy-growing area, riposted that the cost of
producing paddy had been grossly exaggerated.[115]

The GPS price of paddy was increased in the 1977 budget after
remaining unchanged during more than three years of inflation and
thus falling very substantially in real terms.[116] The increase was the
lowest of a range of figures which the Ministry of Finance and Planning
had been considering.[117] Yet it was accepted without demur in
Parliament. The Government (UNP) MPs, who held over four-fifths
of the seats (see Appendix One), expressed reservations about the
adequacy of a number of other budget measures, but had nothing but
praise for this one.

During the Second Reading of the 1979 Agrarian Services Bill the
condition of smallholder agriculture was debated at great length. One
(Opposition) MP, representing a paddy deficit area, demanded more
remunerative output prices for rice farmers. When challenged about
the effect on consumer rice prices he responded that these should also
be reduced and subsidised. Three government MPs, all representing
Dry Zone paddy surplus areas, opposed his demand, as did one other
Opposition MP, albeit ambiguously. Two of the government MPs
argued that increased prices were of no benefit to cultivators as the
benefits were simply captured by middlemen, and that what was
required was more efficient delivery systems for irrigation water,
fertiliser and other production inputs.[118] The elected spokesmen for

the main (Sinhalese) paddy surplus districts – Anuradhapura, Polonnaruwa and Hambantota (see Table 7.1) – thus came out very firmly against the idea of more remunerative output prices for paddy producers.

A slightly less direct kind of evidence on the absence of producer price demands is to be obtained by examining the kinds of demands which actually have been made on smallholders' behalf. For it is the interests of the villager as consumer of subsidies and recipient of state land, rather than as producer of marketed products, which have been most important. For example, the 1976 parliamentary debate on the financial vote to the Ministry of Agriculture and Lands was in various ways dominated by *land* issues: the implementation of land reform; the organisation of the Survey Department; the plight of encroachers on state lands threatened with eviction; whether or not settlers on irrigation schemes should be given full ownership of their land; land alienation procedures; and the threat of the introduction of an effective land tax on colonisation schemes.[119]

The last issue arose because a few months previously the government had been forced by pressures from foreign aid donors to pass the (unimplemented) Land Betterment Charges Act. This was intended as a vehicle for the levying of effective charges on the developed land and irrigation water which the Dry Zone colonists had previously been enjoying at almost no charge. The parliamentary debate provided the opportunity for Opposition MPs to bemoan the plight of the 'poor farmer' groaning under a further 'burden':

The government was trying to get the people to pay for what it was the duty of the government to provide (Dr N. M. Perera, LSSP).

The function of government was to provide welfare facilities to backward areas and not to impose taxes on the poor. The bill contradicted the concept of a welfare state (K. Jeyakody, Federal Party).[120]

An example of the degree to which welfare considerations dominate programmes for smallholders is the popularity of the idea of extending to farmers some kind of state pension or superannuation scheme. Such schemes cover about one-third of the work force,[121] and it has for some years been accepted in principle by politicians of all parties that farmers should also benefit.[122]

This listing of evidence on the lack of price demands can be concluded with a fragment of evidence revealing the attitudes of farmers themselves rather than those of politicians. What was claimed to be the first all-Island Paddy Producers Association was established in 1977. Its aims were better marketing facilities, cheaper fertiliser and implements, and even a foreign exchange allowance on paddy sales to permit the import of machinery and implements. Despite the very evident 'big farmer' bias of such demands, no mention was made of the level of the GPS price.[123]

Paddy and the peasantry in imagery and political discourse

There is no intention here of arguing that there have been no pressures from any source for higher agricultural producer prices. That would be surprising, especially in view of the strong case which can be made for the vigorous promotion of local food production on any long-term view of Sri Lanka's economic prospects. It is precisely from the institutions taking such a long-term view, i.e. the various founts of professional advice on national economic policy, whence the main pressures for higher prices have emanated. The World Bank, which as the coordinator of foreign aid operations has been at times heavily engaged in attempting to influence Sri Lankan economic policy, has, in accordance with its general approach, been a staunch advocate of remunerative agricultural producer prices.[124] The Central Bank of Ceylon has on occasion played a similar role. For example, its *Review of the Economy* for 1979 spoke firmly of the need for an increase to compensate for the rising costs of paddy production. An increase came, but not until almost a year later.[125]

The question at issue here is why output-price demands have not come from MPs. In the case of the export crops the answer seems fairly clear. The large plantation owners have felt constrained from making them, and it is not surprising that smallholder producers of export crops have been similarly quiescent. Although smallholder export crop producers have the advantage of numbers and of being less tainted by association with capitalism and all the negative traits identified with the plantation sector, they have the disadvantage of being far less informed than estate owners of how, and how far, the state taxes imports. The surplus from estate production has been extracted via export levies, taxes on corporate and personal incomes, and most obliquely and above all, through the dual exchange rate system. Smallholder export crop producers do not feel themselves to be directly affected by such devices, and are probably in general unaware that they are heavily taxed.[126]

It is the absence of output-price demands from *paddy* farmers which is especially problematic, for there are in this case no very obvious constraints on such a demand. This problem is not resolved in this chapter; for it is an aspect of the broader issue of the failure of smallholders to make distinct class or occupational demands, and as such is tackled in later chapters.

Party and agricultural policy

The fact that the content of this chapter has been organised thematically rather than chronologically reflects the lack of major divergencies between successive governments over agricultural policy. The main components of rural policy – the priority attached to supplying the public food distribution system at low cost; the heavy taxation of export crops; the maintenance of an overvalued currency penalising all agricultural producers by reducing the profitability of export crops and subsidising imports competing with local food production; the distribution of Crown land to the rural population; the colonisation of the Dry Zone; the subsidies on farm inputs; and the enforcement of land reform legislation – have been common to governments led by both the UNP and the SLFP. Even the restrictions on imports of subsidiary food crops, although promoted more vigorously by the United Front coalition government of 1970–7, originated as an initiative of the previous UNP government. The occasional demands in Parliament for higher prices for paddy producers have largely reflected the intrinsic relationship between government and Opposition. They have been raised by those in opposition at the time, whatever their party, and rejected by government. The combination of demands for increased subsidies to both rice producers and consumers reflects their 'oppositional' nature; they do not represent a definite commitment to producers as opposed to consumers.

Many of the differences between the policies of different administrations appear to be rooted in personal or relatively temporary factors. A few years ago one might have argued a little differently. It did at that stage appear generally true that under UNP governments 'planning strategy was clearly centred on agricultural development',[127] while SLFP governments had, despite their rural electoral base, focused on industrial development in line with the concepts of nationalism, self-reliance, socialism and independence of the world capitalist system, which featured so prominently in the realm of ideas on economic policy shared by the SLFP and its sometime Marxist allies.[128] This interpretation appeared to have special validity in the early 1970s. For the UNP government of 1965–70 had clearly given paddy production (in particular) real administrative priority, and had established and given weight to a number of institutional devices for improving the performance of the state agencies concerned.[129] That government also started restricting imports of subsidiary food crops. By contrast, the United Front government of 1970–7 had given little administrative attention to farmer services despite the rhetoric of 'production wars', for the Ministry of Agriculture and Lands was then preoccupied with land reform.

Recent events have, however, destroyed the UNP's reputation as a party with a special concern for agriculture. Producers of subsidiary food crops have been dealt a serious blow through the complete decontrol of imports, restrictions on coconut exports have been tightened, and the price and import levels of wheat flour and foreign rice have resulted in a large real fall in the market price of paddy.[130] No attempt has been made to give agriculture or even paddy production the administrative priority it had under the previous UNP government, while the first Minister of Agriculture in the new government showed more concern over the price paid for rice by the consumer than the profitability of agriculture to the farmer.[131]

A major reason for this apparent change in the UNP's orientation is probably that all previous UNP governments, except during an interval in 1953–6, have been led by either D. S. Senanayake or his son, Dudley Senanayake. D. S. Senanayake played a major role in promoting the colonisation of the Dry Zone and incorporating this as a major element in Sinhalese nationalist ideology. He was also renowned for his active concern and involvement in agricultural policy more generally, and was followed by his son in both respects.[132] The concern of the 1965–70 UNP government for Dry Zone paddy production was also in part the result of the influence of the Minister of Land, Irrigation and Power, C. P. de Silva, a major figure in irrigation development in the North Central Province, who had led the defection from the SLFP which had brought down the previous SLFP–LSSP government.[133]

However, by 1977, both Dudley Senanayake and C. P. de Silva were dead, and the UNP was led by J. R. Jayawardena. He has always represented Colombo electorates, built his career as a party organiser, and made no special attempt, at least until after becoming Prime Minister and then Executive President, at developing a special image of empathy with the peasantry. MPs sitting for Colombo electorates are represented especially heavily in his Cabinet, and UNP policies of economic liberalisation, including the establishment of a free trade zone, tend to bring material benefits mainly to Colombo and the densely populated southwestern Low Country.

Yet Jayawardena was responsible for what will, in retrospect, probably appear as the most important single decision affecting smallholder agriculture in Sri Lanka for many years: the decision to drastically accelerate the rate of construction of the Mahaweli project – a network of related power and irrigation projects in the Dry Zone. The circumstances of this decision, however, precisely illustrate the importance of individual personalities in making agricultural policy. The decision was taken 'out of the blue' after the general election. None of the agencies responsible for implementing it were in the least forewarned.[134]

Personal factors aside, changes in rural policy between SLFP- and UNP-led governments seem to have reflected mainly the broader policies practised by these parties and the interests of the voters they represent, rather than a response to any specifically rural or agricultural interest. Policy towards the import of subsidiary food crops has largely mirrored the autarkic preferences of the SLFP and their allies and the free-market policies of the UNP respectively. The UNP, representing the wealthier strata, has been willing to alienate relatively large allotments of state land under 'middle class schemes' or 'special leases' in the attempt to give incentives to capitalists in agriculture. It has granted tax concessions for the same end. The SLFP has alienated land only in small allotments to the poor, and abolished tax concessions.[135] The UNP has generally practised a voluntaristic approach to local rural organisations, depending on the 'natural leadership' exercised by the more wealthy to give it control. The SLFP by contrast has 'politicised' the local organisations, using its control of state power to insert its own local cadres into the positions of authority which they could not capture unaided from the 'natural leadership'.[136] The SLFP has tended to enforce a complete state monopoly in the distribution of fertilisers (and the rice ration), while the UNP has permitted a supplementary role for licensed private traders.

Neither party has shown any special solicitousness towards a broad agricultural interest or advocated and promoted rural policies distinct in conception or origin from the broader perspectives which govern their approach to economic policy in the round. The SLFP has not become the spokesman for the small Sinhalese paddy producer in the way that the Malay parties have represented the interests of paddy production in Malaysia; and neither party shows the least sign of the focus on agricultural producer interests which has characterised the various North Indian political parties with which Charan Singh has been associated in recent years.[137]

The Marxist parties have played only a limited role in government, and only once held the Agriculture portfolio – when Philip

Gunawardena was Minister of Agriculture between 1956 and 1959. Probably their most significant impact on rural policy, apart from the 1958 Paddy Lands Act, has been the way in which they have played, within the realm of agricultural policy, much the same role as elsewhere: the vanguard for demands for the extension of the welfare state.[138] In the case of agriculture, attention to 'welfare' has meant, above all, questions of access to state lands: protection of allottees from financial levies of any kind; pleas for lenient treatment for encroachers; and interventions on behalf of farmers whose lands are threatened by large-scale development schemes.[139] One cannot but note that this defence of 'the peasantry' against state action appears as a convenient way of avoiding the question of whether or not 'the peasantry' is without its internal divisions and conflicts. This represents continuity with the failure of the Marxist parties to apply class analysis *within* the smallholder sector.

Political imagery and discourse: pricing and welfarism

I have at various points suggested that the use of the term 'peasantry' has connotations which at least conform with, if they do not actually in some sense promote, the dominant custodial and tutelary treatment of the Sri Lankan rural population in public policy. There is another aspect of the term which is of special relevance here: the way in which it emphasises the traditional and cultural dimensions of the smallholder identity and thus plays down the commercial and material element. An early illustration can, once again, be found in the words of S. W. R. D. Bandaranaike. In a speech made in 1932 before the State Council he complained that the British had discouraged rice farming and diverted the peasantry into rubber production, an activity 'of no real value to the community'. The 'value' was, however, not material, but moral and historic, for he went on to admit that rubber was financially more worthwhile.[140] One is here very close in spirit to the kind of restrictions placed in colonial Malaya on attempts by the Malay peasantry to diversify out of rice and into rubber production. The view that the peasant either was not or ought not to be motivated by commercial profitability in producing crops, especially crops like rice, so redolent of national historic identity, is a close corollary of the tutelary and custodial stance of the Malay state towards the 'native' Malay population and the Sri Lankan state towards the Sinhalese population.[141]

From this tutelary perspective stems a number of more particular attitudes and assumptions about the relative roles of the peasant and the state in the development of smallholder agriculture.

One is that the role of the state is not to provide price incentives but to deliver, if possible to every last peasant, the production inputs which he, unaided, cannot afford or obtain, partly because of the malign influence of middlemen. In his speech referred to immediately above, S. W. R. D. Bandaranaike laid down a plan for agricultural development which involved not only the nationalisation of all land, but also complete and direct state control of all paddy marketing, retailing, input distribution and pricing.[142] The provision of agricultural inputs may not be clearly distinguished from, and indeed may be explicitly described as, aspects of the 'welfare state'.

A further assumption is that the state, directly or in the person of its local representatives, may justly claim the credit for agricultural progress. Thus the District Minister for Hambantota recently claimed 'that he would increase the acreage under cultivation of cotton to 25,000 acres and when that was done he wanted another increase of Rs. 30 per cwt in the guaranteed price payable for cotton'.[143] The second part of this sentence indicates a conception of increased producer prices as a reward for effort rather than an incentive.

The obverse of the assumption that the state has a duty to provide for all the peasant's production requirements is that the peasant in turn has a duty to serve the state even if this contravenes his material interests. Reference has already been made in Chapter Four to the legislation putting the farmer under the legal obligation to make the best use of his land in the national interest. It is at times of crisis that a special appeal is made to this sense of obligation. During a food crisis farmers can be urged to sell their surplus paddy to the Paddy Marketing Board to meet the needs of the rice ration scheme, they can be accused of 'sabotage' if they resort to the more remunerative open market, and (rather implausibly), they can be threatened with a high tax on all such 'anti-national' sales.[144] At the time these threats were made – the food crisis of 1974 – a ban was placed on the private transport of paddy. If enforced this would have been equivalent to compulsory public procurement of paddy from producers at prices far below those obtainable in the open market. It was, however, a failure,[145] such that in his 1975 budget speech the Finance Minister felt obliged to apologise almost for not having introduced direct procurement.[146]

When smallholder economic performance fails to meet expectations then the elite can, and in Sri Lanka it often does, turn for explanation – and implicit diversion of any blame away from government and state – to the darker side of their image of the peasant: a man of limited foresight and responsibility who, if not carefully supervised, will fritter away his substance, especially cash.

In 1958 Philip Gunawardena, Minister of Agriculture under S. W. R. D. Bandaranaike, and the somewhat equivocal champion of the peasantry, ordered that Rs. 2 of the Rs. 12 bushel of paddy paid under the Guaranteed Price Scheme be withheld by the cooperatives and later paid in kind in the form of fertilisers and other farm inputs. He provoked certain MPs (all Tamil or Muslim) to raise an adjournment debate in Parliament for fear that this was a prelude to a reduction in the GPS price. Denying any such intention, Gunawardena expatiated on the unfortunate conservatism of the farming population in their unwillingness to use modern methods, advised the MP who opened the debate to purchase a tractor to improve his own husbandry, and pointed out the advantages of forced saving for fertiliser purchase when the feckless peasant was all too inclined to waste his harvest earnings on celebration and alcohol without making provision for the next season.[147]

In 1979 the District Minister for Hambantota complained in Parliament that 'The provision of cultivation loans has become a joke. How many are using these loans to buy agricultural inputs such as fertilisers, and how many are using them for consumer purposes, such as drinking and festivities?' He elicited only support from his fellow MPs.[148] Preservation of the peasant from the consequences of his own moral weakness is considered a legitimate and proper goal of rural policy. (See also the documents quoted in Appendix Two.) His own dignity, practices, views and material interests are not to be allowed to stand in the way of attempts to improve his lot.

Conclusion

That agricultural and economic policy has been biased in favour of cheap food is no surprise to anyone familiar with Sri Lanka. It seems quite in accordance with one's impressions that, in their study of the rice economies of nine Asian nations, Timmer and Falcon found that consumer welfare ranked much more highly among the range of objectives pursued in Sri Lanka than in any of the other countries.[149] The striking feature of the Sri Lanka case is the lack of any overt competition in the electoral sphere between food producer and consumer interests. The latter are extremely articulate. A decision to withdraw the subsidised rice ration was reversed after a general strike in August 1953, and it has since been conventional wisdom that no government dare openly defy the food consumer. Only with the so far successful attempt of the present UNP government to do so by reducing the rice ration does this conventional wisdom appear suspect. It would not be accurate to say that food producer interests have been cowed by the power of consumers. For food producers have not, with the recent and partial exception of certain minor-food-crop producers, voiced demands for higher output prices.

Supported by (a) an institutional capacity inherited from the colonial era, especially the World War Two period, (b) an ideology in which the responsibility of the state for economic progress is almost unquestioned,[150] and (c) a particular sense of duty to provide the peasant with the means to improve his agriculture, the state has intervened in great breadth and depth in the smallholder sector. The symbolically significant paddy sector has been the main focus of this intervention, and the main recipient, relative to producers of other crops, of a portion of the economic surplus reaped from plantation production. This resource transfer has, however, been very unequally distributed even between paddy producers, while the smallholder sector as a whole has been the loser rather than the beneficiary of government action affecting agricultural prices. While this resource transfer has supported a dense and wide-ranging network of institutions in delivering subsidised services of various kinds to the individual cultivator, the physical performance of these systems has been poor. The most plausible explanation is that this is due, at least in part, to the absence of any 'countervailing power' on the part of the recipient population to press for more efficiency. One might note, for example, that the same cooperative network which regularly fails to deliver fertilisers on time has consistently been delivering weekly rations of rice and other commodities to almost the entire population with very few failures. Some problems appear to have cropped up in early 1978, for the Minister of Food and Cooperatives felt obliged to threaten publicly with dismissal cooperative managers who failed to keep adequate stocks of rice, flour and sugar.[151] Continual failure in respect of fertiliser supply does not seem, to the best of my knowledge, to have ever elicited any such concern or threat.

6

Categorising space:
urban–rural and core–periphery

Introduction

The reasons why Sri Lankan smallholders have failed to articulate
certain kinds of class demand are explored in detail in Chapters Seven
to Ten. This chapter, dealing with the spatial dimension of the Sri
Lankan economy and polity, is an essential preliminary. It justifies the
use in later chapters of the core–periphery continuum as an analytical
tool.

Because the focus of this book is on *rural* politics, and because the
terms 'rural' and 'urban' have been freely used in the preceding
chapters, the reader has thus far been implicitly encouraged to believe
that the rural–urban dividing line is a significant boundary within Sri
Lanka: that the terms 'rural' and 'urban' do indicate significantly
different elements or 'subsystems' within the national economy or
polity. The purposes of this chapter are (a) to expose the falsity of this
assumption and (b) to indicate that, in order both to describe the
economy of Sri Lanka and to analyse the polity, the concept of a core–
periphery continuum based on location is a more useful way to begin to
categorise the population than is the acceptance of the notion of any
fundamental urban–rural dichotomy in terms of occupation or access
to political power. Part of the reason why smallholder class interests
have not been articulated is that there is not in Sri Lanka a clear
objective basis for a rural–urban conflict of interest over agricultural
and food policy. There are conflicts, but to some degree they are intra-
rural and at the same time interregional. The core–periphery concept is
a useful image around which to organise the data relating to these
conflicts. It enables one to begin to analyse the role in the political
system of a variable widely ignored in Anglophone social science –
distance.[1]

The rural–urban dichotomy

A belief in the distinctiveness of rural and urban spheres, each
associated with particular patterns of living, appears extremely

widespread. Such is the tyranny of language that it is often difficult to use the terms 'urban' and 'rural' without appearing to give credence to such images. To dispense with these terms is, however, no solution. They will continue to be used here, but in a context in which their limitations are explicitly recognised.

The pervasiveness of 'rural' and 'urban' as a conceptual dichotomy seems related to looseness and variety of definition. It is perhaps easiest to understand the way in which the terms are used by tracing out a hierarchy of meanings.

At the first and most elementary level the difference between 'rural' and 'urban' is one of ecology or landscape. In this sense 'rural' indicates the predominance of naturally occurring environmental features – vegetation, watercourses, animals – while 'urban' suggests the predominance of structures made from artificial materials, notably buildings, roads and vehicles. It is an extension of this perspective to identify urbanness with densely clustered human populations.

At the second level these landscapes are associated with differences in economic activity patterns. 'Rural' is essentially agricultural, and 'urban' is non-agricultural, although not necessarily industrial.

At the third level these differences in landscape and occupation are compounded by differences arising from characteristic patterns of economic and social relationships. The human geographer, concerned with space, is likely to see urban areas as 'places performing higher grade central place functions'[2] on behalf of the surrounding scattered rural population. Alternatively, both the layman and the sociologist might locate the essential difference in the character of social interaction. In everyday language urban and rural modes of living are commonly contrasted in terms of such dichotomies as: anonymous–personal; tense–relaxed; reserved–friendly; or instrumental–altruistic. In the more formal schemas adopted by social scientists, similar concepts have been encapsulated in the association of rurality with (a) small-scale social networks characterised by intense, enduring and multiplex relationships among individuals; (b) 'traditionality' within the meaning of the Parsonian-derived 'tradition–modernity' continuum, i.e. relationships structured by status rather than contract, allocation of roles by ascription rather than achievement, multi-purpose rather than specialised institutions;[3] or (c) non-capitalist as opposed to capitalist production and social relationships.[4] The notion of some kind of persistent difference between characteristic rural and urban social relationships has lain at the core of much sociological theory from the origins of the discipline, although contemporary empirical evidence is not generally supportive.[5]

Urban and rural in Sri Lanka

Statistical series conventionally divide Sri Lanka's population into either two or three sectoral-cum-spatial categories: urban and rural; or urban, rural and estate. The rural–estate division, which has been discussed in Chapter Four, need not concern us here. If not treated separately, estates are always included in the rural category.

The method used to distinguish urban from rural areas for official purposes is delightfully simple to operate and correspondingly crude in effect. Urban areas are those under the jurisdiction of the three 'urban-type' local government units – municipal, urban and town councils – and rural areas are those under the jurisdiction of village councils.[6] The demarcation of these units and changes of status – as, for example, from village to town council – are affected by many factors, not least the play of political interests. There are no formalised measurable criteria against which such decisions are to be made. There is in consequence a considerable degree of arbitrariness in the demarcations and overlap between the different categories.[7]

It is convenient for our purposes to evaluate these official demarcations of urbanity and rurality against each of the various definitions of the rural–urban dichotomy set out above.

Urban and rural landscapes

The minimal 'landscape definition' of the urban–rural frontier is more difficult to apply in Sri Lanka than in many other countries because it does not accord closely to settlement patterns. The characteristic feature of Sri Lankan settlement patterns arises from the interaction of two separate sets of factors. The first is the concept of the 'homestead', of which the house is but a part, which is deeply rooted in preference and practice. Apart from the house (or adjacent family houses), a homestead includes a good number of coconut, jak and other trees to serve the kitchen, a vegetable garden, a compound around the house which is kept swept, and a toilet standing clear of the house.[8] Half an acre at least is required to realise this preference in a decent manner. An acre is better, and more does not come amiss. Rural settlement is therefore dispersed. Except for a few areas in the Dry Zone,[9] there are few villages nucleated on European or Indian lines. In the densely populated areas where most of the population live – most of the Wet Zone, the Jaffna peninsula and the eastern coastal strip around Batticaloa – distinctions between separate villages or localities often cannot be gauged visually.

Such rural nucleation as does exist arises from the second set of

factors affecting settlement patterns: a high degree of commercialisation of rural life and a very high level of use of road transport by
the rural population.[10] These factors have two related consequences.
One is the high preference for roadside homestead sites, all the more so
because of the importance of access to extra-village resources, and
therefore road transport, in generating high rural incomes. The second
is the importance of small bazaars, invariably clustered around road
junctions/bus stops, as the foci of rural social and economic life.[11]

Except in the centres of large towns, urban settlement follows much
the same pattern as in rural areas. Roadsides are preferred; commercial
establishments are tightly packed together along main thoroughfares
and junctions; but these often back onto quasi-rural landscapes of
clearly separated homesteads incorporating coconut trees and perhaps
even interspersed with paddy fields. There is no clear differentiation
between urban and rural landscapes. The small rural junctions appear
as microcosms of the large urban centres, and roadsides, especially
along main routes, are always populated, although more densely so in
urban areas. The denser the population in general the less evident is
any rural–urban difference in landscape. The traveller on the main
coastal road along the crowded southwestern coastal strip from
Negombo to Matara often has little basis to decide where he is passing
through an urban council, town council or village council area.

Urban and rural occupational patterns

Despite both the lack of clear distinctions between rural and urban
landscapes and a relatively generous definition of 'urban' which
includes many small local centres under the category of town
councils,[12] the official categories are relatively successful in excluding
agriculturalists from urban populations. In 1971 less than 7% of the
urban working population was employed in agriculture or animal
husbandry, leaving rural areas with fully 96% of the agricultural work
force.[13] The association of rurality with the agricultural economy is,
however, far less complete. In 1971 only 59% of the rural work force
was employed in agriculture or animal husbandry, including plantation production.[14] The details and significance of this figure are
discussed below, where it is demonstrated that the involvement of the
rural population in non-agricultural activities is especially high in
some of the rural Wet Zone districts which comprise part of the core
region based on Colombo.

Central places

Some comment on the usefulness of the concept of urban areas as
'central places' is implicit in the discussion above of settlement

patterns. The relatively high levels of commercialisation and personal mobility endow with special importance central places performing commercial and transport functions. These are, however, found at every level, both in rural and urban areas. Admittedly, by restricting oneself to 'higher grade central place functions', one can establish a close identity between central places and urban areas. One is, however, left with considerable rural diversity, with local central places, in some intuitive sense clearly rural in character, standing out clearly in many dimensions – including wealth and power – from the surrounding scattered populations which they serve.[15] There is an especially strong sense of disjuncture in the Kandyan areas, where many bazaars, invariably located on main roads, arose in association with plantation development, and where bazaar traders are unlikely to be local people. There is a strong spatial and conceptual dichotomy between 'village' and 'bazaar', and villages often stand clear of main roads.[16]

Patterns of social interaction

The application to Sri Lanka of the idea that urban and rural areas are each characterised by separate and distinctive patterns of social interaction cannot be tested directly. However, the heterogeneity of patterns of socio-economic relationships within rural areas and the variety of social and economic attributes of rural populations seems adequate to suggest its implausibility. This heterogeneity has several dimensions, and can be observed at both local and regional levels.

At the local level the heterogeneity associated with the existence of central places has already been mentioned. Other diversities have been introduced by the process of alienation of Crown lands to villagers. Through Village Expansion Schemes, poorer and lower-status villagers have been systematically relocated on plots of unused Crown land, which almost inevitably contain poor quality soil, are on difficult terrain, and are relatively remote from main roads and the centres of village life. At the local level socio-economic stratification has a distinct spatial aspect, all the more so since caste identity and place of residence often overlap very closely, especially in the Low Country.[17] In the Dry Zone there are often substantial differences, and sometimes antagonisms, between the old (*purana*) villages and the new and spatially somewhat amorphous communities created in the process of settling outsiders.[18]

Partly for the reasons given above, 'village' is a somewhat arbitrary, flexible and amorphous unit in most of Sri Lanka. It lacks the boundedness and the elements of partial autonomy and self-sufficiency which are normally associated with the term and are more in evidence, for example, in India. Rural economic life is oriented spatially to commercial and transport facilities rather than to local administrative and social units. Administrative divisions cross-cut one another relatively indiscriminately.[19]

Urban–rural boundaries

The amorphousness of 'village' in Sri Lanka and the lack of clear urban–rural boundaries are opposite sides of the same coin. Both are in large part due to the preference for dispersed settlement; the high levels of both the commercialisation of society and the spatial mobility of the population; the many and diverse consequences of state intervention for the pattern of settlement and for the territorial classifications used at local level; and the high density of population. Most of these factors are more evident in what we have chosen to term the 'core', the southwestern quadrant of the Island (see Map Three), than in the more peripheral areas. It is from the urban–rural categorisation to centre–periphery that attention now turns.

Core and periphery

Partly in consequence of the neo-Marxist theories of authors like Andre Gunder Frank,[20] core–periphery models have enjoyed considerable recent popularity in the social sciences.[21] The concept of core and periphery is, however, extremely elastic and may be used in a variety of ways. It is correspondingly important to define the sense and the modesty with which the concept is used here. The starting point is a core–periphery *schema* – a framework for organising data – rather than a *model*, if that term implies any *a priori* specification of the nature of the relationships involved. These relationships are determined empirically. Within political geography core–periphery schemas generally operate in two dimensions: the spatial and the institutional.[22]

The spatial dimension is almost self-evident and can be understood metaphorically by reference to the concept of the wheel whose spokes radiate from the hub (core) to the periphery. The important aspects of the metaphor are the concentration of certain activities in the core; the costs of transport and communication between core and periphery; and, perhaps less importantly, the tendency for various parts of the periphery to relate to one another through the core rather than directly.

The institutional dimension relates to the clustering of important institutions in the core, and the consequent tendency towards domination by the core of the periphery. All core–periphery models appear to contain at least a suggestion of such domination.[23] It may, however, be understood in very different ways. Perhaps the easiest to comprehend is the Frank type of model, in which a putatively unified or homogeneous core dominates and exploits the periphery. This is not the major sense in which the core–periphery concept is used here. Rather, it is argued that the 'dominance' of the core lies in the fact that it is the 'home' in various senses of the Sri Lankan elite; that it was the historic home of the present electoral system; and that the shape of that system – above all, the pattern of inter-party competition and the agenda of political issues – stems from the social and economic structure of, and thus the pattern of political conflict *within*, the core. In short, the core has the political *initiative*. 'Initiative' cannot be considered totally separately from 'domination': as was suggested in Chapter One, the ability to set the agenda for political competition constitutes power. It is, however, useful to keep the concepts distinct.

There is a third dimension to the core–periphery schema as used here: an economic or occupational dimension. The occupational interests of different groups to a large extent overlap with, and can be described within, a core–periphery schema. The *rural* areas of the core are less dependent on agriculture than are those of the periphery, and practise a very different kind of agriculture. The agricultural populations of the core and of the periphery have different – and to some degree conflicting – interests in policy.

The notion of core and periphery is then an extremely elastic metaphor, and is always used at some risk of misunderstanding. Particular contingent features of Sri Lanka's history and geography make it especially appropriate and it is far less misleading than the notion of distinct urban and rural sectors. Yet it is not used as a substitute for the concepts of conflicting rural and urban sectors as they are used, for example, in the work of Lipton.[24] It is put forward more modestly as a framework from which to begin to analyse other conflicts. In particular, there are important conflicts within population groups located within the core.

The evolution of regional patterns[25]

When in the fifteenth century European traders began to encroach upon its trade, Sri Lanka was an important source of such valuable commodities as cinnamon, gems, arecanuts and elephants, and an importer of Indian rice. Control over trade was the material base for the Sri Lankan kingdoms based in the southwestern quadrant of the Island – both the central Kandyan hills (approximately our 'inner periphery' – see Map Three) and the Low Country (approximately our 'core' region) – where most of the population was concentrated. Trade was channelled through a string of ports along the southwestern coast. Muslim traders had a foothold in these ports and also, as they do today, a considerable trading and farming presence along the east coast around Batticaloa. A longstanding Sri Lanka Tamil polity based on Jaffna was closely connected to Tamil Nadu in India across the narrow, shallow Palk Strait, but separated from the Sinhalese areas in the southwest by the wide no man's land of sparsely populated Dry Zone jungle, which more or less corresponds to our 'extreme periphery' region.

The establishment of European (Portuguese) control over the Low Country began in the early sixteenth century and was completed by the early seventeenth century. The loci of this control were the southwestern ports.[26] Urban life, however, did not develop on a large scale, partly because of continual warfare. Apart from European rivalries, each successive conqueror – Portuguese, Dutch and British – had to face the opposition of the Kandyan kingdom, ensconced in the central hills and protected from superior European firepower by difficult terrain. When Kandy finally came under British control in 1815, the Sinhalese of the Low Country had been under European rule for two centuries and subject to major European influences for three.

These contrasting experiences helped to crystallise a divergence between Kandyan and Low Country Sinhalese which continues to have considerable political significance. Coastal location, foreign contact, trade and continual immigration from India had probably already engendered in the Low Country a society which was relatively loosely structured, innovative and entrepreneurial, while Kandy remained feudal, hierarchic, conservative and subject to the rule of those who controlled the land. The adaptation of the Low Country Sinhalese to Christianity, commerce, formal education and European culture only exacerbated this difference, which emerged also at the levels of ideology and consciousness. Having resisted Europeans for two centuries and maintained a Buddhist kingdom, Kandyans saw themselves as the repository of pure Sinhalese and Buddhist traditions and culture. The Low Country people by contrast saw in the Kandyans backwardness, conservatism, lack of education, and commercial naivety. Low Country and Kandyan Sinhalese came to be officially recognised as distinct 'racial' or 'ethnic' groups. They were classified separately in all censuses before 1981, and remain for some purposes subject to different civil laws.

These conflicting perceptions became more pointed after the Kandyan hills were 'opened up' for plantation development, first for coffee production in the 1840s, and then, from the 1870s, for tea. The commercial opportunities which emerged in such spheres as wholesale and retail trade, estate supply, land clearance and development under contract, and transport services were to a large extent seized by the Low Country Sinhalese. The Low Country already had a substantial nucleus of mercantile capitalists, especially from the population groups located on the coastal fringe. The general expansion of the plantation economy provided them with many new opportunities.[27]

A further consequence of plantation development in the Kandyan areas was the emergence of Colombo as the premier port and city in the Island. It had previously been no more than *primus inter pares* among the whole range of southwestern ports, and had been closely rivalled by the southern port of Galle. However, the development of the Kandy–Colombo road (and, later, railway) as the main supply and export route into the plantation areas, and the decline of sailing ships, for which Galle offered technical advantages, in favour of coal power, led to the rapid development of Colombo and the relative demise of Galle and the other ports, none of which offered deep-water anchorages. Today Colombo 'stands like a Triton among the minnows',[28] and has a population fifteen times larger than the second-ranking urban area, Jaffna.

This process of concentrating urban activities in Colombo did not, however, impair the position of the Low Country Sinhalese as a whole, including those from the southern districts of Galle and Matara, as the leaders of commercial, educational and political development among the Sinhalese. Taking advantage of their established position and easy transport along the coast, the Low Country people – and especially the *Karava* and other castes located on the coast – took a large proportion of educational and public-sector posts, sharing them with other minorities, notably Burghers and Sri Lanka Tamils, to the near exclusion of the Kandyan Sinhalese and the total exclusion of the Indian Tamil estate population. When in the early twentieth century Sri Lankan capitalists began to invest in plantations on a large scale, it was the Low Country Sinhalese (along with Sri Lanka Tamils and members of a few other small minority groups of recent Indian origin – Chetties, Borahs etc.) who were most prominent. Most Sri Lankan-owned estates were either in or on the fringes of the Low Country – tea estates in the upland areas of Galle and Matara, rubber estates in the interior of all the Low Country districts, and, above all, coconut estates in the north of Colombo district and in the adjacent Kurunegala and Kegalle districts.

Colombo and its hinterland

There is a sense in which Colombo has often appeared to be cut off from the rest of the Island. The wealthy, Westernised and largely Christian Sri Lankan elite which emerged in the nineteenth century became physically rooted around the 'better parts' of Colombo, such as the Cinnamon Gardens residential area, and English-model public schools like Royal College and St Thomas'. At the same time rewarding, high-level, middle-class (and even blue-collar) positions, most of them located in Colombo, became occupied to a disproportionate extent by either non-Sri Lankans or non-Sinhalese: the British; the Burgher population engaged mainly in public service; a large proportion of Sri Lanka Tamils, who found public service and trade in Colombo more rewarding than life in the Jaffna peninsula; large numbers of Indian Tamils, Malayalis and other South Indians in domestic service and in formal-sector posts, notably in Colombo port; Indian Moors and other small but wealthy Indian groups – Chetties, Borahs, Sindhis, Marwaris and Parsis – engaged mainly in trade, especially international trade; and Malays in the military, the police and a range of other blue-collar jobs.[29]

Colombo, especially at the wealthier levels of society, was thus not a Sinhalese city.[30] Even less, because of the Christianity of many of the wealthier Sinhalese (and Tamil) families, was it a Buddhist city.[31] The fact that many of these ethnic and religious minorities were concentrated there helped mark it off from the rest of the Island.[32] At the level of the elite and in respect of culture and lifestyle this hiatus is still very evident.

It would, however, be a mistake to interpret this particular disjuncture as evidence of a lack of contact between Colombo and its hinterland in other spheres. For in other respects the creation of powerful and enduring connections between Colombo and *some* rural areas was one of the more noticeable consequences of the plantation experience.

To impose causal order in the complicated pattern of interactions between the plantation experience and the pattern of Colombo–hinterland connections is beyond my competence. It is clear that a lot of things happened together and that they are interrelated. For our purposes it seems useful to distinguish four main processes.

The first is the establishment of what was and remains an extremely good rural transport and communications infrastructure. This originated in the needs of the plantation sector, and is therefore especially well-developed in the plantation areas – our core and inner periphery regions. It is partly for this reason that the rural Wet Zone has been described as being in a process of transformation 'into a peri-urban complex'.[33]

The second point is the way in which the rural population of the Low Country – the southwestern coastal region or our core region – has built upon good coastal transport networks and the early diffusion of foreign trade and European institutions and values, to occupy – along with the Tamils from the Jaffna peninsula – a disproportionate share of superior positions in economic, political, educational and cultural institutions. The Sri Lankan capitalist class has largely been based in the Low Country (and Jaffna), and the Low Country plantations of the political elite have played a major role in the development of the political system.[34]

The third point is that the public provision of a physical and social (especially educational and medical) infrastructure to facilitate the development of the plantation economy, generated many public-sector jobs in the rural areas, especially the plantation areas, i.e. our core and inner periphery regions. The use after 1931 of plantation surpluses for the general benefit of the rural Sinhalese has greatly expanded this network of direct contacts between agencies of the state and the rural population.

The fourth point is that rural population densities generally diminish in proportion to distance from Colombo (see Map Three). They are especially high in the plantation areas, and for this reason alone their populations are relatively much better provided with a transport and communications infrastructure and public services generally. They are well placed to organise politically and bring pressure to bear on politicians and public administrators in Colombo.

Contemporary urban patterns[35]

The rise of Colombo to a position of absolute dominance in the urban hierarchy in Sri Lanka was due to its entrepot role between the plantation areas and the world market. Yet the relative decline of the plantation sector within the national economy has not led to any decline in Colombo's dominance. The new industries which have emerged since Independence have either been concentrated around the fringes of Colombo or widely scattered in rural areas. Colombo remains the core of a very centralised polity and of a very centralised system for the physical distribution of goods. The transport network is centralised on Colombo, and most road and rail traffic travels along a few main routes radiating from there and serving the densely populated areas of the adjacent Wet Zone. A very large proportion of the total rural population live within a few miles of these routes and thus have very good access to the capital: in a single day they can (and very frequently do) make a return journey from home and spend several hours in the capital. Daily commuting to Colombo for work is fairly common in much of the Wet Zone.

Apart from Colombo, most of the district capitals marked on Map Two perform mainly local trade, service and administrative functions. Most are old-established in these roles, although Amparai and Moneragala, the capitals of administrative districts created in the 1960s, comprise mainly loose clusters of new public buildings interspersed with scrubland, and have village-sized populations. Two of the district capitals, Galle and Trincomalee, are in relative decline due to the loss of functions associated with their harbour facilities. In an outline of a national core–periphery model there are only three towns apart from Colombo – Kandy, Jaffna and Batticaloa – which require any special mention.

Kandy merits attention because it is the only town apart from Colombo which has a significant national role of any kind. This role is essentially ideological and political, and has its historical basis in the way in which both the town and the region came to embody Sinhalese and Buddhist traditions because of the long period of European rule and Western influence in the Low Country.

Kandy is the site of the main Buddhist temple, the Temple of the Tooth, and the seat of the two oldest, largest and most prestigious of the Buddhist priestly orders, the Asgiriya and the Malwatte chapters of the Siam fraternity. Its national role is most clearly exhibited in the culture and the ceremonies with which it is associated. These include ceremonies which are clearly national and state events, including for example the inauguration of the first Executive President under the new constitution of 1978. The location of such events in Kandy indicates the success of Kandyan claims to represent authentic and pure Sinhalese traditions. The fact that, in 1978, the Executive President delivered his inaugural address from a balcony of the Temple of the Tooth indicates the centrality of Buddhism to the Sinhalese nationalist self-image.

Another important ceremony is the annual Kandy *Perahera*. This has its origins in a military parade under the Kandyan kings and in ceremonies performed at Hindu temples. It was, however, 'captured' for broad political and ideological purposes earlier this century by the Kandyan aristocracy, and has been transformed into an event which is national, Buddhist and Sinhalese, yet at the same time an indicator and reminder of the pretensions to moral and cultural superiority of the Kandyan element.

Kandyan culture and the tourist trade associated with it are part of the economic basis of Kandy town. The town still retains a little of its former role as a regional centre for the plantation economy, especially in the provision of recreation and commercial facilities for the 'planter class'. Peradeniya, adjacent to Kandy, is the site of famous botanical gardens, and has long been a centre for agricultural research. It now also houses the headquarters of the Department of Agriculture, the only government department to be sited outside Colombo. Peradeniya also contains a university campus. As a consequence of these activities and also because of Kandy's pleasant climate and attractiveness for the retired and semi-retired middle class, the town has a high proportion of 'professionals' in its work force (see Table 6.1).

A large professional middle class is a characteristic which Kandy shares with Jaffna (see Table 6.1). Otherwise they differ very much in terms of their role in a core–periphery model. For while Kandy performs national functions over a very limited range of activities, Jaffna is the centre of a secondary Sri Lanka Tamil regional, cultural, economic, political and communications network, which is to some extent independent of the national pattern. Here the name 'Jaffna' refers less to the town in a formal sense than to the very densely populated Jaffna peninsula, which covers only a fraction of the area of Jaffna district but includes the great majority of its population. Within the peninsula rural–urban differences do not appear very evident or significant.

Since the Sri Lanka Tamil minority is of peripheral concern to this thesis, there is no need to go into detail on the Jaffna economy and regional network. The important points are the cultural and political dominance of Jaffna Tamils over the less numerous and more scattered rural Tamil inhabitants of the three other mainly Sri Lanka Tamil districts – Mannar, Vavuniya and Batticaloa;[36] the pattern of migration from Jaffna to the agricultural districts of Mannar and Vavuniya in particular in recent decades;[37] and the clash which recent Dry Zone colonisation has engendered between Tamils spreading south and, more importantly and aggressively, Sinhalese spreading north and east, which has led to a continued orientation of the rural Tamils to Jaffna in response to this perceived threat.

Batticaloa functions in relation to the Sri Lanka Moors as the core of a semi-autonomous network, much as Jaffna does in relation to the Sri Lanka Tamils. Even more than in the Jaffna case, the core is not confined to the city itself. It is rather the densely populated quasi-urban, quasi-rural coastal strip which runs for perhaps forty miles from Batticaloa southwards to at least Kalmunai.[38] This regional network is, however, far less distinctive than the one based on Jaffna: Moors do not dominate numercially or culturally to the same degree that Sri Lanka Tamils do in Jaffna;[39] the majority of Moors are scattered throughout the Island;[40] and east coast Moors are in some small degree culturally distinctive.[41]

Core and periphery: some statistical indicators

The ranking of areas according to the core–periphery continuum is determined by their relative access to the central political, administrative and commercial institutions located in the metropolis. The resultant pattern therefore overlaps closely with the patterns of population density and communications described above. A special weighting is, however, given to the southern Low Country districts of Galle and Matara which, while in terms of distance fairly remote from Colombo, enjoy, by long tradition, high levels of effective engagement in the institutions of the metropolis.

Most statistics are available only on the basis of the administrative district. The unit is, however, sufficiently small for this not to pose a major problem, and many district boundaries, notably the interior boundaries of the Low Country districts of Kalutara, Galle and Matara, run along topographical barriers and thus correspond to real constraints on movement. In the tables below, districts are grouped into five categories: the core (essentially the Low Country); the inner periphery (the Kandyan hills); the outer periphery (the 'Intermediate Zone' in climatic terms); the extreme periphery (the Dry Zone, except Jaffna); and Jaffna (the semi-autonomous Sri Lanka Tamil core region).

This classification, which was borrowed from elsewhere, was based originally on agro-ecological criteria.[42] However, it suits our purposes as it also corresponds to the degree of accessibility to Colombo. It scarcely needs pointing out that the boundaries are not always drawn at the very best place for any given purpose. They do, however, generally succeed in demonstrating relatively distinctive and homogeneous regions. The major exception is the Intermediate Region. While it is true that this basically covers districts falling substantially into the relatively narrow, climatically defined Intermediate Zone between Wet and Dry Zones,[43] and thus has some climatic homogeneity, the districts are otherwise very diverse, and united mainly by virtue of being intermediate between Wet and Dry Zones in spatial and statistical as well as climatic senses.

The statistics presented in Tables 6.1 and 6.2 are intended to demonstrate as economically as possible the correlates of the core–periphery relationship outlined above, and the usefulness of the regional classification. Table 6.1 relates to the degree of access of district populations, classified separately into urban and rural sectors, to education and thus to employment in the formal and state sectors. Table 6.2 records the degree of dependence of rural populations on agriculture in general, and in particular on paddy production – as a rough proxy for non-estate agriculture.

The reason for juxtaposing in Table 6.1 data on education and the attainment of remunerative 'professional' employment is the closeness of the links between the two. The context is much the same in Sri Lanka as in many other countries, especially but not only those classified as 'developing': higher and more secure incomes in the 'formal sector', i.e. large-scale organisations with highly formalised recruitment and work procedures; the preponderance of public-sector organisations in the formal sector; and the gearing of the schooling system to meet the ever increasing levels of formal certification required for recruitment into the formal sector.[44]

For a number of reasons the linkages between education and 'professional' employment are especially close in Sri Lanka, particularly as they affect the rural population. In the first place, the long history of formal education has combined in recent decades with rapid population growth and only moderate economic growth to place the country high on the scale of 'educational inflation'. High levels of certification are required for recruitment to intellectually undemanding jobs.[45] In the second place, policies of nationalisation and state-sponsored industrial development have drawn a large proportion of the formally organised, large-scale employing organisations into the public sector, where educational qualifications, along with political connections, dominate in recruiting procedures. (In 1971 at least 14% of the labour force was employed by the state. This number had increased by nearly 150% by 1979, largely as a result of the nationalisation of the plantation sector.)[46] In the third place, the remaining large private-sector industrial and financial enterprises, almost all based in Colombo, have a tradition of recruiting through personal connections and from relatively privileged social strata. For most rural people the public sector offers the only realistic (if remote) prospect of a good job. Educational certificates are a necessary, if not a sufficient, condition of attaining a good job.

Table 6.1. *School attendance and professional employment: sectoral and districtwise patterns, 1971*

	School attendance: population aged 5–24 years attending school, 1971			Professional employment: economically active population working in a 'professional' job[a]		
	Rural (%)	Urban (%)	Urban/rural	Rural (%)	Urban (%)	Urban/rural
Core						
Colombo	50	48	0.95	7	8	1.20
Kalutara	50	50	1.01	5	11	2.40
Galle	50	54	1.08	4	10	2.32
Matara	51	55	1.07	4	12	2.90
Inner periphery						
Kandy	46	54	1.19	4	13	3.64
Nuwara Eliya	40	42	1.05	1	5	3.43
Kegalle	49	52	1.07	4	11	2.71
Outer periphery						
Matale	42	54	1.25	3	11	4.48
Kurunegala	47	47	1.01	4	12	3.22
Ratnapura	40	53	1.32	3	11	4.28
Puttalam	40	41	1.02	3	8	2.38
Badulla	42	53	1.27	2	9	3.91
Moneragala	36	39	1.09	3	5	1.88

Extreme periphery					
Hambantota	44	1.03	2	6	2.86
Mannar	38	1.26	3	8	2.42
Vavuniya	41	1.24	2	5	2.13
Batticaloa	31	1.41	3	8	2.73
Amparai	37	1.13	4	6	1.45
Trincomalee	34	1.33	2	6	2.73
Anuradhapura	41	1.05	3	9	3.37
Polonnaruwa	42	0.84	3	6	2.38
Jaffna	53	1.08	6	10	1.48
Sri Lanka	49	1.09	4	9	2.37

[a] 'Professional' indicates occupation code 0/1 in the census. Explanation given in the text; note that it excludes government clerical staff.
Source: Census of Population 1971, Volume 1, Parts 1–22: Tables 12 and 16.

The other side of the coin is that a 'good job' seems to offer the income, orientation and connections required to propel children up the ladder to educational success. Patterns of access to education and white-collar employment tend to replicate themselves within families.[47]

The statistics in Table 6.1 on school attendance rates reflect above all variations in population density. A certain degree of randomness is introduced into the urban statistics due to the small size of the urban population of some districts. In the case of the rural population a graph (not reproduced here) reveals a very close association of population density with school attendance rates.[48] The main exceptions are relatively low attendance rates in the Kandyan districts, especially Nuwara Eliya and Kandy, due to their large population of poorly provided Indian Tamil estate populations;[49] especially high rates in the Jaffna peninsula, reflecting the particular orientation of its population to professional and white-collar employment in other parts of the Island and abroad; and low rates on the east coast, reflecting the relative educational backwardness of the Moor population.[50]

The whole of the (densely populated) rural Wet Zone thus emerges as an area of high education involvement, in which attendance rates often exceed those in the urban areas of the Dry Zone districts. The main causal linkage is clearly with population density and thus the average distance to be travelled to school. Density is not, however, a complete explanation. For educational facilities are of only limited use without the incomes to support children to advanced levels of schooling and the connections to help obtain a return on the investment in the form of a good job. The data on professional employment provide a proxy for resources of this nature.

The full title of the census occupational category to which these figures on professional employment relate is 'Professional Technical and Related Workers'. It constituted 5% of the total work force in 1971. Of those included within it 60% were schoolteachers. The other major employments were, in order of magnitude: nurses; *ayurvedic* physicians; mechanical- and civil-engineering technicians; medical doctors; professional midwives; sculptors, painters, photographers and other creative artists; pharmacists; priests and other religious functionaries; accountants; engineers; and lawyers.[51] This category does not coincide with white-collar, public-sector employment. It includes relatively small numbers of independently employed persons whose careers depend little on educational qualifications – priests, artists, athletes and astrologers. More importantly, it excludes the vast army of public-sector clerical, administrative and office staff, who are inevitably concentrated in headquarters posts, especially in Colombo. Representing especially the educational and health sectors, our 'professional' category is a proxy for occupation of skilled posts in the main public-sector programmes serving the rural population.

The core–periphery gradient shows up very clearly in the case of the rural population in particular, with high levels of occupation of professional posts in the rural Wet Zone, especially rural Colombo, and lower levels towards the periphery. For reasons given above both Jaffna and urban Kandy exhibit especially high rates.

It is significant that this centre–periphery patterning exists despite the predominance of schoolteachers in the category and the legitimate expectation that, given widespread access to and demand for public education, the ratio of teachers to population would be more or less constant across districts. Everyday encounters suggest that the reasons are much the same as those that produce similar spatial biases in other national organisations: postings on the periphery are unpopular and posts may remain unfilled, while at the same time new and unnecessary posts are created in the core to help satisfy local aspirations; teachers posted to the periphery may maintain their homes in the core, and be absent from work for long periods; the concentration of good educational facilities in the core region produces a lowering of expectations and demands for good facilities at the periphery; and the more wealthy families in the periphery arrange to send their children to relatives in the Colombo area for advanced education.

Table 6.2 illustrates very clearly the connection between peripheral location and the relative role in the *rural* economy of both agriculture generally and paddy production in particular, since plantations are concentrated in the Wet Zone, especially the Kandyan districts. As one might expect, the degree of agricultural involvement of the rural population is somewhat lower in the districts containing the centres of the Tamil and Moor regional networks – Jaffna and Batticaloa–Amparai respectively – than in the surrounding Dry Zone districts. The proportion of smallholdings operated by females is generally highest in the core, reflecting the high level of engagement of the rural male population in non-agriculture.

Conclusion

Through an examination of history and of spatial variations in contemporary social and economic statistics, this chapter has both established the general case for adopting a core–periphery schema for macro-level social science analysis of Sri Lanka and indicated a useful

Table 6.2. *Agriculture in the rural economy: districtwise patterns,*
1971 and 1973

	Percentage of rural employed population engaged principally in (1971):		Percentage of smallholdings operated by females (1973)
	All agriculture[a]	Paddy production	
Core			
Colombo	22	9	16
Kalutara	45	15	17
Galle	44	16	20
Matara	53	23	19
Inner periphery			
Kandy	65	16	16
Nuwara Eliya	85	11	11
Kegalle	58	19	11
Outer periphery			
Matale	73	39	9
Kurunegala	65	52	12
Ratnapura	70	19	12
Puttalam	46	18	15
Badulla	78	16	12
Moneragala	78	33	12
Extreme periphery			
Hambantota	66	32	16
Mannar	65	46	9
Vavuniya	78	58	10
Batticaloa	62	45	15
Amparai	58	50	10
Trincomalee	67	54	12
Anuradhapura	81	73	8
Polonnaruwa	76	72	9
Jaffna	49	15	16
Sri Lanka	60	27	14

[a] 'Agriculture' includes all those in agricultural, animal husbandry, forestry, fishing and hunting occupations.
Source: Census of Population 1971, Volume 1, Parts 1–22: Tables 16 and 17; and *Census of Agriculture, 1973, General Report*: Table 1.

pattern of classification of districts into relatively homogeneous regions. In succeeding chapters the schema is tested in use. The occupational and spatial aspects are prominent in Chapter Seven, and the institutional or political aspects in Chapters Nine and Ten.

7

A smallholder interest or smallholder interests?

Introduction

At this point the analytic focus of the book shifts. In Chapters Three to Five we were concerned with the observable politics behind rural policy over the past half century or so: the policies pursued in the spheres of Crown land alienation, land tenure reform, agricultural pricing and agricultural service provision, and the factors shaping these policies. The intention was to justify the insistence on the political subalternity of the smallholder population: its general dependence on the elite for political initiatives, and the common failure of these initiatives to articulate and incorporate the kinds of demands and policies which would appear to represent the true interests of the smallholders themselves. Chapter Six represented a kind of interlude: the introduction of the core–periphery continuum as a tool of analysis to be used in this and later chapters. At this point we begin to focus directly on resolving the puzzle set out at the beginning of the book: why has peasant subalternity been characteristic of Sri Lankan politics despite certain expectations to the contrary?

There are a number of dimensions to the answer. We begin in this chapter by examining how far Sri Lankan smallholders have – and are likely to perceive themselves to have – a common interest in relation to agricultural policy. Is there, within the realm of feasible agricultural policies, a viable basis for an agrarian programme which would attract widespread rural electoral support? Or does the smallholder sector in reality break down into a series of groups whose interests in relation to economic and agricultural policy are different or conflicting?

The search for an answer to these questions generates five main conclusions. The first, which is more directly relevant to the arguments of the earlier chapters, is that no major subcategory of the smallholder population has been consistently benefited or penalised through agricultural policy in recent decades. This illustrates the argument already made in Chapter Five that rural policy has not been in any major degree the outcome of conflicts in which smallholder populations have articulated their occupational interests. Agricultural policy instead reflects broader dimensions and imperatives of the national political system.

The second, and main, conclusion is that different subsections of the smallholder population do indeed have interests in relation to economic and agricultural policy which diverge and to some degree conflict. These divergences and conflicts are primarily of an interregional nature, and are essentially between the food deficit rural areas of the core and the surplus-food producers of the periphery.

The third conclusion is that these divergences and conflicts of interest do not arise solely from patterns of differentiation – by crop, farm size, degree of market orientation, type of production technology employed, or regional location – internal to the smallholder economy. They are also in part the product of the interaction between these patterns of differentiation and the way in which the state is organised to regulate agriculture.

The fourth conclusion is that these divergences and conflicts of interest help, but cannot in themselves fully explain, the lack of smallholder occupational consciousness and political action. In the first place, most smallholders have common interests in relation to such matters as land policy and agricultural service delivery, regardless of conflicts over economic policy. In the second place, there is scope for different smallholder categories to bargain among themselves and formulate economic policies which would make most or all smallholders better off, to the general immediate detriment of non-farmers. In the third place, there is something of a puzzle as to why agrarianism should not have emerged in the Dry Zone periphery as a regional movement. For the Dry Zone population would appear to have a fairly unambiguous interest in both higher producer prices for food and improved public agricultural services. The fifth conclusion is, then, that one must pay special attention to the politics of the Dry Zone in resolving our overall puzzle.

Evaluating the consequences of economic policy

Most of this chapter is concerned with the relative costs and benefits to different smallholder categories of different economic policies impinging directly on agriculture. It tackles what is potentially an extremely complex task. For one would, if interested in the full economic consequences of alternative policies, be required to investigate second-order as well as first-order effects. For example, some of the more evident first-order effects of an increase in the market price of paddy would be to enrich those households which are surplus producers and to impoverish those who are dependent on market purchases for (some of) their food. An analysis of second-order effects might, however, modify the starkness of this conclusion. One might find that agricultural labouring or food deficit cultivating households would not suffer as much as first predicted because the greater profitability of paddy cultivation might generate more investment, more employment, and perhaps higher wage rates. No attempt is made in this chapter to investigate second-order effects. Our ultimate concern is not with the economic consequences of these policy changes, but with the way in which these changes might be conceived and therefore supported or opposed by the rural population. Second-order effects are difficult even for economists to assess. It is unlikely that the rural population would be sufficiently aware of or in agreement about them for this to seriously affect their preferences and politics. Our purposes require that the effects of alternative economic policies be painted only in broad strokes.

Organisation

In accordance with the framework of Chapter Five, three main kinds of policy alternatives are considered here: policies on producer prices, policies on the price of farm inputs, and policies affecting the efficiency of the delivery of those agricultural inputs provided by state agencies. In order to assess the impact of these policies on different categories of the smallholder population, one requires criteria for dividing the population into categories. Three main factors seem to determine interests in relation to agricultural policy: crops produced; size of holding, especially as it affects the distribution of food crop output between sales and autoconsumption; and regional location, in relation both to the core–periphery schema, and to the ecology and economy of cultivation. These three factors are not independent of one another in a statistical sense. Some crops are associated with particular regions and particular ranges of holding size, while farm size and regional location are also related to one another independently of cropping pattern. To maintain continuity with the previous discussion, especially with the examination of economic policy in Chapter Five, the analysis will be structured around individual crop categories: paddy, export crops and 'other crops' respectively.

The first three sections deal with the potential consequences for smallholder political unity of differentiation according to crop, farm size, and regional location. The way in which the state organisation interacts with this pattern is discussed towards the end of the chapter.

Objective interests: paddy producers

The marketed surplus

It is spatial variation – the core–periphery pattern outlined in the previous chapter – which stands out above all other factors in shaping the pattern of objective interests associated with paddy production. The data in Tables 7.1–7.3 illustrate two aspects of this conclusion: the very marked dependence of the core on external supplies of paddy and the dependence, in a different sense, of the periphery on income from paddy sales (see Table 7.1); and the accentuation of this regional difference in the post-Independence period (see Tables 7.2 and 7.3).

The statistics in Table 7.1 barely require written elaboration. They do, however, merit a caution, for in one sense they are too eloquent: they exaggerate to some degree the extent of deficit paddy farming (column d). These estimates were prepared for another purpose and on the basis of a number of broad assumptions made necessary by the inadequacy of data.[1] The desire to limit the number of arbitrary assumptions has resulted in biases tending to exaggerate the proportion of paddy-cultivating households who do not sell paddy.[2]

However, even if the true figure for the number of paddy-cultivating households dependent on market purchases of rice (or wheat flour) is, say, 25% less than in column d of Table 7.1, this does not significantly affect the major conclusion to be drawn, which relates to interregional differences in the pattern of objective interests relating to paddy production. The much greater relative dependence of the periphery on agriculture in general, on smallholder agriculture, and on the production of non-export crops has already been observed (see Table 6.2). The periphery is further an area of substantial surplus paddy production. By contrast, not only are the rural areas of the core substantially in deficit over paddy production (see Table 7.1, column c), but the great majority of even those *households* in the rural areas of the core which cultivate paddy do not produce enough for their own needs (see Table 7.1, column d). Correspondingly, part-time farming is also relatively more common in the core (see Table 7.1, column e), although it is also widespread in those coastal fringes of the periphery which house long-established, dense populations historically oriented to trade, notably the lower-level cores of Jaffna and Batticaloa.

In respect of the degree of self-sufficiency in rice, there is a rough continuum from the extreme deficit of the rural core – as measured against the norm that each person requires ten bushels of paddy per year to meet rice consumption requirements[3] – to the substantial surpluses produced in the periphery. There is, however, a marked break in this progression which justifies a simple division of the districts into two classes. On the one hand, seven of the eight districts of the extreme periphery (excluding Hambantota)[4] each produce, at the minimum, twice as much paddy as is required to feed their rural populations, and at least three-quarters of their paddy farmers sell paddy. On the other hand, each of the remaining fifteen districts produces less rice than is required to feed even their rural populations, and at least 40% – and typically many more – of their paddy farmers are deficit paddy producers. In a pattern which stands at odds with the more simplistic notion of 'modernity' as a bundle of intrinsically related attributes such as urbanisation, education and commercialisation, the more 'modern' rural area of Sri Lanka – the Wet Zone, especially the Low Country core – is characterised by subsistence paddy farming.

The statistics in Tables 7.2 and 7.3 illustrate various aspects of the increasing differentiation of core and periphery into paddy deficit and paddy surplus areas respectively in consequence of migration and the heavily subsidised expansion of irrigated Dry Zone paddy production since the 1930s. The physical relocation of the paddy sector from core to periphery is demonstrated by the output figures given in Table 7.2. The more detailed figures in Table 7.3 indicate the interregional differences in the technology and economics of paddy production associated with this shift. The main single conclusion to be derived from Table 7.3 is that the post-Independence period has seen an *accentuation* of already wide interregional differences in the technology and economics of paddy production. To explain this point it is easier to begin from a static presentation of these differences.

For our purposes, and ignoring the somewhat unusual case of Jaffna, whose farming population anyway specialises in non-paddy food crops, we can define three main regional paddy production technologies: the Low Country (the core), the densely populated Kandyan areas (including both the inner periphery and most of the outer periphery) and the Dry Zone, the extreme periphery.[5]

The Low Country is characterised by a climate and topography relatively unsuited to paddy production, an absence of irrigation and drainage infrastructure, and a population relatively well provided with non-agricultural economic opportunities. Part-time farming is especially common (see Table 7.1), and the area has long been noted for the relative uninterest of its rural population in agriculture.[6] Paddy cultivation techniques are simple. Levels of investment and inputs of labour per acre are low. Per-acre yields are correspondingly lower than elsewhere (see Table 7.3, row a).

Table 7.1. *Agrarian structure and food production: districtwise statistics, 1960s and 1970s*

District	Average size of holding, 1961 (acres)		Annual average paddy production per head of the rural population 1970–2 (bushels) (c)	Estimated percentage of paddy farmers who were deficit producers in 1976 (excl. rice ration) (d)	Percentage of smallholders obtaining most of their income from non-agriculture 1961 (e)
	All smallholdings (less than 50 acres) (a)	Paddy holdings (b)			
Colombo	1.8	1.1	2	84	51
Kalutara	2.2	1.3	4	87	35
Galle	2.1	1.4	4	82	35
Matara	2.4	1.6	5	74	27
Kandy	2.0	1.1	5	63	36
N. Eliya	2.2	1.3	5	44	17
Kegalle	2.6	0.9	4	82	18
Matale	2.9	1.4	6	61	14
Kurunegala	3.5	1.6	8	58	11
Ratnapura	2.8	1.2	4	76	17
Puttalam	3.4	2.4	3	83	38
Badulla	2.1	1.1	} 4	79	19
Moneragala	3.3	1.7		65	4

	(a)	(b)	(c)	(d)	(e)
Hambantota	3.3	2.6	9	41	11
Mannar	4.7	6.3	27	19	43
Vavuniya	5.7	5.9	24	15	26
Batticaloa	3.3	6.7	} 22	15	51
Amparai	3.7	4.7		10	35
Trincomalee	3.9	4.2	22	7	10
Anuradhapura	4.4	3.7	} 28	25	9
Polonnaruwa	5.3	4.0		5	20
Jaffna	1.8	2.3	5	74	49
Sri Lanka	2.7	2.0	7	61	29

Sources: Column (a) is from *Census of Agriculture 1962, Volume 1*: Table 1; column (b) is from *ibid, Volume 3*: Table 1; column (c) is estimated from information on paddy production provided by the Department of Census and Statistics, Colombo, and population data given in *Census of Population 1971, Volume 2, Part 1*: Table 4; column (d) is from Moore, 1980b; and column (e) from *Census of Agriculture 1962, Volume 1*: Table 1.

A smallholder interest or smallholder interests?

Table 7.2. *Regional changes in the location of paddy production, 1953/4–1955/6 to 1975/6–1977/8*

Region	Percentage of national paddy output produced in: 1953/4–1955/6	1975/6–1977/8
Core	22	14
Inner periphery	13	10
Outer periphery	23	25
Extreme periphery	39	48
Jaffna	4	3
Sri Lanka	100	100

Sources: The data for the 1950s were obtained from the *Statistical Abstract*, various years, and those for the 1970s from *Agricultural Statistical Information 2*: 13–14; and Central Bank of Ceylon, *Review of the Economy*, 1978: Table 13.

The Kandyan hills by contrast have a long tradition of careful and labour-intensive paddy production methods involving, among other things, painstaking construction of small-scale irrigation facilities[7] and, more recently, the widespread use of the labour-intensive practice of transplanting paddy seedlings from nurseries rather than simply broadcasting seed (see Table 7.3, row c). High per-acre yields are achieved in most Kandyan districts (row a), but at the expense of low levels of output per unit of labour (row b). There is a direct association with the fact that rural poverty is especially common in the Kandyan areas.[8] Were the Kandyan villagers not so poor, they would not be willing to adopt extremely labour-intensive methods for such low returns per unit of work.

In the sparsely populated Dry Zone it is labour rather than land which is relatively scarce. Tractors and buffaloes are comparatively more important than human labour as a source of power. Levels of labour input per unit of land are relatively low. But because of the relative abundance of sunshine and irrigation water, paddy yields per acre are fairly high (row a), and yields per person-day extremely high (row b).

The figures in rows d–j of Table 7.3 illustrate how these regional differences have been accentuated by developments in the post-Independence economy. New land has been brought into production relatively fast in the Dry Zone (row d), while the paddy labour force in the Low Country has grown more slowly than elsewhere (row g) because of the availability of alternative employment, especially in limited industrial development and in the public sector. Increased production owes comparatively more to new land in the Dry Zone and to additional labour in the Wet Zone/core (rows i and j). The margins of error in the data sources, especially the statistics on the paddy work force, are such that only limited significance need be attached to the apparent fall in paddy output per worker in the Kandyan areas (row h). The figures do, however, illustrate that, faced with a static land base and a growing population, the Kandyan villagers have had to run hard to prevent themselves from falling back. This gives added point to the Kandyan hunger for estate land discussed in Chapter Four.

The important conclusion for our purposes is that the existence of a substantial peripherally located population supplying large rice surpluses to the rest of the Island and engaged in a different type of paddy cultivation from the rest of the Island, is to an increasing degree a product of the economic policies of the last few decades, and is a continuing process. The implications are discussed below.

Output prices or input subsidies?

The differing interests of paddy farmers of the core and periphery in relation to the producer price of paddy are very evident from the figures of column d in Table 7.1: the great majority of producers on the periphery stand to gain from high prices, while the majority of those in the core stand to lose. A further dimension to this clash of interests is demonstrated by the statistics in Table 7.4. These statistics relate to a small but relatively reliable sample survey conducted in each of the three main paddy-producing regions mentioned above. They illustrate the relative benefits to paddy farmers in each of the three regions, of hypothetical changes in government policy leading to changes in the farm input and output prices prevailing at the time of the survey. The first three changes take the form of increased subsidies on farm inputs, and the last is an increase in output prices.

The central conclusion, also supported by alternative data series,[9] is that, although per-acre and per-farm use of subsidisable inputs (i.e. virtually all inputs except land, labour and buffalo power) is typically absolutely higher in the periphery than in the core, the much higher ratio of paddy sales to production in the periphery means that the *relative* advantage of paddy producers in the periphery lies in higher paddy output prices rather than in input subsidies. Put another way, if there were x million rupees of assistance to be given by the state to paddy producers, a higher proportion of that assistance would accrue to paddy producers of the core if it were given in the form of input subsidies, while the periphery would benefit more if assistance were given through an increase in output prices. The higher per-acre levels

Table 7.3. *The regional paddy economy: differences in technique of production and changes between the early 1950s (1953/4–1955/6) and the early 1970s (1969/70–1971/2)*

		Region					
		Core	Inner periphery	Outer periphery	Extreme periphery	Jaffna	Sri Lanka
Average yield per net harvested acre (bushels), early 1970s	(a)	34	61	43	54	35	47
Average yield per person-day equivalent of labour input (bushels), Maha 1966–7 season	(b)	0.53	0.35	0.48	1.08	0.68	0.80
Percentage of sown area transplanted or line sown, Maha 1966–7 season	(c)	4	59	21	16	11	17
Percentage change in:							
Net harvested area	(d)	+12	+22	+29	+86	+48	+43
Yield per acre	(e)	+30	+57	+51	+56	+45	+53
Output (quantity)	(f)	+46	+92	+96	+190	+114	+121
Number of paddy workers	(g)	+32	+127	+151	+152	−17	+112
Output per worker	(h)	+11	−15	−22	+15	+160	+5
Ratio of increase in harvested area to change in:							
Yield per acre	(i)	0.40	0.39	0.57	1.54	1.07	0.81
Number of workers	(j)	0.38	0.17	0.19	0.57	1.41	0.38

Note: The years are chosen to fit the availability of census data on the number of paddy workers for 1953 and 1971, and the improvement in paddy statistics after 1953. Note that there has in fact been little change in the proportion of the recorded paddy labour force who are female, despite an increase in the generally female task of transplanting. The fall in the production of paddy per worker in some areas cannot be traced to this kind of statistical artifact. The years selected are fairly typical in respect of the total volume of production. Nuwara Eliya, Badulla and Moneragala districts are *not* included in the estimates for rows (d)–(j) because of the non-availability of data for the early 1950s.

Sources: Data on paddy area and production were obtained from the regular series in the *Statistical Abstract*, various years. Statistics on the number of workers engaged primarily in paddy production – a poor but usable proxy for labour input into paddy cultivation – were obtained from *Census of Population 1953, Volume 4, Part 1*: Table 3; and *Census of Population 1971, Volume 1, Parts 1–22*: Table 17. The statistics in rows (b) and (c) were calculated from the results of the Central Bank's 1966–7 sample survey (Central Bank of Ceylon, 1969, *Survey on Cost of Production of Paddy*: 27 and Appendix Table 3).

Table 7.4. *Relative regional benefits to paddy cultivators of different government policies, Maha 1976–7 season*

Hypothetical alternative policy	Benefit measured as	Dry Zone (Polonnaruwa) (a)	Kandyan Wet Zone (Kandy, Kegalle) (b)	Low Country Wet Zone (Colombo) (c)	Ratio (a)/(c)
Reduce tractor hire charges by 50%	Rs. per acre	68	neg.	27	2.5
	Rs. per farm	242	neg.	20	12.1
	As % of the cost of production	4.4	neg.	3.6	1.2
Reduce cost of agro-chemicals by 50%	Rs. per acre	26	28	19	1.4
	Rs. per farm	93	21	14	6.6
	As % of the cost of production	1.7	2.8	2.5	0.7
Reduce cost of fertiliser by 50%	Rs. per acre	112	72	50	2.2
	Rs. per farm	400	54	37	10.8
	As % of the cost of production	7.2	7.5	6.7	1.1
Increase paddy price by 50%[a]	Rs. per acre	875	174	68	12.9
	Rs. per farm	3,143	132	50	62.9
	As % of net income from paddy per farm	134	48	65	2.1

[a] Note that the benefits of an increased market price are calculated only on that proportion of the paddy harvest which is sold. Official purchase prices are used.

Source: Ranatunga and Abeysekere, 1977: 2, 18–19, 21, 22, 29.

of use of tractors, agro-chemicals and fertilisers in the periphery makes it *seem* as if subsidies on these items are of especial benefit to the producers on the periphery. The picture, however, looks very different if one examines the alternative means available to steer resources to paddy farmers.

Regional variations in the effectiveness of input delivery

The conclusions of the previous section were implicitly based on the assumption that subsidised inputs are actually available to the farmer on demand at a cost no greater than their official selling price. The discussion in Chapter Five of the performance of state agencies in delivering farm inputs reveals this to be false. The system often fails. The consequences of failure are, however, not randomly distributed. They bear unequally on farmers of different regions.

One can divide the services provided to the smallholder by government agencies into two broad categories: those transferable over space and those not. Fertiliser falls into the first category. It is subsidised and scarce, and supply failures are common. Yet to some degree, at least, supply failures affect only the final pattern of fertiliser distribution between farmers, not the total value of the service.[10] If fertilisers do not turn up in X cooperative, they will turn up in Y. By contrast, there is little or no compensation to other farmers and areas if irrigation water is mismanaged, the credit system is blocked, or state tractor pools dry up. It is useful to examine separately for each category of service the relative consequences for different regions of poor service delivery.

Fertiliser delivery

The important conclusions about the pattern of fertiliser delivery are derived from the figures on Map Four. Before these conclusions are discussed a few words are required about the interpretation of the figures.

The mapping exercise was conducted only in relation to paddy fertiliser because it is the only significant subsidised farm input widely used throughout the Island. 'Paddy fertiliser' is not necessarily used only on paddy. Indeed the very high rates of use in Jaffna district in particular are certainly due to the use of paddy fertiliser for vegetables. The available evidence does, however, suggest that the rate of diversion of paddy fertilisers to other crops is not sufficiently large to seriously affect the validity of the results presented here.[11]

Before we can draw conclusions about regional biases in deliveries, we ideally need to know what the pattern of delivery would be like in the absence of such biases. Let us first assume that fertilisers were freely available everywhere at a uniform price. Inter-district differences in use rates would then reflect differences in demand. What shape would these take? To answer this question two main factors would need to be considered: the relative productivity of fertiliser in different locations, and the ability of farmers to pay for it. Lack of information on these variables makes detailed predictions difficult.

Kandyan paddy farmers might be expected to obtain high returns from each unit of paddy because they apply relatively large quantities of complementary labour.[12] They also need fertiliser more regularly than other regions because they exhaust the soil by practising high rates of double cropping.[13] On the other hand, Dry Zone farmers have a more abundant supply of sunshine to help obtain the maximum return from each unit of fertiliser.

Data on the *total* incomes of paddy-farming households in different districts are only fragmentary, but generally conform to the impression that, although per-household agricultural incomes tend to be higher in the Dry Zone, the greater relative importance of non-agricultural earnings in the Wet Zone generally evens out average total income per paddy-cultivating household in the different districts.[14] If it is true, as some sources suggest, that those paddy farmers with non-agricultural earnings use more fertiliser and other purchased inputs because they have ready cash available at the beginning of the season,[15] then the paddy farmers of the Wet Zone might be expected to be relatively heavy users of fertiliser.

One cannot from such inadequate data draw any conclusions about the likely pattern of 'pure' demand for fertiliser, except that it is extremely unlikely to conform to the actual pattern of use shown in Map Four. It is not simply that actual rates of use are higher in the core than the periphery – a pattern also found, somewhat surprisingly, in the Tamil and Moor regional subsystems based on Jaffna and Batticaloa respectively. The additional and more significant point is that the core–periphery gradient is almost perfect: rates of use decline as one moves from the core out along main transport routes towards the periphery. Local differences in terrain have some marginal influence on the figures,[16] and there are small variations in the figures for other years not represented in the figures on the map.[17] Yet overall the core–periphery pattern dominates, for single years as well as in the three-year averages given here.

How can one explain this pattern of fertiliser use? Three possibilities present themselves. The first is that the mileage discount offered transporters by the Sri Lanka Fertiliser Corporation[18] does not cover

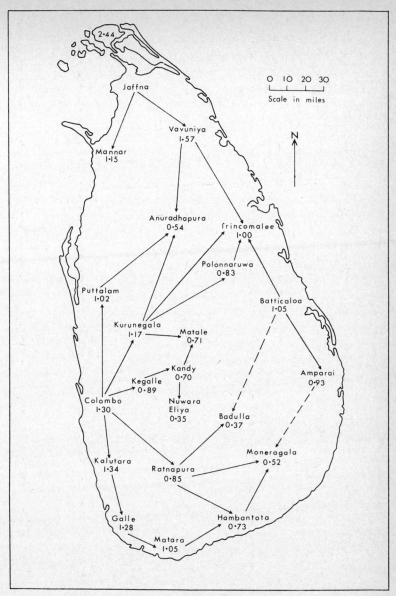

Map 4. Sri Lanka: pattern of use of paddy fertiliser at district level (1972/3–1974/5).
   The figures indicate the amount of paddy fertiliser issued per unit of paddy produced, expressed as a ratio to the national average (1.00) (see text). The arrows indicate main road and rail routes between the district capitals and the implied direction of flow of fertiliser.
   Data on fertiliser issues were obtained from *Agricultural Statistical Information*, Volume 1: 63, and Volume 2: 16; and Central Bank of Ceylon, *Annual Review of the Economy*, 1978: Table 13. Data on paddy production were obtained from *ibid*: Table 13 and from tables supplied by the Department of Economics and Statistics, Colombo.

full transport costs, and that the real cost of fertiliser to the retailer increases in proportion to the distance from Colombo, the point of origin. Charged with selling fertiliser at a uniform regional price, cooperatives on the periphery perhaps respond by purchasing less than they would otherwise have done in order to minimise losses or free their lorries for more profitable activities. The second possibility is that the greater density of population and of transport, storage and distribution facilities in the core increases both the level of effective demand and the ease with which demands can be met. The third possibility is that, because of easier access to Colombo, politicians and other inter-mediaries located closer to the capital can intervene more effectively to influence the distribution of supplies and ensure attention when deliveries are delayed. It is useful to recall that fertiliser distribution has been extremely (and inefficiently) dependent on central storage facilities in Colombo.

The balance between these different explanations for the pattern of fertiliser deliveries is, however, unimportant for our purposes. The point is simply that, regardless of causes, the consequence is to give the paddy farmers of the core, compared to those of the periphery, a greater relative interest than even formal accounting (e.g. Table 7.4) suggests in ensuring that state assistance to paddy farmers takes the form of fertiliser subsidies rather than higher output prices. For the farmers of the core are well placed to obtain scarce fertiliser supplies.

Hence one understands the Central Bank's complaint, quoted in Chapter Five, that 'Delays in fertiliser supplies have been a recurrent experience *in the major paddy growing areas*' (i.e. the Dry Zone, my emphasis). In the absence of deliberate administrative efforts to channel paddy fertiliser into the Dry Zone, 'normal' institutional processes direct it disproportionately to the core.

The delivery of other paddy inputs

Relative to the periphery, the core is less disadvantaged by inefficiencies in fertiliser delivery. The same is true of the other services provided by state agencies. For with the main exception of credit, which is available on an Island-wide basis, these other services are in fact concentrated in the periphery. Almost all state-constructed and -managed large-scale irrigation schemes are in the Dry Zone. The paddy farmers of the core sell a tiny fraction of their paddy output through the GPS, while those on the periphery market most of their paddy in this way.[19] When they were (formerly) in existence, all state (including cooperative) tractor pools were located in the Dry Zone.[20] And poor management characterises all these services.[21] Thus the overall pattern of poor physical delivery of farmer services generally imposes much higher costs on paddy farmers of the Dry Zone periphery than on those of the core.

Interests in paddy production

There are, then, major interregional differences of interest in paddy production. Low output prices and high input subsidies are much more favourable to producers in the core than to those in the periphery. Conversely, inefficient service delivery imposes especially high costs on the periphery. And with respect to paddy (but not other crops), policy has generally been biased in favour of producers located in the core. For policy has been marked by low output prices, relatively generous subsidies, and inefficient service delivery. The major exception is of course subsidised colonisation in the Dry Zone. Even this is not such an exception as it appears. For many of those benefiting from land allotments are in fact from the core.[22]

How is this pattern of interests related to our other criterion for categorising farmers – farm size? The estimates in Table 7.5 indicate the approximate location of big paddy farmers according to district. A 'big farmer' is arbitrarily defined as one producing on average at least five hundred bushels of paddy per year, compared to the estimate of sixty bushels as the average quantity required to meet the consumption requirements of an average farm family. The figures in Table 7.5 are certainly underestimates of the number of big farmers, although to what degree is unknown. As they were collected in 1963, almost a decade before the imposition of an individual paddy land ownership ceiling of twenty-five acres, fear of land reform would not have been such a potent cause of the underreporting of large holdings as in later years. Other considerations probably encouraged underreporting: fear of income tax, and, if later experience is any guide, the existence in the Dry Zone of large unrecorded and illegal paddy holdings created through the cultivation by tractor of large extents of Crown land, and the holding of illegal mortgages on allotments on irrigation schemes.[23]

It is, however, extremely unlikely that the incidence of underreporting was sufficiently skewed across districts to invalidate the main conclusion to be drawn from Table 7.5: the relative concentration of big paddy farmers in a small number of peripheral districts, especially Batticaloa, Amparai, Mannar and Vavuniya. These are mainly Sri Lanka Tamil and Muslim districts, and big paddy farmers are mainly Tamils and Muslims. Agricultural policy is emphatically not clearly biased in favour of the largest paddy producers.

A smallholder interest or smallholder interests?

Table 7.5. *Location of big paddy farmers, 1963*

Region/district	Estimated number of paddy farmers producing more than 500 bushels of paddy per annum[a]		
	Number (a)	Number as percentage of paddy farmers in the region/district (b)	Number as percentage of all big farmers (c)
Core	420	0.3	6
Inner periphery	580	0.7	8
Outer periphery	700	0.4	10
Extreme periphery	4,840	4.2	67
Hambantota	320	1.9	4
Mannar	350	6.9	5
Vavuniya	490	6.5	7
Batticaloa ⎱ Amparai ⎰	1,970	6.8	27
Trincomalee	360	3.7	5
Anuradhapura ⎱ Polonnaruwa ⎰	1,350	2.9	19
Jaffna	730	2.4	10
Sri Lanka	7,270	1.3	100

[a] From districtwise figures on asweddumised acreage (Maha 1962/3 season), net harvested acreage (average of years 1961/2–1963/4) and yield (average of 1961/2–1963/4). Assuming that within each district all these variables were constant across all holding sizes, an estimate was obtained of the acreage required to produce an output of 500 bushels. The number of operational paddy holdings above this size was estimated by graphical interpolation from the statistics relating to the 1962 Census of Agriculture on the size distribution of paddy holdings.
Source: Data on asweddumised acreages are from Bansil, 1971: Appendix 14; those on harvested acreage and yield are from the regular tables published in the *Statistical Abstract*, various years; and data on paddy holdings are from *Census of Agriculture 1962, Volume 3*: Table 2.

Objective interests: smallholder producers of export crops

The objective interests of smallholder export crop producers are so clear that little need be said. All those who sell tea, rubber or coconuts are victims of taxation, exchange-rate and trade policies which transfer large proportions of the world market value of their output either to the state or, in the case of coconuts, directly to consumers. Producers have a direct interest in having these burdens lightened.

The only further point which need be added at this stage is that export crops are concentrated almost entirely on the core or the inner periphery. Coconuts are a partial exception, but even they are relatively rare in the periphery (see Table 7.6).

158

Table 7.6. *Cropped area in smallholdings^a by type of crop, 1962*

Region	Tea	Rubber	Coconuts	Paddy^b	Other crops
			Percentage of cropped area under:		
Core	4	18	37	26	15
Inner periphery	11	16	23	25	25
Outer periphery	2	5	42	29	22
Extreme periphery	1	neg.	13	72	14
Jaffna	—	—	16	53	31
Sri Lanka	3	8	30	39	20

^{a} Smallholdings are defined as holdings of less than 50 acres.
^{b}The asweddumised area, not the gross acreage cultivated during the year, is used for purposes of calculation.
Source: *Census of Agriculture 1962, Volume 2*: Tables 2A and 4.

Objective interests: smallholder producers of 'other crops'

The diversity of the 'other crops' category has already been explained in Chapter Five. It includes food and non-food crops; marketed and non-marketed products; products to which imports pose no threat; those which compete directly with imports of the same product (e.g. chillies, potatoes and onions); and those affected by imports of substitutes (e.g. maize in relation to cheap imported wheat flour). The category also includes tree crops, field crops, crops grown under shifting cultivation, and crops grown in mixtures with permanent shrubs or tree crops. This diversity, combined with the dearth and doubtful reliability of available statistics, makes generalisations about this category difficult. There are two points relevant to the present argument.

The first point is that 'other crops' are especially common on that ubiquitous but ill-defined category of holding termed a 'home garden',[24] and thus on the smallest holdings (see Table 5.2). A paddy land holding is a valued asset, and typically belongs to a household which has in addition a solid chunk of highland. Compared to highland crops, paddy requires large cash outlays in land preparation, which are often beyond the reach of the poor.[25] In the Dry Zone, shifting cultivation (*chena*) is practised most by the poorest farmers.[26] Paddy land tends to belong to the 'middling' rural strata rather than to the poor. Whatever the intention, the 'paddy bias' of post-Independence economic policy has been to the benefit of the politically more significant rural 'middling classes' rather than to that of the rural poor.

The concentration of smallholder subsidies on paddy from the 1940s to the 1960s in part ruled the poorest cultivators completely out of the competition for government assistance.

The association of 'other crops' with the home gardens of the poor is, however, far from complete. Particular crops are concentrated in particular localities, and in regional terms 'other crops' – including sugarcane, tobacco, many vegetables and potatoes – have been especially common on the eastern, southern and northern slopes and foothills of the Central Kandyan hills, i.e. the outer periphery (see Table 7.6). They are not associated with either of the two poles of the core–periphery schema. There is, however, another subcategory of 'other crops' which has become increasingly important during the 1970s, and continues to grow in importance despite substantial changes in profitability induced by changes in import policy. This is a category of 'other food crops', among which the most prominent are chillies, onions, maize, green gram, groundnut, cowpea, millet, gingelly and black gram. These crops are heavily concentrated in the outer periphery, the extreme periphery and Jaffna.[27] The point of significance here is that these food crops are mainly grown in areas which already have a substantial and growing interest in paddy sales. The growing importance of these minor food crops thus contributes to the increasing differentiation of rural Sri Lanka into a food surplus periphery and a food deficit rural core.

Winners and losers?

The material presented above can be related to two broad questions. One is the relative impact on different categories of the smallholder population of the agricultural and economic policies pursued in recent decades. The other is whether there is a real unity of interest among Sri Lankan smallholders. The latter is the main concern of this chapter, but it is useful at this stage to look briefly at the first issue.

It is evident from the information given above and in Chapter Five that no important category of smallholders can be said to have been consistently benefited or penalised through government agricultural and economic policy in recent decades. It is true that smallholder producers of tea, rubber and coconuts have been heavily taxed and that those coconut smallholders with a marketable surplus have suffered from export restrictions designed to keep coconut market prices low for the consumer. If one were to classify smallholders into groups according to single crops grown, then it would be the case that plantation crop producers have fared worse than:

(i)   Paddy producers, some of whom, mainly located in the Dry Zone, have benefited from substantial subsidies, especially for irrigation and land development. Yet it has been much the same people, the producers of marketable surpluses, who have been adversely affected by policies which have depressed paddy market prices.

(ii)   Producers of minor export and home garden crops, who have generally been little touched by economic policy.

(iii)   Producers of subsidiary food crops, whose incomes have been successively inflated and deflated as a by-product of broad strategic oscillations between import substituting and free trade policies.

It would, however, be a mistake to see plantation crop producers as a distinctly different set of people from producers of other crops. The most numerous subgroup, coconut smallholders, generally obtain only a small proportion of their incomes from coconuts. The smallholder areas of the 'coconut triangle' north of Colombo (see Map One) are notorious for part-time farming. The much less numerous tea and rubber smallholders, who currently account for only about 2% of the total smallholder crop production by value (see Table 5.1), generally own other land and produce paddy or some other crop. Since they are nearly all located in the core rather than the peripheral areas (see Table 7.6) smallholder plantation crop producers must number among the beneficiaries of the system whereby the core region obtains an undue share of subsidised fertilisers.

Whether classified by crop, location or farm size, no category of smallholder can be clearly identified as either winners or losers from government economic policy. For the economic policies which do affect their incomes in this rather mixed and arbitrary way stem not from the exercise of political muscle by or on behalf of organised groups of farmers, but from the broader pressures determining state policy. Among these, arguably the most important and most consistent derive from the need for the political leadership to continue to command support from large sections of the population, especially the Sinhalese, by providing them with material and symbolic benefits. Hence the heavy taxes on plantation exports, the cheap food policy, and the expensive Dry Zone irrigation developments justified by reference to national and historic Sinhalese themes.

State organisation and interest groups

It is evident that the differentiation of the smallholder economy along the overlapping dimensions of crops grown, farm size, degree of market involvement, production technology employed and regional location does constitute an obstacle to the emergence of a common national agrarian political programme. There is above all an objective conflict of interest between the food surplus Dry Zone and the food deficit Wet Zone. Aspirant politicians have perhaps been able to foresee the limitations inherent in any attempt to mobilise smallholder votes behind a common national agrarian programme. It is explained below that these intra-smallholder conflicts of interest do not explain as much of our overarching puzzle as they might seem to do at first. In the meantime, however, it is useful to look at another dimension of this intra-smallholder division of interests: that created by the state itself 'in its own image'.

As was mentioned in Chapter One, and is discussed in more detail in Chapter Eleven, the political consciousness and actions of contemporary Asian rural populations are likely to be shaped in large part by the actions of the state itself. The evidence suggests that this general process is also at work in Sri Lanka, for as the Sri Lankan state has generally created separate agencies to deal with the producers of individual crops, producers tend to see their interests in crop-specific ('industrial') rather than in broader occupational terms. This process is probably important because the particular crops – and in the case of paddy, particular production technologies – are regionally concentrated. State organisation interacts with patterns of differentiation within the smallholder economy.

In contemporary Sri Lanka almost all agencies concerned with agricultural development have been crop-specific. In the case of plantation crops, direct state intervention in production was limited while the estate sector was privately owned. The Ministry of Plantation Industries was established only in 1970. The first major direct intervention of the state in the technology of plantation production was the establishment in the 1920s and 1930s of separate Tea, Rubber and Coconut Research Institutes.[28] The decision to create separate sets of institutions to serve each plantation crop was fully consistent with established practice in British colonies and with the fact that the three crops were in large part separate from one another in location and in type of ownership. The practice has been faithfully pursued since that time. In pursuance of international agreements to restrict production, separate Tea and Rubber Controllers were established in 1933 and 1934 respectively to register acreage and authorise expansion.[29] Replanting and new planting subsidies and fertiliser subsidies are granted at different rates for each crop and administered separately. Rates of export duties are set individually for each crop. More recently, special institutions to encourage smallholder production of export crops have also been crop-specific – e.g. the Tea Smallholdings Development Authority.

Although, formally, the Department of Agriculture has a wide-ranging brief, it has in practice tended to concentrate heavily on paddy. A new Department of Minor Export Crops was established in 1971 to take responsibility for this hitherto neglected area. It distributes new planting and replanting subsidies at rates specific to the small range of crops with which it deals. In recent years action to stimulate vegetable production for export has come mainly from the Ministry of Trade. It is on the same ministry that sugarcane producers have focused their demands for protection against imports.

How might this crop-specificity of state organisation affect the potential for smallholder political unity? It could do so in two distinct if related ways. In the first place, the general policy of dealing with each crop separately encourages farmers to believe that the characteristic of the crop is important, and thus to think of themselves as having an interest defined according to crops grown. I was first made aware of this issue when doing research on the cinnamon industry. Officials, politicians, traders and, most interestingly, producers, constantly reiterated suggestions for crop-specific institutions and services – fertiliser depots, official purchasing points, acreage registration – which were specifically justified by reference to the services provided for tea and rubber producers.[30]

In the second place, crop-specific agencies do at least to some degree direct farmers' political energies into separate channels, and thus, everything else being equal, fragment rather than unify the political networks most directly responsive to farmers' interests. Not only do different agencies deal with individual crops, but they also offer a different package of benefits (or costs) to their 'clients'. In dealing with 'their' agencies, tea and rubber producers are mainly concerned with questions of access to and levels of replanting subsidies and with the availability of processing facilities. If they were more aware of their objective interests they might be more concerned with the levels of export taxes levied on their products. Paddy producers, depending on location, are concerned with such issues as credit availability, availability of new seeds, and irrigation water supplies. If they were more aware of their objective interests they might be very concerned about reducing cereal imports.

It is at least plausible that a more unified system of, for example, credit provision, fertiliser supply and pricing, price setting and research funding would have elicited a corresponding response among farmers to see themselves as members of a broad national class or category rather than simply as growers of individual crops.

Conclusion: a smallholder interest or smallholder interests?

Even if smallholders were actively to pursue their occupational interests in politics, there are good reasons for supposing that their action might take the form of the pursuit of particular crop and regional interests rather than any all-embracing national or pan-Sinhalese 'smallholder interest'. Indeed, the recently emergent demands for more favourable prices for minor-crop producers are based on particular localities and regions.

Politicians 'trawling' for potential votes have thus perhaps seen little scope for attempting to unite large numbers of rural voters behind a common set of 'agrarian' economic demands. Yet the extent to which these divergences and conflicts of interest in relation to economic policy contribute to resolving our puzzle about peasant political subalternity could easily be exaggerated.

In the first place, the bulk of the smallholder population have common material interests over such issues as land policy (e.g. the terms of Crown land alienation) and the efficiency of agricultural service delivery by public agencies, which might partly override differences of interest in relation to economic policy.

In the second place, the very fact that none of the various regional, crop or farm size categories has been unambiguously and consistently advantaged or disadvantaged in economic policy illustrates the potential for bargaining among the smallholder categories to their mutual benefit and at the immediate expense of the non-cultivating population. A reduction in the direct or indirect taxation of export crop producers, combined with cuts in public subsidies to non-agriculture and policies to increase open-market food prices, could benefit *most* smallholder cultivators at the expense of non-cultivators.

In the third place, this chapter directs our attention to one important category of smallholders who do have a distinctive set of interests evidently not catered for in present policy: the food surplus producers of the outer and extreme peripheries. The core of this category comprises paddy producers, but they are (increasingly) supplemented by surplus producers of minor food crops. Surplus-food producers have a common interest in high food prices. They also have the advantage of a solid territorial base. In the Dry Zone region dependence on agriculture for livelihoods reaches its highest level (see especially Table 7.7, column f); there is the greatest degree of orientation to a single crop – paddy (see Tables 6.2 and 7.6); there is the lowest level of part-time farming to dilute and divert the attention of

Table 7.7. *Regional variations in the smallholder interest, 1963*

Region	Percentage of the rural population of the Island resident in the region, 1963	Estimated percentage of rural (and estate) households^a (1962/3) cultivating		$\dfrac{(b) \times 100}{(c)}$	Percentage of agricultural operators earning most of their income from agriculture, 1962/3^b	$\dfrac{(c) \times (e)}{100}$
		Paddy	Any agricultural holding			
	(a)	(b)	(c)	(d)	(e)	(f)
Core	31	34	84	40	59	50
Inner periphery	22	27	55	49	74	41
Outer periphery	30	41	76	54	84	64
Extreme periphery	13	58	97	60	77	75
Jaffna	5	37	104	36	51	53
Sri Lanka	100	38	79	48	71	56

^{a} These figures are obtained by making four assumptions, detailed in Moore, 1981d: 319. One of these assumptions – that all land operators are to be found in rural households – explains the figure of 104% for Jaffna, for much of the peninsula is classified as 'urban' while it is in fact neither clearly urban nor clearly rural.

^{b} These statistics relate to all agricultural income, not simply income obtained from cultivation of owned or leased-in land.

Sources: The demographic data used in columns (a)–(c) relate to 1963, and are obtained from *Census of Population 1971, Volume 2, Part 1*: Table 4. The figures in column (b) on paddy land operators are obtained from *Census of Agriculture, 1962, Volume 3*: Table 1. The figures on landholding and sources of income in columns (c) and (e) are obtained from the *Census of Agriculture, 1962, Volume 1*: Table 1.

the farming population (see Table 7.1, column e); and there is the largest population of big paddy farmers likely to be especially concerned with high output prices (see Table 7.5).

If politics were directly to reflect interests arising from the process of production, then there ought in Sri Lanka to be strong demands from surplus-food producers of the periphery for, among other things, high food prices. It is evident that the population supporting such demands would constitute only a minority of the total electorate (see Table 7.7, column a). That, however, might not in itself constitute much of an obstacle. A solid block of electorates united around a clearly defined interest, and anyway occupying a strategic electoral position, is potentially very powerful.

In attempting to explain the political subalternity of smallholders, special attention is paid in the succeeding chapters to the politics of the Dry Zone. After raising in Chapter Eight the issue of socio-cultural identity and its potential relationship to peasant political mobilisation, I show in Chapter Nine that the ethnic conflict between Sinhalese and non-Sinhalese, which has been so prominent in Sri Lanka, has tended to fragment the Dry Zone surplus farmers along ethnic rather than 'class' lines. In the same chapter we explore at the Dry Zone regional level an issue taken up at the national level in Chapter Ten: the historical dependence of the politics of the Dry Zone (and the peasantry generally) on patterns of political conflict and the agenda of political issues which arose in the (mainly non-agricultural) core. Farmers generally, and those of the Dry Zone in particular, have been obliged to participate in patterns of political competition established largely in other places by other occupational groups and at a time when the Dry Zone carried far less electoral weight than it does today.

8

Rural consciousness

Introduction

In this chapter we further explore the answer to our general problem by asking a question which is made very pointed by a comparison of the Sri Lanka experience with that of India and Malaysia: in what ways have collective socio-cultural *identities* – as opposed to the commonalities of material interest dealt with in Chapter Seven – contributed or not contributed to the evolution of a common 'rural consciousness' which could underpin a ruralist economic programme? The Indian and Malaysian experiences indicate that class or socio-cultural categorisations have given broad swathes of the farming population a sense of common identity over and above that generated by simply sharing a common occupation. Ruralist political programmes can be more easily communicated and realised if a large proportion of the farming population can be persuaded that they share, for example, a linguistic, ethnic or caste identity which simultaneously unites them and sets them apart from other social categories – food consumers, industrial groups, public officials, landlords, or urban people generally – who can then be presented as opponents or exploiters. The kinds of collective identity which have been exploited to mobilise Indian and Malaysian farmers – caste, 'peasantness', rurality in a broad sense, or intra-rural conflicts between landlord and peasant, large and small farmers, or agricultural labourers and employers – have not been available to the exploited in Sri Lanka in the same way. Ethnicity has been important in Sri Lanka, but Chapter Nine demonstrates that ethnic conflicts have tended to divide rather than unite the smallholder population by creating cleavages among Dry Zone surplus-food producers.

Collective identities and farmer movements in Asia

It is inherently difficult in typical Asian conditions to organise large masses of small farmers behind a programme of ruralist policy demands. Their wide physical dispersal, poor communications, local and regional conflicts of identity or interest, and the abstract nature of connections between politics, economic policy, and material welfare all pose serious problems to politicians attempting to communicate a few simple messages and generate mass support. It is virtually inevitable that a successful mobilisation of farmers should be based on the association of farmers' occupational demands with broader symbols or messages relating to social and cultural rather than purely occupational identity.

In West Malaysia the Malay community occupies a position in many ways analogous to that of the Sinhalese in Sri Lanka: the 'original' community closely associated with rice cultivation in a society which became socially and economically more diversified as a result of plantation development. The images used to justify pro-Malay policies are very similar to those prevalent in Sinhalese nationalist mythology. Partly no doubt because the Malays have been more closely and exclusively associated with rice cultivation than have the Sinhalese, demands for high rice prices have been fused with general Malay communal demands since the inception of mass electoral politics just before Independence. Major intra-Malay conflicts between large and small farmers appear not to have fractured the united front over the price issue.[1]

In India[2] farmers' movements concerned with higher product prices emerged later and more slowly than in Malaysia and have had a series of regional bases rather than a single national base. But, in marked contrast to Sri Lanka, they do appear to be gradually, if haltingly, gaining momentum. In the 1960s and 1970s a variety of political parties, most of them led by Charan Singh, briefly Prime Minister in 1980, represented the interests of the small and middling farmers of the north, especially Uttar Pradesh and Haryana. The Punjabi regional interest was also closely associated with the demand for high farm output prices. In the late 1970s and early 1980s a series of farmer agitations in the southern states of Tamil Nadu, Maharashtra and Karnataka had higher output prices as their common theme, although they made a variety of other demands. Especially interesting is the emergence in Karnataka of the non-party Farmers Front, which played an important role in defeating the state Congress (I) government in early 1983, and has become a powerful pressure group in the state's politics.

A detailed account of the Indian experience cannot be fitted in here. It is adequate for our purposes simply to note various ways in which socio-cultural identities and class conflicts have helped stimulate Indian farmer movements.

In the first place, an important factor has been the strong sense of a rural–urban dichotomy which is deeply ingrained in Indian culture. Indian cultural traditions, of which one aspect is a broad dichotomy between rural/farming castes on the one hand and, on the other, urban/trading/military/public-service castes, encourage farmers to see themselves as having an interest separate and distinct from that of urban, commercial and state groups. The articulation of farmer price demands is one dimension of a broader and long-term process in which rural groups have over recent decades been increasingly successful in challenging urban, commercial and state-based groups (e.g. Brahmins) for position and power.

In the second place, *farmer* movements have been stimulated by the sense of solidarity engendered by conflicts with other rural groups, notably the conflict with large landlords (*zamindars*), especially in north India from the 1920s to the 1950s, and within the framework of nationalist mass mobilisation; conflicts of interest between small and middle farmers on the one hand and large farmers on the other in Uttar Pradesh in the 1960s and 1970s; and the conflict between famers and landless labour in Tamil Nadu (and Kerala) in the 1960s and 1970s. These conflicts, especially the latter, also have a caste dimension.

In addition to the collective identities located within civil society, farmers' movements in India have also been stimulated by the actions of the state itself, notably widespread attempts to procure grain from producers at less than open-market prices.

It is argued in this chapter that the kinds of collective identities, class conflicts and public policies which have stimulated the articulation of farmer demands in Malaysia and India have not and could not have played a similar role in Sri Lanka. The consequences of ethnic conflict in Sri Lanka are dealt with in the next chapter. We deal here solely with the identities which have not been important. It is first argued that Sinhalese political culture does not incorporate the same kind of notion of a rural versus urban/state dichotomy as does Indian culture. It is then shown that caste is not a good basis for farmer mobilisation among the Sinhalese. The next point is that, unlike India, Sri Lanka has lacked the overt conflicts between different categories of the agricultural population which would tend to mobilise large numbers of the farming population politically. Finally it is demonstrated that public policy in Sri Lanka has not given rise to grievances around which farmers could unite in opposition to the state.

The 'peasantry' in Sinhalese culture

This section is oriented around a comparison between India and Sri Lanka. It is argued (a) that there were important differences between the pre-colonial socio-political structures of Sri Lanka and India; (b) that the Indian tradition conforms in one important respect to the 'peasant studies' model of society – a substantial antagonism between rural society on the one hand and, on the other, the privileged elite, i.e. urban, bureaucratic, commercial landlord and military strata; (c) that the Sri Lankan tradition by contrast is one of substantial non-antagonistic integration of the rural population not only into the structures of a political state, but into a *national* (i.e. Sinhalese) state – there is no 'peasantry' in the Sinhalese tradition; and (d) that these differences in traditional (i.e. pre-colonial) socio-political structures are still in evidence in contemporary politics.

The sketch below of the contrasts between the Indian and the Sri Lankan traditions represents a compromise between the detailed presentation which the topic appears to merit by virtue of its intrinsic importance, and the brevity justified by the fact that the material is intended to support only one of several points made in this chapter. I was emboldened to tackle the issue only because a detailed contrast seemed fully implicit in the work of a range of historians and social anthropologists.[3] The pieces required only fitting together, and that is all that is attempted here. The sources quoted must be consulted for detail. The presentation is necessarily schematic. The word 'traditional' is used to refer to the immediate pre-colonial period, and 'traditional' socio-political structures are presented in a summary and idealised form. The contrasts in traditional structures are first presented, and it is then explained how and why they are considered to have relevance to contemporary politics.

State, society and nation: the Sinhalese tradition

The Sinhalese are heirs to a centuries-old tradition which links them – a particular people having their own distinctive language and culture – with the territory of Lanka, the Buddhist religion, and the state which rules that territory and protects that religion:

> The social history of Ceylon indicates an early and surprisingly persistent unity. That political unity was, over considerable periods, lost in the isolation of the courts and the regional lords, is to be expected. The overall historical view, however, indicates recurrent periods of national oneness and persisting cultural integration between the Sinhalese provinces. This unity rested fundamentally in the theoretical acceptance of a common monarch and the organisation of village society upon a feudal framework in which the ultimate ownership of land and the ultimate authority were vested in the king.[4]

Unlike many other Third World states, independent Sri Lanka has not faced the task of creating a *nation state* out of a territory, a

population and a state structure originating in colonial rule. The idea
and much of the reality of a Sri Lankan national state long predated
colonial rule. 'Nation building' in post-colonial Sri Lanka has involved
mainly the attempt to reconcile the minority communities, especially
the Sri Lanka Tamils, to a Sinhalese-dominated system.[5] For our
purposes it is not necessary to explore in any detail the ambiguities,
confusions and conflicts surrounding the notion that Sri Lanka is
traditionally, uniquely or essentially a Sinhalese and Buddhist territory and polity.[6] As was recorded in Chapter Six, the cultural
distinction between Kandyan and Low Country appears in part to be
the product of the colonial period – the two centuries of colonial rule
and Westernisation experienced by the Low Country before the
Kandyan kingdom was subdued. One consequence of this divergence
is that more is known of Kandyan than of Low Country pre-colonial
social organisation. The latter was subjected to more or less forcible
Westernisation, and substantially modified before it was recorded.[7] As
with other accounts of traditional Sri Lanka, the summary below is
biased by the more ample Kandyan evidence. This is, however, not in-
appropriate, for it is mainly through Kandyan channels that elements of
the traditional order have been transmitted into the contemporary era.

The social organisation of Sinhalese feudalism[8]

Pre-colonial Sinhalese society was organised under a land-service
feudal system in many ways very similar to that of mediaeval Europe.
Perhaps the main difference was that, as in most countries outside
Western Europe, Sinhalese feudalism did not incorporate the
contractual notion of vassalage.[9] Territorial jurisdiction was formally
exercised by direct commission from the ruler and associated with
rights to the produce of specific lands. In practice the occupation of
positions of territorial authority appears to have involved continual
tension between this formal principle and the fact that noble families
derived a degree of independence by virtue of personal or quasi-
personal property and status in particular localities. At all levels the use
of land was associated with service obligations to the state, obligations
due either to the nobility, to temples or, especially in the vicinity of the
capital, directly to the court.[10]

The connection between feudalism as a system of rule and as a
system of social organisation was, however, especially close, more so, it
appears, than under European feudalism. At all levels social and
political structures were to a large degree merged. One can illustrate
this by examining two spheres apparently of especial importance in
traditional society – caste and religion.

Caste in Sinhalese feudalism

Feudalism in temple and state was the skeleton upon which caste was the flesh and blood.[11]

These words from the standard work on the Sinhalese caste system point to a major contrast with the (traditional) Indian one.[12] For the latter, centred around the association of caste status with occupation, around a network of obligations between hierarchically ordered caste groups, and around norms about the behaviour appropriate to the interaction of members of different groups, is fundamentally oriented to relationships within *society*. It is not concerned with *state* organisations. By contrast the Sinhalese caste system is fundamentally concerned – i.e. in principle and in origin – not directly with the relationship between members of different castes but with their individual relationships to the state.[13]

Under Sinhalese feudalism caste was a way of talking about service obligations, whether to court, nobility, or temple. To be a member of the mat weaver caste was to share a collective obligation to deliver a regular quota of mats to the court. To be an elephant worker was to have responsibilities for the capture and care of royal elephants. The individual castes were separately organised, and were almost equivalent to departments of state. Caste administration was an aspect of state administration. Since the state's service requirements were subject to change, so too were caste categories and caste membership. New departments of state/castes might emerge, and old ones grow in size, diminish or disappear.[14]

Caste was associated with occupation only in the performance of service obligations. There was otherwise no caste-related occupational exclusivity.[15] All caste groups appear to have been engaged in cultivation to some degree: land in return for service was the central organisational principle of the feudal system. 'Fundamental to any understanding of Sinhalese caste must be the recognition that the practice of agriculture is caste-free.'[16] The largest and highest-ranking caste, the *Goigama*, is conventionally termed the 'farmer' caste in the English language. This is, however, misleading, for the term indicates a social status rather than simply an occupation. It connotes 'honourable citizens'[17] or the 'good people',[18] i.e. those unencumbered with onerous menial service obligations, and thus left free to pursue agriculture.

There are a number of differences between traditional Indian and Sinhalese castes which stem from the orientation of the one to society and the other to the state. Sinhalese castes were organised by the state for service and judicial purposes. There is, however, scarcely a trace of anything resembling the Indian caste *panchayat* – meetings of representative members of individual castes which served to regulate intra-caste and inter-caste social relations.[19] Only in the jungles of the North Central Province, whose scattered populations were effectively outside the ambit of pre-colonial states, does there appear to have been any comparable caste organisation – the *variga* court.[20]

Since Sinhalese caste is not oriented primarily to relationships within society, it does not require the detailed and strict rules about interpersonal interaction between members of different castes so characteristic of India. 'Pollution', so easily incurred in India if the elaborate behavioural rules are infringed, is among the Sinhalese courted only by eating in the home of a person of lower caste. Similarly, avoidance behaviour is restricted mainly to questions of access to the home.[21] In accordance with the orientation of caste services to the state rather than, as in India, towards members of other caste groups, it is the differences rather than the inequalities or hierarchies involved in caste which are relatively more prominent among the Sinhalese.[22] The physical correlate is the tendency for individual castes to occupy whole villages or village clusters, while the inter-caste service system requires different Indian castes to share the same village. Among the Sinhalese, the hierarchical aspect of caste, inter-caste services and multi-caste villages, are all more common in the Kandyan areas than in the Low Country.[23] Since, however, the main recipients of these services, the *Goigama*, and, more especially, the *Radala* – the aristocratic Kandyan *Goigama* sub-castes – were (and are) themselves occupants of important and privileged positions in the state organisation, services to them were as much state as private services. Relationships in civil society and in the state organisation are not easily separable.

Religious organisation in Sinhalese feudalism

Traditional India was especially marked by the close relationship to one another of religion and society, and their joint separateness from state organisation. By contrast Sinhalese religion was – much more so than in the present day – one of the most evident and important meeting points of social and political/state organisation.

One might begin, at the level of origin and religious precept, by pointing out that 'the structure of Buddhism which is pre-supposed in the discourses of the Buddha and his public activities is that of a triangular relationship between the *Sangha* [the Buddhist priestly orders], the king and the people'.[24] More importantly and concretely, in Sri Lanka as well as in the other Theravada[25] Buddhist countries of Southeast Asia, this dependence of religious organisation on the support of the monarch has been no less evident in practice than in principle.[26] Traditional Buddhism was inherently a state religion. A major Sinhalese Buddhist grievance against British colonial rule was that, by effectively disestablishing the Buddhist religion, the British broke a treaty promise made to the Kandyan people in 1815 to protect their religion. The British on the whole honoured the promise, as they interpreted it, by protecting Kandyan temple lands and not actively promoting Christian missionary activity. The Buddhist view, however, was that it was inherently discriminatory to put Buddhism on the same footing as Christianity, Hinduism and Islam. Buddhism required state sponsorship not merely protection as a private religion.[27] The contemporary demand for a Buddhist state, only partially met by the granting of Buddhism its 'rightful place' in the 1972 Republican Constitution, thus has an historical rationale more profound than simple 'Sinhalese chauvinism'.

The norms and precepts of Buddhism as a system of ideas and the close historical symbiosis of *Sangha* and state are, however, but a small part of the present story. The more important part derives from an examination of temple organisation. For it is as controllers of the resources of particular temples, rather than as members of one of the various orders of the Buddhist priesthood,[28] that the *bhikkhus* – the Buddhist priests – made their main contribution to the integration of political and social organisation.[29]

Under Sinhalese feudalism temples were large landholders, and thus controllers of large populations. Feudal/caste services were due as much to the temples as to the state.[30] The individual temple, or cluster of temples, was, and is, a more important unit of social, economic and political organisation than the orders – the fraternities and chapters – into which the Buddhist priesthood is divided. Headship of the orders derives from headship of the premier temple – typically the largest and wealthiest – of the order. The head of the order has influence and prestige but very little direct authority over incumbents of other temples. Above all, he has no control over recruitment and succession to the headship of the individual temples. Recruitment, succession and the disposal of each temple's economic resources are in the hands of a small and largely self-perpetuating group comprising the chief priest and influential lay members of the 'temple committee' or some similarly termed body. The connection between these laymen and the priests is very close. They are frequently from the same families. For to be a priest, especially a chief priest, is generally very desirable. It brings wealth and power. In the feudal setting all *bhikkhus* were *Goigama*. The distinction between temple resources and the private resources of the locally influential has not always been very clear. Temple organisation thus to a large extent paralleled, replicated and strengthened local patterns of socio-economic stratification.[31]

It is characteristic of traditional Sinhalese social organisation that no trace has been found of major inter-caste differences in religious practices.[32] This corresponds to broader features of the system: centralisation, with the corresponding unimportance of autonomous local or micro-level forms of organisation; unification around a common culture; and the intricate layering of relative privilege and power, with the consequent absence of stark differentiation between large population categories. The *Goigama*, the 'privileged citizens', may have numbered up to half the total population.[33] Although the ancient Dry Zone Sinhalese civilisations clearly had an urban base, urban life and thus urban–rural differentiation were very little developed in the Wet Zone where the Sinhalese were concentrated in the centuries immediately before colonial rule.

The contemporary relevance of these traditions is explained below. In order that their significance may be more easily appreciated, it is useful to present those elements in traditional Indian culture which stand in direct contrast.

Traditional socio-political organisation in India[34]

The standard quotation, often reprinted, on the Indian village as a monolithic, atomistic, unchanging entity is from a report by Sir Charles Metcalfe, one of the founding administrators of British rule in India. The passage begins, 'The village communities are little republics, having nearly everything that they want within themselves and almost independent of any foreign relations.' It goes on to tell that wars pass over it, regimes come and go, but the village as a society always emerges unchanged, unshaken, and self-sufficient. Later writers of considerable influence, among them Sir Henry Maine, Karl Marx and Mahatma Gandhi, reiterated this idea and suggested that the village was so perduring because it was so self-sufficient.[35]

Recent scholars have not dealt kindly with the views on Indian social organisation of Metcalfe and his kindred spirits named above. Their comments on the 'villageness' of Indian society have been quoted only to be intellectually demolished. One major criticism is that the image of village isolation and self-sufficiency is false.[36] Another is that the importance of the village unit is exaggerated and other structural units in Indian society, especially caste, undervalued.[37] As Cohn explains, belief in the unique importance of the village unit was an outcome of the central role of land revenue in the British colonial administration. Because they encountered rural India through the land revenue system, which was organised according to locality (village), and not caste, the British were encouraged to view India as an aggregate of village units. This focus on the land revenue village fitted neatly into the concerns of nineteenth-century social scientists with the evolution of property institutions.[38]

It is, however, quite possible both to agree with their critics and to see that, if their comments on India are interpreted as statements about *comparative* cultural configurations, Metcalfe *et al.* were in fact pointing to certain features which later scholars have, in a more coherent and explicit fashion, viewed as fundamental and almost unique to Indian civilisation: 'small group orientation'[39] cell-like structure, unity in the cultural rather than in the political sphere, and a substantial disjuncture between fragile state-level political organisation and locally organised and largely autonomous rural society. Many scholars have, each from his own perspective, pointed to aspects of this bundle of characteristics. All that can be done here is to mention a few of their summary conclusions and indicate the connections between them.

Srinivas is expressing a widely held view when he argues that India does have a tradition of unity, but in civil society – i.e. in the religious and cultural rather than the political sphere. The basis of this unity is the Hindu caste system, viewed not as a set of beliefs, but as a way of structuring the relationships among groups.[40] The most appropriate metaphor – and it is difficult to discuss such issues other than through metaphor – is of the honeycomb: an aggregate of unordered and unclassified individual cells, greater than the sum of the units only in the sense that the behaviour of the individual cells is shaped and constrained by the fact that they border upon and thus interact with others. Individual cells may be added or subtracted without affecting the structure of the whole.

It is a secondary question how far the cells are to be seen as villages, castes, or some other unit. As Mandelbaum has pointed out, that question must be answered situationally.[41] The more important point is the significance of the largely autonomous micro-units:

India's old regime was – and is – diffuse and decentralised, dominated by micro rather than macro institutions. The traditional society of villages, castes and families has been in considerable measure self regulating.[42]

The framework of this self-regulation was to a large extent Hinduism, a term indicating neither a set of beliefs nor a set of specifically religious institutions like the *Sangha* and temples of Sinhalese Buddhism, but a set of norms about behaviour and social interaction. For caste and Hinduism are in large part different names for the same phenomenon: sets of rules about social behaviour. As Dumont and Pocock express it: 'One might say that all that appears to be social is in fact religious and all that appears religious is in fact social.'[43]

The honeycomb has no head, apex, or framework other than the cells themselves. Echoing Metcalfe, many other commentators have stressed the significance of the state–society gap in traditional India, and seen the state – or rather, the many states – as transitory and fragile structures lacking deep social roots and surviving only through the open and forcible exploitation of (rural) society. 'The Indian system was a loose accommodation between a remarkably stable social order and a transient and unstable political order.' 'One of the principal failures, perhaps *the* greatest failure, of India throughout its long history was its inability to function politically, to construct a viable political authority. It failed to build a center. It is this that is meant when we characterise India as an apolitical society.' 'The general gap between society and politics . . . continued through the Hindu period'.[44]

States were rooted in urban centres, and both were transient.[45] The state–society gap was thus nearly equivalent to the urban–rural gap. The consequences can still be observed in contemporary India. We noted above the continuing separateness of rural and urban caste groups. The rural–urban division is accorded great importance in Indian culture. Sharad Joshi, the leader and spokesman for a militant farmers' movement in Maharashtra in the early 1980s, rallied his followers around the idea that there were two separate nations within the country's boundaries: 'Bharat', the exploited rural 'nation', and 'India', the exploiting urban 'nation'.[46]

The antagonism of Indian rural populations towards towns has a substantial historical justification, for the latter have long lived very openly from the surplus extracted from the countryside. In the Mughal period it is estimated that about a third of the value of gross agricultural output was extracted by the state through land revenue.[47] By contrast pre-colonial Sinhalese monarchs, with their substantial trading revenues and their far more structured and stable methods of extracting economic surpluses, especially via caste services, levied land revenue at a far lower rate.[48] Much of the surplus extracted was redirected locally, especially to temples. The objective basis for rural–urban antagonism was far smaller than in India.

Traditional socio-political structures and contemporary politics

The traditional Indian socio-political system outlined above has been changed considerably as a result of colonial rule and the reactions to it. In the spheres of culture, religion and law the 'little traditions' of localities and groups have been – and are still in the process of being – supplanted by a national 'great tradition' of essentially urban and Brahmanic origins.[49] Under the impact of mass electoral politics and modern communications, small, locally oriented caste groups are amalgamating at the regional level.[50] A sense of Indian national identity is being built.[51] With the expansion of electoral politics, the gap between society and polity has been narrowed:

the Indian model of development is characterised by politicisation of a fragmented social structure through the penetration of political forms, values and ideologies. Operating against the background of an essentially apolitical condition of society, such a process involves the building of a political center, the diversification of this center through a network of benefits and obligations, and the mobilisation of diverse sections of society in this network, thus closing the gap that has traditionally divided village society from the polity.[52]

Yet as this quotation implies, the influence of traditional socio-political structure and culture is manifest in many ways in contemporary Indian politics. The author of the quotation, India's best-known political scientist, sees the traditional as the key to the contemporary.[53] Two particular aspects of this continuity are especially relevant to the analysis of the articulation of Indian smallholder interests: the exploitation of rural–urban separateness and antagonism; and the penetration of politics into local economic and social institutions – castes, cooperatives, education foundations, village councils – such that they in large part supplant the politician's need for a solid *party* political base. The contemporary Indian political system represents an accommodation of the expansionary force of central state power to the structure of 'non-political' local institutions.[54] These continuities from the traditional structure have encouraged Indian farming groups to articulate their own class interests independently.[55]

Are there grounds for expecting comparable continuity between traditional and contemporary socio-political structure and culture in Sri Lanka? One immediate response might be that the likelihood is less than in the Indian case because the Indian tradition is, by its very nature, in large part independent of the character of the holders of state power, and therefore more likely to perdure under colonialism. Nevertheless, *in the Kandyan areas* of Sri Lanka, the British colonial state helped perpetuate tradition by incorporating many aspects of the Kandyan structure. It is true that some elements of the pre-colonial structure disappeared: Buddhism ceased to have the backing of the state; and the ending of caste services to the royal court and the abolition in 1832 of *rajakariya*[56] – compulsory labour service to the state – removed some of the rationale for caste distinctions and led to the disappearance of some caste categories. Yet in many other respects the Kandyan structure survived. The British refrained from any wholesale assault on caste or feudalism.[57] Indeed, after a period of suspicion and distrust of the Kandyan aristocracy, they came, as much through the absence of viable alternatives as through clear preference, to rely heavily upon them for local-level administration.[58] Traditional titles and areas of jurisdiction were maintained, and the various ranks of Kandyan headmen commanded considerably more power and prestige than did their Low Country counterparts. Ryan, writing in the early 1950s, states:

it is notable that there is a high concentration of land ownership in lordly families in many parts of the Kandyan interior. Where the manorial lord or his descendants still maintain their *valuavva* (manor house), village relationships hew to a feudal design even under nominally contractual rent arrangements. The household of the *valuavva* is set apart by economic position, economic and political power, and caste. Dignity and prerogatives of high birth are preserved, both as a due to those of lordly heritage and as an effective demand exerted upon land hungry peasants.[59]

Nindagam lands – the official holdings of the Kandyan aristocracy cultivated by tenants under service tenure – continued to cover about 80,000 acres until formally abolished and handed over to the cultivators in 1968.[60]

Although compulsory labour services to the state were abolished, temple *rajakariya* – the obligation to perform caste services at temple ceremonies in return for land[61] – remained and has survived to the present day despite radical land reforms in other spheres. Temple lands were officially registered by the British in the mid-nineteenth century and, it has been suggested, monastic landlordism has been strengthened in consequence.[62] The exact extent of temple landholdings is unknown. It has recently been suggested that *viharagam* – the land attached to Buddhist monasteries and temples – accounts for about a tenth of paddy land holdings in the area of the former Kandyan kingdom. The extent of *devalagam* – land attached to temples of 'non-Buddhist' gods – is reckoned to exceed that of *viharagam*.[63] Violation of legal rent ceilings on sharecropped temple paddy land seems frequent.[64]

Connections of interest and of personnel, both official and unofficial, between Kandyan temples and the Kandyan aristocracy remain close.[65] Indeed, competition between Kandyan aristocrats to occupy leading lay positions in temple administration has become entangled with their competition in the electoral arena. In particular, the Guardianship of the Temple of the Tooth in Kandy, and thus control of the annual Kandy *Perahera*, has become a major prize. It is decided by an electoral college comprising the lay trustees of major Kandyan temples and Assistant Government Agents for the Kandyan areas.[66]

The survival of important elements of the structure and culture of Kandyan feudalism is of more than purely regional significance. For Kandyan traditions have on the whole assumed national stature. How can one demonstrate the influence of these traditions on contemporary politics? One cannot make a cast-iron case, but can only argue on grounds of plausibility and coincidence.

A few comparisons with India can, without establishing cause, illustrate continuity into the contemporary era of contrasts in traditional socio-political structures. The tradition of local socio-political autonomy and fragility of state control persists in India in the form of, for example, organised banditry in certain localities and the frequency of direct resort to violence to settle local conflicts, especially caste conflicts. Sri Lanka has by contrast very little recent history of the local use of *organised* private (i.e. non-state) violence.[67] It is only in the last decade, with the growth of Tamil separatist violence and the alienation of the Sri Lanka Tamil population from the state, that such a tradition has emerged. The much closer involvement of the Sinhalese with the state is illustrated by the eagerness with which, in comparison to Indians and to Sri Lanka Tamils, they have taken to electoral politics. One might also note the enormous degree of familiarity with leading public figures implied in the way in which ordinary Sri Lankans discuss politics. The gossip in the village *boutiques* (small shops) is of 'J. R.' (Jayawardena), 'Dudley' (Senanayake), 'Lalith' (Athulathmudali) and 'Felix' (Bandaranaike).[68] Sri Lankans have similarly resorted more frequently to the use of state institutions to mediate in personal and social conflict. In the nineteenth century they turned to the law courts in pursuit of interpersonal conflicts far more frequently than Indians – or indeed, the British and Irish. The fact that in the late nineteenth century *recorded* crime rates were proportionately four to nine times higher in Sri Lanka than India seems to indicate a greater degree of interaction in Sri Lanka of formal state institutions with civil society.[69] It is demonstrated in Chapter Ten that locally based institutions have been less common and played a less important role in recent politics in Sri Lanka than in India.

Any discussion of the causes – the transmission mechanisms – for the continuity into contemporary Sri Lankan politics of the pre-colonial socio-political structure and culture must be very speculative. We have already noted the general persistence of a traditionalism identified with the Kandyan kingdom. Michael Roberts, who has been working independently on the same theme, has suggested that two important mechanisms have been Buddhism and the *'walauwa-hami* life style' – the retinue-oriented involvement of contemporary planters and local notables in local affairs in the style of feudal lords.[70]

Although much scholarly work remains to be done, one can reasonably conclude that these are good grounds for believing that the pre-colonial socio-political structure and culture have influenced the development of the contemporary Sri Lankan polity. It is consistent with the evidence relating to both India and Sri Lanka that the failure of Sinhalese smallholders to articulate class demands independently is in some degree due to the absence from their traditional political culture of any precedent or support for the concept of a distinctive rural population and interest separate from and antagonistic to the urban-based apparatus and personnel of the state. The Sinhalese have no such 'peasant' tradition.

One might conclude by noting the failure of one very overt attempt to legislate for rural Sri Lanka on the assumption that it had a village-based social structure like that of India. In the nineteenth century the absence of an empirical investigation into local Sinhalese social organisation led colonial officials to transfer uncritically to Sri Lanka the notions of 'village community' derived from the work of Sir Henry Maine and others in India. The 1871 Village Communities Ordinance was based on the assumption that the *gansabha*, the Sinhalese village 'committee', could be utilised as an administative body comparable to the Indian village *panchayat*. In fact the *gansabha* had in recorded history only ever fulfilled very limited dispute-settling functions, and the attempt failed.[71] More recent attempts to revitalise the 'village community' have met the same fate.

Caste and farming

The role of caste in Sinhalese[72] politics is uncertain and the subject of much dispute.[73] I tend to believe that caste is politically significant mainly at the local level. Moreover, even if it were of greater and more national significance in shaping political competition (mainly intra-party), this would not materially alter the point to be made briefly here: that, among the Sinhalese, caste divisions and consciousness cannot contribute to the emergence of a farmer identity in the way that, for example, caste identity has done in India. For there is neither a distinct farmer caste among the Sinhalese – almost all castes engage in cultivation – nor any correspondence, in tradition or in practice, of caste divisions with the rural–urban division.

The absence of intra-rural class conflict

It is a commonsensical kind of observation, supported also by evidence,[74] that in a situation of nascent class conflict the mobilisation of one contender will tend to elicit comparable action from the other. No significant intra-rural class confrontation has occurred in Sri Lanka to stimulate the class mobilisation of cultivating smallholders. Here, three potential kinds of conflict are examined: landlords versus tenants; smallholders versus engrossing large (mechanised) farmers; and employing farmers versus hired agricultural labourers.

Landlord and tenant

Sri Lanka on the whole lacks anything resembling the stereotypical Asian landlord: the owner of hundreds or thousands of acres divided on exploitative terms among large numbers of small sharecroppers. This in itself is partly a reflection of the long stability of the pre-colonial feudal order and the absence of any trace of foreign conquest in the establishment of that order. Although confined mainly to paddy land, sharecropping and other forms of tenancy are widespread. These are, however, relatively small-scale transactions, generally intra-village, and often among kin.[75] In the words of one observer: 'the typical tenancy in Ceylon is not as oppressive as elsewhere'.[76]

A stereotype far more valid for rural Sri Lanka – and one likely to feature in conversations among villagers themselves – is the village schoolteacher who has used his salary to purchase the kind of holding – say, ten acres of paddy – which places him among the village elite.[77] It is a stereotype with a great deal of truth in it, especially if extended to cover all villagers with some secure external or non-agricultural source of income. There is ample evidence of the connection between extra-village income and the acquisition of paddy land.[78] The intimacy of the connection between land purchase and reliable external income, especially teachers' salaries, is fully comprehensible if one recalls some points about the historical context: the spread of public employment, especially teaching, into the rural areas of the Wet Zone; the high status attached to paddy land ownership; and the depressed state of paddy prices as a result of the strength of the plantation export sector, with the consequent severe restriction on the possibilities of purchasing land from the profits of food production. A study undertaken in the 1960s, when paddy prices were remunerative in comparison to earlier decades, suggested an annual rate of return of only 4% on the purchase of paddy land. Demand remained brisk, but for motives other than financial accumulation.

It is in fact the land-purchasing activities of public employees and others with non-agricultural incomes which have given rise to the sole case of overt class conflict between landlords and cultivators among the Sinhalese. This has taken place in Hambantota district, especially the eastern part which, unusually among the Sinhalese districts, was the site of *both* state-financed irrigation development and state-sponsored land colonisation in the late nineteenth and early twentieth centuries, before the planned large-scale peasant colonisation described in Chapter Three.

The story of the colonisation of Hambantota has been told by Herring.[79] Both there and in the adjacent district of Batticaloa, large blocks of land were sold to 'capitalists' in the hope and expectation that they would be able to promote the kind of economic progress which was beyond the penniless peasant. Batticaloa was at this stage separated from the Sinhalese areas by jungle. Its main communication route was by sea to Jaffna. It was developed by Tamils and Muslims and oriented in part to feeding Jaffna. Batticaloa interests us here only insofar as it was later cited, along with Hambantota, as the only district where tenant exploitation was so dire as to require the passing of the 1953 Paddy Lands Act. The diagnosis of Batticaloa as having a landlord–tenant problem similar to that of Hambantota was false. The fact that the two were singled out, however, illustrates the failure of the project for capitalist development of paddy production.

The agrarian structure of both districts was the outcome of the interaction between a small number of wealthy outside entrepreneurs and a local population of poor and backward peasants living in a climate and physical environment harsher than anywhere else in Sri Lanka. Public servants, especially those from the adjacent Matara district, were especially prominent among those who purchased land in Hambantota. They became absentee rentiers, using local agents, known as *gambarayas*, to organise their cultivation and collect their rents.

The agrarian structure of Hambantota has become somewhat diversified, and includes large-scale mechanised cultivation, share-cropping, and the heavy use of wage labour – often by the tenants themselves.[80] What characterises Hambantota and distinguishes it from all other districts is both the sharpness of the gap which separates the mass of cultivators, tenants and labourers, from a small number of wealthy men – landowners, tractor and buffalo owners, the landlords' agents – and public awareness of this. In Herring's terms, it is 'discontinuities' in access to land and working capital which characterise the district.[81] The term *'gambaraya'* no longer relates specifically to the landlord's agent: 'it has come to mean in village parlance any wealthy person involved with paddy cultivation'.[82] Popular reference to 'the *gambaraya* system' in Hambantota is, however, not inaccurate in that it indicates an agrarian structure distinctively different from that of the other Sinhalese districts.

It is consistent with the unusually pronounced rural inequality there and the very evident discontinuity between *gambarayas* and the mass of small farmers, tenants and labourers, that the only evidence I have been able to unearth of substantial overt intra-rural Sinhalese class conflict relates to Hambantota district.[83] In addition, and unusually for a Dry Zone district, Hambantota has a certain tradition of ideological polarisation between the UNP and the SLFP, the latter having locally a strong 'left' element.[84] The import of radical traditions from neighbouring Matara and the virtual absence of ethnic minorities[85] may have helped provide a favourable environment for this kind of ideological polarisation, but it seems very likely that it also reflects the conflictual elements inherent in the local agrarian socio-economic system. The focus of the conflict is not principally the landlord–tenant relationship. This is but one issue in a broader pattern of the articulation of the poor's grievances against a few wealthy and powerful men. It is labourers' and tenants' unions which the radicals have attempted to promote, not single-class movements.

Hambantota provides, then, only a partial exception to the general political invisibility of the tenant class. It does, however, help to explain the reasons for this invisibility. Organised assertion of tenants' interests is feasible where there is a wide structural gap between landlords and tenants, and where landlords are at least in some degree absentees. Elsewhere tenants are too closely under surveillance and too firmly tied to landlords by personal ties of kinship and dependence for resistance to be feasible.[86] Tenants have at best managed in some areas to take advantage of the provisions of the 1958 Paddy Lands Act once it was passed on their behalf. While the legislation was under debate the landlords established local associations to press their interests.[87] The fact that these associations seem to have melted away quickly after the issue was settled indicates the absence of any perceived threat from the tenants themselves.

Small farmers and big farmers

One element in the evolution of Indian farmers' movements has been the hostility of small cultivators to large mechanised farmers who, by evicting tenants and cultivating large acreages with a small work force, appeared to threaten the small farmers' livelihood. Given that in Sri Lanka's Dry Zone tractor ploughing has been widespread since the 1950s[88] one might expect to find a similar phenomenon there. The few reliable data which are available confirm the widespread impression that ownership of four-wheeled tractors leads to the control of more land.[89] While there is undoubtedly considerable resentment against the wealth, success and hire charges levied by tractor owners, there is no sign of any attempt to articulate this politically. The reason appears to be that the activities of tractor owners or indeed of other big farmers do not yet pose an apparent threat to small-scale agriculture generally.

In the first place, Sri Lanka has not experienced a 'green revolution' – a sudden shift to a new experimental and risky package of production practices – of a kind which excludes the small farmer and leaves him fearful of being squeezed out of agriculture by the wealthy and successful big farmer.[90]

In the second place, by virtue of the programmes of Crown land alienation and Dry Zone development and of the shift of price ratios in favour of food rather than export crop production since Independence, there has been if anything an expansion of the small-farm sector over the last half century.

In the third place, and probably partly because of the relatively depressed state of food prices, Sri Lanka has witnessed, unlike, say, India, very little development of capitalist forms of production in the smallholder sector. Tractors have served to enrich their owners rather than to help promote any broader development of rural capitalism.[91]

Far from Sri Lankan smallholders as a class being under threat from large mechanised and capitalist farming, the past half century or so has seen something of a 'peasantisation' of rural society – the spread and consolidation of family-scale farming. The process is in some ways analogous to that described for Kenya by Leys.[92] Rather than experiencing rural class differentiation as some Marxists had mechanically posited, the Kenyan peasant or family sector had actually expanded due to the subdivision of former European farms. In Sri Lanka the physical subdivision of estate land has played only a marginal role in the expansion of the smallholder sector. However, the surplus extracted from estate production through the taxing of exports and income has played a major role in financing the colonisation of the Dry Zone. Both Kenya and Sri Lanka have expanded the smallholder sector at the expense of the large-scale agricultural enterprises which originated under colonial rule.

Employer and labourer

How important is the use of hired labour in Sri Lanka's smallholder sector, especially in the symbolically potent paddy field? Two different kinds of source supply very different answers.

On the one hand, farm management data reveal that the use of hired labour is widespread. Depending upon location, a representative sample of paddy farmers will obtain between 50% and 90% of all their labour through hiring.[93] Such a high figure is in part due to the characteristic requirement of paddy cultivation for large amounts of labour in a short period. Individual families cannot cope unaided.[94] In addition, the tendency for paddy land to be concentrated in the hands of the 'village elite', who do not themselves engage in field labour, leaves wide scope for labour hiring.

On the other hand, official sources of data, especially censuses and the beliefs implicit in official action, suggest a different, far less explicit, but nevertheless unmistakable answer: that hired labour is not important in the smallholder sector. That it is unimportant is suggested first of all by the confusing and incomplete presentation of census statistics on hired labour.[95] It is difficult to avoid the conclusion that this is in some way related to the non-recognition of an agricultural labouring class in Sri Lankan politics generally. The 'official' view of agrarian class structure corresponds to a simplified version of that implied in the statistics in Table 8.1: a fundamental dichotomy between the estates employing a (mainly alien) proletariat and the family-farming rice-based smallholder sector. In the second place, official data series (e.g. Table 8.1) imply that the proportion of the rural work force recorded as engaged mainly in hired labour is far lower than that recorded in farm management surveys.

One could compare the various sets of occupational data from the censuses and other sources in search of evidence to support the suspicion that the census figures understate the degree of dependence of the rural poor on hired employment within the smallholder sector.[96] That would, however, still leave one with estimates of uncertain accuracy: the status attached to being considered as a farmer rather than as a labourer is such that census-type enquiries are of very doubtful accuracy. The more important point to be made here is that there are several structural reasons why, with the exception of certain

Table 8.1. *Distribution of persons engaged in agriculture and animal husbandry according to occupation, employment status and sex, 1971*

Occupational category	Number of persons in the category as a percentage of the total engaged in agriculture and animal husbandry	Percentage of those in the category who were	
		Paid employees	Female
Farm managers and estate supervisory staff	1	94	2
Cultivators of:			
paddy	45	13	15
vegetables	3	12	19
minor export crops	neg.	72	15
other or mixed crops	8	12	15
Livestock farmers	neg.	52	10
Rubber tappers and rubber labourers	7	92	40
Tea pluckers and tea estate labourers	30	99	56
Coconut estate labourers	1	96	24
Toddy tappers	neg.	62	—
Other agricultural labourers	3	96	11
Farm machinery operators	neg.	93	1
Total	100	50	29

Source: Census of Population 1971, Volume 2, Part 1: Table 4.

stirrings in Hambantota district, there has been no sign of any attempt by agricultural labourers in the smallholder sector to organise themselves to bargain for wages or make other class demands.

In the first place, there is a substantial overlap between small farmers and hired labourers. As the ownership of at least a house plot and a small home garden is widespread, a large proportion of those gaining most of their income from hired labour may still tend to identify themselves as small farmers rather than as labourers. As cultivators of even very small paddy plots need to engage hired labour at some points in the year, they themselves also need to work for others to reciprocate and to obtain the necessary cash. It has frequently been observed that a large proportion of all hired labour in paddy farming is provided by those who themselves have a small paddy plot.[97] It is my impression that it is this practice more than anything else which accounts for the apparent paradox that paddy is cultivated mainly by hired labour while hired labourers are relatively few in number.

In the second place, the most important single source of demand for hired labour in paddy cultivation among the Sinhalese – the Dry Zone colonies – is to a large extent met by seasonal migrants from the Kandyan hills. Apart from the fact that some are small landowners at home, they are clearly in no position to organise as a class for wage demands. Their terms are often negotiated *seriatim* by a number of intermediaries before they leave home.[98]

In the third place, the highly seasonal nature of paddy work means that those dependent on rural labour characteristically engage in a range of activities under different conditions and for different employers.[99] In the Wet Zone in particular, due to ecological diversity and the high incidence of non-agricultural activities, the rural poor engage in a wide range of activities which, while generating income, detract from any sense of a distinct class interest in agricultural labour. Agricultural and non-agricultural labour overlap.

Insofar as there is in Sri Lanka a distinctive agricultural proletariat – a landless population dependent mainly on agricultural employment and relatively numerous in comparison with the employing households – then this is to be found in the Tamil and Muslim areas of the Eastern and Northern Provinces. This is in major contrast to the Sinhalese Dry Zone districts where locally resident hired labourers are in comparison very scarce.[100] The significance of the existence of this Tamil and Muslim agricultural proletariat is beyond the scope of this study. One might simply note that it conforms to the more hierarchical and traditional nature of Sri Lanka Tamil and Muslim social structures. Among the Sinhalese there is plenty of hiring of labour within agriculture but no distinct agricultural proletariat to challenge the concept of the Sinhalese as a smallholding peasantry, or, of more immediate relevance to our concerns, to organise around wage demands, confront their smallholding employers, and thus stimulate farmers to organise themselves in response.

Public policy and political identity

The most important elements at work in changing India's mass political culture are the vast amounts of directives and regulations emanating from the state and central government.[101]

Duncan has shown that the consolidation of North Indian agriculturalists around the leadership of Charan Singh, which was later to result in the very strident articulation of small-farmer demands, was stimulated by Singh's exploitation of small-farmer concerns about the threats of forcible collective farming, increased land revenue, low legal ceilings on landholdings and, above all, widespread forcible procurement of foodgrains from producers.[102] By extending the scope of its action, the state may generate the sense of grievance and of commonality of interests necessary for the political mobilisation of groups hitherto non-existent from the political point of view. This is but one sense in which politics may be said to reproduce itself, rather than to simply reflect categorisations and conflicts arising in the social and economic spheres.

Perhaps more through chance than as the result of any conscious intention, the Sri Lankan state has, for the past half century or so, steered clear of creating through its own action occasions for the political mobilisation of smallholders.

After a long and well-publicised agitation which mobilised small farmers in at least some areas,[103] the grain tax was abolished in 1893.[104] Since that time there have been no significant effective direct taxes on smallholder production. Mainly nominal taxes on land and water have been widely ignored. There was thus no Sri Lankan equivalent to the agitation of Indian farmers, both within the framework of the nationalist movement and after Independence, against land revenue and the landlord intermediaries (*zamindars, jagirdars,* etc.) who collected it on behalf of the state.

The land issue in Sri Lanka has been the terms of and the mechanisms involved in the alienation of the large extents of Crown lands. There appear to be two reasons why this did not provide the occasion for an independent articulation of the small-farmer interest.

The first and perhaps the most important is that the state has not on the whole put up much resistance to demands for this land. There is no doubt that the needs of plantation capitalists guided the original assertion of state claims to so much land and the adoption of alienation procedures favouring the rich. However, even by the latter part of the nineteenth century, purchases of very small lots were common. Purchases may have been beyond the means of the average villager, but the more articulate and influential 'village elite' had little cause for dissatisfaction. The 1928 Land Commission then established a system for the wholesale block alienation of land to the poor before the poor had themselves collectively articulated a demand for such a policy. Legalisation of encroachments and toleration of environmentally destructive shifting cultivation have become *de facto* state policy. Obstacles to the satisfaction of peasant land hunger have mainly been experienced in the Kandyan plantation areas, where little Crown land has been left for distribution. The resultant demands have been directed against estates rather than the state.

The second reason why the Crown lands issue has not stimulated supra-local smallholder political action lies in the nature of land – its immovability and the fact that it is fixed in quantity. The individual's first demand is not for land in the abstract, but for a particular piece of land within his immediate locality. Abstract 'land' is likely to become a demand only if there is mass frustration of demands for individual 'lands'. While there exist mechanisms for satisfying these latter demands, and where land is so scarce that there is evident competition among the population of each locality for access to such Crown land as remains, the demand for land is – and in Sri Lanka has been – locally and particularistically oriented: it is for the supporters of the ruling party in 'Kurunugama', not for the rural population as a whole.[105]

Despite the priority given to feeding consumers through the ration system and the normative justification implicit in attitudes to the peasantry, the Sri Lankan state has avoided the direct compulsory procurement of foodgrains from producers. Apart from World War Two, such a step was attempted only in an oblique and unsuccessful manner during the 1974 food crisis. In this case at least, a conscious desire not to antagonise the rural population appears to have been a significant consideration.

Finally, producer prices – at least monetary prices – of the single most important locally grown food crop, paddy, have not been allowed to fall significantly; with the exception of the descent from the peak achieved during the 1974 food crisis, they have on the whole been allowed to increase gradually. Coconut prices have been kept low rather than allowed to rise and then fall. Price policy has politicised agricultural producers only in the recent, although potentially significant, case of minor food crops.

The Sri Lankan state has thus avoided creating a grievance around which the smaller population might mobilise, and develop a collective identity.

Conclusion

The image of the Sinhalese as an essentially peasant nation, which is intrinsic to the Sinhalese nationalist historical myth, does not accord with the facts of Sri Lankan culture, social organisation or political evolution. At the same time, the 'objective' conflicts among the different social strata obtaining livelihoods from smallholder production have not resulted in political mobilisation along class lines. Neither Sinhalese cultural traditions, caste divisions, intra-rural class conflicts nor public policy have provided the kind of stimulus to the political mobilisation of large categories of the farming population which they have in comparable Asian countries.

9

Ethnic conflict and the politics of the periphery

Introduction

This chapter brings together two issues which were introduced in Chapters Seven and Eight. In Chapter Seven it was suggested that in explaining the absence of an explicitly agrarian party or political programme, one should look especially closely at the Dry Zone periphery. For this contains a population apparently united around a clear objective interest in high domestic food prices. In Chapter Eight it was shown that the kinds of collective identities which have helped stimulate agrarian political movements and policy demands in India and Malaysia have not played an equivalent role in Sri Lanka. Yet it was at the same time noted that ethnic conflict has been a salient feature of Sri Lankan politics. Given the symbolic place of the peasantry in the Sinhalese nationalist myth, one needs to ask why the Sinhalese ethnic identity has not underpinned a Sinhalese agrarian political movement extending its scope beyond cultural, religious and linguistic issues to those of agriculture and economic policy

The main argument in this chapter is that the Sinhalese versus non-Sinalese ethnic conflict – especially that of the Sinhalese versus Tamils – has probably played an important role in preventing the emergence of an agrarian movement in the Dry Zone. For the ethnic divide has fragmented the Dry Zone surplus-food producers and has left the Sinhalese farmers in particular without the leadership that most large surplus-paddy producers could have given – for the latter tend to be Muslims and Tamils. This is followed by a discussion which leads into the argument developed in Chapter Ten.

There is among the Sinhalese Dry Zone population a division between Kandyans and people from the Low Country. This is significant mainly because the latter tend to dominate in positions of local political and economic power. Traders and politicians are especially likely to be of Low Country origin, and politicians to have a background in public service rather than cultivation. Insofar as the personal backgrounds of the local leadership influence the style and content of local Dry Zone politics, they tend to orient these politics to the conditions and conflicts of the core region (the Low Country) rather than to the issues which arise from the local Dry Zone economy. As a relatively new society largely created by public colonisation projects, the Sinhalese Dry Zone remains oriented to the politics of the core.

Ethnicity and politics

Before we tackle the two issues summarised above, it is necessary to take a position on the question of the role of ethnic identities in politics. For to begin simply by using such categories as 'Sinhalese' or 'Tamil' is to run the risk of appearing to support two related fallacies. The first is that politics itself plays no role in the generation of collective identities. The second is that a collective identity is a homogeneous, unitary and fixed phenomenon which cannot vary in content or emphasis over time, over space and according to situation.[1] Rather than attempt to broach seriously what might require a separate volume in itself – the nature of collective identities in contemporary Sri Lanka – I shall profess general allegiance to the concept of the plasticity of collective identities, indicate some of the evidence which supports this belief in relation to contemporary Sri Lanka,[2] and note one reservation. The reservation is that ethnic or communal identities in Sri Lanka are neither infinitely plastic nor in any major degree the product of recent history and politics. As was indicated in Chapter Six, the major ethnic groups, especially the Low Country Sinhalese, the Kandyan Sinhalese, the Sri Lanka Tamils, and to a lesser extent the Sri Lanka Moors, each have a long history of cultural distinctiveness based on their predominance in one particular region. The distinctiveness of the Indian Tamils arises from their close association with estate labour in circumstances generating antagonism with Sinhalese villagers. Over recent decades ethnic conflict in national politics has been associated, as both cause and effect, with enhanced ethnic consciousness and the hardening of the lines of division between ethnic groups.[3] But in no sense are the main ethnic categorisations mainly the product of *recent* history and politics. They have long been available to be exploited by politicians and indeed have been exploited since at least half a century ago.

Sinhalese and non-Sinhalese in the Dry Zone

Community and rice farming

As the ideology of Sinhalese nationalism attempts to convey, albeit often in a grossly exaggerated form, there is indeed a peculiar affinity between the Sinhalese and paddy cultivation. The Sinhalese account for a higher proportion of paddy farmers than their proportion of the total population.[4] The Sinhalese connection is, however, with paddy cultivation, not with the production of large paddy surpluses. Surplus paddy production is concentrated in seven Dry Zone districts – Mannar, Vavuniya, Batticaloa, Amparai, Trincomalee, Anuradhapura and Polonnaruwa (see Table 7.1) – which generally, and especially in the first five cases, contain non-Sinhalese majorities (see Table 9.1). The former district of Batticaloa, now divided into Batticaloa and Amparai, was the traditional 'rice-bowl' of the Island, in which rice was produced on a commercial scale, often, it seems, for export to Jaffna. Big paddy farmers, i.e. those producing large marketed surpluses, are currently especially common in Batticaloa and Amparai (see Table 7.5). Big farmers comprise a relatively large fraction of all paddy farmers in four of the non-Sinhalese rice surplus districts – Mannar, Vavuniya, Batticaloa and Amparai (see Table 7.5). It is in these same districts (and also in Jaffna), that one finds the only substantial non-plantation agricultural proletariat in the Island.

The big paddy farmers of the east coast are by tradition Moors and Tamils. The east coast Moors in particular appear to have provided the few really large paddy farmers and landlords in the Island.[5] Landownership statistics are not classified by ethnic group, and so one cannot illustrate these points with precise numbers. It is, however, worthwhile to produce some illustrative figures by reworking the tentative estimates of the numbers of deficit paddy farmers and big paddy farmers given in Tables 7.1 and 7.5 respectively. The resulting estimates are somewhat 'timeless' in the sense that they are built up from data series relating variously to 1962, 1971 and 1976. It is, however, the broad magnitudes which are important. In 1946 the Sinhalese accounted for about 87% of all paddy farmers. They accounted, however, in these 'timeless' estimates, for only 72% of surplus-paddy farmers, and for 49% of all big paddy farmers.[6]

It is, then, no great surprise that the few parliamentary spokesmen for big farmer interests have been Tamil and Muslim MPs from the Northern and Eastern Provinces.[7] It is, however, emphatically not the case that the Sinhalese–non-Sinhalese political divide corresponds to any division between the rice purchasers and rice producers. For the non-Sinhalese are also divided. The east coast Muslims have a trading base, and their own heartland – the Batticaloa–Amparai coastal fringe – has a large rice-purchasing urban population. More importantly, the Sri Lanka Tamils, the group most clearly alienated from the Sinhalese-dominated polity, have as their heartland the densely populated Jaffna peninsula, which is both in chronic rice deficit (see Table 7.1) and a

Table 9.1. *Percentage distribution of district populations among the main 'ethnic' groups, 1971*

District	Low Country Sinhalese	Kandyan Sinhalese	Sri Lanka Tamils	Indian Tamils	Sri Lanka Moors
Colombo	80	3	6	2	6
Kalutara	86	1	1	5	7
Galle	94	1	1	2	3
Matara	94	neg.	neg.	3	3
Kandy	11	51	4	24	8
Nuwara Eliya	7	33	4	52	2
Kegalle	8	77	2	9	4
Matale	12	63	4	15	6
Kurunegala	17	76	1	1	5
Ratnapura	17	63	1	17	1
Puttalam	72	9	7	2	10
Badulla	8	51	3	34	3
Moneragala	19	72	2	6	2
Jaffna	1	neg.	95	3	1
Hambantota	96	1	1	neg.	1
Mannar	3	1	51	17	25
Vavuniya	5	11	61	15	7
Batticaloa	2	2	69	2	24
Amparai	11	19	22	1	46
Trincomalee	15	14	35	3	32
Anuradhapura	21	69	2	1	7
Polonnaruwa	29	61	3	neg.	7
Sri Lanka	43	29	11	9	7

Source: Census of Population, 1971, General Report: Table 6.5.

specialist area for cash crops such as onions and chillies. Let us recall the demand voiced in Parliament in 1964 by Dr E. M. V. Naganathan, a leading Sri Lanka Tamil politician, that the producer price of paddy be *reduced* and more incentive be given to producers of subsidiary food crops.[8] As representative of the Nallur electorate in the Jaffna peninsula, Naganathan was accurately reflecting the interests of his constituents, who are buyers of paddy and sellers of subsidiary food crops.

The point is not *simply* that the large surplus-producing paddy farmers are divided between the conflicting ethnic groups, and for this reason have been unable to assert a collective demand. This is certainly true, but there is more to it. For one has to ask *why* the Dry Zone surplus-paddy farmers have accepted the ethnic conflict definition of their interests. There is nothing causally prior about ethnic over class or occupational group conflict. The Dry Zone Tamil, Muslim and

Sinhalese paddy farmers could have united on a regional basis to demand higher farm output prices, and would have been very well placed to determine which party won general elections (Chapter Two). For the reasons why this did not happen one must look more closely at the causes of ethnic conflict, and at relations between core and peripheral areas among both the Sinhalese and the Sri Lanka Tamils. For the surplus-rice producers are located in peripheral areas in both subsystems.

Ethnic conflict and core–periphery relations

In both the Sinhalese (or national) core–periphery network and in the Jaffna-based Sri Lanka Tamil network there is a clear 'objective' conflict of interests between the core rice-deficit and the peripheral rice-surplus populations. Why have the peripheries not united against the cores? That this is not an idle or fantastic question is illustrated by Sivathamby's discussion of the substantial cultural and socio-structural differences between the Sri Lanka Tamils of Jaffna and those of the Vanni, basically Vavuniya district. He points out the hostility which has developed among the latter to the immigration of Jaffna Tamils in recent decades, and goes on to say:

In terms of economic demands the Vanni peasant is one [*sic*] with the Sinhalese peasant of the *Rajarata* region [literally country of the kings – the North Central Province]. In fact during the period of SLFP rule there was some understanding forged with the Tamil politicians of the Tamil Vanni districts. But the action of successive governments in settling Sinhala peasant colonists in and around the Vavuniya district and the corresponding increase of Sinhala residents of the area has always given rise to Sinhala–Tamil conflict and confrontation in this district.[9]

Sivathamby implies that, but for the provocation of public colonisation policy, some kind of political unity might have been built among the Tamil and Sinhalese farmers of the Dry Zone. This is very plausible, especially when one considers the sources of Sinhalese–Tamil conflict nationally and the basis for Tamil separatism. Let us take the latter first.

The Sri Lanka Tamil separatist demands which sparked off the communal violence of 1983 have always been based on and mainly restricted to the Sri Lanka Tamil core – the Jaffna peninsula.[10] With one short-lived exception, all elected Sri Lanka Tamil MPs who have represented their community in national cabinets since Independence have sat for electorates *outside* the Jaffna district.[11] Even in the presidential election of 1982 and the succeeding national referendum on extending the life of the existing Parliament, when communal tensions were high, Sri Lanka Tamils outside Jaffna mainly supported the UNP, not Tamil separatist parties.[12]

The reason for this seems quite clear. The origin of the Sinhalese–Sri Lanka Tamil conflict lies in the disproportionate share of places in higher education, public-sector white-collar employment, and commerce which accrued to Sri Lanka Tamils (and other minorities) during colonial rule. Independence has seen a continuing and largely successful campaign of 'Sinhalisation' of the state in both symbolic and material terms.[13] And the material brunt of this has fallen on the Jaffna Tamils. They lack natural resources, but are specialised in higher education, public-sector employment and Island-wide business enterprise. Thus it is they, not the poorly educated Tamil farmers of Vavuniya, Mannar, Trincomalee and Batticaloa districts, who have suffered, and feel correspondingly frustrated.

The Jaffna Tamils comprise the majority of the Sri Lanka Tamil population,[14] and have the great political advantage of being densely clustered and highly educated, while the Sri Lanka Tamil farmers of the Dry Zone are scattered. Since the latter include many large farmers they appear better able than the Sinhalese Dry Zone farmers to speak up for themselves. But the Tamil farmers' voice is weak within the Tamil community as a whole, and they have generally accepted, albeit reluctantly, the political leadership of Jaffna. Their interests, like those of the Sinhalese farmers, find little place in a conflict which, while apparently 'ethnic', is to a large extent a conflict between two well-placed and well-educated urban or quasi-urban populations over access to jobs and state resources generally.

As Sivathamby indicates, it is the publicly funded and organised Sinhalese colonisation of areas traditionally considered Tamil (and Muslim) which appears to have turned the scales against *de facto* political cooperation across ethnic lines in the Dry Zone, and thus reproduced the ethnic conflict between the cores in the very different conditions of the Dry Zone.[15] How far this was an inevitable outcome of colonisation is a matter of debate. For there has been no significant displacement of Tamil or Muslim farmers by Sinhalese colonists. In the past the concern of the Tamils has probably been more with the symbolic than with the material effects: with the diminution of the area which the separatists could validly claim as a natural part of a separate Tamil-speaking state; and with the way in which Tamil cultural and religious monuments and locations in the Dry Zone have been ignored by an archaeology department apparently seeking only evidence of past Sinhalese occupation. It seems likely that the conflict over land has gradually become more acute as the Dry Zone has been populated, and the former 'no man's land' between Tamils and Sinhalese obliterated. For example, a contribution to the communal tension preceding the 1983 violence was conflict over the allocation of land under the Maduru Oya irrigation scheme in Batticaloa district. This is perhaps the last area available for large-scale colonisation. Conflict developed over large-scale intrusions by mainly Sinhalese squatters, allegedly supported by politicians.[16] However, in a longer-term historical perspective it would be a mistake to see conflicts over land as the prime reason for antagonism between the different farming communities in the Dry Zone. Their respective orientations and subordination to core regions which are in conflict over access to state resources were probably more important. It is to another aspect of this orientation of peripheral politics to the politics of the core that we now turn.

Kandyan versus Low Country identities and the politics of the Sinhalese Dry Zone

Intra-Sinhalese divisions in the Dry Zone

The obverse of the failure of the Tamil, Muslim and Sinhalese surplus-paddy farmers of the Dry Zone to unite politically has been the continuing orientation of the politics of the Dry Zone Sinhalese to the politics of the core: the engagement of the Dry Zone farmers in a pattern of electoral competition in which none of the contestants seems to stand squarely for their (the farmers') interests. There are two ways in which the ethnic division between Kandyan and Low Country Sinhalese has helped foster this subordination of the Dry Zone regional political agenda to the core-based agenda.

The Sinhalese Dry Zone population is divided between Kandyans and Low Country people, with the latter being especially obtrusive as they have come into what is considered, at least by the Kandyans, to be a traditionally Kandyan area.[17] Since there is a long-established, albeit fluctuating, tradition of political conflict and social antagonism between Kandyan and Low Country Sinhalese, including a weak attempt in the 1920s to assert Kandyan separatism,[18] there have quite naturally been many instances of local antagonism between Kandyans and Low Country Sinhalese in the Dry Zone.[19] There have in addition been similar antagonisms between immigrants from the Kandyan hills and the original residents of the Dry Zone, the so-called *purana* villagers.[20]

These divisions have undoubtedly constituted some kind of obstacle to the evolution of a sense of common identity[21] and interest among

Dry Zone farmers. It would, however, be a mistake to make too much of this particular point, as local antagonisms of this kind are not unusual, and not necessarily a major obstacle to common action in relation to national politics. Far more important is the *nature* of the Kandyan–Low Country antagonism, and the way in which the local politics of the Dry Zone has been dominated by (mainly Low Country) traders and public servants, who could not be expected to identify so easily and immediately with farmers' interests as would political leaders who had emerged purely from farming.

Patronage and brokerage in Dry Zone politics[22]

The 'dependence' of Dry Zone colonists on the government is an extremely common complaint among Sri Lankan public servants, and no less prevalent is the belief that the settlers have failed to create 'real communities', or 'lack the community spirit'. These complaints are closely connected and clearly relate to the environment in which the settlers find themselves. The settlers are initially uprooted from their home areas. Although not necessarily from among the poorest, they are people who owned little or no land at home. They thus include relatively few people who are socially and politically competent to deal with politicians and administrative agencies on equal terms. Yet such dealings are absolutely crucial, for effective access to government agencies is the *sine qua non* of economic success. In the colonies it is public-sector agencies which allocate irrigation water, credit and fertiliser; purchase much of the crop; and decide whether the subdividing or the mortgaging of allotments is to be formally accepted or informally tolerated.[23] Colonists cannot help but appear dependent on government; they are in truth very dependent. And the political skills required to make this dependence tolerable are likely to emerge but slowly, as some farmers become prosperous, a little leisured, and familiar with the worlds of politics and government institutions. In the earlier stages the allottees are likely to be preoccupied with their own cultivation.

There is, then, a potential political vacuum on the new irrigation schemes. It is filled by non-farmers of various kinds. Low Country traders,[24] endowed with mobility, connections, and close personal contacts with individual farmers through retail trading, are well placed to exploit the possibilities. Their position is strengthened by the substantial requirements for credit arising from the seasonality of paddy production. In contrast to the relatively aseasonal agricultural economy of the Wet Zone, that of the Dry Zone colonies is geared in large part to the seasonal fluctuations of crop production, especially paddy. Once or twice a year the farmer needs to spend heavily to get his fields ploughed, sown, and perhaps transplanted. He must then wait for three or four months until harvest. This is then followed by a spending spree in the bazaars and taverns. There are ample opportunities for the trader to purchase political support, grudging or grateful, through moneylending.

It is especially in local-level politics that Low Country *mudalalis* seem to predominate.[25] At the higher levels public-sector employees, who are often even better placed to build up networks of support, are more prominent. The pathway from being a public officer serving in the Dry Zone to becoming an MP is so well-beaten that it can be said to be traditional. The earliest example is Major H. R. Freeman, a British former Government Agent serving in the North Central Province who was very actively involved in early colonisation projects. In the first State Council elections in 1931 he was elected as the member for Anuradhapura with 90% of all votes cast, and in 1936 was returned unopposed.[26] C. P. de Silva followed the same path. He was from the Low Country and, as Minister of Lands in the 1950s and early 1960s, a major political figure in Dry Zone development. A network of his family and connections, many of them from his own caste in his home town of Balapitiya in Galle district, have continued to play a major role in the politics of Polonnaruwa district since de Silva's death in the early 1970s.[27] Maithripala Senanayake, a stalwart of the SLFP since its inception, Deputy Prime Minister between 1970 and 1977, and leader of the faction opposed to Mrs Bandaranaike in the first of a series of major splits in the SLFP in the early 1980s, also used his position as a public official to become the most powerful political figure in Anuradhapura district.[28] The figures in Table 9.2 relating to the background of the MPs elected in 1977[29] reveal that these are not just isolated cases.

With respect to Sinhalese and Muslim MPs, the differences between Wet and Dry Zones are very clear. In the Wet Zone the two largest occupational categories are lawyers and planters – the very stuff of the national elite – while in the Dry Zone former public servants stand out way above all other categories. Farmers account for the same small proportion of MPs in both zones. (There is a very substantial contrast with India, where those identified as 'farmers' have accounted for over 30% of MPs since 1967, and have increased their representation almost steadily since 1952.)[30] Given the historic preponderance of Low Country people in public-sector employment, it is likely that they account for a large fraction of Dry Zone Sinhalese MPs. The problem, as Kandyans tend to see it, of people from the Low Country 'carpetbagging' Kandyan electorates has been in existence since the introduction of elections.[31]

Table 9.2. *Main occupations of Sinhalese and Muslim MPs elected in
1977*

Occupation[a]	Wet Zone electorates[b]		Dry Zone electorates	
	Number	Percentage	Number	Percentage
Government service[c]	13	13	15	35
Lawyer	21	20	4	9
Businessman	15	14	6	14
Planter[d]	17	16	—	—
Landed proprietor[d]	2	2	1	2
Farmer/cultivator[d]	7	7	3	7
Professional politician	11	11	3	7
Doctor/*ayurved*[e]	3	3	3	7
Other non-agriculture	—	—	2	5
Not given	15	14	6	14
Total	104	100	43	100

[a] Information on occupations is obtained from the brief biographies of the MPs. These are neither standardised nor always precise. On occasion a certain amount of 'interpretation' was necessary. Where this could not be undertaken confidently, the occupation was left unclassified.
[b] For this purpose electorates (as mapped in Lake House, 1977: 346), were divided as accurately as possible into Wet Zone and Dry Zone on the basis of the climatic map (*Ceylon: Climate*, issued by the Survey Department, Colombo, 1972). The Wet Zone comprises the entire districts of Colombo, Kalutara, Galle, Matara, Ratnapura, Nuwara Eliya, Kandy and Kegalle, plus the electorates of Chilaw, Nattandiya and Wennappuwa in Puttalam district, and the electorates number 112 (Wariyapola) to 121 (Dodangaslanda) in Kurunegala district. (For names and numbers of electorates, see Lake House, 1977: 346.)
[c] This category excludes doctors in government service. It includes all employment in the para-statal sector, notably in cooperatives.
[d] The term 'planter' implies one actively engaged in the management of estates, and 'farmer' or 'cultivator' one managing non-estate production, while 'landed proprietor' is someone leaving direct management to others. The practical distinctions are unlikely to be so clear as the terms suggest.
[e] An *ayurved* is a practitioner of indigenous homeopathic medicine.
Source: Biographies of MPs in Lake House, 1977: 55–204.

The significance for the present argument of the dominance of Low Country traders and public servants in the local politics of the Dry Zone can only be presented in a hypothetical fashion. It is best tackled by speculating about the alternative. What would have happened had the Dry Zone farming population been individually less dependent on the brokerage and credit services of public servants and traders? It is likely that they would have found their MPs and local political leaders more from farming backgrounds than from trade and public service, and more from among those of Kandyan than Low Country backgrounds. The implication is that the problems and interests of the cultivating population – especially product prices – would have received more attention. As it is, the Low Country leadership appears to have 'imported' from the core region ideas about policy and the role of government. Perhaps the most dramatic example is when Maithripala Senanayake, the dominant figure in the politics of Anuradhapura district for several decades, left the UNP to join the SLFP in the early 1950s. The reason he gave was the rice price – not that the farmers' price was too low, but that the consumer price was too high![32]

This general notion introduced here that the politics of the smallholder areas are derived from those of the core region is elaborated in detail in the next chapter.

10

The Sri Lankan polity

Introduction

Our explanation of the political weakness of smallholders as a class has so far been advanced mainly from a 'bottom-up' perspective: it has treated factors in the sphere of social and economic organisation rather than those in the realm of state and national polity. Chapter Seven focused mainly on the divisions and conflicts of interest among smallholders which arise from variations in the natural, technical and economic features of agricultural production systems. Chapter Eight was concerned mainly with the ways in which traditional social organisation and culture, and contemporary agrarian socio-economic relationships, create or fail to create sets of social categorisations which may be exploited in the competition for mass political support. Chapter Nine dealt with the consequences for mass political consciousness and action of ethnic conflict and of the nature of local-level political leadership in the Dry Zone. However, the influences of state and polity on smallholder political action have not been entirely ignored. It has been argued that the state has made the local rather than the national political arena the focus of demands for access to state land (see Chapter Three); helped particularise smallholder demands and consciousness along individual crop lines (see Chapter Seven); and avoided stimulating smallholder political mobilisation by refraining from taking provocative policy initiatives like compulsory crop procurement and rural taxation (see Chapters Five and Eight). But the book has not so far lived up to the claim made in Chapter One that mass political action must be explained from within the political system itself as well as by reference to the pressures which emerge from social and economic structures and conflicts within civil society. It is on the consequences for smallholder political consciousness and action of the national political system that this chapter focuses.

The causal relationship between smallholder political action and the national political system has been reciprocal: smallholders have been influenced by the national system, as well as influencing it, in the process of becoming socialised into participation in the competitive electoral system. For the representative political system predated universal suffrage; and a system of party competition, oriented in large part to capital–labour conflicts in the plantations and in the semi-urban Low Country, predated the full participation in competitive politics of most of the Sinhalese population from the 'genuine' smallholder areas, especially those of the migrant-created society of the Sinhalese Dry Zone. Smallholders, and especially those of the peripheral areas, thus came rather late to competitive electoral politics, and were faced with a number of constraints in imposing their own class concerns on the agenda of party competition. One set of constraints took the form of their own relative inexperience and ignorance of electoral politics: limited education and access to mass media, and subordination to local patrons much more aware of the issues at stake and the techniques for manipulating elections.[1] The other took the form of the existence of an already well-developed system of party competition and an established agenda:

(i)   By the late 1930s there had already evolved a pattern of left–right party competition which has persisted since. This has more or less effectively subsumed and contained other political issues – especially anti-colonial nationalism and anti-minority 'Sinhalese chauvinism' – which do not fall neatly into the left–right spectrum in a conventional sense, and which might otherwise have led to a more multi-polar party constellation which would have opened the political agenda to a wider range of relatively small interest groups (e.g. Dry Zone surplus-food producers).

(ii)   The political elite had already established a firm hold on politics and the party system, and had thus established the capacity to impose its own definition of the political agenda.

(iii)   By the late 1930s the meta-agenda of political competition was already well-established. This meta-agenda is what we have called 'welfarism', i.e. competition for a share of the very substantial material resources redistributed by the state. This has encouraged members of particular occupational or class categories to compete among themselves for a share in the resources already in principle available to them, rather than to mobilise as class or occupational groups against other such groups. The provision of welfare without prior political mobilisation of groups and classes helps prevent that mobilisation at a later stage.

The literature on Sri Lankan politics is relatively copious. Apart from much historical material and a very large number of scholarly articles and contributions to edited books, not all of them listed in this volume, there are several books covering politics 'in the round', generally in the post-Independence period.[2] This material is in certain respects disappointing and deficient. It exhibits two related biases: a tendency to concentrate on 'the politics of legislative institutions';[3] and a tendency to eschew theory in favour of description. The most common organising framework – not one that can very accurately be ennobled with the title 'theory' – is the attempt to account for the 'deviant' (from a comparative international perspective) survival in Sri Lanka of liberal democracy.[4]

I have suggested elsewhere[5] that these two biases are causally related: that the openness of Sri Lankan politics and the political elite seduce the political science researchers into concentrating on Colombo and on the minutiae of parliamentary and intra-elite politics at the expense of investigation into both the political system as a whole and local-level politics – especially at levels above the individual village, which social anthropologists have covered.

While I rely largely on other observers for primary material, some of my interpretations are either not found in the published literature or not accepted generally. The questions asked here are in many respects different from those to which the source literature is oriented. This chapter is organised in such a way as to help clarify the extent of the novelty of the analysis. In the succeeding section a list is made of those aspects of recent Sri Lankan politics which are relevant to the present argument and on which most other observers appear to agree, either overtly, or implicitly by their failure to record disagreement openly. The main body of the chapter comprises my account, in quasi-chronological sequence, of those aspects of the emergence and character of the political system which require investigation in order to sustain the argument of this chapter.

Summary features of Sri Lankan politics

One convenient consequence of the descriptive and atheoretical bias of the literature on Sri Lankan politics is that its authors are rarely in much disagreement with one another. The 'facts' of the situation seem fairly clear. One can read one book after another without encountering much disagreement, finding instead a great deal of approving cross-referencing between one author and another.

On the following points, all of them at least mentioned in previous chapters, there appears to be general agreement.[6]

(i)   Politics is still to a large extent dominated by the national elite which emerged through commercial and plantation enterprise and English-model public-school education in the nineteenth and early twentieth centuries, and which exhibits substantial family continuities.[7]

(ii)   The party system emerged in classic European fashion out of alliances of notables formed in the context of competition within the legislative assembly.[8]

(iii)   The parties and the party system have since been extended and strengthened such that the notables – the elite – now have little individual power independent of that exercised through parties.[9]

(iv)   There is within Sinhalese politics what is from the comparative viewpoint a more or less clear ideological continuum from right (UNP), to centre (SLFP), to left (LSSP; the Communist Party; what are currently no more than the remnants of Philip Gunawardena's MEP; the JVP – the insurrectionary youth party of 1971, now 'parliamentary' in orientation; and various unstable smaller Marxist groups).[10]

(v)   In the late colonial period nationalism, i.e. anti-colonialism, was broadly correlated with leftism. In particular, the left took the lead in *popular mobilisation* under the banner of anti-colonialism.

(vi)   In the post-Independence period Sinhalese nationalism (or 'chauvinism') has become a feature of all shades of the left–right political spectrum of Sinhalese politics.

(vii)   When formed in 1951 and elected to power in 1956 the SLFP was oriented mainly to Sinhalese linguistic, religious and cultural nationalism. It has since acquired, under the leadership of Mrs Bandaranaike, a firmer orientation to economic and social issues. This places it squarely between the Marxist parties on the left and the UNP on the right, even if there is considerable overlap on both sides.

(viii)   *De facto* cooperation between the SLFP and the Marxian parties has been based on two factors. The first is that their relative strengths lie in different locations – the Marxists in urban areas, along the southwestern coastal strip between Colombo and Matara, and in the rubber plantation areas of Sabaragamuwa Province; and the SLFP elsewhere. The two have been able to win power only if allied against the UNP.[11] The second is that nationalisation and the extension of public-sector activities – classic Marxian demands – serve also to increase Sinhalese control over and their share in the fruits of the national economy, and thus to nourish the SLFP's cadres and its electoral base.[12]

(ix)   Sri Lankans, especially the Sinhalese, are highly politicised.

The elite

Origins and character

Sri Lanka constitutes a glaring exception to the generalisation that in less developed countries 'the domestic bourgeoisie is usually quite weak'. Indeed, a better point of departure, and one which relates back to the discussion of 'peasantry' in Chapter Eight, is the view of Sri Lanka's foremost social anthropologist: 'I do not see the peasantry as a class in any meaningful sense, but I do see the elite as one.'[13] Sri Lanka has long had a highly developed bourgeois class, with a firm base in the ownership of the means of production rather than simply, as in many developing countries, in the occupation of professional and public-service posts and in trading. The Sri Lankan political system is so much the creation of the upper stratum of this bourgeoisie, here termed 'the elite', that it is difficult to discuss the system without first giving a sketch of the nature and origins of this elite.

Social science research in Sri Lanka has been heavily concentrated in Sinhalese villages, especially in remote and putatively 'traditional' villages.[14] Very few investigations have been conducted among the middle classes or the elite.[15] Partly for this reason no attempt is made here to define in detail what is meant by the term 'elite', or to specify any division between it and the 'middle' classes.[16] The term 'elite' is used broadly to indicate a relatively homogeneous group which is dominant in political, economic, social and cultural spheres. The relative dearth of published material on this elite is partially compensated for by the ease with which the English-speaking foreigner can conduct informal 'research' on the Sri Lankan elite and middle classes.

The obituaries of E. J. Cooray, who died in 1979, provide a useful illustration of some important dimensions of this elite. Cooray's father, a Catholic and a member of the *Karava* caste living at Wadduwa, on the coast south of Colombo, began life as a distiller of liquor. He was successful in business and then purchased estates. Cooray attended St John's College, Pandura, a school not quite on a par with Royal College or St Thomas' in Colombo, but nevertheless 'the educational cradle of many an eminent personality'. After a spell at the Ceylon University College he proceeded to the UK, where he took an honours degree in classics at London University. This was followed by the Masters of Laws degree. Cooray then topped the London Civil Service examination list but, rather than choosing to serve in India, he returned home to enter public service. After a quarter of a century of service, including posts as Registrar of Cooperative Societies and Chairman of the Cooperative Wholesale Establishment, 'he plunged into the whirlpool of politics and was immediately made a Senator and Minister of Justice'. 'In 1962 when British businessmen began to pack their bags and to leave Lanka's private sector in the hands of the sons of the soil he became Chairman of the Browns' Group of 18 companies, covering such diverse interests as engineering, hire purchase, finance, tourism, airline agencies, banking, transport and hoteliering.' Among his other achievements was receiving the Légion d'honneur, personally bestowed by General de Gaulle.[17]

This case may be somewhat untypical in that a dominant characteristic of the elite – involvement of the same individuals and families in all spheres of economic and political endeavour – is taken to extremes. In two generations the Cooray family achieved eminence in capitalist production in the unorganised sector, plantation ownership, advanced Western education, the public service, politics, and modern sector large-scale business. The point is, however, made.

The various elements of this elite do specialise to some degree.[18] Ownership of property in Colombo on a commercial basis has been to a large extent a Muslim monopoly. Sri Lanka Tamils have specialised in the professions and public service. Foreign trade has been to a large extent in the hands of various minorities identified with India. Among the Sinhalese, the capitalist class has been disproportionately of *Karava* caste origin, while the *Goigama* have been more eminent in electoral politics. But in comparative terms the elite has been and remains very representative of the nation in three important senses. In the first place, its members generally have capital invested in all spheres of economic activity – plantations, property, commerce, industrial production, finance, transport services and, more recently, tourism. In the second place, the ownership of capital is combined, at the level of the individual or the family, with domination over the higher levels of the public service, politics and the professions. One might note for example that S. W. R. D. Bandaranaike, whose family owned large estates, financed the SLFP from his own private resources, even when the party was in power and many additional sources of finance could have been tapped.[19] In the third place, the elite is representative of the nation in the sense that it is made up, albeit not always strictly proportionately to population, of families from almost all ethnic, caste, linguistic and religious categories. There are a few significant exceptions. Some of the low-caste groups among both Sinhalese and Sri Lanka Tamils are underrepresented.[20] As is explained below, the elite, especially the Sinhalese element, is based in the core region and has limited direct links with the economy and society of the extreme periphery. However, from a comparative perspective it is the homogeneity and representativeness of the elite which is most striking.

Individual mobility from one sphere of activity to another is one indicator of the homogeneity of the elite. Despite a diversity of backgrounds and the rarity of intermarriage across caste and communal boundaries, it has been made homogeneous around a Westernised lifestyle in which a small number of English-style Colombo public schools have played a major role. These schools have served the same function as their English equivalents: the induction into a leisured and gentlemanly lifestyle of the sons of those who had made their fortunes in commercial enterprise.[21] Whereas in India, for example, Western education and subsequent public-sector employment was the source of a distinct white-collar elite, in Sri Lanka the pattern of causality was to some degree different: public-school education served to 'civilise' commercial wealth. The widespread engagement of the elite in plantation ownership played a useful ancillary role, providing a milieu for indulgence in a lifestyle in some respects analogous to that of the English squirearchy.[22] The price – at least from the traditionalist nationalist viewpoint – of the apparent homogenisation of the elite around the model of the English upper classes was a loss of national culture. As was mentioned in Chapter Six, Colombo appeared in a cultural sense a city cut off from the rest of the Island.

'Cultural denationalisation' was, however, not a major political issue or liability until the general election of 1956. In the meantime, plantation ownership provided the base from which the elite was able to tame and turn to its own purposes that threat posed by the somewhat unwelcome introduction of universal suffrage in 1931. Members of the elite contested and won elections on the basis of the support they were able to muster in their 'home' areas – i.e. the areas in which their family estates were located, and where they were able to exercise additional patronage through their ownership of large numbers of paddy holdings, purchased perhaps more as a source of patronage than for immediate financial gain.[23]

These local patronage networks appear to have provided one of the mechanisms through which a high voter turnout was achieved – 55% in the State Council elections of 1931 – prior to the emergence of political parties. Only very slowly have party organisation and the party 'ticket' elbowed out the independently minded politician assured of considerable personal support in his home area regardless of his programme or party affiliation. It still pays the party, whether UNP, SLFP or Marxist, to nominate members of the elite in the areas in which they have family connections. The SLFP, for example, has always found its most solid and loyal support in a block of Colombo district electorates where the Bandaranaike family estates are located.[24]

The political 'reach' of the elite through plantation ownership is, however, geographically limited. Not only are plantations in general confined to the Wet Zone, but Sri Lankan-owned estates have historically been confined mainly to the plains and the foothills of the southwestern seaboard – to the 'coconut triangle' north of Colombo and to the rubber, tea and coconut estates of the Western, Southern and Sabaragamuwa Provinces. These are the immediate hinterlands of

Colombo and easily accessible. An active role in estate management is compatible with the location of the main family house in Colombo itself. By 1924 two-thirds of those who had been elected or appointed to the national legislature had at least one family residence in the Western Province, i.e. either in Colombo or Kalutara district.[25]

This Colombo-centricity is related to one important aspect of economic activity in which the elite is not fully represented: although a significant owner of paddy land, at least until the 1972 land reform, its involvement has been in large part motivated by 'land-is-to-rule' rather than by strictly commercial considerations, and paddy land has been insignificant in comparison with other sources of income. Paddy production in the Wet Zone is relatively unprofitable and the elite appears to have been almost entirely uninvolved with food production in the Dry Zone.

There are severe spatial constraints facing any members of the Colombo-based bourgeoisie interested in investing in the Dry Zone. The search for land takes one round the Kandyan hills (see Map One), either south into Hambantota district or north, beyond the 'coconut triangle', into Kurunegala district. In the late nineteenth and early twentieth century some capital, apparently more middle class than elite, did go into paddy cultivation in Hambantota district. An active interest in paddy production in the deep South is, however, inconsistent with playing an active role in political and social life in Colombo. It is no surprise that these Hambantota paddy capitalists became absentees. Kurunegala is more promising because it is closer to Colombo and to the 'coconut triangle' where many of the elite have their estates. There is little doubt that Kurunegala district is currently the one Sinhalese district of Sri Lanka where there is significant urban-based capital (from Colombo) going into the production of paddy and other field crops.[26] The scale of this investment is, however, as yet inadequate to cause one to revise the conclusions that the elite both had and have little financial interest in the profitability of paddy and field crop production generally; and that their personal patronage networks have in most cases not extended into the Dry Zone,[27] and have thus left political leadership there to traders and public servants. It is at least very likely that these conclusions point to a partial reason for the failure of members of the elite to place the commercial profitability of paddy production on the public political agenda. There is little incentive either in terms of material self-interest or in the character of their electoral bases, which are firmly in the core rather than the periphery, to do so.

The continuity of elite dominance[28]

The dominance of the elite in the period leading up to Independence does not seem especially problematic. It is, however, in many ways surprising that this dominance should have survived beyond, say, 1956, in an era of mass politics of a distinctly radical tone. Indeed this combination of elite dominance and apparently radical politics is one of the most remarkable features of contemporary Sri Lanka. The reasons for this perpetuation of elite dominance are clearly relevant to the main argument of this study. For the lack of any wholesale replacement of the old elite by new leaders from less elevated social strata is clearly likely, everything else being equal, to inhibit the expression of political demands at grassroots levels. Sri Lanka has exhibited instead a pattern of gradual absorption of new elements into the national political leadership, with a consequent high degree of continuity in political culture at the elite level.

To explain continuing elite dominance is too ambitious a task. All that can be done here is to indicate what appears to be one of the major contributory factors: the flexibility of the elite in various senses.

The first is the very high degree of flexibility which members of the elite have shown in anticipating and therefore in some degree helping shape popular electoral demands: Crown land alienation in the 1920s and 1930s, the creation of a welfare state and of a Marxian labour movement in the 1930s and 1940s, the cultural nationalism of the SLFP in the 1950s, and the nationalisation of estates in the 1970s. This flexibility in turn seems to stem from the very diverse nature of the elite's material base, the relative ease with which members can switch emphasis and efforts from one activity to another,[29] and the consequent willingness to make or accept sacrifices in the material sphere in order to maintain political dominance. The plantation interest in particular has been placed on the sacrificial altar with the acceptance of a ban on the alienation of state land for expansion in the 1920s, the low prices for coconuts since Independence, and the nationalisation of estates in the 1970s with the consequent loss of local patronage networks.[30]

A second aspect of elite flexibility is the way in which it has been able to provide from within its own ranks changes of personnel for national leadership positions to meet changing political situations.

The Sinhalese commercial fortunes which were made in the nineteenth century accrued not simply to people of the Low Country rather than to Kandyans. Additionally, these fortunes were concentrated very heavily in the hands of the three minority coastal castes of the Low Country, the *Karava*, the *Halgama* and the *Durava*, especially the *Karava*.[31] This small minority still accounts for the bulk of the Sinhalese commercial elite. It played a leading role in the early nationalist movement when this remained restricted to discrete pressures for more power for themselves from a small wealthy class represented by nomination in the councils of state and organised in particular in the Low Country Products Association, originally an association of Sri Lankan planters.[32]

Members of these coastal castes were, however, never quite accepted as equal to the *Goigama*, either by the British – who preferred to nominate *Goigama* to the leading honorary positions – or by the *Goigama* themselves. Even before the introduction of democratic elections there was something of a shift of leadership from this older, conservative and non-*Goigama* group, which was generally unable to command the allegiance of ordinary villagers,[33] to that of those Low Country Sinhalese who combined wealth with *Goigama* status. One of the more notable elements in this newer Low Country *Goigama* nationalist leadership was the Senanayake family, which provided two Prime Ministers, D. S. Senanayake and his son Dudley.[34] The Kandyan aristocracy, still enveloped in traditionalism and oriented to rule through control of land and their occupation of the various ranks of headman, generally allowed opportunities to participate directly in commercial and plantation development to pass them by. They appear to have benefited from plantation development, but mainly indirectly, through, for example, leasing out land to plantation capitalists.[35] There then emerged something of a cleavage between the traditionalistic and aristocratic Kandyan *Goigama* elite and the capitalist Low Country elite,[36] including the politically prominent *Goigama* element. Resentment at the Low Country dominance of the nationalist movement was one motivating factor behind the unsuccessful initiative for a separate Kandyan state taken in the 1920s by a group of Kandyan aristocrats. More successful was Mrs Bandaranaike's partial reconstruction of the SLFP, after the assassination of her husband, around a leadership comprising in part her relatives among the Kandyan aristocracy. Ironically, the very conservative and traditionalistic nature of this Kandyan element in the elite, as indicated by its 'feudal' rather than 'capitalist' background, made it an especially credible leadership for the expression, in a broadly nationalist idiom, of the resentments of the rural poor against the plantation sector. Its own hands could be shown to be relatively clean.[37]

Thus the relative social, economic and cultural homogeneity of the elite was no bar to vigorous intra-elite political competition. Indeed it is this competition which in large part accounts for the perpetuation of competitive representative politics in Sri Lanka.

The final aspect of the elite's political flexibility relates to its composition, especially the way in which this is affected by the Sinhalese kinship system. In a summary of the work of a number of social anthropologists, I have explained elsewhere[38] that a central feature of Sinhalese kinship is that all relatives by marriage are potentially kin of the same status – and addressed by the same kinship terms – as cognates, i.e. relatives by blood. This gives kinship a very long potential 'reach': an individual can easily find large numbers of others with whom a potential kinship link could be cultivated. Although the Sinhalese elite is highly intermarried, at least within caste categories – such that, for example, the Bandaranaikes and Senanayakes have numerous traceable kinship connections – it is not especially exclusive. For the wide range of potential kin enables it to draw into national political leadership, and through the idiom of kinship, those who were previously living in relative obscurity. Conversely, many close relatives of leading politicians themselves live in obscurity. In other words, the elite is less exclusive than many are led to believe by accounts of the kinship connections which unite its various members. The range of tactical choice open in recognising, claiming and denying kinship links, permits, in some degree at least, new wealth and power to be incorporated and fading relatives to be dropped from sight.[39]

This brings us on to the final comment on the elite, which is the reality of the claim that it remains dominant. There is indeed some evidence that its dominance has declined somewhat, but the absence of detailed quantitative investigations makes it impossible to judge the extent of this trend. There is a fairly popular theory, originating on the political left[40] but also taken up at the rhetorical level by the UNP,[41] that the periods of SLFP rule have seen the birth of a 'new bourgeoisie', commonly termed a 'national bourgeoisie', as opposed, in the Marxist idiom, to the 'comprador bourgeoisie' represented by the UNP. A standard Marxian formula is often applied: this 'national bourgeoisie' is said to have its material base in the limited import-substituting industrialisation fostered by the semi-autarkic economic policies of SLFP governments. There is unfortunately no solid evidence to support this claim. It is my impression that too much weight is put upon one or two individual cases, notably the support given Mrs Bandaranaike by one wealthy self-made businessman, 'Dasa Mudalali'. The evidence, such as it is, suggests that the capital and enterprise devoted to new activities, notably for example the tourist sector, which grew rapidly in the 1970s, come in large part from the old elite. Rather than suffering a sudden eclipse, it is probably undergoing a slow mutation, as indeed it always appears to have done.[42]

The evolution of the political system

The Buddhist Revival, the temperance movement and early nationalism

This extended discussion of the elite sets the stage for a brief statement on the early nationalist and proto-nationalist movements, the latter including in particular the Buddhist revivalist and temperance movements of the late nineteenth century.[43] The main point is simply that these were almost entirely Low Country movements led mainly by members of the Low Country capitalist class,[44] i.e. they were phenomena of the core.

The Buddhist Revival is of particular significance.[45] For, despite the name, it was more than simply a revival. It involved rather the creation of a new kind of Buddhism, which has been termed 'Protestant Buddhism', in recognition of the way in which, in attempting to halt and reverse the inroads of Christianity among the Sinhalese, its promoters adopted many of the practices and organisational forms of Protestant Christianity: lay Buddhist organisations, Sunday schools, a Buddhist flag, and the general attempt to convert Buddhism into a distinct and exclusive religion comparable to Christianity.[46] The militancy, assertiveness, populism, and lay involvement which accompanied this Revival were alien to the temple-based traditional Buddhism of the Kandyan areas. A prominent feature of the Revival was the emergence of new non-*Goigama* priestly orders and the creation of a new kind of temple in the Low Country: one without property and therefore dependent on, and closely involved with, the population of its neighbourhood, including financial sponsors from among the elite.[47] These new elements – the propertyless and generally socially and politically activist and non-*Goigama* Low Country priestly orders and temples, and militant lay Buddhist organisations, notably the All Ceylon Buddhist Congress – have coexisted uneasily with the traditional Buddhism of the more prestigious and wealthy Kandyan orders and temples.[48] The *bhikkhus* who became actively involved in organising on behalf of S. W. R. D. Bandaranaike's MEP in the 1956 general election were mainly from the Low Country. One reason why Buddhism has not become the state religion is fear on the part of the Kandyan religious orders that this would open the way to lay control through bodies like the All Ceylon Buddhist Congress.

The rise of the labour movement and the emergence of a left–right party continuum[49]

Following on from the Buddhist Revival, the temperance movement and nationalism, the fourth great socio-political movement to affect Sri Lanka in the late nineteenth and early twentieth century was the rise of an organised labour movement, and its acceptance of Marxist political leadership. This, too, was a Low Country-based movement. The consequences were considerable, and included above all a basically unidimensional pattern of inter-party competition on a left–right continuum familiar, for example, in much of Northern Europe. This, it is argued, is one reason for the non-emergence of a smallholder movement. It is also an outcome which appears to have been treated remarkably casually by the political scientists writing on Sri Lanka. For they appear to have accepted as automatic or natural this 'European' pattern of alignment, to the extent of accepting as somehow intrinsically justified and unquestionable the SLFP's claim to be a social democratic party, as counterposed to the 'conservatism' of the UNP and 'Marxian socialism' of the left parties. A 'European' party alignment in a country with a large peasant or smallholder population seems more problematic than automatic.[50] If one is to accept the validity of European comparisons, then one ought at least to be looking for a 'centre' or 'agrarian' party of a German or Scandinavian type representing small farmers.[51] The SLFP is not such a party.

To some degree the creation of trade unions preceded the activities of the Marxists.[52] However, the Sinhalese labour movement went from infancy to strength during the 1940s and 1950s under Marxist leadership,[53] and after the creation in 1935 of Sri Lanka's first 'modern' political party, the LSSP. The LSSP survives to the present day, and it is not for our purposes necessary to trace the history of its continual splits and reunifications. On that point it is adequate to say that it has given birth to two main alternative mass Marxian movements: the Communist Party, and the group, now virtually defunct, which has under various names followed Philip Gunawardena and, later, his son.

The LSSP was formed, and is still led, by a group of people from elite and mainly Low Country backgrounds who, apart from their Marxist beliefs, tend to be distinguished from the UNP and SLFP leadership by two main factors: their far more intellectual approach to politics, and their origins in minority non-*Goigama* groups, especially the castes of the Low Country coastline, the *Karava*, the *Salagama* and, to a lesser extent, the *Durava*.[54] In the very narrowest sense the LSSP was not created from on high from among the ranks of parliamentarians: its two early leaders, N. M. Perera and Philip Gunawardena, were not elected to the State Council until 1936.[55] That is, however, rather a quibble. For the Marxist leadership has, at least as much as the leadership of the other Sinhalese parties, placed emphasis on, and excelled in *parliamentary* performance and skills.[56] They have behaved very much as if they were, for example, members of landed elites in nineteenth-century Britain, where political issues were indeed in large part decided within the legislative assembly. The LSSP was Sri Lanka's first organised mass political party, but its leadership has never quite behaved accordingly.

The Marxist/labour movements came to have, and generally still retain, bases in three occupations and in three localities. The occupations are transport services, especially the railways, the ports and, later, the nationalised bus service; the clerical service in the large government, financial and mercantile offices in Colombo; and some plantations.[57] The localities are Colombo city; the coastal strip south from Colombo to Matara, where high levels of education, and high rates of employment in the modern sector and in Colombo combine with a certain degree of resentment on the part of the coastal castes against *Goigama* social and political dominance; and the Sinhalese plantation proletariat of the Low Country and of the rubber estates of the Kelani valley – parts of Ratnapura and Kegalle districts. In the 1930s and 1940s the Marxists had strong links with the highly organised and militant Indian Tamil estate proletariat,[58] but these disintegrated after the Indian Tamils were disenfranchised by the UNP immediately after Independence in 1948, and the Marxists, in a (vain) bid to stem the steady erosion of their electoral base, abandoned their cosmopolitan line and accommodated themselves to explicitly pro-Sinhalese styles and policies.[59]

The Marxian contribution to the emergence of a left–right political spectrum was first to pose a challenge to the dominance of the loosely organised and somewhat eclectic nationalism associated with the Ceylon National Congress.[60] The UNP was founded just in time to fight the pre-Independence general election of 1947, in which they garnered 41% of the total vote and the three Marxist parties 21% – the highest proportion the latter were ever to attain.[61]

Two great political issues divided the Sinhalese in the 1930s and 1940s: the capital–labour conflict in the plantations and in the supporting transport and commercial sectors; and the degree of pressure to be put on the British to grant independence. The Marxist contribution to the political future of Sri Lanka was to bring these conflicts into line with one another: to make militant nationalism a left-wing cause and to associate the mainstream national elite with a less strident nationalism – and one with which their political opponents have been taunting them ever since. The fusion of nationalism and Marxism was facilitated by the fact that capital still remained largely in British hands.[62] The demands of organised labour could be merged with demands not merely for legal political independence, but also for the ending of colonialism as a system of economic domination.[63] To the degree that it was compatible with their cosmopolitan beliefs and background, the Marxist leaders confirmed their nationalist credentials by adopting a more populist style than that associated with their opponents in the Ceylon National Congress.[64] The Marxists were also committed democrats whereas some elements in the mainstream nationalist leadership appeared to have hoped to wrest control of the country from the British without conceding universal suffrage.

It has been convincingly argued that, in the 1930s and 1940s, the Sri Lankan Marxists in effect functioned as a 'national bourgeoisie', very much like the industrial and commercial class which supported the Congress Party in India.[65] The Marxists' electoral support appears to have been offered as much for nationalist and democratic reasons as on grounds of working-class solidarity. The steady decline in their vote since 1947 seems due more than anything to the fact that, after the foundation of the SLFP in 1951, they (the Marxists) were outflanked by the SLFP's Sinhalese, as opposed to Sri Lankan, nationalist programme.

Had the Marxists not managed to fuse class and nationalist perspectives then it is unlikely that Sinhalese political party competition would have commenced from a situation of bipolarity. If the labour–capital and nationalist conflicts had been fought separately, a multi-polar party system would probably have emerged. This in turn would have increased the likelihood that politicians would have sought the support of particular spatially concentrated minorities, including perhaps the surplus-food producers of the Dry Zone. National party-political competition along a single dimension constitutes a hindrance to the representation of minority regional interests.

One might note in conclusion that the 1947 general election, unlike the State Council elections of 1931 and 1936, was fought mainly on party lines. Only one (Muslim) MP was elected without a contest. The UNP and the three Marxist parties returned forty-two and eighteen MPs respectively in a House of ninety-five elected members. Only a dozen Sinhalese MPs were returned as Independents. Only three of these Independents came from our core region, where they accounted for 11% of the seats. Two of these three seats were located in the very southern extremity of the region – Akuressa and Deniyaya in Matara district. In the inner periphery (the Kandyan hills), only one out of eight Sinhalese seats (12%) returned an Independent, and that was the Minipe seat, which, although in Kandy district, lies at the eastern extremity on the Dry Zone plain at the foot of the Kandyan hills. By contrast, eight (25%) of the remaining Sinhalese seats – those located in the outer and extreme periphery – returned Independents.[66] The greater significance of party labels and party contests in the core region reflected the fact that the party system was born there.[67]

1956

The broad nature and significance of the 1956 general election have been discussed in Chapter Two. Our interest here lies in the fact that this great political resurgence of the Sinhalese Buddhists, especially the *rural* Sinhalese Buddhists, which has been described as the 'Green Uprising',[68] would seem *a priori* to have provided an opportunity for the Sinhalese smallholders to gain a voice, either directly through the SLFP, or indirectly through the introduction of a new dimension to party competition – that of Sinhalese chauvinism – that would perhaps have led to a multipolar party system and to the possible consequences mentioned above. Neither of these things did happen, although, admittedly, the latter looked distinctly possible around 1960 when the SLFP was in total disarray in the interval between S. W. R. D. Bandaranaike's assassination and his widow's assertion of control over the party. The SLFP split and appeared in danger of disintegration, while minor Sinhalese communal parties began to proliferate, and indeed won a number of seats in the first (and inconclusive) of the two general elections held in 1960.[69] Yet the SLFP settled down to a 'centrist' position between the UNP and the Marxists[70] and has shown no special regard for the occupational interests of the smallholding population.

The SLFP is indeed mainly a rural Sinhalese Buddhist party.[71] It has little support in urban areas, which are mainly UNP strongholds, or among the non-Sinhalese minorities. Its sweep to power in 1956 was, unlike the other major turning-points in Sri Lankan politics, not in any special sense a product of the Low Country.[72] Its support was, and is, fairly widespread throughout the Sinhalese areas, except that it remains relatively weak in the Colombo–Matara coastal strip, where the Marxists have been strongest and provided the main opposition to the UNP. One should, however, note that it was mainly the more radical *bhikkhus* of the Low Country who rallied to the SLFP-led MEP coalition in 1956.[73]

The reason that the emergence of the SLFP did not result in the addition of a second, Sinhalese nationalist, dimension to inter-party competition seems fairly clear in general terms: the other parties, the UNP and Philip Gunawardena's group eagerly, and the LSSP and the Communist Party more slowly and reluctantly, got in on the act. Soon differences in the degree of Sinhalese chauvinism were greater within parties than between them.[74]

Why, given especially its strength in the Dry Zone, the SLFP failed to become the spokesman for smallholder surplus-food producers is a question which does not seem to have such a satisfactory answer. I can but point to three aspects of the explanation, other than those given in previous chapters.

The first is the very elite nature of the SLFP leadership, especially at the time of its creation. S. W. R. D. Bandaranaike[75] was a member of an old-established elite family[76] and the son of the *Maha Mudaliyar*, the occupant of the most prestigious position available to a Sri Lankan under British rule. There is truth in the claim that S. W. R. D.'s quarrel with the UNP leadership, arising mainly from frustrated personal ambition, was embittered by his own snobbery. S. W. R. D.'s wife was a member of a leading Kandyan aristocratic family.[77] In very recent years, it is the SLFP rather than the UNP which has appeared as the vehicle of an old elite family. 'Family-bandyism' was a charge used against the SLFP with great effect in the 1977 general election.

Despite his 'common touch' – his ability to create an image of empathy with the Sinhalese villager[78] – S. W. R. D. Bandaranaike's views epitomised the paternalism of the elite towards the peasantry. He was the last person to encourage the smallholder population to formulate their own demands, especially price demands. The future which he envisaged for the peasantry was very carefully mapped out, and included nationalisation of all paddy land and total state control of input provision, marketing and food distribution.

The second reason for the failure of the SLFP to represent smallholder class demands is that, contrary to the impression conveyed by much of the literature, the eruption of support for the SLFP in 1956 did *not* involve the politicisation of (peasant) populations hitherto outside the electoral system. Those who took part in the 'Green Uprising' were not rising for the first time. Admittedly they rose on a wave of Sinhalese cultural, linguistic and religious enthusiasm which was unprecedented, and the outcome was a change in the style of politics and a thorough politicisation of those spheres of society and the economy which had hitherto remained 'non-political'. Yet no new population was inducted into politics. At the level of local leadership,

Roberts has demonstrated that the SLFP cadres, the rural middle classes, had long been politically active, but were frustrated at playing second fiddle to the elite represented by the UNP. More importantly – and a point which seems to have escaped the attention of other commentators – the 1956 election witnessed not an increase but a slight fall in the proportion of the population voting compared to the previous election in 1952: 71% of the electorate voted in 1952, and only 69% in 1956.[79]

By far the biggest increase in electoral turnout in Sri Lanka took place between 1947 (56%) and 1952 (71%).[80] Admittedly the SLFP had been founded in 1951 and contested the majority of Sinhalese seats in 1952. Yet this in no sense explains the big increase in electoral turnout: the increase between 1947 and 1952 was on average smaller in the seats contested by the SLFP than elsewhere.[81] These figures appear to run counter to widespread impressions, and raise a number of questions which cannot be answered here.[82] I suspect that much of the reason behind the increase in electoral turnout between 1947 and 1952 is to be found in the combined consequences of the rapid spread of state welfare activities, especially the rice ration, in the war and post-war periods and fears that the government was contemplating cutting or abolishing the rice ration for financial reasons.[83] There is indeed broader evidence to support this suggestion: the second largest increase in electoral turnout took place between 1956 (69%) and 1960 (78%), following the rapid expansion of the scope of state activities after 1956. It is likely that it is the expansion in the scope of public-sector activities, with a consequent increase in the significance of politics, which explains the extent of and changes in levels of electoral participation.

The conclusion for our purposes is that the SLFP did not tap the support of the hitherto unpoliticised. The population which supported it had conceptions of the nature and purpose of politics affected by their previous participation in electoral politics. And, as will be explained below, this participation was in a system oriented to welfarism.

The third reason for the failure of the SLFP to articulate smallholder class demands is probably its *de facto* dependence on political allies who, more than any other parties, represent food consumers – the Marxists. This dependence has two main dimensions. On the one hand the Marxists and the SLFP are 'natural allies' in the sense that they separately constitute the main opposition to the UNP among the rural Sinhalese in different localities – the Marxists in parts of the Low Country and Sabaragamuwa Province and the SLFP elsewhere. For most of its existence the SLFP has been in political alliance with at least one of the Marxist parties, and has only once, in July 1960, managed to win a general election without an electoral agreement with the left. That was at a time when Sinhalese communalism was an especially attractive electoral formula. Yet even the SLFP government elected in July 1960 was obliged to take the LSSP into government before its term was up.[84]

The second aspect of the dependence of the SLFP on the Marxists is that it is in many ways their historical successor. The SLFP inherited the Marxists' combination of nationalist and leftist opposition to the UNP,[85] although substituting Sinhalese (i.e. mainly anti-Tamil) nationalism for the Marxists' Sri Lankan (anti-colonial) nationalism. Both depend mainly on rural Sinhalese Buddhist votes,[86] with the SLFP gradually replacing the Marxists. The SLFP has inherited many of its cadres and leading personalities from the LSSP in particular, and has been very dependent on them for ideas.[87] S. W. R. D. Bandaranaike appears to have recognised the basic similarity between the two parties, and indeed suggested a merger before his victory in the 1956 general election made that unnecessary.[88] In more recent years the apparent differences between the SLFP and the Marxists have probably been exaggerated by the frictions engendered by the Kandyan aristocratic element in the SLFP leadership. Even so, the SLFP has been in alliance with at least one Marxist party continuously from 1964, until a few months before the 1977 general election. Since 1977 relationships between the (fragmented) SLFP and the left have been unstable and unclear.

Had the SLFP started more from scratch with new cadres and new voters hitherto uninvolved in politics, and had it been able to win a parliamentary majority without entering into alliances with the left, then there would have been a greater likelihood that it would have become oriented to the interests of the smallholding population, especially the Dry Zone food producers. As it is, it has tended to extend and perpetuate a pre-existing pattern of party competition rather than initiate a new one. As Jupp says, 'it is not a peasant party in any real sense'.[89]

The JVP Insurgency[90]

After 1956 – and apart from planned military coups – the only major initiative to change the shape of Sri Lankan politics was the unsuccessful Insurgency of the JVP youth party in 1971. The JVP was, like both the SLFP and the Marxist parties, with which it had strong historical links and a relationship that was in many ways close and in others antagonistic, a mainly rural Sinhalese movement. Yet it was, like the

Marxists but unlike the SLFP, very strongly based in the Low Country, especially the Colombo–Matara coastal strip. The leaders of the JVP were mainly of the coastal *Karava* caste, and had strong links with the town of Ambalangoda,[91] mid-way between Colombo and Matara, which has played an especially prominent role in almost all major Sinhalese social, cultural and political movements over the past century.[92] JVP activities were concentrated in this area.[93] Widespread popular support for the JVP was forthcoming in only two localities: around Elpitiya inland from Ambalangoda, and in a low-caste area of Kegalle district. Despite its rural base the JVP had no 'agrarian programme' to speak of. Like the SLFP it was rural rather than agricultural in orientation.

The nature of the political system

This completes our selective account of the significant incidents and processes in the evolution of the political system whose outlines were listed at the beginning of the chapter. The remainder of the chapter is devoted to an examination of three significant structural features of the system: the socio-economic basis of party support; the content of the political agenda; and the dominance of political over social organisation. Each helps explain why smallholder interests have not been articulated.

The socio-economic basis of party support

We have seen that the major Sinhalese parties fit fairly clearly into a left–right ideological spectrum, and that their policies are differentiated accordingly: the UNP generally favours private enterprise and a 'liberal' economy, and the SLFP and, even more strongly, the Marxists, state enterprise and state control of the economy. Allowing for the fact that the Marxists' unionised supporters might often be less poor than the unorganised working class in the rural and urban areas, one might otherwise expect that there would be a clear correlation of party and socio-economic status. That indeed is implied in much of the literature on Sri Lankan politics.[94] It is, however, a conclusion which is not often strongly stated, and coexists with a certain degree of doubt and ambiguity. For example, the author of one of the more recent and authoritative books on Sri Lankan politics talks as if the only social cleavages affecting party allegiance were those of 'religion, race, caste, language and region'.[95]

In their reluctance to claim a correspondence of party with socio-economic status the political scientists seem more cautious than most

Sri Lankans, among whom it is in my experience accepted almost as a matter of course that the UNP represents the rich, and the SLFP and the Marxists the poor and, in the latter case, organised labour. Part of the reason for caution lies in the non-availability of any statistics relating voting to voters' characteristics.[96] The only detailed set of quantitative data relating to voting preferences and socio-economic characteristics that I know of were in fact collected on my behalf, and under conditions which ensured accuracy, in one village during the 1977 general election. These data show a very high degree of correspondence of voting to wealth and income – the poor support the LSSP, the rich the UNP, and the in-betweens the SLFP – and indeed a correspondence which amazed me, previously familiar as I was with each of the sixty-two households interviewed.[97] This locality, just inland from Ambalangoda town, may be untypical in the strength of its radical traditions. However, other local-level evidence, published and unpublished, indicates the same conclusion. At the grassroots level the SLFP and/or the Marxists command the allegiance of the poorer strata, and the UNP the allegiance of the rich.[98]

Apart from the lack of reliable survey data, there appear to be four other reasons why political scientists have been unnecessarily cautious in associating party with socio-economic strata. One is the prevalence of the idiom of caste in discussions of local-level politics. Yet caste does correspond broadly to socio-economic ranking. To appeal to the poor is in large part to appeal to members of the lower castes, and vice versa. The second is the continuing importance of patron–client linkages, a phenomenon which is, however, not antithetical to strata-based electoral behaviour. The third reason is the elite nature of the leadership of *all* parties, especially at national level. And, as was noted above, political commentators have not delved below the national level sufficiently often. The fourth – and rather more speculative – reason is that observers of Sri Lankan politics appear to have operated with an unnecessarily restricted conception of the possible range of party systems. One has the impression that they feel obliged to choose between two possible models: a North European pattern of 'ideologically based' parties,[99] each grounded on distinct socio-economic classes; or a purely transactional model of parties as aggregates of caste, linguistic, regional, religious and other groups united purely for immediate instrumental reasons. Since the Sri Lankan party system evidently does not accord with the first model – there are no national or pan-Sinhalese socio-economic classes – then there is a tendency to associate it with the second model.[100] In reality it appears as something intermediate between the two: parties broadly unite the less privileged or the more privileged strata on a national basis, but the characteristics of each category – their occupations, caste, educational levels – can vary widely from locality to locality.

The main exception to this association of party with socio-economic status may be found in the Dry Zone, especially in the colonisation schemes. Here, where there is anyway no Marxist political presence and thus a relatively low overtly ideological content to politics,[101] competition between the UNP and the SLFP tends to be more purely instrumental than elsewhere, and to have relatively little basis in socio-economic differentiation. The Dry Zone colonies anyway have no large permanently disadvantaged populations such as landless labouring groups, and very little by way of an established local elite. There is less scope than elsewhere for party competition along the lines of socio-economic strata.[102] It is only for Dry Zone localities that I have encountered evidence of pattern allegiance distinctly contrary to the more typical national pattern.[103]

If Sinhalese parties do indeed receive nationwide support on the basis of identification with particular socio-economic rankings, how is this perceived and communicated by their supporters themselves? In what way does the coconut estate labourer conceive of himself as having an identity in common with the low-caste paddy land tenant, the cinnamon peeler, the lorry cleaner or the baker's labourer? What are the codes or symbols by which they recognise themselves? The answer on the whole and in most areas is not the language of occupational categories or class in the strict sense. While it is true that this – the appeals to 'the working class and the peasantry', or 'the working class, the middle class and the peasantry' – is part of the established discourse of politicians of all parties, it seems to be used to appeal to the Sinhalese collectively. Among ordinary Sinhalese it is the language of socio-economic *stratification* which is used – 'the rich', 'the middling people', and 'the poor'. It is in these terms, rather than by reference to occupation or class, that villagers tend to rank themselves. They do not talk of themselves as 'farmers', 'tenants', 'potters', 'labourers' or 'toddy tappers'.[104] This is scarcely surprising in the light of the diversity of the rural economy, the widespread practice of combining agricultural and non-agricultural activities, and the lack of clear differentiation between the various categories of agriculturalists – farmers, labourers, tenants and landlords. Seneratne has made much the same point in his analysis of ranking criteria and terms used in a Low Country village: in a community with many kinds of material resources, individuals are ranked according to the composite concept of *thathwaya* ('status'). Wealth, income levels, occupation or landholdings do not individually tell one very much.[105] Ranking according to socio-economic strata rather than class or occupation is an outcome of the diversity of the rural economy and the lack of clear boundaries between occupational and class categories.[106]

One is dealing here with issues beyond the scope of proof in the strict sense. There is, however, at the very least an interesting consistency between the three phenomena identified above: the conceptualisation of socio-economic inequality by villagers in terms of strata rather than in class or occupational terms; social stratification as the basis of party support; and the absence of a distinct rural occupational or class identity in politics. Were inter-party competition framed in terms of the interests of particular rural class or occupational categories, then one would expect to find villagers evaluating one another in similar terms, and vice versa.

The political agenda

We have talked of the lines of inter-party competition, but said nothing about the content, about what the stakes are. They are of course various, and change from time to time. However, one major item has remained prominent on the political agenda since the inception of a representative politics in the 1930s: access to resources distributed through state agencies – public-sector jobs, subsidies, permissions, places in schools, medical treatment, etc.[107] Although conducted in the language of class conflict, and structured in fact around strata rather than class categories, Sri Lankan politics is ultimately oriented mainly to the question of who shall enjoy privileged access to services distributed by the state. There is thus ultimately less at stake in political conflict than at first sight appears. No party is aiming at fundamental socio-economic change. Change is restricted mainly to the political sphere, and this change is in large part cyclical.

The implication of this point for the present book is fairly clear: a stable pattern of inter-party competition over publicly distributed resources encourages voters to define themselves in terms of their roles as actual or potential consumers of these resources. Politics is about who will be employed by the Ceylon Transport Board as bus conductors. Conversely, it is not mainly about the interests of different occupational groups. Political action involves an implicit choice between alternative role definitions: between, for example, acting as a plantation labourer interested in better wages and conditions, as an inhabitant of Region X wanting to obtain a good share of public investment and jobs for the region, or as a Buddhist concerned to see Buddhism declared the state religion. If voters are habituated to acting according to one set of roles – in this case roles as consumers of services distributed through state agencies – then it is correspondingly more difficult to mobilise them according to a different set of roles and the interests to which these give rise – e.g. roles as smallholder producers.

The significant question is, then, why access to publicly provided services has so dominated the Sri Lankan political agenda. There appear to be two parts to the answer. The first is the very abundance of the resources which the state has taken into its hands through assertion of control over Crown lands, nationalisation, the expansion of public-sector activities, and the taxation of the estate sector. On these issues no more need be said here,[108] except perhaps to add that the ratio of public-sector jobs to population is very high in Sri Lanka compared to other countries with large, private economic sectors and competitive electoral systems.[109] The second part of the answer to our earlier question is that the state became a major distributor of material resources at an early and formative stage in the development of representative politics.

In 1931, when universal suffrage was introduced, the Sri Lankan electorate was already relatively highly politicised. In the 80% of State Council seats which were contested in that year's general election, 55% of the voters turned out to vote. I have seen no serious attempt to explain this early politicisation,[110] although the reasons appear in large degree to be almost self-evident. Most relate in one way or another to the plantation experience.[111] Since 1931 rates of electoral turnout have generally been highest among the Sinhalese villagers of the Kandyan hills[112] – the area affected by large 'alien' estates – despite the relative political backwardness of the Kandyans in other respects.

The large extent of Crown land and of the acreages alienated, and the fact that many people could reasonably expect to obtain an allotment, probably made the rural population particularly aware of the usefulness of access to administrative decisions. Good transport and communications systems and high rates of literacy[113] were by-products of the plantation economy. The high level of the economy's dependence on plantation production and international trade meant that the economic depression of the 1920s and 1930s struck deeply even in the Sinhalese villages.[114] The plantations themselves used a higher proportion of female labour than did smallholder agriculture, and probably helped to make females politically aware by bringing them out into the public domain.[115] The plantations in many ways irritated the villagers, especially the Kandyans. And, perhaps above all else, the welfare services – the schools, school meals and medical services – which the plantations provided their permanent resident (i.e. mainly

Indian Tamil) work force provided a stimulus and a model for Sinhalese demands:[116]

Thus the origins of welfare legislation in Ceylon were closely identified with a specific sector of the working class [the Indian Tamil estate workers] and were, in inspiration, unrelated to trades union pressures. [The origins lay in the paternal watchfulness of the colonial government of India over the interests of estate labour originating in India.] However, when an indigenous trades union movement emerged in the 1920s, one basic trend in the pressure they used lay in their efforts to win for the Ceylonese working class the statutory benefits which immigrant labour enjoyed, and which had been denied to the indigenous population.[117]

The government elected in 1931 very quickly began to construct for the Sinhalese a welfare state on the British model. A modest system of unemployment relief and public works was introduced in the major urban areas in 1931. The 1930s also saw the introduction of a workmen's compensation scheme, maternity benefits, employment exchanges and free school meals, and the expansion of free medical and educational facilities. Wartime saw the introduction of free milk to infants and expectant mothers and, far more importantly, subsidies and rations for rice and wheat flour.[118] 'By 1947, the total expenditure on social services absorbed a staggering 56.1% of the government's revenue.'[119] The size of the welfare budget has dominated discussions on Sri Lanka's economy ever since. And subsidies of various kinds have been a major feature of economic policy towards the smallholder sector.

Representative politics and the party system thus emerged and matured in an environment in which questions of individual or group access to publicly distributed resources were of very great significance. The plethora of programmes and the volume of resources distributed have meant that individual welfare is to a very large degree shaped by administrative decisions about, for example, the eligibility for a 'public assistance' allowance of those lacking other means of support;[120] acceptance of an application to be allowed to plant an additional half acre of tea and to receive a new planting subsidy; registration with the cooperative as a legitimate handloom weaver entitled to subsidised supplies of yarn; the legalisation of an encroachment on Crown land; permission to make a cart track across Crown land to one's paddy field; acceptance of children into an urban secondary school equipped with a science stream; allocation of the post of 'watcher' of the village cooperative branch; re-registration of a ration book so that the rice ration may be obtained at a different cooperative outlet; eliciting from the Central Bank documentation to prove that contributions have been made to the Employees Provident Fund; and enforcement of regulations which prohibit regular employment of labourers on estates without giving them the favourable status of permanent employees.[121]

All these decisions are likely to require political mediation. It is with this kind of mediation that grassroots politics is to a large extent concerned. The change from a UNP to an SLFP government determines which population categories shall receive the most effective support and mediation. As in all other polities, politics in Sri Lanka is represented as the pursuit of the public good. There is, however, a particularly strong 'welfarist' seam in the language of Sri Lankan politics. More generally, government support for any activity, locality or population is commonly couched in terms of the granting of 'relief'[122] or of 'due privileges',[123] while allegations of past failure to provide support are termed 'Cinderella' or 'stepmotherly' treatment. The implication is that the 'public good' is conceived in 'welfarist' terms, i.e. in terms of the ability of the government to perform its duty of distributing largesse widely rather than, for example, in terms of its ability to mobilise the population to achieve national development goals.

The dominance of political over social orgnisation

The final point about the structure of Sri Lankan politics is perhaps the most abstract. It is certainly the most difficult point to document satisfactorily, mainly because it relates to issues not raised by most other observers. Much of the evidence is oblique.

The best starting point is the contrast between traditional Sri Lankan and Indian socio-political organisation and the way this is evidenced in contemporary politics. Traditional India was characterised by a hiatus between (urban, state-level) 'politics' and (rural, local) 'society'. In the contemporary era representative politics, spreading from the political centre, has reached down to the grassroots through locally rooted economic and social institutions – castes, cooperatives, educational foundations and local self-government bodies (*panchayati raj*). These institutions constitute powerful political bases in their own right, and give those who control them substantial independence of particular political party links and organisations, especially now that the Congress Party has lost its assured dominance. Firmly ensconced in their local bases, politicians are able to shift support from one party to another, or to create new parties, with relative impunity. The traditional autonomy of local social organisation is still in evidence.

The Sri Lankan tradition by contrast is one of the integration of social and political organisation in the framework of a national state, and the corresponding absence of autonomous local social institutions. There are strong traces of tradition in the contemporary political system, which is characterised by the dominance of national, political over local, social organisation. Politics is shaped mainly by initiatives from the centre.

This general picture is muddied somewhat by the political role of the national elite. For in the early stages of the development of representative politics *individual* members of the elite did indeed have independent local political bases around their estates. They were able to secure election to the legislature independently of party organisation. This was, however, only a very restricted kind of local political autonomy, affecting only members of the elite in the electoral sphere. It has almost disappeared with the strengthening of the party system, and has not been matched by any increase in the ability of local-level organisations to influence the party system or act independently of it. The contemporary party system is very centralised. 'Tickets' to contest elections are allocated by the party leaderships in Colombo, and with only limited local consultation.[124]

Sri Lankan politics is generally characterised by a concentration of power in national-level – and therefore centrally located – institutions, including the elite, and by a corresponding weakness of local political and politico-administrative institutions.[125] Some of the more significant illustrations of this point are as follows:

(i) As a result of the welfare system, Sri Lanka has achieved an excellent record of enhancing the physical quality of life of its citizens. Infant and total mortality, malnutrition, and illiteracy all stand at levels which are, by the standards of international comparisons, very low for such a poor country. Yet this performance has been achieved almost entirely through state-provided services. The contribution of local-level initiatives, self-help, etc. is negligible.[126]

(ii) Local government bodies in Sri Lanka are, although long-established, notoriously weak and ineffective, and stand in large part outside the system of national-level party politics.[127]

(iii) The record among the Sinhalese of local-level voluntary, quasi-statutory and statutory representative organisations is poor.[128] Rural Development Societies, Cultivation Committees, and a range of other local organisations, although supported in various ways by the state, tend barely to function at all. The widely admired Sarvodaya social service organisation originates in a Colombo-level initiative, is highly centralised, and has few durable links at local level.[129] The only organisations which generally thrive at village level are those which serve specific and immediate needs, notably Death Donation Societies and Temple Societies. Ryan has argued that Sinhalese village social organisation is incompatible with sustained local formal organisation.[130] By contrast, the Sri Lanka Tamils have a very creditable record of local-level organisation and cooperation, and one which appears long-established. Among others, S. W. R. D. Bandaranaike drew attention to this contrast between the two peoples in a speech in the State Council in 1932.[131] The strength of local organisation among the Sri Lanka Tamils conforms to the more 'Indian' nature of their social organisation, and thus to the broad arguments set out in Chapter Eight.

(iv) So-called 'cooperative' organisations originated mainly on state initiatives and have become entirely state-controlled.[132]

(v) In the 1970s, Sri Lanka borrowed from India the idea of 'District Ministers', each responsible for the general progress of public programmes in one particular district.[133] In India, District Ministers are Cabinet Ministers (at the state level), are generally appointed to their home district, and become especially powerful spokesmen for the interests of that district. They are a mechanism for articulating, more directly, local-level demands. Although justified in Sri Lanka in terms of 'decentralisation', District Ministers have in fact served the opposite purpose. They are appointed from among the relatively junior MPs remaining once both Cabinet Ministers and Deputy Ministers have been selected, have sometimes been appointed to districts other than their home district, and, as Sri Lanka's foremost constitutional expert has recently argued – and indeed as others foresaw – they have become instruments for the assertion of greater central control over the public service at the district level.[134]

(vi) In conformity with the rootedness of the national elite in Colombo and its immediate hinterland, the more powerful MPs – those appointed to Cabinet posts – are especially likely to represent electorates in Colombo district and in the core region generally.[135]

(vii) Although a great deal of patronage is distributed by Sri Lankan politicians, there is no smoothly running system for the distribution of predictable and reliable flows of patronage down to the local level comparable, for example, to that in India. A great deal depends on the whims of the national leadership.[136]

The implications of this dominance of national political organisation for the argument of this book are fairly straightforward, and in many senses the obverse of the point about elite dominance discussed at the beginning of this chapter. As power is not strongly rooted in local social organisation, the interests of locally organised categories – e.g. smallholders – are less likely to be represented in national-level politics.

Conclusion

The Sri Lankan political system has dynamics of its own which are independent of the pressures arising from social and economic relationships within civil society. Insofar as the system does reflect phenomena arising in the socio-economic sphere, then these are not necessarily contemporary. To an important degree the political system reflects the socio-economic situation of an earlier period, the formative stage when representative politics and the party system were emerging.[137] At that time the capital–labour and nationalist issues were more politically salient than they have been since; it was possible to expand the welfare system rapidly for the benefit of the Sinhalese without running up against acute economic and financial constraints; and, prior to the expansion of the smallholder economy in the Dry Zone through colonisation, the plantation-related social and economic structures of the Wet Zone weighed more heavily than they do currently.

The political system which emerged in the core in the 1930s and 1940s, and which quickly became national (pan-Sinhalese) in scope, incorporates a number of features which interlock with one another and restrict the scope for the representation of minority, regionally concentrated, producer interests: the continuing dominance of a well-established elite with local bases in all areas except those where surplus-food producers predominate; the concentration of power in national-level – and therefore centrally located – political institutions; the location of political initiatives which have, or might have, significantly changed the political system, in the core region, where smallholder production is relatively unimportant; an established and comprehensive national system of party competition on a single left–right continuum; and a political agenda dominated by issues of access to (substantial) publicly provided resources.

11

Concluding remarks

The changing Sri Lankan polity

This book has been concerned with the continuities in Sri Lankan politics over a period of several decades. Nothing has happened in the few years since the arguments presented here began to crystallise to suggest that there has yet been any very marked change in the way in which the farming population relates to the political system. At the same time, it is becoming increasingly clear that the political system itself has undergone very substantial changes in recent years. It is likely that future observers will look back and see 1977 as an important turning-point. The new UNP government elected in 1977 introduced a policy of economic liberalisation and integration into the global capitalist system which has had far-reaching consequences for the economy and, less certainly, for the social structure. And the relationships between the Sri Lankan state and the Jaffna-based Sri Lanka Tamil population, which had been deteriorating slowly in earlier years, took a marked turn for the worse after the widespread attacks on Tamils in August 1977.

Since it has been argued that the way in which smallholders use politics is in large degree shaped by the national political system, the book would be incomplete without some reference to these recent changes in the system. It would be convenient if the nature and direction of changes in the polity were sufficiently clear for one to hazard a few predictions about how they are likely to affect the representation of smallholders' occupational interests. But this is not the case. As of early 1984 there are too many uncertainties over even the short term. The UNP's economic policy, while looking increasingly bedraggled, still cannot be said to have failed completely. The economy has continued to expand at a respectable rate during the depths of the global recession. Whether this continues depends on such unpredictable factors as the state of the world economy in the immediate future, the confidence of foreign investors in Sri Lanka, and, more immediately, the support which foreign governments and international financial institutions will provide to help Sri Lanka ride its problem of a massive external debt. It is not yet clear how far the latter two factors have been affected by the explosion of violence against the Tamil community in July 1983 and the continuing state of near war between the armed forces and the Tamil population of Jaffna. It is clear that further uncertainties have been built into the situation by the emergence of the government of India, heavily pressured by the people of Tamil Nadu state, as a major actor in internal Sri Lankan politics. A period of several decades, in which Sri Lanka was largely insulated from the direct political pressures of global and regional 'superpowers', seems to have come to an end. Unlike during most of the period covered by this book, in the foreseeable future Sri Lankan politics, like those of most other poor, small countries, will be very directly affected by external political influences.

Some of the information suggesting changes in Sri Lankan politics is too flimsy to be taken as evidence of clear trends. For example, what significance can one attribute to a recent newspaper report that government MPs had joined with members of the Opposition to complain in Parliament that the UNP's economic policy was adversely affecting farmers, and to request that imports of agricultural commodities be reduced?[1] This certainly looks like a departure from the previous situation, but it is not possible to say if it heralds the emergence of the kind of political movement whose previous absence has been treated so exhaustively in this volume. There is, however, more solid evidence of other changes in the Sri Lankan polity. These are dealt with below under two broad headings. Their potential significance for smallholder polities can at best be hinted at.

The resource base of the polity

Perhaps the most important factor to consider is the rapid exhaustion of the material bases for the welfarist policies which have been quantitatively and politically so important in Sri Lanka since the 1930s. This applies to both Crown lands and to the financial surpluses taxed from exports of plantation crops.

The disappearance of the 'bank' of Crown land has been gradual. Most of the land which currently remains formally in Crown hands is occupied by squatters. Once the current Mahaweli irrigation-cum-settlement programme is completed, little further land will be available for new public settlement schemes in the Dry Zone. Population is still growing rapidly, albeit less fast than in earlier decades, and the agricultural population is still increasing in absolute numbers. Pressures to find additional land for redistribution are likely to be felt long into the future. Since the larger estates are already in public hands, any attempt to meet this demand will involve either the subdivision of these publicly owned estates, where the existing labour force would anyway have a strong claim, or an assault on the remaining small private estates or the larger holdings in the non-estate sector. The latter in particular would probably generate a degree of intra-village political polarisation and conflict hitherto unseen in Sri Lanka.

Of more immediate significance is the rapidly diminishing scope for continuing to fund Sri Lanka's generous public welfare programmes by taxing tea, rubber and coconut exports. Three trends are at work here.

Firstly, the long-term downward trend in the real world market price for tea in particular, allied to the continuing mediocre production performance of Sri Lanka's estate sector, means that the taxable surplus is shrinking rapidly, especially in relation to growing public expenditure. Between 1978–9 and 1981–2 public revenue from export levies on tea, rubber and coconuts fell in cash terms in a period of high inflation, and declined from 32% to 17% of total government revenue.[2] The rise in world tea prices in late 1983 can alleviate the situation only temporarily. As most of the estate sector is in public hands the main result of any attempt to raise the rate of taxation would be an increase in the operating deficits of the public plantation corporations.

Secondly, it is for political reasons becoming increasingly difficult to continue the long-established policy of keeping plantation production costs low by exploiting the captive and semi-servile status of the plantation labour force. The Sinhalese proportion of the plantation labour force continues to increase, especially since the nationalisation of the estates. The trades union representing most of these Sinhalese employees, the Lanka Jathika Estate Workers Union, has become an important source of pressure for higher wages. In early 1984 it negotiated a big increase in the estate wage bill, when female wage rates were levelled up to equal those of males.[3] At the same time the Indian Tamil estate population, having largely been without citizenship, the vote or political power since 1948, has in recent years gained considerable political leverage. This is mainly due to the increasing separatism of the Sri Lanka Tamils, and the consequent need for the government to forestall an effective alliance between the two Tamil groups.[4] The CWC, the main trade union-cum-political party representing the Indian Tamils, entered into a tacit alliance with the UNP just before the 1977 election, and has been part of the governing coalition since the election. Those of its members who are Sri Lankan citizens, and therefore have the vote, supported the government very strongly in the two 1982 elections – the presidential poll and the referendum to extend the life of Parliament by six years.[5] The idea of giving citizenship to most or all of the stateless Indian Tamils has been an increasingly likely prospect.[6] In early 1984 the Supreme Council of the *Maha Sangha*, the apex organisation of the Buddhist priestly orders, became advocates of such a move, having become persuaded that this would remove a potential excuse for direct Indian political or military intervention. Soon after, the President declared that the necessary legislation was being prepared.[7] The CWC felt sufficiently confident of its power to call a successful nine-day national wages strike in May 1984, the first such flexing of estate labour muscle since the 1940s.

Thirdly, and least importantly, there are signs that the nationalisation of the estate sector has had the unwelcome side effect of providing smallholder tea producers with a stimulus and a mechanism for putting pressure on the government to guarantee them relatively high prices for their green leaf. For a large number of tea factories have come into public hands, and they purchase green leaf from a substantial number of smallholders. The implicit pressures are such that factory managements feel unable to reject or pay lower prices for poor quality leaf.[8]

The redistribution by the state of the financial surplus appropriated from capital and labour in the plantation sector has been central to the political economy of Sri Lanka since World War Two. This process is rapidly ceasing to underwrite the public economy, and this is likely to have major consequences for the polity. Apart from those in the estate sector, Sri Lankans have become used to a high level of public expenditure and a low level of taxation. Despite the 'free market' interpretation which it gives its economic policy, the UNP government has vastly increased public expenditure. Cuts in food subsidies have been largely offset by a very large public housing programme. Caught between continuing demands for high public expenditure and the erosion of the government's revenue base, the Minister of Finance warned Sri Lankans in mid-1983 that they would in future be obliged to pay much more in taxes.[9]

The pattern of political competition

It was argued in Chapter Ten that the absence of any distinct 'farmer interest' is related to the long-established pattern of relatively clear left–right party competition. Since 1977 the future stability of this pattern has become more questionable. There are several dimensions to this, and the causal connections between them are not generally clear.

In the first place, J. R. Jayawardena's efforts to reorganise and revitalise the UNP after he became party leader in 1973 helped to bring into the UNP fold many low-caste voters who had previously been relatively inactive participants in politics and/or supporters of the SLFP.[10] Having very successfully and ostentatiously freed the UNP of the influence of the Senanayake family, who had dominated it since its creation, Jayawardena was able to use the charge of 'family-bandyism' against the SLFP very effectively at the 1977 election. For the SLFP remained, as it had been since the early 1960s, dominated by mainly Kandyan notables connected closely by kinship to Mrs Bandaranaike.

The failure of the SLFP to reform itself in the same way as the UNP seems partly to explain why the party has been subjected to continuing factional conflict and overt divisions from 1977 until the present day. This extended to the failure of the bulk of the party leadership to support, verbally or organisationally, its official candidate for the Presidency in 1982, the late Hector Kobbekaduwa. (Mrs Bandaranaike was ineligible to stand due to the loss of her civic rights.)

The fragmentation and electoral failures of the SLFP since 1977 are probably also due to the loss of the effective support of the Marxist parties, who had previously provided ideological coherence and guidance, and organisational muscle.[11] The LSSP in particular has almost disappeared as an electoral force.[12] It has been replaced by the JVP, reconstituted in a 'parliamentary' form from elements of the 'old' JVP which led the 1971 Insurgency. Mainly because it was the United Front government formed by the SLFP, the LSSP and the Communist Party which presided over the repression which followed the failure of the Insurgency, the JVP is hostile to both the SLFP and the 'old' Marxist parties. It has not established close working relationships with any of the various smaller Marxist parties or groups, and is especially opposed to any cooperation with the SLFP.

The demise of the working relationship between the SLFP and the Low Country-based Marxists is in turn probably related, both as cause and effect, to the decline in the political influence of organised labour. Since 1977 organised labour has been in part brought under the wing of UNP-led unions, and attempts by other unions to assert their power have been crushed.[13] Since 1977 the salaries of many groups of public-sector employees, notably schoolteachers, have fallen considerably relative to other groups.[14] With the exception of the plantation sector, organised labour appears to have lost, at least temporarily, the political power it once enjoyed. If the decline in the power of organised labour should continue, then the chances that the left–right party alignment will persist are correspondingly diminished.

These changes in the pattern of party competition have occurred in the context of two broader changes in the framework of political decision-making. One is the increasing intrusion of military issues into politics as a result of the urgency of the 'Tamil question'. Senior members of the armed forces and the police are increasingly involved directly in political issues, while leading members of the government are assuming military roles. To this extent the sphere of party politics is becoming less significant. The other change is the new 1978 so-called 'Gaullist' constitution.[15] Among other things, this created a directly elected Executive Presidency, introduced proportional representation at district level for future parliamentary elections, and established a set of procedures which, at least in principle, enable party leaderships to exercise tight control over their MPs.

How far these constitutional changes have in the past, or will in the future, affect party competition and politics more broadly is not clear. The objectives of the new constitution have not been achieved. Although a number of UNP MPs have lost their seats at the behest of the party leadership in response to complaints about corruption or because they failed to follow the party line on the Sinhala–Tamil conflict, neither J. R. Jayawardena nor the SLFP leadership, itself divided, has established firm control over their parties. Indeed it seems that the attacks on Tamils in July 1983 were to some degree instigated and organised by senior UNP personnel.

Despite its centralising provisions, the new constitution could become the framework within which politics becomes more regionalised. For the system of proportional representation on a district basis means that any locally based political group with support only in one or two districts has some incentive to set up in business on its own – provided it can wait a few years to be recognised as a political party.[16] In the June 1981 elections to the newly created District Development Councils a group of SLFP politicians in Polonnaruwa district defied the national party decision not to contest and stood as independent candidates.[17] This is perhaps an illustration of how regionally based groups, such as Dry Zone surplus-food producers, might begin to organise independently of the existing national political parties.

The state and peasant politics

From the uncertainties of current Sri Lankan politics one can turn in conclusion to firmer ground: to the relationship of the analysis presented here to the literature on peasant political action. The interpretation of Sri Lankan history offered here is essentially catholic in tone, and represents particularistic rather than nomothetic social science: it is an attempt to understand the peculiar features of the Sri Lankan case rather than to develop or test general explanatory models of farmers' political action. Yet the interpretation necessarily reflects the adoption of a particular broad theoretical stance, and thus the implicit rejection of certain alternatives. The result hopefully justifies the position adopted, and thus has implications for the way in which social scientists attempt to understand the political action of small farming populations in countries other than Sri Lanka.

In summary, the distinctive feature of the present analysis is the emphasis placed on the role of politics, the polity or the state, in addition to socio-economic relations within civil society, in shaping the evolution of the political action of groups within civil society. This is an emphasis which is in fact appearing increasingly frequently in recent social science, and is not confined to students of peasant politics. It is an aspect of a broader reaction against a tendency, broadly inspired by a simplistic version of Marxism,[18] to reduce the analysis of politics to the study of the conflicts generated by relations of production within society. The similarities between the present book and this broader current of scholarly reformism can be clarified by looking at the relationship of the present analysis to the literature on peasant politics generated over the past two or three decades.

In the 1950s and 1960s there emerged within the rapidly expanding Western social science establishment a corpus of researchers with considerable first-hand experience of the social structures of poor agrarian societies. While always engaged in debate among themselves, these scholars were united by a general sympathy with the rural poor whom they studied, a theoretical perspective attuned to the virtual rediscovery in the 1960s of Marxism as a scientific paradigm, and a certain fascination and sympathy with the historical and contemporary peasant revolutions in France, Russia, Mexico, China, Algeria, Vietnam, Angola and Mozambique.[19] These scholars related sufficiently closely to one another and established a sufficiently distinctive institutional base to justify the label of the 'peasant studies school'.[20]

Their analysis of peasant politics was loosely characterised by three unifying intellectual perspectives. One was the assumption, or working hypothesis, that there were sufficient commonalities in the pattern of relationships between peasantries and superior social strata (landlords, merchants, the state bureaucracy, the military) to make at least plausible the search for generic patterns of peasant political action across time and space.[21] The second was that peasants were so subordinated to these superior social strata that in normal (non-insurrectionary) situations they were virtually powerless, almost regardless of the formal character of the political system. It was argued, most memorably by Barrington Moore,[22] that, even when on the winning side in social revolutions, peasants were so little able to frame and enforce public policies to suit their interests that they were likely, as a class, to be among the victims of programmes of economic modernisation pursued by post-revolutionary regimes. The third perspective, implicit in the two above, was a broad adherence to the mainstream Marxian approach to the explanation of politics: that politics was largely a reflection of conflicts among socio-economic groups or classes determined by their relationships in the economic sphere, and therefore that politics was to be explained primarily by examining the structure of civil society and the interests and conflicts which that generated.

There are certain affinities between the 'peasant studies' paradigm and the argument of this book. At the substantive level there is convergence in viewing the physical dispersal of peasantries as an important obstacle to effective autonomous political mobilisation. There is also apparent convergence in the focus on the political weakness of peasantries. But this convergence is apparent rather than real. For within the 'peasant studies' paradigm the political weakness of peasantries is seen as more axiomatic than problematic. In the Sri Lankan case this weakness is not only taken as analytically problematic but is also substantively far from complete. The Sri Lankan peasantry has not been subject to naked exploitation through state action. The state has in large part fulfilled its claim to be the guardian of the peasant interest. The puzzle to be resolved is that the peasantry has permitted the state to define where that interest lies. The resolution offered for that puzzle involves two major divergencies from the 'peasant studies' paradigm.

There is, firstly, a difference of approach to the question of the generic nature of peasant political action. The 'peasant studies' paradigm seeks generic patterns. This book, by contrast, focuses explicitly on the differences in the patterns of peasant political action between Sri Lanka and other Asian countries, especially India and Malaysia. It is argued in Chapter Eight that there is a marked contrast between Sri Lanka and India in the traditional relationship between peasant society and the state, and that this helps explain differences between the two countries in the degree to which, in the era of competitive electoral politics, farmers have emerged as a politically self-aware interest group. While the 'peasant studies' hypothesis that there are generic patterns of peasant political action has not been directly tested here, the comparison between Sri Lanka and India implies that any similarities may be narrow in scope. Particular historical features of individual societies, even societies which in the broad global context are relatively similar, play a major role.

Secondly, and more importantly, there is a major difference of emphasis, in the factors which are held to explain peasant political action, between this book on the one hand and, on the other hand, the 'peasant studies' paradigm and the mainstream Marxian tradition from which it draws inspiration. This book does not, of course, ignore the consequences for the pattern of smallholder political mobilisation of socio-economic relationships essentially located in civil society rather than in state–society relationships. They constitute much of the explanation of our puzzle. But the explanation at the same time places equal emphasis on variables located essentially at the level of the national polity or state: the influence of long-established programmes which redistribute public resources, in shaping the way in which farmers conceive of and organise for politics; the 'failure' of public policy to stimulate smallholder occupational solidarity through taxation, through initiatives which appear to lay new burdens on the farming population, or by violating expectations about the beneficent role of the state; and the way in which smallholder voters have been obliged and encouraged, partly through successive radical initiatives on the part of members of the political elite, to fit into an established pattern of party competition which is oriented to the historical circumstances and political conflicts of the urban and quasi-urban Low Country region.

This insistence that politics cannot be viewed solely or even mainly as an expression of the conflicts arising within civil society, and that the sphere of politics plays a role in its own reproduction, is not new to political science or even to the study of the politics of South Asian peasantries. A few quotations from Kothari's study of the Indian political system illustrate this:

The transformation taking place in India is largely a political-bureaucratic transformation. India seems to us to be the clearest refutation of the reductionist viewpoint which takes politics and government as phenomena whose explanation must properly be sought in social and economic forces.

it will not do to look at political institutions as some kind of superstructure that presides over more basic relationships in society and economy, or look at elites as simple recipients of inputs from society to which they respond in the form of various governmental outputs. Instead the whole process starts here through the establishment of a constitutional and political superstructure which then, through the actions of elites, penetrates into society at various levels and, by stages, leads to responses from below in the form of new coalitional structures.[23]

Weiner, writing even earlier, argues along the same lines that the 'most important elements at work in changing India's mass political culture are the vast amounts of directives and regulations emanating from the state and central governments'.[24]

That relatively conventional political scientists like Kothari and Weiner should emphasise the state-level determinants of mass political action, while 'peasant studies' theorists should emphasise societal determinants, appears to reflect the fact that the latter came to study peasant politics 'from below': through contact and/or empathy with the peasant masses rather than through national-level political and bureaucratic institutions. The 'peasant studies' paradigm has, however, not stood still. The most notable recent contribution to the study of the role of peasantries in social revolution, Theda Skocpol's *States and Social Revolutions*,[25] represents an attempt to integrate both perspectives. Traversing much the same terrain as Barrington Moore's earlier monumental work, and explicitly shaped in a mixture of sympathetic response and reaction to it,[26] Skocpol begins by criticising earlier theories of revolution partly on the grounds that they focus excessively on relationships within society and pay too little attention to the role of state structures.[27] This deficiency is remedied by emphasising the importance of variation in state-related phenomena in explaining the different trajectories and outcomes of the peasant involvement in the French, Russian and Chinese social revolutions. The opportunities which peasants have to revolt are shaped by both the extent to which local peasant social organisation is autonomous of state administrative structures and by the degree to which state structures themselves broke down due to the combination of internally and externally generated political crises.

Skocpol's much acclaimed work implicitly illustrates, much more effectively than the present book, the limitations of the society-centred analysis of politics common to the 'peasant studies' paradigm and to conventional Marxism more broadly. She also establishes a much stronger claim to the inclusion of the term 'state' in the title of her book by examining the subject both theoretically and practically. I cannot claim to have even begun to present a coherent account of the Sri Lankan state, either theoretically or descriptively. 'State' appears in the title to signal the adoption of a particular perspective in the analysis of the determinants of mass political action.

There are very justifiable qualms about using the concept of 'the state', which is so popular in contemporary social science but the focus of so much basic conceptual disagreement and uncertainty. Its popularity cannot, however, be attributed to mere fashion. It is, at least in my view, symptomatic of an increasing tendency among social scientists reared in an academic environment much influenced by Marxism, to question whether the prime focus on relationships within society and the economy provides an adequate basis from which to explain politics. From a variety of particular perspectives and concerns many social scientists reared in a Marxian environment are beginning to realise that the sphere of politics and public policy has a certain autonomy; that politics cannot be reduced to a concentrated expression of class forces; and that polity on the one hand and society and the economy on the other interact mutually.[28] Apart from any contribution it may make to our understanding of Sri Lanka, this book is conceived as a part of this same current and is intended to help re-establish the validity of explaining politics by reference to politics itself.

APPENDIX 1

Results of general elections, 1947–77: percentage of parliamentary seats won

	1947	1952	1956	1960 (March)	1960 (July)	1965	1970	1977
UNP	44★	57★	8	33★	20	44★	11	83
LSSP	11	9	15	7	8	7	13★	—
Communist Party	3	4^a	3	2	3	3	4★	—
Other Marxist parties	5^b	—	—	8^c	3^c	1^c	—	—
SLFP	n.a.	9	54^d★	30	50★	27	60★	5
Federal Party	n.a.	2	10	10	11	9★	9 ⎫	10^e
Tamil Congress	7	4	1	1	1	2	2 ⎭	
Other parties	7^f	1^g	—	4^h	1^i	3^j	—	1^k★
Independents + minor parties	22	13	8	5	5	4	1	1
Total	100	100	100	100	100	100	100	100

★ Parties forming the government immediately after the election.
^{a} The Communist Party was in an electoral alliance with the VLSSP (Viplavakari Lanka Sama Samaj Party) of Philip Gunawardena.
^{b} Bolshevik-Leninist Party.
^{c} MEP (Philip Gunawardena) and People's Liberation Front.
^{d} Includes a few MPs from the VLSSP and the Language Front, who joined with the SLFP in the MEP electoral and governmental coalition.
^{e} Tamil United Liberation Front.
^{f} Ceylon Indian Congress and Labour Party.
^{g} Labour Party.
^{h} Three short-lived parties.
^{i} Ceylon Democratic Party.
^{j} Sri Lanka Freedom Socialist Party and Ceylon Democratic Party.
^{k} Ceylon Workers Congress.
Source: Lake House, 1977: 211–18.

APPENDIX 2

The myth of the plantation impact on the Sinhalese village: two accounts

The term myth is used here, as in the text, *not* as an indication that the account is necessarily false, but that it is accepted and transmitted without regard for, or enquiry into, its veracity.

Both of the accounts reproduced here have been influential and widely quoted. The significance of the first, the *Report of the Kandyan Peasantry Commission (1951)*, has been discussed in Chapter Four. The book by Sarkar and Thambaiyah, entitled *The Disintegrating Village*, appeared a few years later in 1957, and was the outcome of a rural survey in the Kandyan areas.

There are differences of interpretation and emphasis between the two accounts. These are of a kind one might expect to find between an official report and the work of independent social scientists. The former places more emphasis on the alleged harmony and unity of pre-colonial social and economic life, on the integrating cultural role of Buddhism in this life, and in the loss of 'community' as a socio-cultural phenomenon. The latter is more willing to trace contemporary poverty to exploitation and inequality *within* village society. The commonalities between the two accounts are, however, striking, and virtually complete when they are assessing the material, cultural and socio-economic impact of plantation development/commercialisation.

All emphases are my additions.

The Report of the Kandyan Peasantry Commission

(Kandyan Peasantry Commission 1951: 10–13)

Historical background

38. It is difficult to assess the social conditions of the peasantry in the two Provinces and the present social problems without some idea of the historical background of the rural society as it existed in ancient times. The picture we formed was somewhat as follows:

39. The rural population of the two Provinces, as elsewhere in the Island, resided in villages in which the family lived as a unit. The main occupation of the elder members of the household was agriculture and ownership of land was the main qualification to social status. The families were dependent for their livelihood on their paddy fields, smallholdings and chenas. With agriculture as the base, there were other occupations all calculated to supply the needs of a

243

peasant economy. The basic principle of this economy was to achieve *self-sufficiency* in food and employment. *Its nucleus was the paddy field* which supplied the main article of diet. Gardens and chenas produced additional supplies of food, and the village forests the building material for the village home. Sufficient employment was found in agricultural operations and subsidiary pursuits and it could be said that for an agricultural people with a primitive *peasant* economy there was a *sufficiency of food and employment*.

40. The status of a family in the village society depended on its occupation. As land was the principal asset and agriculture the main occupation, that section of the village society that owned land and pursued agriculture laid claim to the higher social status. Other sections that followed other occupations were regarded as holding places which varied in position according to traditionally accepted notions of their importance: hence in Ceylon, as in many other countries, there prevailed and was recognised a social system based on what is termed 'the caste system'. Under conditions which then existed, this system, whatever the defects may have been, played an important part. Distinctions based on services and functions, however, cannot now exist, as services and functions are not now assigned to particular sections of the people or to communities. Modern conditions leave little or no place for these distinctions. In the areas which came under our investigation, they are not as defined as they appear to have been in ancient times and are fast disappearing, but inasmuch as they still exist, they cannot be ignored in a consideration of relevant problems.

41. Just as families that comprised the *village society* were knit together by a common language and religion, *common cultural traditions* and agricultural and other pursuits, so also each family was united by a high sense of *family obligation*. The family income was used not merely for the support of the household, but also to assist dependants. The aged and the young were all *equally assisted* and so also relations. State Aid in the sense in which it is now understood was not available and, indeed, was unnecessary in a society in which every member of the family was entitled to maintenance from the *joint family property*. Ties of this nature are also fast disappearing due mainly to economic reasons and it is now recognised that it is the function of the state to look after the poor, the sick and the destitute.

42. The recreations and amusements of the village population sprang primarily from and were centred round agriculture and religious institutions. The *peasant* led a strenuous outdoor life and therefore did not need vigorous physical exercise. In the village tradition there was no communal playground and no sport of any intensive nature. Their place was taken by games, usually associated with agricultural operations and indulged in mostly by younger men. *Country dancing* and '*Kandyan dancing*' were popular in both Provinces and music appears to have played a prominent part in the life of the village. The New Year, Wesak and Poson festivals also provided occasions for entertainment. The great majority of the *peasant* population professed the *Buddhist religion* and often sought relaxation in the form of pilgrimages to distant Buddhist shrines. Other avenues of recreation were found in peraheras and festivals organised on public or religious occasions.

Present conditions

43. With the advent of British rule and the impact of a plantation economy based on the exploitation of cultivable land for commercial purposes, there was a *disruption* of the old *peasant* economy. Most of the forests, chenas and uncultivated land passed into the ownership of the Crown. The villages were neglected and *new land* was *unavailable* for village expansion. *Village Councils*, which under the leadership of the more progressive members, took all decisions on behalf of the village community, fell into *disuse* and in their place were appointed *state officers* in the nature of chief and minor headmen under the control of Government Agents.

44. The village society itself could not withstand these new forces and was *broken up*. The importation of *Indian labour* took away the opportunity for subsidiary forms of employment; the high lands and paddy fields became insufficient with the growth of population. Private *capitalists* began to buy up all available land and the villagers were unable to protect even their rights to the property which they owned. The prospect of the Crown claiming jungle and chena prompted numerous sales of land to *speculators*. The consequence was that the *old unity of village life began to disappear* and there was no new system which took its place. These factors have mainly contributed to create the present problems, some of which are discussed in the paragraphs that follow.

45. The *village community*, with its communalities and obligations, has in a great measure *disappeared* and so also the old conceptions of community effort. Family ties and obligations do not now have the same attraction. Whatever may be the advantages of a different social system, the elimination of the old system has not yet been followed by the substitution of a new one. The state does not provide the social services which in olden times the village community provided for itself. There exists therefore an obvious gap between community action and state aid and the needs of the rural population are not adequately met by either effort.

46. The pressure on land, aggravated by the growth of population, has placed an intolerable burden on the village household. There are more mouths to feed, but no land to cultivate and no housing accommodation. Apart from the low level of living standards and insanitary houses, which we have dealt with elsewhere and which must necessarily reflect adversely on *moral and social standards*, the want of food and employment has led the village population to seek any possible method of escape, however unsatisfactory. One such is *child marriage*; girls of the age of ten to fourteen are given in marriage to men of various ages in order to lessen the burden on the family household. Another is the giving out of children for domestic service, which often is tantamount to *child slavery*. It is a common incident in the lives of the poorer class of *peasant* to give away little children to anyone who wants them, for whatever they can get, and thereafter the whereabouts of the child or the treatment it meets with cannot be ascertained. Instances have not been wanting of *extreme cruelty*.

47. The prevalence of the caste system has led to considerable abuse and hardship in the less educated and non-progressive areas. Persons who are

considered to be of lower social status have less opportunities of employment and sometimes of education and certain customs still exist which subject them to humiliation. Rajakariya service in its present form may be cited as an instance. As we have said, these distinctions are disappearing. There are however instances where they can lead to abuse. The Rodiya (sweeper), and Kinnaraya (mat weaver) communities are examples of backward communities which require special attention and assistance. In other cases, the equality or non-equality of treatment would ordinarily depend on the educational and social standard of the locality in which different communities exist and the progress which their members have made in regard to their own advancement.
48. A matter to which reference was made and which we feel requires careful investigation is the selection of allottees in the colonies established under major irrigation schemes. The schemes are intended to release the pressure of population in rural areas and the colonists are intended to be peasants. The impression we gathered was that there is a grave danger of *persons of non-peasant character* and of *doubtful antecedents* getting into colonisation areas either as peasants or as employees with the object of exploiting the colonists. The camp-followers of this type of adventurer are *gambling, drink and immorality*. They are not incapable of *intimidating peasants* living away from their own villages and in strange surroundings and inducing them to adopt *evil habits*. They *demoralise peasant society. The supervision in the colonies should be of a stringent character*.
49. In certain areas stress was laid on the *laxity of the administration of the Kandyan Divorce Laws*. Kandyans, who have contracted a marriage according to the Kandyan Law, can obtain a divorce by mutual consent. The spouses need only appear before a provincial registrar and express a desire to divorce each other. It has been suggested that the sanction of the officer authorised to grant the divorce should not be lightly given and should be preceded by some investigation and that a time limit should be fixed for reconciliation. The present system leaves room to inflict hardship on a wife who is lightly divorced and may even have to support the children and the execution of maintenance orders is beset with difficulties.

The disintegrating village

(Sarkar and Thambaiyah, 1957: xi–xii)

The basis of rural economy in ancient Ceylon was paddy cultivation. The social beliefs, customs and institutions were closely integrated with the system of paddy production.

A *well-integrated and self-sufficient* social and economic system, well adapted to certain ecological factors, evolved.

The *invasion of this system by the plantations* struck a *damaging blow* to its stability; for, it *destroyed the balance* that existed between high land cultivation, paddy production and *chena* cultivation, and other uses of forest land. The story of the conversion of the forests into plantations, a process from which the village high land often did not escape, is well-known and need not be retold here. What we want to remind the reader of is that the destruction of the forests not only affected the supply of water for the paddy fields, but also reduced the fertility of the soil by the double process of soil erosion and sedimentation and the reduction of the supply of vegetable and organic manure. Furthermore a number of irrigation channels having their source in forests were lost to the villagers when they became estate property.

The long-run effect of the opening of the plantations on the village was equally *disruptive*. The accompaniments of plantation economy were better roads, English education, a money economy and a modern form of government which provided health services to the people. The death rate was reduced and the population in the rural areas increased. The colonial system did not provide much scope for the expansion of employment. In ancient times, if the population increased, forests and waste lands were cleared and new paddy lands were created from the valleys and the slopes of the hills. This avenue for relieving population pressure on the soil was no longer existent.

The situation was made worse by the destruction of cottage and rural industries which followed the importation of cheap foreign goods.

Thus while an increasing number of mouths demanded sustenance from the same acre of land, the opening up of roads, the growth of trade and the introduction of money provided the more fortunately placed members of the village community with an opportunity to *exploit* the less fortunate and to add to their own property and wealth. They did this by advancing loans at an exorbitant rate of interest, by taking mortgages on land, by buying crops in advance and by supplying requirements at unfair prices. The process worked remorselessly and within a generation or two produced a large *landless or semi-landless* class in the rural areas. This sequence was accelerated by the laws of inheritance by which property was sub-divided among heirs, thus leading to acute fragmentation of land. Once a landless under-employed class was created, a competition amongst them for land and jobs grew more acute, and it became possible for the land-owning and the well-to-do persons in the village to exploit their cheap labour more effectively, and to extort higher rent and interest by giving land on a share-cropping basis, by buying and selling on credit and by advancing money on mortgaged land.

The picture revealed by our survey is that of a vast mass of landless under-employed labourers with no definite means of livelihood, continually growing in number not only through natural increase but also through *victimisation and exploitation by the middle classes, merchants and estate owners*. The competitive laissez-faire economy as it operates in the rural areas of Kandy today does not seem to achieve the best results for the community but, on the contrary, continually *degenerates* it, converting it into a machine that extracts more and more of rentier income than making greater and greater additions to output.

NOTES

1   Puzzles and agendas

1. Meyer, 1982: 244. My translation and emphasis.
2. Lipton, 1977.
3. Westergaard, 1974: 29.
4. For a critique of this perspective, see Nordlinger, 1981: Chapter 1.

2   Methods, scope and elaborations

1. Much of what might be written here under the heading 'method' would constitute *post hoc* rationalisation of procedures, practices and events which originated in chance, in outcomes very different from expectations, and in speculative or unfocused interests and curiosity. For both the problematic of this work and the resolution offered emerged only slowly and discontinuously in the course of a long period of doing research in and on Sri Lanka on a number of topics connected with rural development policy. As a description of the intellectual processes through which the present argument emerged, the term 'iterative' appears as something of an understatement. They include research, both detailed and cursory, in a number of different rural areas of Sri Lanka; interaction, formal and informal, with politicians, public servants and the Anglophonic Colombo middle-class; study of the relatively copious historical and contemporary social science literature on Sri Lanka; some primary research into recent political history; many hours spent applying a calculator to the relatively ample and reliable statistics on the Sri Lankan rural economy; discussion and cooperation with fellow social scientists, including attempts to present aspects of the present argument; and a comparative perspective provided by earlier research on India. Given this methodological opportunism it would not be useful to offer more than a few particular comments on the sources of data used.

This book owes more than is evident at first sight to conventional sociological 'fieldwork', i.e. research undertaken among rural people. Its contribution is veiled in two ways. Firstly, it was especially important in drawing my attention to the paucity of cultivator demands, while secondary macro-level and historical materials have been relatively more significant in explaining this phenomenon and thus appear more prominent here. Secondly, most of the detailed results of this fieldwork have already been published. The conclusions are summarised where appropriate and the reference given; they are not, however, repeated in detail.

Just as important as the formal fieldwork conducted in the village arena has been my informal fieldwork, i.e. the sum of the social interaction and observation arising from over two years' residence and eight years of intermittent visits and contacts. This informal fieldwork was especially important in turning my attention to what became a prominent aspect of this work: the study of discourse and ideology, i.e. the ways in which Sri Lankans represent and understand their world. It is a matter of regret that shortage of time and my incomplete grasp of Sinhala have limited the scope of these investigations, and led to more reliance than is desirable on written English language sources. The issue is, however, important and little touched by other scholars, except Roberts (especially 1972, 1978, 1979a and 1979c) and Smith (1979). I therefore feel justified in pursuing a 'second-best' strategy.

I have benefited enormously from the relative depth and quality of literature on contemporary Sri Lanka. It has been possible to pursue a fairly narrow topic in detail and with only limited dependence on primary source materials because of the excellence of the secondary material.

Four sources of published information have been especially important. The first is an especially comprehensive, continuous and relatively reliable supply of official statistics. The second is the excellent work of a cluster of Sri Lankan contemporary historians, most of them at one time or another associated with Peradeniya University. (See especially de Silva, K. M. (ed.), 1973 and 1977; and Roberts (ed.), 1979.) The third, not totally separable from the second, comprises a number of books by both Sri Lankans and expatriates on recent politics, notably Jiggins, 1979; Jupp, 1978; Kearney, 1971 and 1973; Roberts (ed.), 1979; Wilson, 1979; Woodward, 1969; and Wriggins, 1960. Although often biased towards description and somewhat weak on theory, these books constituted an invaluable base for the present work. The fourth source comprises a disparate but considerable volume of published work relating to sociological, economic and social anthropological investigations into the Sinhalese peasantry. This work in general merits more appreciation than criticism, and much of it deservedly has a reputation beyond the circles of scholars interested in Sri Lanka (notably, Leach, 1961; Obeyesekere, 1967; and Yalman, 1967). It is, however, inconvenient and probably inefficient that so much social science research should have been conducted on and in villages, especially Sinhalese villages, while equally interesting and pressing questions relating to other levels and sectors of society remain uninvestigated. (A recent study by Jayanntha (1983) exemplifies brilliantly the advantages of studying local politics at the level of the electorate rather than at the village level.)

2. The debate is neatly and clearly summarised in Lukes, 1974. See also Connolly, 1974: Chapter 3.
3. E.g. Lukes, 1974; and Connolly, 1974.
4. Lukes, 1974: Chapter 8. See also Newby *et al.*, 1978: 243–4.

5. The fact that in the main statistical series 'estates' are defined purely by acreage rather than crop or organisation makes the demonstration of this point slightly complicated. The following data, however, serve. In the 1962 Census of Agriculture, 'estates' were defined as holdings of fifty acres or more. Of all holdings of paddy, the main smallholder and food crop, 0.4% were of more than fifty acres, and 91% were of less than five acres (*Census of Agriculture 1962, Volume 3*: Table 2). Looking at the same issue from another perspective, one finds that 91% of the cropped area of estates (i.e. holdings of fifty or more acres) was under 'plantation crops' – tea, rubber, coconut, cinnamon and cacao – 2% under grass, and only 4% under paddy (*Census of Agriculture 1962, Volume 2*: Table 2a).

6. *Census of Population 1971, Volume 2, Part 1*: Table 10.

7. *Ibid*: Table 9.

8. These points are made in Jupp, 1978: Chapter 5.

9. This phenomenon is clearly illustrated in Indian historiography, within which there has recently arisen an explicitly revisionist school challenging some of the most cherished canons of nationalist ideology and history, e.g. the belief that the Raj was uniquely a tool for *British* rule, capable of powerfully reshaping the prostrate and oppressed Indian society, rather than a weak facade crucially dependent on the willing and self-interested cooperation of Indians; and the unquestioned assumption that those politicians later labelled 'nationalists' were motivated above all by the desire for independence rather than by more prosaic goals. For a brief statement of the 'revisionist manifesto', see Seal, 1973. One of the most impressive examples of this revisionism at work is Washbrook, 1977. A sense of the flavour of the revisionist case is provided by the following quotation:

> I would question the utility of the commonly-used metaphor of a British impact on India, with its implications of a dynamic force – expansive Europe – hitting a static object – Indian society. I believe that we are much better able to understand the effects of the British intrusion if we take account of the fact that the pattern of relationships among Indian elites was subject to constant change in periods before the European arrival, as much as in the period of European dominance. (Broomfield, 1968: 553)

10. This latter point is made by Roberts, 1979a: 10.

11. The current of revisionism which Roberts (1979a: 1) detects in Sri Lankan historiography is far less radical than the Indian product referred to above.

12. *Ibid*: 1.

13. *Ibid*: 17 and *passim*.

14. *Ibid*: 22.

15. For a scholarly statement see Jayawardena, 1972: xii–xiv; and for a programmatic statement see the 1977 general election manifesto of the (mainly LSSP and Communist Party) United Left Front (Lake House, 1977: 302–11).

16. Roberts, 1979a: 9–11.

17. Jayawardena, 1972: 264–9.
18. Lake House, 1977: 268.
19. The phrase is widely used by those sympathetic to the 'Bandaranaike policies'.
20. On Bandaranaike's intentions, see Jupp, 1978: 272. The SLFP's pride in the new constitution is indicated by their 1977 general election manifesto, in which it receives first place in the list of the achievements of their seven-year rule (Lake House, 1977: 265).
21. Details of two appeals to the British Privy Council in the 1960s are given in Wilson, 1980: 98–9. The mixture of pride felt by the LSSP leadership over the new constitution, and disappointment at the lack of popular appreciation, is revealed in the following quotation from the party's official post-mortem on its United Front experience:

> Of the greatest significance was the New Constitution of the Republic of Sri Lanka. However, it should be realised that the remnants of the forms of imperialism that the Constitution sought to abolish were not felt mass issues. Besides, laws are generally understood more in the concrete results of implementation than in the abstract form of their enactment.
>
> That a fundamental objective of the government under the New Constitution is the social ownership of the means of production, the means of distribution and the means of exchange is important, but this is not widely known. For these reasons the New Constitution did not generate the exhilaration of national liberation. Nevertheless, the realisation that domination by British imperialism is now over and even more the fact that constitutionally the source of parliamentary power is the people have served to heighten the consciousness of the progressive intelligentsia (Lanka Sama Samaj Party, 1978: 21).

22. Perhaps the main qualifications to this claim, and a point I owe to Michael Roberts, is that Independence was significant in that it led to the immediate disenfranchisement of the Indian Tamil population and the consequent electoral impotence of an important ally of the Marxist parties. This helped free the Marxists to adapt themselves to 'Sinhalese chauvinism'.
23. De Silva, K. M.: 1973b.
24. Wilson, 1979: 136–7; Lake House, 1977: 242–6; Jupp, 1978: 74; de Silva, K. M., 1973b: 507–9; Woodward, 1969: 62; Wriggins, 1960: 124–138.
25. See the statistics on cultivated area in Snodgrass, 1966: 49.
26. *Census of Population 1971, General Report*: 80.
27. Meyer, 1978: 1.
28. Wickremeratne, 1973c: *passim* and 488.
29. *Census of Population 1971, Volume 2, Part 1*: Table 4. For discussion of the relative stability of the urban–rural population ratio, see Gunatilleke, 1973; and Abeysekera, 1980.
30. The figures relate to the industrial classification, and include the entire 'Agriculture, Forestry, Hunting and Fishing' sector, in which 'Agriculture and Animal Husbandry' predominates overwhelmingly, accounting

for example for 97% of the population of the sector in 1971. The data are from *Census of Ceylon 1953, Volume 4, Part 1*: Table 3; *Census of Population 1971, Volume 2, Part 2*: Table 9; and *Labour Force and Socio-Economic Survey, 1980/81, Preliminary Report*: 21.

31. The sources are as in note 30. The figures for 1971 are derived directly from the figures in the source. For 1953 there is no published simultaneous breakdown of the agricultural work force according to both crop and employment status. Since however (a) in 1971, 97% of the total work force engaged in the production of tea, rubber and coconuts did so as hired labourers, and (b) the relative importance of smallholder production of these crops increased after 1953 (see, for example, Snodgrass, 1966: 49), it seems reasonable to assume that in 1953 the total work force engaged in producing these crops could be considered practically equivalent to the hired work force.

32. *Census of Population 1971, Volume 2, Part 2*: Tables 9 and 10.

33. Agricultural censuses were conducted in 1962 and 1973. There are, however, several reasons for suspecting the latter to be relatively unreliable. The 1962 data are to be preferred, and have been used throughout this book where possible and appropriate.

34. The figures on the number of agricultural holdings were obtained from *Census of Agriculture 1962, Volume 1*: Table 1. It is assumed here, as at various other points below, that statistics on the number of *operators* can be taken as equivalent to the number of *operating households*. Holdings of more than fifty acres were defined as estates for the purposes of this census, and are included in the total. Since, however, they numbered only 0.5% of all holdings, their exclusion or inclusion does not affect the broad magnitudes. The population statistics used for estimation derive from the 1963 census (*Census of Population, Volume 2, Part 1*: Table 4). They were converted into numbers of households – not given in the census – by using the average household sizes enumerated in the 1969/70 Socio-Economic Survey (Department of Census and Statistics, 1974, *The Population of Sri Lanka*: 54). The total number of agricultural holdings equalled 64% of the total number of households in the Island, and 78% of rural households. If it is assumed that a small proportion of urban households operate agricultural holdings, the figures suggest that about 75% of rural households did so.

35. Exceptions were made if smaller holdings housed a minimum quantity of livestock (*Census of Agriculture 1962, Volume 1*: 25, 33).

36. *Ibid*: 33. There are two small doubts about the concepts used in these statistics. It is only implied in the way the questionnaire was set out, not firmly stated, that the reference is to household incomes and not the individual incomes of the land operators (*ibid*: 320). Similarly, it is only implied that the term 'agricultural income' relates both to income from own farming activities and income, if any, from hiring out labour to other cultivators (*ibid*: 51, 320). Note that the 1973 Census of Agriculture indicates very similar magnitudes (*Census of Agriculture 1973, General Report*: 14).

37. *Ibid*: 33.
38. The 53% figure is obtained from estimates, quoted in the text, that in 1962 75% of rural households operated holdings, and 29% of these obtained most of their income outside agriculture.
39. *Census of Population 1971, General Report*: 80, 83, 96.
40. Under the first 'republican constitution', in force between 1972 and 1978, Parliament was officially termed the National State Assembly, although its members continued to be addressed as MPs in almost all contexts. The established terminology, reinstated under the second 'republican constitution' of 1978, is used throughout this book.
41. Jupp, 1978: 190. The original intention of this measure, introduced by the nationalist leadership of what was to become the United National Party, was to weight the electoral system against the Marxist parties, which have their strongholds in the densely populated southwestern maritime areas and which, in the 1940s, constituted the main parliamentary and extra-parliamentary threat to UNP rule (Wilson, 1979: 195–200; Kearney, 1973: 133–4; Jupp, 1978: 190). This weightage has been diluted in the proportional representation system introduced under the 1978 constitution (see 'Proportional Representation System', *Ceylon News*, 4 December 1980).
42. Wilson, 1979: 195–200; Kearney, 1973: 135; Jupp, 1978: 190. This bias was eliminated in the 1978 constitution (see 'Proportional Representation System', *Ceylon News*, 4 December 1980). The disenfranchisement of the Indian Tamils was generally justified in nationalist terms, but an important motivation was their high level of political organisation and links with the Marxist left (Wriggins, 1960: 222–4). The UNP was certainly motivated to act by partisan electoral considerations and probably also by class interests, since it generally represented the Sri Lankan plantation capitalist class.
43. The figures are calculated from data contained in de Silva, G. P. S. H., 1979: 409–29; and Lake House, 1977: 436.
44. For information on political parties in the pre-Independence period, see de Silva, K. M., 1973b; Jupp, 1978: 1–6; and Woodward, 1969: Chapter 2. At the 1947 general election the UNP polled 40% of the votes, and the three main Marxist parties between them collected 21%. Two Tamil parties received 8%, and independents, always stronger among the Tamils and the Muslims than the Sinhalese (Jupp, 1978: 195), received 29% (Lake House, 1977: 218).
45. In 1952 the SLFP, contesting only forty-eight electorates, won 16% of the votes cast and 9% of the seats (Lake House, 1977: 217).
46. Jupp, 1978: Chapter 1. The only significant exceptions were the very short lived Parliament of March 1960 and that of 1965–70.
47. Jupp, 1978: Chapters 3, 5 and 7.
48. For example, in 1947 the total number of registered voters amounted to 91% of the number of persons aged twenty-one years or more, enumerated in the census of 1946 (Lake House, 1977: 219; and *Census of Ceylon 1946, Volume 1, Part 2*: Table 15). See also Jupp, 1978: 193.

Notes

49. Figures calculated from data given in de Silva, G. P. S. H., 1979: 91–107.
50. Lake House, 1977: 219.
51. Jupp, 1978: 189.
52. On the nature and consequences of the 1956 general election, see Jupp, 1978: 7–11, 63–7; Wilson, 1979: 125–9; Wriggins, 1960: Chapter 10; Woodward, 1969: Chapter 4; and Phadnis, 1976: 175–90.
53. In 1947 fewer than a quarter of all MPs were elected as independents, and only one succeeded in 1977 (Lake House, 1977: 211, 218). For information on the growth of the party system see Woodward, 1969, and, on its current strength, Jupp, 1978: Chapter 4. Data illustrating the importance of the emergence of the SLFP in the rapid shrinkage of votes for independent and minor party candidates are given in Woodward, 1969: 244.
54. Jupp, 1978: 94, 162.
55. *Ibid*: 94; and Kearney, 1971: especially Chapter 4.
56. Jupp, 1978: 162.
57. E.g. 'Although articulate and militant, the numerically smaller urban working class and middle class have much less political clout than the peasantry in general elections' (Abeysekera, 1980: 35).
58. Herring, 1972: 99–100.
59. On the structure of the colonial economy, see Snodgrass, 1966: especially Chapters 2–4.
60. Gavan and Chandrasekere, 1979: 26.
61. On the post-Independence economic and balance of payments situations, see Snodgrass, 1966: Chapters 5–8; Gunasekere, 1977; and Wickremeratne, 1977a.
62. The conceptual and terminological problems of talking of 'nationalism' in relation to Sinhalese and Sri Lanka Tamils are discussed by Roberts, 1979a.
63. For a general discussion of the various socio-cultural categories and the relationships between them, see Samaraweera, 1977a. There are no contemporary statistical series in which occupation is cross-classified by socio-cultural category. The general point about the trading/urban orientation of the minorities is, however, unquestioned. Statistics from the 1946 Census of Population illustrate the concentration of the minorities in Colombo city, the dominant urban node. For evidence on the low representation of Sinhalese, especially Kandyans, in professional occupations in the early part of this century, see Roberts, 1973a: Table 4.
64. The qualification about 'recent years' arises from the fact that, in the early 1980s, the government appeared to be making a serious attempt to accommodate many of the demands of the minorities. Some of the main elements were the relaxation of the extent of discrimination against Sri Lanka Tamils in admission to higher education; continuing negotiations about a degree of federal devolution for Tamil-speaking areas; and the establishment of Hindu and Muslim cultural departments to balance the fact that, since its establishment in 1958, the Department of Cultural Affairs has in fact operated as the Department of Sinhalese Buddhist

Culture. The communal violence of mid-1983 has extended the willingness of the government to concede some Tamil demands.
65. See Jupp, 1978: especially 347–55.
66. Moore, 1981d: Chapter 3.

3 Crown lands

1. Bansil (1971) fulfils the task for the period between Independence and 1970.
2. See in particular the work of Roberts (1973b and 1973c), on the nineteenth century, and for this century, Samaraweera (1973b, 1977b and 1981).
3. I have elsewhere helped draw attention to the social and economic significance of the local-level spatial differentiation associated with the process of the alienation of Crown lands to the rural poor (Moore and Perera, 1978; Moore *et al.*, 1979). See also Seneratne, 1970: 69–70.
4. Roberts, 1973b: 121–2; Ellman *et al.*, 1976: 16–17; de Silva, K. M., 1964. On previous and succeeding policy, see Roberts, 1970/2b.
5. Moore and Perera, 1978: 39.
6. Stenson, 1980: 14–15.
7. Moore, 1981d: Chapter 3.
8. *Administration Report of the Settlement Officer for 1975*: 15; and Ministry of Lands and Land Development, 1979: 5–6.
9. Peiris, 1981b: 16; and Roberts, 1973c: Appendix Table A.
10. ESCAP, 1975: 79.
11. de Silva, K. M., 1977a: xv.
12. The implementation of the restrictions on *chena* is discussed by Roberts, 1973b: 129–31; Leach, 1961: 61–4; and Samaraweera, 1973b: 448.
13. Gooneratne *et al.*, 1978: 6.
14. Roberts, 1970/2b: 16–18.
15. Land Commission, 1929: 12–14; Samaraweera, 1973b: 447; Roberts, 1973b: 125–6.
16. Roberts, 1973c: Appendix Table B.
17. The statistics do not distinguish between Sri Lankans and other non-Europeans, but the latter are reckoned to have been unimportant (Roberts, 1973c: 149).
18. Roberts, 1973c: Appendix Table A. Roberts (149) comments that: 'These statistics should also lay to rest the popular theory that land was only sold in large units and could only be bought by large capitalists.' I have been unable to consult what is perhaps the best secondary source of information on the alienation of Crown land in the plantation era: a 1973 doctoral thesis of the University of Chicago by Patrick Peebles.
19. Leach, 1961: 49–50, 218–19.
20. *Census of Population 1971, General Report*: 18.
21. Snodgrass, 1966: 49.
22. Samaraweera, 1973b: 447.

23. Roberts, 1972.
24. Roberts, 1973c: 153.
25. Corea, 1975: 94.
26. On the structure of the colonial plantation economy, see Snodgrass, 1966: Chapter 3.
27. Wickremeratne, 1973b: 441.
28. Herring, 1972: 109.
29. Roberts, 1970a: 142; and 1973c: 1158.
30. Roberts, 1973c: 158–9; see also Herring, 1972: 109–111 and 123–4.
31. Snodgrass, 1966: 38.
32. Meyer (1978) gives some account of the cultural stereotyping surrounding recruitment of estate labour.
33. Accounts of these initiatives can be found in Samaraweera, 1973b: 449–54; Farmer, 1957: Chapters 5 and 6; Roberts, 1973c: 153–6; Roberts, 1972; and Bansil, 1971: 374–6.
34. Herring, 1972: 109.
35. Samaraweera, 1973b.
36. Roberts and Wickremeratne, 1973: 101; and Wickremeratne, 1973c: 476–9.
37. Wickremeratne, 1973a.
38. See Birnberg and Resnick, 1975: 67–8 and Chapter 11.
39. Snodgrass, 1966: Chapter 3.
40. Samaraweera, 1973b: 446.
41. See, for example, the quotation from the Secretary of State in Wilson, 1973: 361.
42. This is a quotation from a British former public servant – Collins, 1966: 457.
43. For statements of this concern see Samaraweera, 1973b: 447–53; and Blackton, 1978: 35–6.
44. In 1920 a third of the officers in the Ceylon Civil Service were Sri Lankan, and between 1920 and 1937, 59% of all new recruits were Sri Lankan (Collins, 1966: 467–8).
45. Snodgrass, 1966: Chapters 1 and 2.
46. *Ibid*: Chapter 1.
47. Wilson, 1973: 361–2 and *passim*.
48. Roberts, 1973a and 1979b.
49. Meyer, 1980a: 6.
50. Samaraweera, 1973b: 448.
51. For an account of the impact of depression and malaria, see Meyer, 1980b; also Snodgrass, 1966: 49–51.
52. Samaraweera, 1981.
53. *Ibid*: 136.
54. Skocpol, 1979: 168–71.
55. Abercrombie *et al.*, 1980.
56. Bansil, 1971: 14.
57. Samaraweera, 1973b: 448–56.
58. *Ibid*; and Land Commission, 1929.

59. The main sources for this interpretation are Samaraweera, 1981, and 1973b: 449–54; and Land Commission, 1929.
60. Samaraweera, 1973b: 455–60; and Bansil, 1971: 67–8.
61. Leach, 1961: 51–2; and Amunugama, 1965: 143.
62. See *Land Development (Amendment) Act, No. 27 of 1981*. The UNP's 1977 election manifesto is reproduced in Lake House, 1977: 249–64.
63. Samaraweera, 1973b: 456.
64. For a discussion of the characteristics of the different schemes see *Report of the Land Utilisation Committee, August 1967*: 34–42.
65. *Administration Report of the Land Commissioner for 1969–70*: Schedule Q. It was recently officially noted in relation to Village Expansion Schemes that 'so far no meaningful action for development of these lands has been taken' (Ministry of Lands and Land Development, 1979: 20).
66. *Administration Report of the Land Commission for 1969–70*: Schedule R.
67. *Ibid*: Schedules G and F.
68. The eight main Dry Zone agricultural districts – Hambantota, Mannar, Vavuniya, Batticaloa, Amparai, Trincomalee, Polonnaruwa and Anuradhapura – contained 14% of the Island's population in 1971 (*Census of Population 1971, Volume 2, Part 1*: Table 4), and had received 44% of the allotments under Village Expansion Schemes up to 1970 (*Administration Report of the Land Commissioner for 1969–70*: Schedule A).
69. *Administration Report of the Land Commissioner for 1969–70*: Schedule A.
70. *Ibid*: Schedule A and Table 2.1.
71. Richards and Gooneratne, 1980: 124; *Report of the Land Utilisation Committee, August 1967*: 35–8; and Ranatunga *et al.*, 1981: 3.
72. This estimate is obtained from the figures quoted in the text, and by assuming that almost all land alienated in the last four categories of schemes in Table 3.1 is cultivated.
73. This claim that almost all those recorded as 'agricultural operators' owned at least some land can only be inferred from the results of the 1962 Census of Agriculture. For cultivated highland (i.e. non-paddy land) is far more widely distributed and fragmented into smaller lots than paddy land, and yet renting of land is almost completely confined to paddy. In 1962, 0.5% of all enumerated paddy holdings were of less than a quarter of an acre in extent, compared to 8.1% of all agricultural holdings (*Census of Agriculture, 1962*: Volume 3: 28). See also Table 5.2. Complete landlessness among those recorded as agricultural operators could be widespread only if it took the form of the renting in of relatively large paddy plots by those owning no highland. This is both intrinsically unlikely and not recorded anywhere to my knowledge.
74. Some estate Tamil households do have the use of small plots of estate land, and cultivate these intensively in the Up Country vegetable-growing areas. Some have purchased land of their own (Barrie Morrison, private communication). The overall incidence of own cultivation among households living on estates is, however, unknown.
75. Moore and Perera, 1978: 41.

76. Information obtained from my own fieldwork, especially discussions with numerous public servants. See also ESCAP, 1975: 102.

77. Richards and Gooneratne, 1980: 74.

78. Official pronouncements that Indian Tamil encroachers will be evicted appear fairly frequently, although this may in fact indicate their relative ineffectiveness. For example, in his latest available report the Land Commissioner records having regularised 90% of encroachments dealt with, but concludes that 'The position regarding encroachments by non-Ceylonese was constantly kept under review, and swift action was pursued to evict them' (*Administration Report of the Land Commissioner for 1969–70: 216*).

79. The statistics have deliberately been rounded because various accounts give differing totals. This may reflect the difficulty of the exercise of tracing all such encroachments, and thus the large margin of error in the statistics themselves. See *Ceylon News*, 14 August 1980 (which states that about 580,000 squatters were to be found occupying 900,000 acres of Crown land); and *Ceylon News* 20 November 1980. An official Ministry publication records almost 900,000 acres in 23 of the 24 districts (Ministry of Lands and Land Development, 1979: 16). In a survey conducted in 1978 in one village in Anuradhapura district, Perera (1982: 94) found that 60% of the highland area permanently cultivated by the villagers was encroached Crown land to which they had no legal title.

80. *Ceylon News*, 20 September 1979; and Ministry of Lands and Land Development, 1979: 16–17. See also *Ceylon News*, 20 November 1980.

81. Detailed accounts of how allottees are *actually* chosen do not exist. Two trends are very clear. The first is that, as the Dry Zone has become more attractive, there has been more competition for allotments. It is no longer used as a dumping ground for the undesirable (see Robinson, 1975: 265). The second trend is that, formally at least, more effort is made to select persons thought likely to make good settlers. It seems, however, likely that politicians in fact have a dominant say. I am indebted to John Harriss for information on the selection process.

82. Leach (1961: 51) describes how the lack of any definition of 'landlessness' allowed the sons of relatively wealthy villagers to obtain Crown allotments. Allegations of this kind of 'malpractice' are rife, and probably contain a great deal of truth.

83. Richards and Gooneratne, 1980: 126–7; and Hameed *et al.*, 1977: 83.

84. The latest figures available to the author relate to the year 1969–70. The Rs. 6.5 million due that year represented less than Rs. 5 per acre on all land at that stage alienated under the Land Development Ordinance (see Table 3.1). Yet only 44% of dues were collected in the course of the year, and at the end of it accumulated arrears amount to Rs. 22 million (*Administration Report of the Land Commissioner for 1969–70*: Schedule L).

85. This paragraph is based on my own field observations.

86. Eric Meyer, private communication.

87. Samaraweera, 1973b: 456–8; and Farmer, 1957: 143–5.
88. See Smith, 1979; Roberts, 1979a and 1979b; and Obeyesekere, 1979.
89. Jiggins, 1979: 111.
90. I am referring to innumerable speeches and other reports in the Sri Lankan mass media.
91. Letter in *Lanka Guardian*, Volume 6 (16), 15 December 1983.
92. For a case study see Wanigaratne, 1979b: 8.
93. 'In order to accommodate a greater number of settlers in the schemes, the allotment size has been progressively reduced from eight acres (5 irrigated and 3 highland) to 3 acres (2 irrigated and 1 highland). The present allocation in the Mahaweli project is 2.75 acres (2.5 acres irrigated and 0.25 acres homestead)' (Richards and Gooneratne, 1980: 123). It may or may not be coincidence that official projections of labour requirements, and thus of the need for hired labour, for the current large-scale Mahaweli settlement programme seem to be gross underestimates (Fieldson and Farrington, 1980). The usual pressures in a project such as this would tend to lead to an exaggeration of the employment potential.
94. Smith, 1979.
95. Connolly, 1974: 1–2.
96. Ryan, 1953: 180–1.
97. I am grateful to U. L. Jayantha Perera for this point.
98. Wiener, 1981: especially 46–64.
99. For an analogous argument, see Samaraweera, 1981: especially 142–3.
100. To give but one example, the United Front of the SLFP, LSSP and the Communist Party claimed in their 1970 general election manifesto that 'the rich have got richer while life has become harder for the workers, peasants and middle class' (United Front, *Joint Election Manifesto of the United Front, 1970*).
101. Samaraweera, 1977a: 99.
102. de Silva, K. M. 1973f: 253.

4 Land reform

1. Note that these figures exclude paddy land on estates (*Census of Ceylon 1946, Volume 1, Part 2*: Table 69). For other later statistics, see Wanigaratne *et al.*, 1980: 26; and for comments on their reliability, see Peiris, 1976: 24; and Richards and Gooneratne, 1980: 101.
2. In the Sinhalese areas only 4% of paddy land was held under leasehold in 1946, as opposed to 30% under *ande* tenure. The corresponding figures for the Northern and Eastern Provinces, i.e. the Tamil and Muslim areas, were 22% and 0.5% respectively (*Census of Ceylon 1946, Volume 1, Part 2*: Table 69).
3. I am referring for example to Gold, 1977: Chapters 2, 3 and 7; Hameed *et al.*, 1977: 33–7; Richards and Gooneratne, 1980: 100–9; Sanderatne, 1972a; Wanigaratne *et al.*, 1980; Weerawardena, 1975; and Wickremeratne, 1977b: 248–50.
4. Herring, 1972.

5. *Ibid*: 114–17.

6. *Ibid*: *passim*; and Peiris, 1976: 25–30.

7. Sources as note 6.

8. This case was not proven at the time (Herring, 1972: 112–13; and Peiris, 1976: 34), and later research has failed to find any support for it (Peiris, 1976: 34, 41; and Moore and Wickremesinghe, 1980: 106–7), despite 'a forceful case in logic . . . to show that share tenancy . . . is an obstacle to higher productivity'. A recent attempt to review the evidence for all developing countries on the productivity consequences of sharecropping has been similarly inconclusive (Berry and Cline, 1979: 25–7).

9. Herring, 1972: 103.

10. *Hansard*, Volume 30, 12 and 13 December 1957: 1958. The MP is Mr. E. L. B. Hurulle, currently (1984) Minister of Cultural Affairs. His brief biography is given in Lake House, 1977: 171–2.

11. Woodward, 1969: Conclusion.

12. This paragraph is based on Herring, 1972: 102–18.

13. *Ibid*: 119–23. The two quotations are from the speech by P. H. William de Silva, a leading member of the Revolutionary Lanka Sama Samaj Party and Minister of Industries and Fisheries (see *Hansard*, Volume 30, 12 and 13 December 1957: 2092–3). See also the (English language) speeches by Leslie Goonewardena (LSSP), T. B. Subasinghe (MEP), E. Samarakkody (LSSP), Pieter Keunemann (Communist Party), Colvin R. de Silva (LSSP), Anil Moonesinghe (LSSP), and A. H. Macan-Markar (then an Independent of radical persuasion) (*Ibid*: 1875–1930, 1947–2030, 2074–2184, 2313–2462).

14. Herring, 1972: 121; Peiris, 1976: 35–6; and Gold, 1977: 193.

15. Herring, 1972: 102–11.

16. Jupp, 1978: 72–81; and Wriggins, 1960: 124–43.

17. See Herring, 1980a; and 1980b.

18. Wriggins, 1960: 125.

19. Herring, 1972: 120. The need to nationalise land in the interests of national economic efficiency had long been a theme of Bandaranaike's. See for example the report of his speech to the State Council on 18 October 1933 (Bandaranaike, 1961).

20. *Hansard*, Volume 30, 12 and 13 December 1957: 2379–81.

21. Herring, 1972: 102; and Peiris, 1976: 28, 30.

22. For discussions of Gunawardena's role, see Herring, 1972: 119–23; Jupp, 1978: 10, 172–3; Peiris, 1976: 31–4; Wanasinghe, 1980a: 240; Weerawardena, 1975: Preface; Wilson, 1979: 72; Wriggins, 1960: 294; and Gold, 1977: Chapter 3.

23. Wriggins, 1960: 125. Gunawardena or his wife continually held the Avissawella seat, the location of his family estates, despite several changes in his political orientation, from 1947 until his defeat in 1970 (de Silva, G. P. S. H., 1979: 125). In the 1977 general election, after Philip's death, his son Dinesh scored a very respectable 37% of votes cast as one of the few,

and the only really serious, candidate for the remnants of his MEP party (*ibid*).

24. Wriggins, 1960: 127–8, 331.

25. Gunawardena's following, which took the name of MEP (People's United Front) after his expulsion from office in 1959, gradually became more Sinhalese communalist in nature (Jupp, 1978: 76). From being the largest of the three Marxist parties in the general election of March 1960 (*ibid*: 370), it steadily lost support until it became little more than the personal political vehicle of Philip's son (*ibid*: 371; and note 23 above).

26. They were S. A. Wickremesinghe and P. Keunemann (Communist Party); Colvin R. de Silva, Anil Moonesinghe and Edmund Samarakkody (LSSP); P. H. William de Silva from Gunawardena's own Revolutionary LSSP; and T. B. Subasinghe, a left-wing SLFPer, who was to leave the SLFP from the left in 1977 (see *Hansard*, Volume 30, 12 and 13 December 1957: 1875–1930, 1947, 2074–2184, 2313–2462).

27. *Ibid*: 2461–2; Wriggins, 1960: 362; and Lake House, 1977: 216.

28. For example, Roberts (1970c: 1) lists the following eight characteristics of what he calls 'the revivalist elite within the MEP coalition of 1956': 'the upper-level of the Sinhalese-speaking intelligentsia'; 'the lower middle-class traditionalists'; 'Sinhalese educated lower middle-classes'; 'new village leadership'; 'alternative village leadership'; 'national bourgeoisie and petit bourgeoisie'; and 'the rural middle classes and the Sinhala-Buddhist intelligentsia'.

29. The latter argument is made by Roberts, 1970c. The quotation is from page 37.

30. The original proposal was to limit rents payable to five bushels per acre (Gold, 1977: 29), at a time when average paddy yields were thirty-four bushels per acre.

31. This account of the struggle over the Paddy Lands Bill is based on Gold, 1977: Chapter 3; Herring, 1972: 119–23; Jupp, 1978: 65–7, 172–3; Peiris, 1976: 31–4; and Wriggins, 1960: 294–5.

32. Jiggins, 1979: 13.

33. S. W. R. D. Bandaranaike's speech in the closing stages of the debate on the Second Reading of the Bill is felt to have been especially influential in quelling opposition. See Bandaranaike, 1961: Speech made on the Second Reading of the 1958 Paddy Lands Act, 19 December 1957.

34. Gold, 1977: 32.

35. Herring, 1972: 122; and Jupp, 1978: 10.

36. For details, see Gold, 1977: especially Chapters 3 and 7; and Weerawardena, 1975.

37. Gold, 1977: 198.

38. *Paddy Lands Act, No. 1 of 1958*: 3.

39. *Agricultural Productivity Law, No. 2 of 1972*; *Agricultural Lands Law, No. 42 of 1973*; and *Agrarian Services Act, No. 58 of 1979*.

40. See the Acts themselves and Moore, 1980a.

41. This framework for analysing the conceptions behind the 1958 Act owes much to the work of Herring (1972), although it is not transferred directly.
42. Quoted in Peiris, 1976: 34.
43. For details of the *thattumaru* system, see Moore and Wickremesinghe, 1978b; and Gold, 1977: Chapter 6. For a reference to the debate, see note 26. The MPs were Pieter Keunemann, Communist Party (p. 2107) and Colvin R. de Silva, LSSP (p. 2356).
44. Herring, 1972: 118–24.
45. See the parliamentary debate on the Second Reading referred to in note 26, especially pp. 2019–22, 2089; Gold, 1977: 30–2; and Peiris, 1976: 32–3.
46. *Paddy Lands Act, No. 1 of 1958*: 3, 29.
47. Herring, 1972: 118.
48. *Paddy Lands Act, No. 1 of 1958*: 29, 33, 35.
49. *Agricultural Productivity Law, No. 2 of 1972*: 1–6; *Agricultural Lands Law, No. 42 of 1973*: 29–30; and *Agrarian Services Act, No. 58 of 1979*: 21–5, 36–7.
50. In a speech to Parliament in 1979 the acting Minister of Agriculture stated that no land transfers had ever taken place under these provisions of the law (*Hansard*, 4 July 1979: 1144).
51. Weerawardena, 1975: 17.
52. See *Ceylon News*, 8 November 1979.
53. See the parliamentary debate on the Second Reading of the 1958 Paddy Lands Bill referred to in note 26 (p. 2006). The speaker was Sir Razik Fareed.
54. Moore, 1981d: Chapter 2.
55. Leach (1961: 28–30) reports a different arrangement, in which the *Vel Vidane* exercised general authority at the small village level, in part of the North Central Province. See also Perera, 1982: 59–62.
56. See sources quoted in Moore, 1981d: Chapter 2, especially Warnapala, 1974: 339–43; and also Ryan, 1953: 182.
57. For example, by refusing to register documents in new names, headmen could prevent members of low castes from disguising their caste origins (Wanigaratne, 1977: 5; and Perera, 1982: 62).
58. De Silva, K. M., 1973b: 518, 525.
59. Peiris, 1976: 32–3; and Gold, 1979: 29–32.
60. Wilson, 1979: 72; and Gold, 1977: 29–32.
61. Herring, 1972: 120.
62. See sources quoted in note 3.
63. E.g. Weerawardena, 1975: 24.
64. Moore, 1979; and Weerawardena, 1975.
65. See the debate on the Second Reading, referred to in note 26.
66. Note that the only other occupational category he used was 'industrial work'. Does one detect here a usage of 'peasantry' in relation to the economy analogous to the way in which the Marxists used 'feudal' in

Notes

relation to agriculture, i.e. anything non-modern? (Bandaranaike, 1961: Speech made on the Second Reading of the Paddy Lands Act, 19 December 1957, p. 891.)

67. *Census of Ceylon 1953, Volume 4, Part 1*: Table 3.
68. Paddy cultivation at this stage was the main activity of 13% of the work force (*ibid*).
69. *Agricultural Lands Law, No. 42 of 1973*.
70. Herring, 1972: 122.
71. On this convergence between Marxist and conservative prescriptions, see Herring, 1972: 123.
72. For example, Colvin R. de Silva, a leader of the LSSP (Herring, 1972: 113).
73. This comprised the LSSP, the Communist Party and a fragment of ex-SLFPers.
74. Lake House, 1977: 306.
75. Colvin R. de Silva, quoted in Herring, 1972: 123.
76. *Paddy Lands Act, No. 1 of 1958*: 25–6. This omission was pointed out in the Second Reading debate by the MP for Kalkudah, A. H. Macan-Markar. Reference as in note 26, p. 1991.
77. The MP in question is once again A. H. Macan-Markar (*ibid*: 1992).
78. Gold, 1977: 38–9; and Weerawardena, 1975: 33–6.
79. Weerawardena, 1975: 33. Weerawardena was a director of the Agrarian Services Department at the time he wrote this.
80. Herring, 1972: 124.
81. In its abortive attempts to establish a base in the smallholding areas, the Communist Party has operated through a very weak front organisation called the Ceylon Peasant Congress (Gold, 1977: 196–7).
82. Gold, 1977: 35–40; Weerawardena, 1975: Chapter 2; and Wanigaratne *et al.*, 1980: 29.
83. Peiris, 1976: 42; Moore and Wickremesinghe, 1980: 53; Weerawardena, 1975: 5, 47; Gold, 1977: 188; and Central Bank of Ceylon, 1969: 18.
84. The author is referring especially to Gold, 1977: 35–40; and to Weerawardena, 1975: Chapter 2; but does not exclude any of those commentators listed in note 3.
85. It was only in 1963 that the Act was applied to the final nine districts of the Island (Weerawardena, 1975: 31).
86. *Ibid*: 75.
87. *Ibid*: 10. The Department of Agrarian Services also inherited from Gunawardena's associates a tradition of independent investigation into rural conditions. For details of this tradition, see *ibid*: Preface; and Gold, 1977: 28. Publications representing the continuation of this tradition include Weerawardena, 1975; and Weerawardena and Collonnege, 1971.
88. Weerawardena, 1975: 10 and *passim*; and Moore, 1979: 243.
89. *Agrarian Services Act, No. 58 of 1979*: 26–8, 32–4, 39; and Moore, 1980a.
90. Weerawardena, 1975: 10.
91. *Ibid*: *passim*; and Gold, 1977: 35–40.

263

92. I am referring to Mr I. K. Weerawardena.

93. Moore, 1980a.

94. See the debate on the Second Reading of the Agrarian Services Bill in *Hansard*, Volume 5 (10, 11), 4 and 5 July 1979. The main critics of the Bill were the SLFP MPs, S. D. Bandaranayake, Ananda Dassanayake and R. P. Wijesiri, the latter two representing Kandyan electorates (Kotmale and Harispattuwa respectively). R. P. Wijesiri is well known as a spokesman for the poor and low-caste Kandyans, and for his opposition to the Kandyan landowning classes. For these MPs' criticisms of the provisions to permit landowners to resume tenanted land, see pp. 1170, 1248, 1256–8.

95. My own 'exposé' of the tenurial provisions of the 1977 Agrarian Services Act (Moore, 1980a) is, as far as I have been able to discover, the sole public demonstration of concern about this issue.

96. For details of this legislation, see Sanderatne, 1972b.

97. For details, see Peiris, 1978: 611–12; and Wanigaratne *et al.*, 1980: 66.

98. Peiris, 1978: 616–17.

99. *Ibid*. Statistics on the asweddumised acreage in 1972–3 were obtained from the Department of Census and Statistics, Colombo.

100. *Ibid*: 613. There was a vague commitment to do something about estates in the election manifesto of the United Front which came to power in 1970 (United Front, *Joint Election Manifesto of the United Front, 1970*: 6).

101. Wanigaratne *et al.*, 1980: 4; and Richards and Gooneratne, 1980: 85.

102. In 1970 tea accounted for 55% of all exports by value, and rubber and coconut products jointly contributed a further 33%. The corresponding figures for 1977 were 53% and 10% respectively (Central Bank of Ceylon, *Review of the Economy*, 1978: Tables 81–4). For details of this dependence on plantation exports, see Snodgrass, 1966; and Gunasekere, 1977.

103. On the general process, see Snodgrass, 1966: 211. On state assistance, see Oliver, 1957: 75–6.

104. Peiris, 1978: 613.

105. Herring, 1972: 100.

106. E.g. de Silva, Colvin R., 1975; Shanmugaratnam and Siriwardana, 1979: 49–56; Abeysinghe, 1978; Balasuriya, 1977; and Obeyesekera, 1973: 358–69.

107. E.g. Sarkar and Thambaiyah, 1957: xi–xii.

108. For a relatively elaborated representation of this element in the myth, see Shanmugaratnam and Siriwardana, 1979: 49–59.

109. The concern of the Kandyan Peasantry Commission with divorce and early marriage (pp. 12–13) is symptomatic of the 'bourgeois outrage' with which the Sri Lankan elite and middle classes have greeted information on the relatively relaxed sexual mores of the Kandyan villagers (Yalman, 1967: 64, 108–14, 159–60, 170).

110. Kandyan Peasantry Commission, 1951: 13.

111. Meyer, 1980a. Meyer would, however, be the first to object to any attempt to generalise from the conclusions of this work.
112. On this point, see also Roberts, 1966; and Ameer Ali, 1970/2.
113. Meyer, 1978.
114. Roberts, 1970b.
115. Meyer, 1980a: 8. He is worth quoting in detail:

> *It seems to me that the problems resulting from the contact between the 'territory' of the village and that of the plantation were of a 'political' rather than economic nature.* The villagers used to fence their paddy fields and to let their cattle graze freely over the rest of the village area. When forests and chenas were converted into estates, the animals continued to wander in their favorite areas and developed a taste for young tea leaves (and even rubber milk, if I can rely on my informants . . .). Some plantation workers, especially beef-eater Paraiyars, used to hunt cattle in the estate and even to lift it in the village. These 'border incidents' became the source of strained relations between village headmen and planters; the peasants blamed the planters for not enclosing their estates, while they themselves fenced their fields; the planters, resting on the western notion of abstract property, and some of them, actually obsessed by a quasi-caste complex of agoraphoby heightened by their way of life, resented as intolerable any presence of 'native elements in British territory' (in the humorous words of a civil servant of the time, W. E. Davidson); most of them could not speak a word of Sinhalese, many considered the village as an unknown territory, the hotbed of lawlessness where 'their' coolies were led astray, attracted by illicit arrack and toddy taverns and gambling dens, where daily petty thefts were planned etc. Some of them got an idea that the development of small village plantations was in every case the result of the theft of seedlings in their nurseries, and the planting lobby obtained from the colonial authorities the right to make use of corporal punishment in these cases, in the 1870s. Many superintendents refused to let the villagers use footpaths and cattle tracks across the estates, but they never scrupled to widen their access roads to the detriment of the village gardens, while the peasants sometimes retaliated by closing to the plantation workers the paths across fields.

116. The spatial segregation of tea estates and tea smallholders is greater than the information in Table 4.2 implies. For example, in 1962 the six Kandyan districts of Kandy, Matale, Nuwara Eliya, Badulla, Ratnapura and Kegalle accounted for 88% of the registered tea acreage in estates (i.e. holdings of fifty acres or more), and 68% of the tea area in smallholdings. By contrast, the two Low Country districts of Galle and Matara contained only 9% of the tea estate area but 30% of the smallholder tea area (*Census of Agriculture 1962, Volume 2*: Table 4). A more disaggregated set of spatial categories would reveal a more marked spatial separation between estates and smallholdings.
117. Scholars adopting this perspective in their analyses of Sri Lanka include Snodgrass (1966: 56–7) and Shanmugaratnam and Siriwardana (1979). The characterisation in this paragraph relates both to their work and to elements of the conventional myth of the plantation impact discussed above.
118. E.g. Snodgrass, 1966: 57.

Notes

119. Examples of this perspective are provided by the work of Roberts (1973a and 1973c); and Meyer (1978 and 1980a).

120. Tea estates are particularly concentrated in the Up Country districts of Badulla and Nuwara Eliya, and in some of the higher and less accessible parts of Kandy and Ratnapura districts. In 1962 Badulla and Nuwara Eliya contained 38% of the total acreage of tea in holdings of more than fifty acres (*Census of Agriculture 1962, Volume 2*: Table 4). In 1971 they contained 38% of the Indian Tamil population, and only 6% of the Sinhalese population (*Census of Population 1971, General Report*: Table 6.4).

121. For an example of almost complete integration of estate and village in a Low Country tea-producing area, see Moore and Wickremesinghe, 1980: 37–43. The importance of local purchases by a foreign-owned rubber estate in another Low Country village is detailed by Seneratne, 1970: 176.

122. Snodgrass, 1966: 49; and Peiris, 1978: 614–16.

123. Meyer, 1978: 1.

124. *Census of Population 1971, General Report*: 79, 80.

125. *Census of Ceylon 1946, Volume 1, Part 2*: Table 48; *Census of Population 1971, Volume 2, Part 2*: Table 9; and *Census of Population 1971, General Report*: 124.

126. This emphasis of the 'Kandyan connection' is very close to the interpretation of land policy made by Samaraweera (1981) and Peiris (1981b: 2), although drafted before their work was available.

127. *Census of Population 1971, General Report*: 32–3.

128. For a recent case study, see Morrison, 1979.

129. Moore, 1981d: 176, fn. 270.

130. *Ibid*: 176, fn. 271.

131. See Chapter Eight; and Ryan, 1953: 56.

132. Moore, 1981d: 270, fn. 273.

133. 'In the Kandyan areas . . . turnout reaches the maximum found possible in other voluntary systems' (Jupp, 1978: 189).

134. Wriggins, 1960: 124–43; and Jupp, 1978: 374–9.

135. Jupp, 1978: 199.

136. Jiggins, 1979: 115–19; and Roberts, 1979a: 46–9.

137. It is significant that R. P. Wijesiri, who has directly represented the low-caste Kandyan poor in Parliament between 1965 and 1970 and since 1977, has not been 'at home' with the SLFP because of the character of its leadership. But neither has he been fully at home with the UNP. His party affiliation while MP has changed as follows: UNP, Independent, SLFP, UNP (Lake House, 1977: 98; and my own fieldwork).

138. Examples of three such villages are those studied by Robinson (1975); De Mel and Fernando (1980); and Yalman (1967: Part 2).

139. For details, see Bansil, 1971: 73–4.

140. *Census of Agriculture 1962, Volume 1*: Table 1 ('Plantation' is here defined as a holding of more than fifty acres); *Administration Report of the Land Commissioner for 1969–70*: Schedule D. The bias in this programme

266

towards the Kandyan districts would have been more marked had the acquisition of estates not been even more rapid in Colombo district, where the more rapid expansion of population made this a greater 'objective' necessity (see *Census of Population 1971, General Report*: Table 2.9).

141. The original commission was dated 13 January 1949 (see *Report of the Kandyan Peasantry Commission, 1951*: iii). The chairman, N. E. Weerasooria, was of mixed Kandyan and Low Country origin, and oriented politically to Kandyan issues (M. Roberts, private communication). Each of the other four members sat for Kandyan seats – C. E. Attygalle for Ratnapura; M. D. Banda for Maturata; H. R. U. Premachandra for Kadugannawa; and T. B. Panabokke for Galaha (de Silva, G. P. S. H., 1979: 349, 350, 377, 381). Messrs Panabokke and Banda were members of prominent Kandyan 'aristocratic' families, and the latter was to be a prominent member of all UNP cabinets between 1950 and 1970 (*ibid*: 307–9, 313, 317).

142. In 1946, five districts were recorded as having 40% or more of their paddy land under *ande* tenure. Four of them were the Kandyan districts of Kandy, Matale, Nuwara Eliya and Ratnapura (*Census of Population 1946, Volume 1, Part 2*: Table 69).

143. *Report of the Kandyan Peasantry Commission, 1951*: 109–10.

144. See *Administration Report of the Kandyan Peasantry Rehabilitation Commissioner for 1969–70*: 19.

145. For comparable comments on the ideological implications of 'rehabilitation' and 'upliftment', see Samaraweera, 1981: 131–2.

146. Among the other SLFP members of the Cabinet, T. B. Ilangaratne had long been the main broker between the SLFP and the Marxists, and T. B. Subasinghe had an LSSP background (de Silva, G. P. S. H., 1979: 391) and was to desert the SLFP along with a handful of other 'radicals' just before the 1977 general election. See also Jupp (1978: 294) on the left-wing orientation of some of the SLFP leadership.

147. See Jupp, 1978: 70–2, 78–81, 294–5.

148. Godfrey Gunatilleke, private communication.

149. Jiggins, 1979: Chapter 7.

150. Herring, 1972: 101; and Obeyesekere, 1974.

151. On the circumstances of this decision, see Wanasinghe, 1980a: 247–9; and Gold, 1977: 209–11. I am also grateful to Godfrey Gunatilleke for his account of them.

152. It was reported in the *Ceylon News* of 26 June 1980 that half of the total number of 423 appeals against 'punitive' treatment of landowners, i.e. allocation of particularly poor land, had been 'finalised', presumably accepted. As of the end of 1980, former owners dispossessed under the 1972 law had been given back 9662 hectares, 4.4% of the land originally acquired under the law (Central Bank of Ceylon, *Review of the Economy*, 1980: 40).

153. Sanderatne, 1972b: 13–14; and Wanasinghe, 1980b: 251. By June 1980,

442 appeals had been made to the Land Reform Commission on the grounds that discretion had been used punitively in withholding land from children aged more than eighteen years (*Ceylon News*, 26 June 1980).

154. Sanderatne, 1972b: 15.
155. For an example, see Perera, 1979a: 262–3.
156. The Bandaranaike family appear to have been guilty of a certain degree of manipulation, but on a relatively minor scale. The truth is difficult to get at because it is a highly emotive and political topic.
157. Gold, 1977: 210.
158. This section is based in large part on my personal experience in Sri Lanka. Other main general sources of information include Peiris, 1978: 618–28; Wanasinghe, 1980a: 247–61; Wanigaratne *et al.*, 1980: 65–94; and Richards and Gooneratne, 1980: 91–9.
159. Strong hints of this 'productionist' attitude are given in the LSSP's official 'post-mortem' on the results of its participation in the United Front government (Lanka Sama Samaj Party, 1978). It makes much of the general corruption, inefficiency and lack of planning which characterised the government's activities (pp. 12–13), and, in relation to the nationalised estates, talks of the 'criminal plunder of estate assets and a scramble for soft jobs' (p. 26).
160. Examples of the kind of conflicts which took place are recorded in Wanigaratne *et al.*, 1980: 83–4.
161. Wriggins, 1960: 129.
162. Peiris, 1978: 620.
163. For an illustration of how its estates were managed, see Wanigaratne *et al.*, 1980: 78.
164. See, for example, Jayatilleke, 1980: 37–8. I am aware of one local exception. The then Deputy Minister of Finance, Neil de Alwis, ensured the relatively efficient management of the estates under his control in the Baddegama electorate. Not only had he a career in plantation management, but was an LSSP MP who stayed with the SLFP when the majority of LSSP MPs were expelled from the coalition in 1975.
165. Then the head of the National Youth Service Council.
166. For example, Wanigaratne *et al.* (1980: 78) demonstrate that the *Janawasa* they studied was under the control of the local SLFP party organisation.
167. No *Janawasas* seem ever to have paid dividends to their worker-members. I know of one case where the worker-members went on strike against 'their' management, who responded by bringing in 'blackleg' labour. Ellman and Ratnaweera (1974: 61, 227), in a study of *Janawasas* and other forms of collective agriculture, demonstrate that members were kept in considerable uncertainty about long-term plans for organisation and landownership.
168. Peiris, 1978: 623.
169. Moore, 1981d: 179, fn. 320.

170. Richards and Gooneratne, 1980: 95; and Peiris, 1978: 625.
171. Moore, 1981d: 180, fn. 322.
172. Central Bank of Ceylon, *Review of the Economy*, 1978: 41.
173. See Ministry of Lands and Land Development, 1979: 21.
174. Wanigaratne *et al.*, 1980: 82; and Richards and Gooneratne, 1980: 95.
175. The sources include my own personal observations and reports of numerous informants, as well as Wanigaratne *et al.*, 1980: 91–4.
176. Wanasinghe, 1980a: 251; and Moore *et al.*, 1979: 207.
177. Lake House, 1977: 276.
178. Illustration of the covetousness with which the Kandyan village poor looked on the holdings of the village temples and the landed during the period of the United Front government, is provided by Morrison, 1979: 104–6.
179. Wanasinghe, 1980a: 251.
180. See Gold, 1977: Chapter 4; and Weerawardena, 1975: Chapter 7.
181. Richards and Gooneratne, 1980: 99.
182. The extent of the deleterious economic consequences of management practices after the land reform is a subject of considerable dispute, and opinions are of course highly influenced by party political considerations (Peiris, 1978: 623–8).
183. One might note here the prohibition on alienation of paddy land to non-citizens in the preamble to the 1958 Paddy Lands Act reproduced above in the text. The evolution of the concept of land as 'patrimony' to be protected from Indian Tamils is traced by Samaraweera (1977b).

5 Pricing and agricultural services

1. Bandaranaike, 1961: 891.
2. See, for example, Appendix Two; Tambaiah, 1963: 75; and Morrison *et al.* (eds.), 1979: 16.
3. Morrison *et al.* (eds.), 1979: 16.
4. Moore, 1981d: Table 5.6.
5. Here 'imagery' is used to refer to largely implicit models of the world and stands in contrast to 'ideologies' which are relatively coherent social theories. For this distinction, see Newby *et al.* 1978: 279–85.
6. Richards and Gooneratne, 1980: 60.
7. A fairly detailed account is provided in Bansil, 1971.
8. Samaraweera, 1973b: 452.
9. Bansil, 1971: 82, 157, 259, 261.
10. In Sri Lanka as in most Asian countries, 'government policies with regard to food and agriculture prices and production took shape during and immediately after the Second World War' (FAO, 1958: 1).
11. Edirisinghe and Poleman, 1976: 17, 58; and Bansil, 1971: 82.
12. Samaraweera, 1973b: 453. A recent study shows that an attempt to orient the Department of Agriculture's extension system to other crops in

addition to paddy has had no success (A. M. T. Gunawardena, private communication).

13. Samaraweera, 1973b: 456–7; and de Silva, K. M., 1973b: 525.
14. Adam Pain, private communication.
15. For details, see Bansil, 1971: 259–60; Hussain, 1977: 50–3; and the regular *Review of the Economy* and the *Bulletin* of the Central Bank of Ceylon.
16. Moore, 1981d: Appendix Two.
17. Sathasivampillai, 1973: 15, 54–6; and Chapter 7 of this volume.
18. Central Bank of Ceylon, *Review of the Economy*, 1977: 20.
19. My own fieldwork. This argument is to be found in Sathasivampillai, 1973: 57.
20. In her study of the operations of local cooperatives, Harriss, B. (1978: 287–9) demonstrates that managers are often obliged to use private resources or unofficial procedures if they wish to fulfil many of their responsibilities.
21. For these points I am indebted to Mr J. Broersma, formerly of the West Germany–Sri Lanka Fertiliser Project Team. Some of their conclusions are summarised in Kuruppu, n.d.; and Volz, n.d. The latter provides statistics on the extremely poor performance of the public distribution system (pp. 1–2). One point about the range of different fertiliser mixes is that the difference in specifications was often smaller than the likely range of error in the mixing operation. See also Kuruppu, 1979.
22. One might cite in particular the efficiency with which a regular rice ration was delivered to almost all households between 1942 and 1978 (see Edirisinghe and Poleman, 1976: Chapter 5; and Gavan and Chandrasekere, 1979: 27–33). Other examples include the efficiency and relative fairness with which the operation of withdrawing rice ration books from half the population was conducted in 1978, and the enormous speed with which the programme of the current Prime Minister (R. Premadasa) to build 100,000 houses, begun in 1977, has been conducted.
23. A useful summary may be found in the *Economic Review* (Colombo), April–May 1979: 3–18.
24. *Ibid*: 7.
25. The quotation of survey 'evidence' that crop failure is the biggest single cause of non-repayment of loans (e.g. *ibid*: 7) suggests a rather naive trust in the simplicity and honesty, not to say stupidity, of the smallholder population.
26. International Labour Office, 1971a: 98.
27. Harriss, B., 1978: 284.
28. An excellent case study of the use of such discretion to benefit especially the staff of cooperatives allocating credit is provided by the report of a committee which investigated the abuses of loans for sugarcane production in Amparai district. (See Ministry of Plan Implementation, 1978.)
29. *Economic Review*, April–May 1979: 12.
30. *Ibid*: 15.

31. For details of the scheme, see *ibid*: 15–17.
32. For example, for the nine paddy seasons from Yala 1975 to Yala 1979, only 19% of premia due were collected (Central Bank of Ceylon, *Review of the Economy*, 1979: 44). The greatest success by far was obtained during the Maha 1977–8 season, when the volume of rural credit was, in historical terms, enormous. Yet, even then, less than 50% of premia due were collected (*ibid*: 44 and Table 5.1). In the course of the nine seasons referred to above, premia collected exceeded indemnities paid only twice, and the total indemnities paid equalled 122% of the premia collected (*ibid*: 44).
33. Commissioner of Agrarian Services, 1973: 41.
34. I am referring here to my own experience in the Wet Zone, where total failures of the paddy crop are rare.
35. Central Bank of Ceylon, *Review of the Economy*, 1979: 204 and Table 2.
36. The general case is argued in Lipton, 1977: Chapter 7.
37. International Labour Office, 1971b: 111; see also Richards and Gooneratne, 1980: 124.
38. Details of how this guesstimate was made are provided in Moore, 1981d: 232, fn. 55.
39. Richards and Gooneratne, 1980: 124–5; and Farmer, 1957: 324–8.
40. *Census of Population 1971, General Report*: 80.
41. *Census of Ceylon 1946, Volume 1, Part 2*: Table 28; and *Census of Population 1971, General Report*: 33, 84. Note that the percentage increase would have been higher had it not been necessary to include in this list the present Batticaloa district, which was created in the early 1960s, along with Amparai district, by division of the old Batticaloa district. The Sinhalese population of the new (and still large) Batticaloa district is very small and relatively constant.
42. For details of the pattern of migratory flow between districts since 1946, see *Census of Population 1971, General Report*: Chapter Four.
43. An account of the movement of Sinhalese settlers into Gal Oya is provided by Pieris, 1965.
44. International Labour Office, 1971b: 109.
45. For details of this provision, see Farmer, 1957: especially Chapter 16; and Richards and Gooneratne, 1980: 123.
46. *Ibid*: 123.
47. For some details, see *Administration Report of the Land Commissioner for 1969–70*: 215 and Schedules C and E.
48. This paragraph is based mainly on my own research on the subject of water management. See also Moore, 1981a; Moore, 1980c: especially 7–8, 14–23, 25–31; and Murray-Rust and Moore, 1983.
49. Wickremeratne, 1973e: especially 36–40.
50. Such controls have been especially important during periods of SLFP government. For details, see Snodgrass, 1966: Chapters 7 and 8; Gunasekere, 1977: 186–8; and Wickremeratne, 1977a.
51. Gavan and Chandrasekere, 1979: 29. In fact the monopoly lost statutory

backing in early 1980 (*Ceylon News*, 13 March 1980) in consequence of
the policy of economic liberalisation introduced by the UNP government. However, to the best of my knowledge the Food Commissioner
remains *de facto* almost a monopoly importer of rice, wheat flour and, to a
lesser extent, sugar.

52. These figures are calculated from those given by Gavan and
    Chandrasekere (1979: Table 8 and Table 10). Here, as in other
    calculations, no account is taken of the minor quantities of locally
    produced, non-rice cereals, i.e. millet, sorghum and maize.

53. In 1978 there was on average one cooperative retail outlet for every 1850
    persons in the Island (*ibid*: 29).

54. *Ibid*: 31.

55. The following quotation from a recent report of the Central Bank
    represents an indication of, and a warning against, the way in which
    pressures to supply the ration scheme physically have tended to dominate
    the activities of the FC (Food Commissioner, responsible for food
    supply) and the PMB (Paddy Marketing Board, responsible for paddy
    procurement and milling):

    As much as the PMB should not measure its achievements by the proportion of the
    annual harvest it purchases from the farmers, but by its ability to stabilise the
    paddy/rice market to the farmers, the FC should not feel obliged to stand-by to
    exchange food stamps for food items at predetermined prices, but to stabilise the
    consumer market by efficient supply management at the wholesale level (Central
    Bank of Ceylon, *Review of the Economy*, 1979: 31).

56. See FAO, 1958: 8. The proportion of the Sri Lankan rice crop procured
    by the state was far higher than in all other countries except
    (industrialised) Japan.

57. The only publicly available price index of any depth is the Colombo
    Consumers Price Index, which grossly underestimates the rate of
    inflation and is unusable for economic calculations. It is possible to derive
    an implicit 'GDP deflator' from data series on the Gross Domestic
    Product, but this gives a heavy weight to international trade prices and so
    is not very suitable for use in relation to domestic consumer or producer
    prices. A wholesale price index dating from 1974 is now published, but,
    apart from its lack of temporal depth, it is not altogether trusted by
    independent economists.

58. For the price series themselves, see Moore, 1981d: 202.

59. For statistics and analysis, see Central Bank of Ceylon, *Review of the
    Economy*, 1978: 32–3 and Table 12.

60. The consumer price of flour was increased by 150% in six steps between
    May 1978 and January 1980 (Central Bank of Ceylon, *Review of the
    Economy*, 1978: 214; and 1979: 249; and *Bulletin*, January 1980: 5).

61. Central Bank of Ceylon, *Review of the Economy*, 1979: 31. For details of
    changes in the 1970s in price ratios affecting paddy producers, see Moore
    1981d: Appendix Three.

62. *Census of Agriculture 1962, Volume 2*: Table 2. The category 'plantation crops' actually includes producers of cocoa and cinnamon as well as tea, rubber and coconuts. The numbers of producers of each plantation crop are not given separately. Since, however, cocoa and cinnamon accounted for less than 3% of the total smallholder acreage under plantation crops (*ibid*: Table 4), it can safely be assumed that they constitute a correspondingly tiny proportion of growers.
63. *Ibid*: 27 and Table 2a.
64. Snodgrass, 1966: 82–3, 114–15, 187–90; and Wilson, 1979: 77–8.
65. Central Bank of Ceylon, *Review of the Economy*, 1979: 21, 24, 27, 194 and Table 14.
66. International Labour Office, 1971b: 92. See also IBRD, 1975: Annex 6.
67. Central Bank of Ceylon, *Review of the Economy*, 1979: 194.
68. Central Bank of Ceylon, *Review of the Economy*, 1978: 33.
69. *Economic and Social Statistics of Sri Lanka*, 1 (2): Table 4.3.
70. See *Ceylon News*, 13 December 1979.
71. Moore, 1981d: Appendix 2.
72. The word 'public' is important here. Levels of taxation of plantation crops have in recent years been a major item of contention between the government of Sri Lanka and its foreign advisers, especially the World Bank (my fieldwork). The issue did briefly become public in 1979 when the Minister of Plantation Industries, M. D. H. Jayawardena, was obliged to resign after his outspoken criticism of the level of taxation on plantation products.
73. This point was expressed thus to me by Mr Godfrey Gunatilleke.
74. On the ratios between GPS and local market prices see Hussain, 1977: 57; *Economic and Social Statistics of Sri Lanka* 1 (2): Table 4.6; Bansil, 1971: 82–5; Gavan and Chandrasekere, 1979: 48; and Edirisinghe and Poleman, 1976: 80–6.
75. Moore, 1981d: Appendix Two.
76. Snodgrass, 1966: 207–15.
77. For example, in the period 1973 to 1977 an average 17% of public revenue was obtained from the sale of FEECs (Central Bank of Ceylon, *Review of the Economy*, 1975: Table 36; and 1977: Table 38).
78. Gavan and Chandrasekere, 1979: 49.
79. *Ibid*: 25.
80. Moore, 1981d: 202.
81. *Ibid*: 236, fn. 106.
82. Wheat flour was briefly available only on ration during the period of food crisis in 1973–5 (Gavan and Chandrasekere, 1979: 28).
83. The financial magnitudes involved are presented in Moore, 1981d: Table 5.5.
84. *Ibid*: 209.
85. Gavan and Chandrasekere, 1979: 12.
86. Moore, 1981d: 209 and Appendix Two.
87. The value of the subsidy on tractors was not included in the source given

above. That it was substantial in the 1970s is a point the author owes to a private communication from John Farrington.

88. These crops are justly labelled 'minor'. Almost the entire output is marketed, and for statistical purposes exports are reckoned as equivalent to total production. In 1978 minor export crops accounted for only 2.6% of all exports by value (Central Bank of Ceylon, *Review of the Economy*, 1978: Tables 81 and 85).

89. Wickremeratne, 1973e: 32–6; and Peiris, 1981b: Table 1.

90. Bansil, 1971: 286–7.

91. Snodgrass, 1966: 167–8; Bansil, 1971: 100–1; and *Statistical Abstract*, 1977: Tables 90–108.

92. Wickremeratne, 1977a: 161.

93. For statistics on imports, see *Agricultural Statistical Information 1*: Table 68.

94. Statistics on the area and production of subsidiary food crops are not very reliable. Those on manioc and sweet potato vary widely according to source. The trend is, however, very clear. The area under *kurakkan*, maize, chillies and red onions increased by 113% between 1970 and 1976 (*Statistical Pocketbook of Sri Lanka*, 1977: 46).

95. Jayanath, 1980; and Moore, 1981d: 210–11.

96. *Ceylon News*, 21 February 1980; and Central Bank of Ceylon, *Review of the Economy*, 1978: 38.

97. Central Bank of Ceylon, *Review of the Economy*, 1979: 33.

98. Jayanath, 1980: 31. For further evidence, see *Tribune*, 18 October 1980: 11, and *Sri Lanka News*, 27 October 1983.

99. Central Bank of Ceylon, *Review of the Economy*, 1979: Table 16.

100. Moore, 1981d: 237, fn. 127.

101. See *Hansard*, Debate on the Economic and Financial Situation of the Country, 25 August 1964: 2445–6.

102. See *Sun*, 24 May 1978; *Tribune*, 7 October 1978; and *Ceylon Daily News*, 5 February 1980.

103. For example, see *Tribune*, 29 July 1978: 1, 32; 18 October 1980: 11; 14 June 1980: 32; 19 January 1980: 32; 12 January 1980: 9–14; and 22 November 1980: 1.

104. Moore, 1984a.

105. Moore, 1981d: 238, fn. 134.

106. My fragmentary knowledge of the potato industry owes a great deal to information provided by Evan Due, W. M. Wijepala and Barrie Morrison.

107. For example, in the 1977 parliamentary debate on the financial vote for the Ministry of Agriculture, the MP for Uva-Paranagama (Badulla District) asked not for higher output prices or protection against imports, but subsidies on imported potato and cabbage seed (*Ceylon Daily News*, 21 December 1977).

108. In January 1978, immediately after the announcement of almost complete import liberalisation in the November 1977 budget, the (government) MP for Haputale, a sugarcane area, complained publicly

about the effects on the industry (*Weekend*, 8 January 1978). The details of the conversion of the UNP to some protection for the sugarcane industry are given in *Tribune*, 14 June 1980: 32. Later in the same month the Minister of Trade publicly announced that protection would be granted (*Ceylon News*, 26 June 1980).

109. Details of the proposal and its origins are given in the *Ceylon News*, 15 January 1981. The only potential investors specifically mentioned in the announcement were interested in sugarcane.

110. See *Sri Lanka News*, 8 March 1984, and 5 May 1984 for an indication of the success of domestic sugar producers in at least making cheap sugar imports into a public political issue.

111. I refer particularly to conversations with Godfrey Gunatilleke and the late Raju Coomaraswamy.

112. For an elaboration of this point, see Moore 1981d: Appendix Six.

113. Source as note 101.

114. *Sun*, 15 December 1973.

115. *Ceylon Daily News*, 10 December 1976.

116. See Moore, 1981d: Appendix Three.

117. I am grateful to Mr A. S. Ranatunga for information on this decision.

118. Details of these speeches, all in Sinhalese, are to be found in *Hansard*, Volume 5 (10, 11) of 4 and 5 July 1979. See speeches by S. D. Bandaranayake (SLFP, Gampaha) on pp. 1172–3; H. B. Abeyratne (UNP, Yapahuwa) on p. 1173; R. Atapattu (UNP, Beliatta) on pp. 1189–90; H. G. P. Nelson (UNP, Polonnaruwa) on pp. 1210–11; and R. P. Wijesiri (SLFP, Harispattuwa) on pp. 1260–1.

119. *Ceylon Daily News*, 10 December 1976.

120. See reports of the Second Reading of the Land Betterment Charges Bill in the *Ceylon Daily News*, 8 and 10 October 1976.

121. Moore, 1981d: 239, fn. 151.

122. The demand for farmers' pensions was accepted in principle by the Minister of Finance in his 1973 budget speech (*Budget Speech*, 1973: 61). It has been repeated more recently by the Minister of Agriculture (*Sun*, 14 July 1978; and *Ceylon News*, 10 August 1978). The most recent account I have of a demand for such a measure is of a parliamentary motion put down by the MP for Laggala in March 1980 (*Ceylon Daily News*, 25 March 1980).

123. See the report of the founding meeting in the *Ceylon Daily News*, 5 November 1977.

124. The evidence for this claim lies partly in my own involvement as a consultant in the policy-making process in relation to food prices and partly in information from a number of other persons similarly engaged either as consultants or as public officials. Among the latter, the late Raju Coomaraswamy and Godfrey Gunatilleke have been especially helpful.

125. Central Bank of Ceylon, *Review of the Economy*, 1979: 31. The *Review* was published in April 1980, while the GPS paddy price was increased from Rs. 40 to Rs. 50 per bushel in the budget of January 1981.

126. This latter observation is based on my investigations in a Low Country

tea-growing village. I am especially grateful to Gamini Wickremesinghe, who was resident in this village at the time.

127. Wickremeratne, 1977a: 152–3.
128. On some of the roots of this partial symbiosis of nationalist and socialist economic ideas, see Roberts, 1979e; and Oliver, 1957.
129. Particularly important were authoritative coordinating committees at cabinet level (chaired by the Prime Minister or the Minister of Agriculture and Food) and at district level (chaired by the Government Agent), which were designed to improve the level of cooperation among government departments. Senior public servants were appointed as government agents to important food-producing districts (Wanasinghe, 1980b: 188–91).
130. Moore, 1981d: Appendix Three.
131. This statement is based largely on my own experience in Sri Lanka, especially my work as a consultant in economic planning. It is evidenced in the Minister of Agriculture's boast in a speech in early 1980, that the consumer price of rice was low and that further reductions could be anticipated (see *Ceylon Daily News*, 19 April 1980).
132. Wanasinghe, 1980b: 192; and Farmer, 1957: 144–5.
133. For an account of C. P. de Silva's political career, see Jupp, 1978: pages as in his index.
134. This paragraph is based on data I collected while in Sri Lanka. The total unexpectedness of the decision is illustrated by the fact that there was considerable gossip, verbally and in the press, about the identity of the person who could have planted such an idea in Jayawardena's mind.
135. See *Budget Speech*, 1977: 53; and Duncan, 1979: 303–5.
136. Morrison *et al.* (eds.), 1979: 32–3.
137. Moore, 1981d: Chapter 3.
138. The author has nowhere seen this argument explicitly developed. Evidence may, however, be found, for example, in Roberts, 1979e: 404.
139. See, for example, the speech by Colvin R. de Silva in the debate on the 1976 financial votes for the Ministry of Agriculture and Lands (*Ceylon Daily News*, 10 December 1976), and the speeches by P. O. Wimalanga, A. Seneviratne, Vasudeva Nannayakara, N. M. Perera, Colvin R. de Silva, and L. C. de Silva, all LSSP MPs, in the earlier debate, mentioned in the text above, on the Land Betterment Charges Bill (*Ceylon Daily News*, 8 and 10 October 1976). A couple of years later Dr N. M. Perera and Dr Colvin R. de Silva, the LSSP's two most prominent personalities, were to assume the role of spokesmen for those Dry Zone farmers whose lands and small irrigation systems were being overrun or destroyed by state development agencies in the rush to accelerate construction of the large Mahaweli irrigation-cum-power project.
140. Bandaranaike, 1961: 880–4. The quotation is from p. 880.
141. Moore, 1981d: Chapter 3.
142. See note 140.
143. *Ceylon News*, 10 January 1980.

144. See reports in the *Ceylon Daily News*, 1 and 2 February 1974, of speeches made in Hambantota district by the Minister of Agriculture and the Minister of Fisheries.
145. The proportion of paddy crop actually sold through the GPS declined continuously from 40% in 1972 to 21% in 1975 (Gavan and Chandrasekere, 1979: 31–3).
146. *Budget Speech*, 1975: 3.
147. See *Hansard*, Volume 30, Adjournment (Price of Paddy Under Guaranteed Price Scheme), 6 March 1958: 3855–3895. Gunawardena's suggestion that the MP for Vavuniya buy a tractor is on p. 3863, and his discussion of the fecklessness of the peasantry on p. 3891.
148. See *Hansard*, Volume 5 (11), 5 July 1979: 1191–2, 1201–2.
149. Timmer and Falcon, 1975: 401.
150. Oliver, 1957. Herring (1972: 118) talks of 'a dominant theme in land reform ideology for Sri Lanka, the legitimacy of societal claims on land and land utilisation against the traditional prerogatives of private ownership'.
151. See *Ceylon Daily News*, 21 February 1978.

6 Categorising space: urban–rural and core–periphery

1. The greater significance attached to spatial analysis in Francophone rather than Anglophone social science is discussed, for example, by Claval, 1980: 63, 69.
2. Mills, 1980: 20.
3. Parsons, 1951: 67 and *passim*.
4. Newby, 1978: 3–5.
5. *Ibid*: 4–5; and Moore, 1984a.
6. Since this section was first written the functions of the village, town and urban councils have been taken over by the District Development Councils created in 1981.
7. Moore, 1981d: 283, fn. 13.
8. Moore and Perera, 1978: 38.
9. Moore, 1981d: 250.
10. *Ibid*: 250, 284, fns. 17, 18.
11. These factors were discussed, for example, by Denham (1912: 27–8) in his commentary on the results of the 1911 population census.
12. In 1971 forty-one out of eighty-six town council areas had populations of less than 5,000 people (*Census of Population 1971, Volume 1, Part 2*: Table 5).
13. *Census of Population 1971, Volume 2, Part 2*: Table 5.
14. *Ibid*.
15. See, for example, a case study by Moore *et al.*, 1979.
16. Ryan, 1953: 197; Yalman, 1967: 53; and Farmer, 1957: 95.
17. The general case is argued by Moore and Perera, 1978. See also

Wanigaratne *et al.*, 1980: 42; Seneratne, 1970: 69; and Ryan, 1953: 191, 265.

18. ESCAP, 1975: 105–8.
19. Moore, 1981d: 253–4.
20. Frank, 1969.
21. Gottman, 1980: 13.
22. *Ibid*: 15–17.
23. *Ibid*: 17.
24. Lipton, 1977.
25. This section is a summary of a more detailed account given in Moore, 1981d: 255–67. Many of the references given there have been omitted here.
26. Chilaw, Puttalam, Negombo, Colombo, Kalutara, Beruwala, Galle, Weligama, Matara and Tangalle.
27. See especially Roberts, 1982.
28. Farmer, 1972: 812.
29. For the details of this ethnic diversity and the occupational patterns with which it was associated, see Samaraweera, 1977a. This paragraph is not an attempt to deny the undoubted poverty of many members of the minorities in Colombo (Michael Roberts, private communication).
30. In 1946 the population of Colombo Municipality was classified as follows: Sinhalese – 47%; Sri Lanka Tamils – 10%; Indian Tamils – 13%; Sri Lanka Moors – 12%; Indian Moors – 4%; Eurasians – 5%; Malays – 3%; Europeans – 1%; Others – 6% (*Census of Ceylon 1946, Volume 1, Part 2*: Table 26a).
31. In 1946, although 47% of the population of the city were Sinhalese, only 39% were Buddhist (*Ibid*: Table 37a).
32. In 1946 two-thirds or more of the total populations in the following categories were to be found in Colombo Municipality: Indian Moors, Burghers, Malays, Europeans and 'Others' (*Ibid*: Tables 26 and 26a). Because of the large Catholic fishing population along the coast, only 14% of Christians were located in Colombo Municipality (*Ibid*: Tables 37 and 37a). This figure, however, included most of the Sri Lankan members of the high-status Anglican community.
33. ESCAP, 1975: 111. See also Gunatilleke, 1973: 41–2.
34. For a more detailed account of this point, see Moore, 1981d: 262–5.
35. This section is a summary of a more detailed account given in *ibid*: 267–73.
36. In 1971 the number of Sri Lanka Tamils living in Jaffna district was over twice the combined numbers of those living in Mannar, Vavuniya and Batticaloa districts, and amounted to almost half the Sri Lanka Tamil population of the Island (*Census of Population 1971, General Report*: 83). The greater use of educational facilities by Jaffna Tamils of the various parts of the Northern Province is indicated by Sivathamby, 1980: 19.
37. *Census of Population 1971, General Report*: 53.

Notes

38. Many of the people living along the coastal strip own and cultivate land in the interior (M. U. Ishak Lebbe, private communication; and Selvanayagam, 1977: especially 211–14).

39. In 1976 Sri Lanka Moors accounted for only a half of the population of five coastal electorates from Batticaloa southwards – Batticaloa, Padiruppu, Samanthurai, Kalmunai and Pottuvil – and Sri Lanka Tamils for most of the remainder (de Silva, G. P. S. H., 1979: 133, 192, 250, 258, 266–7).

40. In 1971 Batticaloa and Amparai districts contained only 23% of the Sri Lanka Moor population (*Census of Population 1971, General Report*: 83).

41. M. U. Ishak Lebbe, private communication.

42. ESCAP, 1975: 16.

43. For a discussion of these zonal boundaries, see Peiris, 1977a; and Farmer, 1972: 810.

44. Dore, 1976.

45. *Ibid*: Chapter 4.

46. Moore, 1981d: 291, fn. 111.

47. The connection between educational performance and parental socio-economic status is high (Moore and Wickremesinghe, 1980: Chapter 7).

48. For parallel evidence of high intra-district inequality in access to education, transport, and health facilities according to location and population density, see Peiris, 1981a.

49. In 1971 Indian Tamils accounted for 52% of the population of Nuwara Eliya district, 24% of Kandy district, and 9% of Kegalle district (*Census of Population 1971, General Report*: Table 6.5). Although in the past the estate population was considered well-provided for educationally, estate schools have remained confined to the elementary grades while the public system serving the non-estate population has expanded enormously.

50. Samaraweera, 1979a: 250–7.

51. Data from *Census of Population 1971, Volume 2, Part 1*: Table 5.

7 A smallholder interest or smallholder interests?

1. Moore, 1980b.

2. The estimates were obtained by subtracting assumed paddy consumption requirements from estimated total paddy availability. The number of households estimated to sell paddy would have been larger if allowances had been made for:

(i) The fact that larger farms probably support larger than average families. Various different samples do suggest that there is on average a positive relationship between household size and farm size, but this varies considerably from place to place. See, for example, ARTI, 1974a: 111; 1974b: 105; 1975a: 89; 1975b: 72; 1975c: 53.

(ii) The availability of the rice ration to most cultivating households. The rice ration has been available indiscriminately to food producers for most of the period since it was introduced. Its quantitative impact on the food supplies of farming households has, however, varied considerably over time. Entitlements and costs have been changed regularly (Gavan and Chandrasekere, 1979: 28) and, although the free component of the ration has generally been utilised to the full, rates of offtake of that component provided at subsidised prices have varied considerably.

(iii) The fact that poorer paddy-cultivating households depend in part on home-grown 'inferior' staples – maize, millet, sorghum, jak fruit, cassava and other root crops – rather than rice alone. The cheapness of so-called 'inferior' staples as a source of calories and proteins is demonstrated by Edirisinghe and Poleman, 1977: 18. It is quite possible that dietary surveys underestimate the consumption of these 'inferior' (i.e. low-status) foods. The information in these surveys is, however, not presented in such a way as to allow one to determine whether cultivators do indeed consume 'inferior' foods themselves in order to have more rice for sale (e.g. Perera *et al.*, 1973). Brow argues that this was the practice in Anuradhapura district in the past (Brow, 1978: 92–3).

3. For the derivation of this figure, see Moore and Wickremesinghe, 1980: 164–5.

4. Hambantota district devotes an unusually large proportion of its cropped area to the miscellaneous 'other crops' category, and is less oriented to paddy production than other Dry Zone districts (*ibid*: 23).

5. For a more extended discussion of these regional differences in paddy production technologies, see *ibid*: 24–8.

6. For a sociological village case study oriented around this point, see Seneratne, 1970.

7. Evidence of the careful and labour-intensive nature of paddy production in the Kandyan areas in the seventeenth century is provided by Knox, 1686: Chapter 3.

8. For evidence of this from comparative wage rates, see Chapter Four.

9. Moore, 1981d: 323, fn. 15.

10. This point is simplified and exaggerated here for heuristic purposes. Fertiliser is most useful if delivered on time.

11. Many of the allegations of diversion of paddy fertiliser to other crops seem to relate to the 1960s, when only paddy fertiliser was subsidised. The fact that Hussain (1977: 69) has found annual rates of offtake of paddy fertiliser to be a statistically significant determinant of paddy yields implies that the use of paddy fertiliser for other crops is limited.

12. For example, those paddy farmers to which the data in Table 7.4 relate applied the following quantities of labour per cwt of fertiliser in the survey season: Dry Zone (Polonnaruwa) – 26 person-days; Kandyan areas (Kandy and Kegalle) – 44 person-days; and core region (Colombo) – 34 person-days (Ranatunga and Abeysekera, 1977: 31, 43).

13. Moore and Wickremesinghe, 1980: 27.

14. An example is provided in the data from a sample of paddy farmers in five

districts given in ARTI, 1975d: 30. The main exception is that in the fertile and well-watered Dry Zone district of Polonnaruwa, household incomes are, not surprisingly, distinctly higher than elsewhere.

15. This is suggested by Sathasivampillai, 1973: 54–5; and Morrison, 1979: 92–3.
16. Moore, 1981d: 323, fn. 22.
17. *Ibid*: 323, fn. 23.
18. *Ibid*: 324, fn. 24.
19. *Ibid*: 324, fn. 27.
20. Burch, 1979: Appendices 7–10.
21. For evidence of poor water management, see Chapter Five. Information on the poor performance of state tractor pools is given in Burch, 1979: 182–7. Inefficiencies and corruption in the purchase of paddy under the GPS are a perennial topic of complaint by Dry Zone farmers.
22. Up to the end of 1953 allottees on new irrigation schemes were equally divided between local people and outsiders, and the latter tended to come especially from the hilly Kandyan areas (Farmer, 1957: 208–9). More recent figures on the origin of colonists do not seem to be available, but it is known that an increasing proportion are tending to come from the Dry Zone itself, especially the children of the original settlers on older schemes (Moore and Wickremesinghe, 1980: Chapter 1).
23. I obtained information about the existence and landholdings of such individuals from the field staff of the Agrarian Research and Training Institute/University of Reading research project on farm power and water use in the Dry Zone.
24. According to the 1973 Census of Agriculture, where an attempt was made to treat home gardens as a separate category, 44% of all smallholdings comprised home gardens only. The decision as to whether a holding was a home garden was, however, left to the subjective judgement of the investigator. The unhelpful, if substantively accurate, definition offered was a holding other than 'a regular farm' where 'the land is primarily meant for cultivation'. See *Census of Agriculture 1973, Smallholdings, Final Tables – Stage 1*: Table 4 and p. 4.
25. Some illustrative statistics are to be found in ARTI, 1979b: 44–5.
26. *Ibid*: 55–6.
27. See Moore, 1981d: Table 7.8.
28. Wickremeratne, 1973b: 445.
29. *Ibid*: 433–6.
30. For references to some aspects of this study, see Moore, 1978. One might note that these demands for a separate agency were successful, at least insofar as they received the approval of a Parliamentary Commission established to investigate the industry. It recommended the establishment of a Cinnamon Development Authority. One might note also that the newspaper report was headlined: '*Uplift* of cinnamon industry proposed' (my emphasis). (See *Ceylon News*, 15 March 1979.)

Notes

8   Rural consciousness

1. For a detailed account of the Malay experience, see Moore, 1981b: Chapter 3.
2. For the Indian experience, see *ibid*; and Nadkarni, 1983.
3. Two scholars have been particularly influential in planting in my mind the seeds of this comparison. Bryce Ryan (1953) continually touches upon aspects of it in explaining differences between the Sinhalese and the Indian caste systems. Mark Holmstrom of the University of East Anglia made some very perceptive – although epithetical and at the time enigmatic – comments on the contrasting natures of 'urban bias' in India and Sri Lanka at an academic gathering some years ago. Much the same kind of contrast between Sri Lanka and India as the one developed in this chapter has recently been suggested by Meyer (1982: 228) in his reference to the much higher levels of village solidarity in India.
4. Ryan, 1953: 10.
5. The first half of this paragraph is the author's paraphrase of Roberts (1979a). It does not, however, do justice to the subtlety of his more differentiated and useful terminology for describing the various different kinds of phenomena which are conventionally bundled together under the label of 'nationalism'.
6. In general, see Roberts, 1979a. The long autonomy and/or South Indian orientation of a separate Jaffna-based Tamil polity and culture raises questions about the notion of Lanka as a distinctively Sinhalese Buddhist territory and polity (de Silva, K. M., 1977b: 37–48). Indeed the last kings of Kandy, for two centuries a Sinhalese stronghold against the European rulers of the lowlands, were in fact from a South Indian Tamil dynasty. Although a cause of some embarrassment to latter-day Sinhalese nationalists, this does not throw serious doubt on the distinctively Sinhalese nature of the Kandyan polity. These kings were recognised and often resented as foreigners at the time (Dharmadasa, 1979: 103–9 and *passim*). Similarly, the essential homogeneity of the Sinhalese tradition does not appear to have been affected by the fact that immediately before the European conquest the Island was divided between rival Sinhalese rulers (de Silva, K. M., 1977b: 47–58). After the European conquest the 'Sinhalese of the Maritime Provinces seldom failed to respond to the wishes of the Kandyan King whom they regarded as the legitimate ruler of all Sinhalese' (de Silva, K. M., 1973e: 12).
7. Ryan (1953: Chapter 3) and Pieris (1956) provide information on historical sources for pre-colonial and colonial Sinhalese social and political organisation.
8. The nature of pre-colonial Sinhalese socio-political organisation has been explored by historians in some detail and, because of substantial continuities, material relating to the colonial period is also relevant. Apart from specific references given, the main sources for this section are: for the general historical context, de Silva, K. M., 1977b; for the nature of

Notes

Sinhalese, and especially Kandyan, feudalism, Pieris, 1956; Ryan, 1953; and Seneviratne, 1977 and 1978; for the connection between religious and social organisation, Seneviratne, 1977 and 1978; Evers, 1972; Ling, 1976: especially Chapters 10 and 12; Obeyesekere, 1979; and Ryan *et al.*, 1958: Chapters 6 and 7.

9. This point was made to me by Michael Roberts. For a sketch of the socio-political dimensions of European feudalism, see, for example, Poggi, 1978: Chapter 2; and for an analysis of the implications of the absence of vassalage in Russia, see Pipes, 1977: 49–52.
10. For a detailed account of the land tenure basis of Sinhalese feudalism, see Pieris, 1956.
11. Ryan, 1953: 50.
12. A brief summary of the traditional Indian caste system is provided by Srinivas, 1969. For a more detailed account, see, for example, Mandelbaum, 1970a: Parts 3 and 4; and 1970b: Part 6.
13. This point is argued in great detail by Ryan, 1953: Chapter 1, 45–7, Chapter 3, and *passim*. See also Pieris, 1956: Part 5.
14. Pieris, 1956: 171; and Ryan, 1953: 107–9.
15. The main apparent exception to this, at least in the contemporary era and probably long before, is the *de facto* near monopoly of fishing held by the *Karava* caste. Although the *Karava* are currently engaged in a wide variety of occupations, these have mainly been developed from a fishing base (Ryan, 1953: 185; and Roberts, 1979d).
16. Ryan, 1953: 180.
17. *Ibid*: 78.
18. Pieris, 1956: 171.
19. Ryan, 1953: 78–9.
20. *Ibid*: 16, 245. For a recent social anthropological study of a community still exhibiting traces of the *variga* court, and therefore autonomous local control of caste membership, see Leach, 1961.
21. Ryan, 1953: 31 and Chapter 7.
22. For a discussion of these two dimensions of intercaste relationships, see, for example, Harriss, J., 1982: Chapter 6.
23. Ryan, 1953: 11–12, 87–8, 197–8 and *passim*.
24. Ling, 1976: 213.
25. For the distinction between Theravada and Mahayana Buddhism, see *ibid*: 19–20.
26. *Ibid*: Chapters 10 and 12; Seneviratne, 1978: 15; Phadnis, 1976: 40–3; and Wriggins, 1960: 180–2.
27. Wriggins, 1960: 262–5; de Silva, K. M., 1973d: 189–92; and Phadnis, 1976: 56–7.
28. The contemporary *Sangha* in Sri Lanka is divided into three fraternities (*Nikaye*), and each is subdivided into sects (Phadnis, 1976: Chapter 3).
29. Apart from specific references, this account of temple organisation derives mainly from Ling, 1976: Chapter 12; Seneviratne, 1978: 11–12 and *passim*; Evers, 1972: Chapter 1 and *passim*; Phadnis, 1976;

Carrithers, 1979; Ryan, 1953: Chapters 1, 2 and *passim*; and Malalgoda, 1976: especially Chapters 1 and 2.

30. Ryan, 1953: 48–50.

31. The association of the priesthood with (generally modest and local) material wealth and privilege has correlates in the ideology and practice of priesthood. While it is true that the norm of the priest as a quasi-hermit retreating into the forest for a life of contemplation has never been very strongly adhered to, the principle itself points to important aspects of Buddhist priesthood: its orientation to learning and the personal religious devotions of the priest, and its lack of a tradition of pastoral care in the Christian sense, i.e. concern with the worldly and personal problems of a 'flock'. Interaction between priest and villagers is often very close. The emphasis is, however, on the duty of the villagers to support the priest, as illustrated by the rota for the provision of the priest's meals by villagers. The priest is under little obligation to interrupt his devotion, or leisure – depending upon one's point of view – to serve the spiritual needs of those who serve his material needs. For this purpose Buddhism has always coexisted with a very wide and diverse 'non-Buddhist' magico-religious universe inhabited by planets, demons, ghosts, spirits and gods of all kinds, many of them of Hindu form and origin. They communicate to mankind through astrologers, devil dancers, and a wide range of other 'non-Buddhist' religious practitioners, few of them measuring up to the *bhikkhu* in status or material well-being. This harmonious coexistence of Buddhist and what are often formally but inaccurately termed 'non-Buddhist' elements in Sinhalese religion – physically represented in the existence of a shrine to 'Hindu' or other gods in the compounds of many 'Buddhist' temples – may be viewed, if one accepts a materialist analysis of religion, as a necessary correlate to the privileged lifestyle of the *bhikkhus*. In terms of our concerns it is an outcome of the way in which religious organisation replicates and strengthens the hierarchies of material privilege and political power in the non-religious sphere (Ling, 1976: 268–80; Ryan, 1958: Chapters 6 and 7).

32. Ryan, 1953: 12.

33. Thus Pieris (1956: 171) says of the *Goigama*: 'This farmer aristocracy . . . was far from being a ruling minority, for it included the bulk of the population.' Caste membership has not been recorded in population censuses since 1824. In that year, the *Goigama* accounted for 54% of the Low Country Sinhalese (Ryan, 1953: 145 and *passim*; Jiggins, 1979: 29, 75), and one would expect that the proportion of *Goigama* would increase over time. They appear, according to the only recent attempt actually to count numbers, to comprise only a half of the Sinhalese population (Jiggins, 1979: 35). The accuracy of this count has, however, been very much questioned.

34. All the points made in this section are to be found in one form or another in Kothari, 1970.

35. Mandelbaum, 1970b: 327–8.

36. For example, Srinivas and Shah, 1960.
37. See for example Dumont and Pocock, 1957b; the reply by Bailey, 1957; and also Dumont, 1966.
38. Cohn, 1968: 18–20.
39. Kothari, 1970: 26.
40. Srinivas, 1962: 98–111.
41. Mandelbaum, 1970b: 336.
42. Rudolph, 1968: 530–1. See also Kothari, 1970: 25–6 where he talks of 'local solidarity' and 'small group orientation'.
43. Dumont and Pocock, 1957a: 20.
44. The quotations are all from Kothari, 1970: 25, 11 and 31 respectively. See also Mason, 1967: 26.
45. This point is made by Chaudhuri, 1978. Although explicitly concerned only with the Mughal period, he implies continuity with the pre-Mughal period. See also Kothari, 1970: 31; and Habib, 1963.
46. Kothari, 1970: 351; for Joshi's ideology, see Nadkarni, 1983.
47. Chaudhuri, 1978: 81; see also Habib, 1963.
48. Roberts, 1970a: 144.
49. On the concept of 'little' and 'great traditions' and the expansion of the latter into contemporary rural India, see Marriott, 1965. On the urban and Brahmanic origins of the 'great traditions' of contemporary India, see Shah, 1974: 119–20 and, with special reference to the spread of Brahmanic law, Rudolph and Rudolph, 1967: Part 3. On the general Brahmanisation (i.e. Sanskritisation) of contemporary Indian culture, see Srinivas, 1962: Chapter 2. On the revival of Hinduism and Hindu power (as opposed to Islam) as a result of British rule, see Kothari, 1970: 63.
50. Moore, 1981d: Chapter 3.
51. On the nature and problems of this process, see Weiner, 1963: Chapter Two.
52. Kothari, 1970: 11.
53. *Ibid*: *passim*.
54. *Ibid*: 17 and *passim*.
55. Moore, 1981d: Chapter 3.
56. For the role of *rajakariya* in early British administration and its abolition, see Samaraweera, 1973c: 37, 41; and 1973d: 58–62; and 1973a: 86.
57. Ryan, 1953: 198, 54–5.
58. For an account of the evolution of the relationship between the colonial rulers and the Kandyan aristocracy, see Samaraweera, 1973c: 46–7; 1973a: 81; and de Silva, K. M., 1973c: 220–1.
59. Ryan, 1953: 56.
60. Gold, 1977: 54–5. Note that this measure, the only 'land to the tiller' land reform programme conducted in Sri Lanka, was carried through by a UNP government. It is likely that part of the motivation lay in the fact that the SLFP leadership was at this time in large part occupied by members of the Kandyan aristocracy, and at the top levels the UNP–

SLFP divide appeared to some degree as a contest between Low Country *Goigama* and Kandyan *Radala* (a high-status *Goigama* subcaste) respectively (see Jiggins, 1979: 94).

61. These caste services are mainly those of the *Berava* (drummers) and similar performers.
62. Roberts, 1973c: 161.
63. Evers, 1972: 18–19.
64. Gold, 1977: 55.
65. Evers, 1972: 19–20 and *passim*; Ryan, 1953; and Seneviratne, 1978: Chapters 6–8.
66. Seneviratne, 1978: especially Chapters 6–8; and 1977: 70.
67. This point is, to the best of my knowledge, nowhere written. It is justified by a knowledge of recent Indian and Sri Lankan history. To make this claim is not to deny that physical violence does play a role in local-level Sri Lankan politics (e.g. Perera, 1982: Part Three). It is, however, not as prevalent or as organised as in India.
68. See Jiggins, 1979: 6; and my fieldwork.
69. Samaraweera, 1979b: 80; and Rogers, 1984: 2.
70. I am indebted to Michael Roberts for the opportunity to read an undated draft paper entitled 'The Past in the Present: The Asokan Persona As a Persisting of Authority in Sinhalese Political Culture'. See also Roberts, 1975: 46–7.
71. Samaraweera, 1978.
72. Caste remains strong among the Sri Lanka Tamils (Samaraweera, 1977a: 106).
73. See, for example, my review of Jiggins (1979) in *Modern Asian Studies*, 15 (1), 1981; and that by Samaraweera in *The Ceylon Journal of Historical and Social Studies* NS 8 (2), 1978
74. For some evidence in relation to farmers' and agricultural labourers' organisations, see Wilson, 1978: 37.
75. See the references given in Chapter Four and, for particular case studies, Robinson, 1975; and Moore and Wickremesinghe, 1980: 87.
76. Gold, 1977: 193.
77. For a village case study, see Yalman, 1967: 54–5. See also Moore, 1981d: 363.
78. Seneratne, 1970: 57–8.
79. Herring, 1977; and 1972: 106–8.
80. In addition to Herring's work cited above, see Dias and Wickramanayake, 1977; Harriss, J., 1977a; and ARTI, 1974a.
81. Herring, 1977: 139–40.
82. *Ibid*: 136. See also Dias and Wickramanayake, 1977.
83. Harriss, J. (1977b: 251) talks of attempts to establish tenants' and labourers' unions in Hambantota district under the aegis of a group of relatively active SLFP MPs in the early 1970s. He has amplified this point to me in a private communication. In their study of agricultural labour the only examples Perera and Gunawardena were able to find of

the development of class-like horizontal organisation among the rural poor related to Hambantota district (1980: 118–20).

84. Moore, 1981d: 381, fn. 133.
85. On the importance of emigration from Matara to Hambantota, see Moore, 1981d: Appendix Five; and Herring, 1977: 119, 122. On the ethnic homogeneity of Hambantota district, see Table 9.1.
86. A local-level example of the ease and automaticity with which Kandyan village landlords assumed local control of the machinery intended for the enforcement of tenants' rights under the 1958 Paddy Lands Act is provided in Robinson, 1975: 189–91.
87. Gold, 1977: Chapter 3.
88. Burch, 1979.
89. See Ranatunga *et al.*, 1981: 48–9; and Farrington and Abeyratne, 1982.
90. This is the conclusion of a team which originally set out to examine Sri Lanka's 'rice revolution'. See Hameed *et al.*, 1977: 71.
91. Burch, 1979: Chapter 7; and Farrington, 1983.
92. Leys, 1971.
93. See, for example, ARTI, 1975d: 18; Ranatunga and Abeysekere, 1977: 34; Central Bank of Ceylon, 1969, *Survey on Cost of Production of Paddy*: 29; Moore and Wickremesinghe, 1980: 94.
94. Thus Moore *et al.* (1979: 205) found that of a sample of forty-eight paddy cultivators in a village where the average paddy holding was only 1.4 acres, only three managed to prepare their land in the survey season without recourse to non-family labour.
95. Moore, 1981d: 382, fn. 147.
96. e.g. *ibid*: 383, fn. 148.
97. See Wickremasekera, 1977: 82; Gunawardena, 1979: 190; Moore *et al.*, 1979: 205–6; and Perera and Gunawardena, 1980: 18–20.
98. For information on the organisation of this seasonal labour, see Perera and Gunawardena, 1980: Chapter Five; and Ranbanda, 1980.
99. Wickremasekera (1977: 77–8), for example, has provided a case study of a single household whose members at various times engaged in the following income-earning activities: own cultivation; employment on road maintenance; employment in making sheet rubber; toddy tapping and jaggery making; seasonal migration to the Dry Zone for agricultural labour; mat weaving; carpentry and masonry work.
100. Moore, 1981d: 383, fn. 153.
101. Weiner, 1963: 113.
102. Duncan, 1979: 94–103, Chapter 4, and 312.
103. Wesumperuma (1967: 138) reports cases of peasants organising to resist grain taxes in the 1880s.
104. Moore, 1981d: 82.
105. This paragraph is based on my fieldwork observations and on Stinchcombe's (1971) account of the particular impact on social and political relationships of the immobility of land and of the fact that it cannot be reproduced.

9 Ethnic conflict and the politics of the periphery

1. Perhaps the classic demonstration of the fallaciousness of these beliefs in relation to contemporary South Asian politics is the work of Brass on North India (1974).

2. The best single source of information on the nature of collective identities in contemporary Sri Lanka is the recent volume on the subject edited by Michael Roberts, especially Roberts' own contributions (Roberts, 1979a; and 1979c). Obeysekere (1979) has described the change over time in the significance of Buddhism to the Sinhalese identity. There is evidence from 'frontier' regions between Sinhalese and Tamils of the very recent emergence of distinct and opposed Sinhalese and Tamil identities in response to the increasing salience of ethnic identities in public life (Yalman, 1967: Chapter 14; Roberts, 1979a: 55–7). Evidence was quoted in Chapter Four of the cultural assimilation into the Indian Tamil category of Sinhalese employed on estates. Roberts (1979a: 39) quotes evidence of movement in the opposite direction of Indian Tamils who have 'escaped' from the estate sector. References are given in Moore (1981d: Chapter 6) to some of the ambiguities about the labels placed on the various Moor categories.

3. This is probably true of the divisions between the Sinhalese and other groups. In the case of the intra-Sinhalese divisions between Buddhist and Christian, Kandyan and Low Country, the opposite may be true. Stirrat (1984) has demonstrated how among the Catholics religious identity was primary in the nineteenth and early twentieth centuries, but has been replaced by ethnicity, leaving the Sinhalese and Tamil Catholics, and the Sri Lankan Catholic Church generally, now bitterly divided.

4. No recent or precise figures are available on the ethnic composition of the farming population. One can, however, produce a reliable estimate for rice farmers. It is reasonable to assume that in 1946, before substantial Sinhalese colonisation of traditional Muslim and Tamil areas, all paddy farmers in the Moor and Tamil Eastern and Northern Provinces were non-Sinhalese, and that in the rest of the Island all paddy farmers were Sinhalese. Errors are likely to be self-cancelling. Calculations suggest that at that time 87% of all paddy farmers were Sinhalese, while the Sinhalese accounted for 69% of the total population. (For information on the district populations by communal group and on paddy holdings see *Census of Ceylon 1946, Volume 1, Part 2*: Tables 26 and 69.) The 'Sinhalese bias' of Dry Zone colonisation would suggest that the disproportionate involvement of Sinhalese in rice cultivation has tended to increase rather than decrease since that time.

5. In the parliamentary debate preceding the passing of the 1958 Paddy Lands Act, Sir Razik Fareed, a leading Moor politician, while arguing that the large paddy landlord was a rare bird, declared that he knew of one man in the Eastern Province – implicitly a Moor – who owned about four thousand acres of paddy. *Hansard*, Volume 30, 12 December 1957: 2006.

6. For the purpose of these calculations it was assumed (a) that each category of paddy farmer (e.g. 'big farmer', 'deficit farmer') was divided among the different ethnic groups in the same proportion as these ethnic groups are found in the total non-estate population of the district; and (b) that the estate population comprised the Indian Tamil population of the main plantation districts – Kandy, Nuwara Eliya, Kegalle, Matale, Ratnapura and Badulla. The data on the distribution of the district populations among ethnic groups were obtained from *Census of Population 1971, General Report*: 84. The estimated number of deficit farmers are those from which the figures in column (d) of Table 7.1 are derived. For sources, see Moore, 1980b. The number of paddy holdings in each district are as given in the *Census of Agriculture 1962, Volume 3*: Table 1. The estimated number of big paddy farmers are as given in column (a) of Table 7.5.

7. Evidence is given in Chapter Five that the MPs who have expressed concern about the adequacy of output prices for rice farmers have tended to be Tamils and Muslims. The parliamentary debate on the 1979 Agrarian Services Bill was generally premised on the common (although erroneous – see Chapter Five) assumption that the tenancy provisions were oriented to the needs of the paddy land *tenant*. The Muslim MP for the east coast electorate of Pottuvil was, however, willing to step out of line to the degree that he publicly praised the provision to allow the landlord to resume control of land in the event of rent default (see *Hansard*, Volume 11 (5), 5 July 1979: 1240).

8. *Hansard*, 25 August 1964: 2445–6.

9. Sivathamby, 1980: 19.

10. Moore, 1981d: 335.

11. Moore, 1984b.

12. Moore, 1984a.

13. For recent figures on the declining proportion of Sri Lanka Tamils in higher education and public-sector employment, see *Lanka Guardian*, Volume 13 (6), 29 October 1983. For discussions of ethnic conflict, see Kearney, 1973: Chapter 5; Roberts, 1979a; and Arasaratnam, 1979.

14. In 1971 only 28% of the total Sri Lanka Tamil population resided in the food surplus Tamil districts – Mannar, Vavuniya, Trincomalee, Batticaloa, and Amparai (*Census of Population 1971, General Report*: 83).

15. Thus one of the flashpoints of the 1958 communal disturbances was what has been the biggest single Sinhalese 'intrusion' – the large Gal Oya irrigation scheme in Amparai district (Wriggins, 1960: 261). On the general issue, see Wilson, 1980: 116, 121–2.

16. See *Sri Lanka News*, 3 November 1983, 10 November 1983, and 24 November 1983; and *Lanka Guardian*, Volume 6 (16), 15 December 1983.

17. In 1946 Low Country Sinhalese accounted for 17% of the Dry Zone Sinhalese population, and in 1971 for 24% (Moore, 1981d: 374, fn. 30).

18. Moore, 1981d: 337; and Moore, 1984a.

19. Moore, 1981d: 339.
20. *Ibid*: 338.
21. But there is evidence of cultural assimilation of Low Country Sinhalese into the Kandyan category in the Dry Zone (*ibid*: 343).
22. Apart from specific sources cited, this section relies heavily on my own field observations. None of the sources quoted below presents the issue in quite the same terms as I have done. In particular, the central role played in local politics by *mudalalis* – businessmen, traders, contractors etc. – is characteristically seen as bad, and implicitly deviant from some kind of norm or ideal. The following are the sources of information which I recall most clearly: conversations with John Harriss and with R. D. Wanigaratne in relation to his research on the Minipe colonisation scheme; Wanigaratne, 1979a: especially 138–40; and 1979b; Farmer, 1957, who provides generally useful background as well as evidence of the dependence of colonists on government (p. 288), the particular intensity for colonists' indebtedness to traders (pp. 274–5), and the 'lack of community spirit' (pp. 296–9); Ellman and Ratnaweera, 1973; Perera, 1979b: especially 144; the comparison made by Robinson (1975: Chapter 10) between the social life of a Kandyan village and that of a group of ex-villagers settled in a Dry Zone colony; the account by Dias and Wickramanayake (1977) of the socio-political consequences of the economic insecurity and risks to life in the Dry Zone; Amunugama, 1965; ESCAP, 1975: 105–7.
23. An illuminating individual case study of the importance to land allottees and their heirs of favourable administrative decisions over land rights and the legality of marriage is given in Wanigaratne, 1979b: 54–7.
24. There appear to be no large-scale surveys which would support the claim that people from the Low Country dominate among Dry Zone traders. The point is very sensitive. Some supporting evidence is, however, given in Perera, 1982; and in the results of a recent survey in the Galnewa area in Anuradhapura district (Dr D. Wanasinghe, private communication). The point is, however, easily established in any visit to the Dry Zone.
25. Amunugama, 1965: 50–4; Jupp, 1978: 197; Wanigaratne, 1979a: 138–40; Perera, 1979b: especially 144; and 1982: especially 120.
26. For details of Freeman's career, see Jupp, 1978: 195. The election results are in de Silva, G. P. S. H., 1979: 91.
27. Jiggins, 1979: 54–5, 90–1; Jupp, 1978 (references in his index); and de Silva, G. P. S. H., 1979: 302–28.
28. Jupp, 1978 (references in his index); and de Silva, G. P. S. H., 1979: 302–8.
29. It is for two reasons especially appropriate to use the 1977 election results. The first is that the UNP won over 80% of all seats, and almost swept the board in the Sinhalese and Muslim electorates, leaving, apart from the TULF's Tamil seats, only eight for the SLFP and one for an independent. Inter-party differences in the background of MPs cannot therefore seriously affect the calculation. The second reason is that, since the UNP had itself been reduced to sixteen seats in the previous (1970) general

Notes

election, most of the MPs elected in 1977 had in the previous few years been engaged in occupations other than full-time politics. Tamil MPs are not included because the distinctive nature of the Tamil political subsystem would bias the results. In many ways very conservative, this is still dominated by the legal profession (Lake House, 1977: 55–204).

30. Sharma, 1979: 33.
31. See, for example, Jiggins, 1979: 99.
32. Woodward, 1969: 108.

10 The Sri Lankan polity

1. Jayanntha (1983) provides an illuminating account of the use of malpractices in elections in the early decades of universal suffrage.
2. See Kearney, 1973; Jupp, 1978; Woodward, 1969; and Wilson, 1979.
3. The phrase is from Roberts, 1979a: 11.
4. Moore, 1981d: Appendix Six.
5. See my review of Jiggins (1978) in *Modern Asian Studies*, 15 (1), 1981. Recent work by Jayanntha (1983) is, however, an important breakthrough in the study of politics at the level of the electorate.
6. Support for all these points can be found in Jupp, 1978.
7. The neatest single account of continuing elite dominance is perhaps Fernando, 1973.
8. On the evolution of the Sri Lankan party system, see especially Woodward, 1969: Conclusion and *passim*. On the origin of European parties as cliques of 'notables', see, for example, Bottomore, 1979: 49.
9. Woodward, 1969: Conclusion; and Jupp, 1978: Chapter 4.
10. See Jupp, 1978: Chapters 1 and 51.
11. See Jupp, 1978: especially Chapter 7.
12. See Roberts, 1979a: 75–6.
13. Roxborough, 1979: 41; and, for the quotation, Obeyesekere, 1974: 382.
14. Among the better-known social scientists who have contributed to the study of Sinhalese village life, Brow (1978), Leach (1961), Obeyesekere (1967), Robinson (1975), and Yalman (1967) have worked solely or mainly in remote villages and in explicit search of tradition. The main exception is Ryan *et al.* (1958), who worked in a Low Country village. So too did Seneratne (1970), but his work is unpublished and therefore little known, although very valuable.
15. On the middle classes, see Gunatilleke, 1978: 78; and Tambaiah, 1963: 55–64. The main source of information on the elite, information which I draw on heavily in this section, is the historical work of Michael Roberts (especially 1978 and 1979b). Jayawardena (1972) also provides useful historical background. Singer (1964) provides a very useful account of the changing composition of what he defines as the 'political elite', i.e. those elected or appointed to national legislatures. Additional contemporary information is provided by Jiggins, 1979: especially Chapter 6; Meyer, 1982; and Obeyesekere, 1974.
16. For some discussion of the confusions surrounding the loose and variable

use of terms such as 'elite', 'bourgeoisie' and 'middle class', see Roberts, 1975. For some attempts to explore the usefulness of a 'local elite–national elite' distinction, see Roberts, 1970c.

17. This information on the late E. J. Cooray is obtained from his obituaries in the *Ceylon News* of 15 November 1979 (brief) and 29 November 1979 (extended). The quotations are from the latter.

18. For the information in this paragraph I am indebted to Tara Coomaraswamy for indications of some results of her current research.

19. Manor, 1979: 31.

20. Of the two numerous Sinhalese castes, the *Batgam* or *Padu* are very poorly represented in the elite while the *Vahumpura* are represented mainly through a single family, the Mathews.

21. In relation to Sri Lanka this point is made by Dore, 1976: 54. See also Wriggins, 1960: 32.

22. See the account of the lifestyle of the Bandaranaike family in Manor, 1978: 17.

23. Jayanntha, 1983; and Roberts, 1975: 48.

24. Jupp, 1978: 198.

25. Singer, 1964: 67.

26. I derive this conclusion from the consistency of a number of fragmentary pieces of evidence: personal knowledge of a number of wealthy individuals who have recently invested in field crop production in Kurunegala district; the location in Kurunegala town of one of the Island's leading tractor dealers, Sathyawadi's; the fact that the first all-Island Paddy Producers Association was formed in 1977 in Kurunegala and made 'big farmer' demands, notably a foreign exchange allowance against paddy sales to permit the private import of tractors and implements (*Ceylon Daily News*, 5 November 1977); and the fact that in 1973 half of all land in smallholdings (i.e. all holdings of not more than twenty acres and having ten or more resident labourers) held by registered companies was located in Kurunegala district (*Census of Agriculture 1973, General Report*: Table 5). The average size of these company holdings in Kurunegala district was thirty-nine acres, as opposed to nine acres for the whole Island.

27. Perhaps the main significant exception is that the Bulankulame family has exercised political leadership in Anuradhapura district that is rooted in their aristocratic status in the traditional Kandyan social order. Their leadership is, however, gradually weakening in the face of political challenges from other groups (Brow, 1978: 216).

28. One of the most comprehensive – although now somewhat dated – attempts to investigate the extent of the continuity of elite dominance (Singer, 1964) is possibly somewhat marred by the definitions he adopts. He defines the political elite as persons elected or appointed to national legislatures in the period 1924–60 (p. 52). Yet over this period the number of such posts grew very rapidly from 37 in 1924 (Kearney, 1973: 30) to 187 in 1960 – 30 senators (Wriggins, 1960: 95) and 157 elected and nominated MPs (Kearney, 1973: 41). This represents an increase of

460%. It is not surprising that Singer detected a decline in the socio-economic standing of the elite, as he defined it, over this period (e.g. p. 47 and Chapter 7). This cannot, however, be considered to be reliable evidence of the decline of elite dominance in the sense in which we have used the term.

29. This point is made, *inter alia*, by Herring, 1972: 101n.
30. Jayanntha, 1983.
31. Roberts, 1979b.
32. Roberts, 1979a: 15, 73.
33. But see Jayanntha, 1983, on the Weligama electorate.
34. Roberts, 1979a: 73.
35. Meyer, 1982: 231–2.
36. Wickremeratne, 1975: especially 61–7.
37. Roberts (1970/72a: 26–9) gives an account of the integration of Kandyan concerns about plantations, 'the Indian menace', etc. into the mainstream of the nationalist movement and ideology, which partly replaced the earlier, more secular and cosmopolitan nationalism of the Low Country.
38. Moore, 1981b.
39. Empirical details to support this argument may be found in Jiggins, 1979: especially Chapter 6. Ironically, Jiggins actually used these data to argue the 'reality' of family clusterings.
40. See, for example, the quotation from Dr Colvin de Silva, the LSSP's leading theoretician, in *Lanka Guardian*, Volume 3 (10), 1980: 4.
41. See the UNP's 1977 general election manifesto, reproduced in Lake House, 1977: 249.
42. De Silva, Mervyn, 1979: 4–5. But for a recent and important restatement of the Marxian case, see Gunasinghe, 1984.
43. On the 'proto-nationalist' nature of the Buddhist, temperance and labour movements in the late nineteenth and early twentieth century, see Jayawardena, 1972: Part 1.
44. Of the Buddhist Revival, de Silva, K. M. (1973d: 201) says: 'the leadership of the Buddhist revival was largely in the hands of traders who belonged to the rising non-*goyigama* castes of the littoral, the *karava*, the *salagama* and the *durawa*'. On the Low Country basis of the temperance movement, see de Silva, K. M. 1973f: 259–60. On the Low Country basis of nationalism, see de Silva, K. M., 1973f: 258; and 1973a.
45. On the Buddhist Revival, see Malalgoda, 1976; Phadnis, 1976: 67–72; and de Silva, K. M., 1973d: 201–7.
46. For an account of the rise and nature of 'Protestant Buddhism', see Obeyesekere, 1970; and Malalgoda, 1976: Chapters 6 and 7.
47. Jayanntha, 1983.
48. On the Low Country basis of the Buddhist Revival, see Malalgoda, 1976: Chapters 2 and 3; and Phadnis, 1976: 55–6, 72, 106–7.
49. Apart from specific references, this section is based on the accounts of the early history of the left movement in Sri Lanka in: Jupp, 1978: 72–81; Wriggins, 1960: 124–42; and de Silva, K. M., 1973b: 507–24.

50. The uncritical description of the SLFP as a 'social democratic' party is to be found, for example, in Wilson, 1974: 41. The more general point about the lack of any major sense of puzzlement about the 'European' pattern of party alignments seems to apply equally to Wilson, 1979; Jupp, 1978; Kearney, 1973; and Woodward, 1969, to name the more prominent writers on Sri Lankan politics.
51. Bottomore (1979: 53) observes that in Europe peasant populations have been associated with multi-party systems under electoral democracy.
52. For an account of the origins of trade unionism, see Jayawardena, 1972.
53. For statistics on the growth of trade unionism, see Kearney, 1971: 16. On the relationship of the trade unions to political parties, see *ibid*: especially Chapters 3 and 4.
54. On the origins of the Marxist leadership, see Wriggins, 1960: 124–32; and Jiggins, 1979: 82–4.
55. De Silva, K. M., 1973b: 508.
56. Probably the three best parliamentarians – i.e. parliamentary performers – in the post-Independence period have been S. W. R. D. Bandaranaike (SLFP), Dr N. M. Perera (LSSP), and Pieter Keunemann (Communist Party). (See Woodward, 1969: 97.)
57. On the evolution of a proletariat in these sectors, see Jayawardena, 1972: especially 6–13.
58. Roberts, 1979a: 69.
59. On this gradual adoption by the Marxists of a pro-Sinhalese stance, see Jupp, 1978: 72–81.
60. Woodward (1969: 53–4), for example, demonstrates that fear of the Marxists was the main reason for the creation of the UNP. On the eclectic nature of the nationalism of the Ceylon National Congress, see Roberts, 1979e.
61. See the electoral statistics in Lake House, 1977: 211–18. The percentage of votes polled by the Marxist parties was as follows in the general elections of 1947–77: 1947 (LSSP + Communist Party + Bolshevik/ Leninist Party – 21%); 1952 (LSSP + Communist Party + VLSSP) – 19%; 1956 (LSSP + Communist Party, excluding VLSSP) – 15%; 1960 March (LSSP + Communist Party, excluding MEP) – 15%; 1960 July (LSSP + Communust Party) – 10%; 1965 (LSSP + Communist Party) – 10%; 1970 (LSSP + Communist Party) – 12%; 1977 (LSSP + Communist Party) – 6%.
62. It was estimated in 1947 that over 80% of Sri Lanka's capital was foreign-owned (Wickremeratne, 1973c: 483).
63. On the nationalism of the early Marxists, see Roberts, 1970c: 33; Jupp, 1978: 73; and de Silva, K. M., 1973b: 517–19.
64. Particularly significant was the relief work organised in the rural areas of Kegalle district by the Marxists during the malaria epidemic of 1934–5 (de Silva, K. M., 1973b: 508).
65. Siriwardena, 1979.
66. These figures are calculated from the electoral data given in de Silva,

G. P. S. H., 1979: 112–293. The electorates which returned Independent Sinhalese MPs in 1947 were, in alphabetical order: Akuressa, Chilaw, Dambulla, Dandagamuwa, Deniyaya, Hambantota, Kurunegala, Matale, Matugama, Minipe, Nikaweratiya and Welimada.

67. Woodward (1969: 68) demonstrates that in 1947 the UNP was more organised and ideologically coherent in the Western and Southern Provinces, where it faced Marxist competition.

68. Huntington, 1968: 433, 438–51.

69. Woodward, 1969: 141; and Jupp, 1978: 11–14.

70. Jupp, 1978: 14 and Chapter 1; and Woodward, 1969: 156–7.

71. On the rural electoral base of the SLFP, see Jupp, 1978: Chapter 7. The SLFP identifies itself as an explicitly rural party (Woodward, 1969: 207).

72. This conclusion was reached by examining the spatial distribution of SLFP candidates and votes in the 1952 and 1956 general elections. The raw electoral data are provided in de Silva, G. P. S. H., 1979.

73. Phadnis, 1976: Chapter 5, especially 200–4.

74. Jupp, 1978: Chapters 1 and 11.

75. On S. W. R. D. Bandaranaike's personality and its relation to his politics, see Manor, 1978 and 1979; and Wriggins, 1960: 119–20.

76. Five of the six persons who between 1833 and 1912 served as the nominated Low Country Sinhalese representative in the Legislative Council were from the Obeyesekere/Bandaranaike family. All, like S. W. R. D. Bandaranaike himself in his youth, were Protestant Christians (Jayawardena, 1972: 62).

77. On the kinship connections of the Bandaranaikes, see Jiggins, 1979: Chapter 6.

78. Jiggins (1979: 76) describes the contrast between Bandaranaike's populist electioneering style and the more remote style of the other members of the elite.

79. Lake House, 1977: 219.

80. *Ibid*.

81. Moore, 1981d: 423, fn. 84.

82. One might note that the disenfranchisement of the Indian Tamil population in 1948 in no sense contributed to this increase in voter turnout between 1947 and 1952. Indeed it tended to have the opposite effect, for the turnout level among Indian Tamils was high (*ibid*: 423, fn. 85).

83. When the rice subsidy was withdrawn in 1953, after the 1952 election, there was a general strike and the government had to reverse its position (Wriggins, 1960: 76).

84. On these points, see Jupp, 1978: Chapter 1.

85. One might note that S. W. R. D. Bandaranaike had never been a very loyal or trusted member of the UNP (Woodward, 1969: 54–5), and had long had leftist sympathies (*ibid*: 72).

86. Jupp, 1978: 196–9.

87. de Silva, Mervyn, 1979: 4.

88. Woodward, 1969: 112.
89. Jupp, 1978: 63.
90. On this incident, see in general Jiggins, 1979: Chapter 7.
91. Almost the entire Politburo of the JVP originated from the southwest coast, and a large group were graduates of Dharmasoka College in Ambalangoda (Keerawella, 1980: 54–5).
92. See Moore and Wickremesinghe, 1980: 44.
93. For example, Jiggins' account of the activities of the JVP leaders prior to the Insurgency involves repeated reference to meetings in the coastal strip from Colombo to just south of Matara: at Colombo and Vidyodya campus (p. 140); and in Ambalangoda, Kamburupitiya and Dondra (p. 141).
94. See, for example, Woodward, 1969: 166–7, 245–6; Jiggins, 1979: 78; and Jupp, 1978: 208.
95. Wilson, 1980: 11–13. The quotation is from p. 11.
96. The very high levels of political awareness among Sri Lankans and their concern at the potential costs of being identified as an opponent of the government have made experimental public opinion polls on party affiliation worthless.
97. See Moore *et al.*, 1979: 231–2. My research assistants and I had been doing field research in this village for almost a year before the election. I was absent during the election, and the data were collected by a research assistant who fortunately exceeded his brief, which was to keep a general eye on events.
98. For example, writing of the early 1950s, Ryan (1953: 289) reports that in Kalutara district villages the *Goigama* generally supported the UNP, and the poor, low-caste people supported leftist candidates. He also provides evidence of the strong resentment felt by the village poor towards the village landowners even at that early stage, both in the Kandyan hills (p. 211) and in a remote Dry Zone *purana* village (p. 253). Writing of a Colombo district village in the 1970s, Wanigaratne *et al.* (1980: 42, 62) report that the poorer locality provided strong support for the SLFP, while in a Kandy village the wealthy supported the UNP (*ibid*: 78). Seneratne (1970: 138, 215, 252) describes the general association of poverty/low caste/leftism and wealth/high caste/UNP support in a Kalutara village. For other village-level studies which indicate that the UNP draws support from the wealthier strata and the SLFP from the poor, see Perera, 1979a; Perera, 1982: Part Three, in relation to the village of Palliporuwa; Jayatilleke, 1980: 147; Silva, 1979: 67; Lebbe *et al.*, 1977: 18; Robinson, 1975: 104, 191, 217, 219; and Kemp, 1982: 277.
99. This is a paraphrase of Jiggins' caricature of Westminster-style politics (Jiggins, 1979: 1–2).
100. Because of the atheoretical bias of so much political science literature on Sri Lanka, the nature of the party system has not been explicitly debated. This claim about what other observers *seem* to be thinking can only be inferred from their work – especially Jupp, 1978; Jiggins, 1979; and Wilson, 1979.

101. In those electorates which Jupp classifies as the 'Kandyan Dry Zone' none of the Marxist parties has even bothered to put up a candidate since 1960 (Jupp, 1978: 379).

102. One might note that it was from a Dry Zone base that the most important single inter-party defection since the establishment of the SLFP occurred – the defection from the SLFP of C. P. de Silva and a small group of supporters, which brought down the SLFP–LSSP coalition government in 1965. C. P. de Silva, who had led the SLFP in the general election of July 1960, had his base in the Dry Zone (Jiggins, 1979: 54–5, 90–1, 117).

103. Thus Perera (1979b: 145; and 1982) quotes the case of the population of a very poor locality in Anuradhapura district who supported the UNP because of local factional conflict. In a locality of the Minipe colony Wanigaratne (1979a: 142–3) found in 1976 that the Rural Development Society, alone among the local institutions, was run by a leadership which was mainly both UNP and from the lower income categories.

104. The earliest reference I have to this point is from Ryan's (1958: 130) study of a Kalutara district village:

> The existence of an economic class terminology is evident, but these levels are not conceived as social classes possessing distinct interests, cohesion, or self-contained levels of social interaction. Such groupings are construed in terms of material goods, security, and varying living levels.

He talks of four categories – 'monied', 'middle', 'ordinary' and 'poor'. The use of similar categories is confirmed by Tambaiah (1963: 106); Wanigaratne *et al.* (1980: 42); and my own fieldwork. In a village within the relatively radicalised rural areas around Ambalangoda, Jayatilleke (1980: 71) reports an even more radical terminology in everyday use. People there use the categories of *danapathi panthiya* (rich or capitalist class), *madiama panthiya* (middle class) and *peeditha panthiya* (oppressed class).

105. Seneratne, 1970: 306 and *passim*. See also Tambaiah, 1963: 97–107.

106. More generally, the Sri Lankan rural stratification system appears to be based on what Weber termed *Erwerbsklassen* ('acquisition classes', i.e. classes determined by the opportunities in markets for goods and services), rather than on the *Besitzklassen* (i.e. classes formed mainly on differences in possessions) characteristics of peasant societies (see Linz, 1976: 365).

107. It is difficult to cite any precise references for this claim because it is such an intrinsic feature of Sri Lankan politics, and so evident to the external observer.

108. For a general account of economic policy and public-sector economic activities, see Wickremeratne, 1977a; and Balakrishnan, 1977.

109. In a seminar at the University of Sussex in June 1982, Tony Michel gave figures for public-sector employees per head of the population for a number of industrial countries, which ranged from one job per 254 people for Korea to fifty for Australia. In Sri Lanka in 1971, before the

nationalisation of the estate sector brought about a vast increase in the number of public-sector employees, the figure was twenty-four. (For sources, see Moore, 1981d: 291, fn. 111.)

110. There are four relatively recent books covering Sri Lankan politics 'in the round' which might be expected to provide some explanation of the unusually high levels of politicisation or, more narrowly, electoral turnout. Jupp is very explicit about the facts of high politicisation (1978: 162, 189). He does not, however, give any clear explanation, and tends to imply that the 1956 election was crucial (e.g. p. 162). Kearney suggests, in passing, the importance of the stimulus provided by conflicts over the respective roles of the Sinhala and Tamil languages, 'party agitation' and 'propaganda', high levels of literacy and education, and the long experience of the franchise (1973: 17, 144–5). Neither Wilson (1979) nor Wriggins (1960) appears to attempt any explanation.

111. In addition to these plantation-related reasons, it is possible that the salience of ethnic conflict has tended to increase political participation rates in Sri Lanka. The evidence from other countries appears to suggest that low-status persons tend to participate actively in politics – often as actively as high-status persons – where group issues such as ethnicity, religion, race and region are at stake (Verba et al., 1978: 11–14).

112. Jupp (1978: 189) remarks that 'In the Kandyan areas . . . turnout reaches the maximum found possible in other voluntary systems.' In the seven general elections from 1947 on, the average (unweighted) voter turnout has equalled or exceeded 77% in seven districts – Kandy, Nuwara Eliya, Badulla and Kegalle; Hambantota, Mannar and Puttalam. The first four are Kandyan. (Calculated from data given in de Silva, G. P. S. H., 1979: 405–29.)

113. For example, in 1921 40% of the population aged more than five years was recorded as literate. By 1946 this had increased to 58% (Snodgrass, 1966: 318).

114. Meyer, 1978: 3–4.

115. In 1946 females accounted for 47% of the labour force employed in tea production, 32% in rubber, 19% in coconut and only 8% in other agriculture (Census of Ceylon 1946, Volume 1, Part 2: Table 48).

116. An illustration of this point can be found in S. W. R. D. Bandaranaike's speech to the State Council on 7 May 1937 (Bandaranaike, 1961: 524–30).

117. Wickremeratne, 1973c: 477.

118. Ibid.

119. Ibid: 488.

120. There are various 'public assistance' schemes for those in distress. For details, see Social Services Department, 1974. In 1971–2 assistance was given to 160,000 people, 1.4% of the total population (ibid: 106).

121. This list includes only issues over which my assistance was requested during village field research.

122. In a speech in 1979 the Minister of Finance promised that the government 'will continue to give as much relief to the people as possible'

and 'would always safeguard and protect the people' (*Ceylon News*, 9 August 1979). For a couple of other examples of the use of this very common term, see the headlines relating to the budget in the *Ceylon Daily News*, 16 November 1979; and the report on the import policy of the Trade Minister in the *Ceylon News*, 24 February 1980.

123. The quotation is from a speech by the Minister of Agriculture (*Sun*, 10 October 1977).

124. Jupp (1978: 94–5) confirms that local party members have very little influence over major decisions. Power is shared between the locally influential individuals and the central party organisation in Colombo.

125. Apart from the specific instances and references below, the general point is argued by Manor, 1979; and Leitan (1979) provides a detailed critique of the centralisation of government procedures and structures. See also Dawson, 1978.

126. See Isenman, 1980a; and Mattis, 1978: 7.

127. See Manor, 1979: 24–9; and, for more detailed supporting data, Leitan, 1979: especially Chapters 3 and 4. See also Dawson, 1978: 11. One might also note in addition that the new District Development Councils, which are, in the name of decentralisation, to replace other local government units, appear, constitutionally at least, to be under tight central ministerial control (Ponnambalam, 1980).

128. I make this case elsewhere (Moore, 1979). To discuss it in any detail would require a chapter in itself, for the subject of local organisations has been dealt with at enormous length in recent applied social science research on Sri Lanka.

129. My fieldwork.

130. Ryan *et al.*, 1958: Chapter 10.

131. See Bandaranaike, 1961: Speech delivered to the State Council on 9 June 1932, pp. 230–1.

132. Uphoff and Wanigaratne, 1982: 500–1; and Leitan, 1979: 155–8.

133. The District Minister scheme in Sri Lanka actually emerged out of a system of so-called 'Political Authorities' – MPs with special (extra-constitutional) powers in each district – introduced by the 1970–7 United Front Government (see Leitan, 1979: 257–8).

134. Wilson, 1980: 67–8; and Dawson, 1978: 16.

135. Moore, 1981d: 145; and 1984b: Table 2.

136. Manor, 1979.

137. The point is made, *inter alia*, by Verba *et al.* (1978: 13) that party systems may freeze a pattern of party competition long after it ceases to be 'relevant'.

11 Concluding remarks

1. *Sri Lanka News*, 15 December 1983. It may be significant that the only UNP MP cited by name as having criticised the effect on farmers of government economic policy, H. M. Lokubanda of Galgamuwa, describes

himself as a cultivator in his parliamentary biography (Lake House, 1977: 159) and represents, not a sugarcane-growing area, but one dependent on paddy, vegetables and subsidiary food crops. A few weeks later it was reported that the plant in Polonnaruwa processing locally produced milk had lost a large share of the processed milk market to imports (*Sri Lanka News*, 19 April 1984).

2. Central Bank of Ceylon, *Annual Report*, 1982: Table 30.
3. *Sri Lanka News*, 12 April 1984.
4. The Indian Tamils' trade union, the CWC, was briefly and only nominally a partner to the Tamil United Liberation Front in the mid-1970s.
5. Moore, 1984a.
6. In March 1980 an official committee was established to review the issue of the stateless population. Mr S. Thondaman, CWC leader and Minister of Rural Industrial Development, was a member. In July 1981 an amendment to the 1967 Indo-Ceylon Agreement (Implementation) Act increased the number of stateless people eligible for Sri Lankan citizenship. In September 1982 President Jayawardena hinted strongly at the possibility of extending citizenship in a speech to the Ceylon Planters Society (*Observer* (Colombo), 12 September 1982).
7. See the article by the Director of the Supreme Council of the *Maha Sangha* in *Sri Lanka News*, 5 April 1984; and the interview with President Jayawardena in *Sri Lanka News*, 26 April 1984.
8. This paragraph is based on my fieldwork.
9. *Sri Lanka News*, 28 July 1983.
10. Two of the UNP's most powerful ministers are from low-caste backgrounds. R. Premadasa, the Prime Minister since 1978, is believed to command the personal allegiance of a large number of UNP MPs, not all of them of low-caste background. Cyril Mathew, Minister of Industries and Scientific Affairs, is believed to command fairly solid support from the *Vahumpura* community. The *Vahumpura*, along with the *Padu*, are very numerous, but until 1977 had played a relatively limited role in politics. They are physically rather dispersed and have historically been economically depressed groups dominated locally by higher castes (Jiggins, 1979: references as in her index). For some written evidence on the revitalisation of the UNP before 1977 and the enhanced role of low-caste politicians at local level, see Jayatilleke, 1980: 148, 168–9; and, more especially, Perera, 1982: Part Three.
11. At the 1982 presidential election the campaign of the SLFP's official candidate, the late Hector Kobbekaduwa, was in large degree organised by the Communist Party.
12. Moore, 1984a.
13. A one-day general strike called by opposition parties in September 1978 led to the dismissal of large numbers of employees in the public sector. A further strike call in July 1980 produced a limited response and was withdrawn without achieving anything.
14. Central Bank of Ceylon, *Annual Report*, 1982: Table 17.

15. For details, see Wilson, 1980.
16. *Ibid*: 89.
17. *Ceylon News*, 11 June 1981.
18. Dissatisfaction with the conventional Marxian approach to the explanation of politics and to the characterisation of 'the state' is now widespread among Marxian scholars. It is the subject of a voluminous recent literature, including attempts to argue that Marx himself had a much more sophisticated view of 'the state' than that implied, for example, in the much quoted phrase from *The Communist Manifesto* that 'the state' is but a 'committee of the bourgeoisie'. For a small sample of this literature, see, for example, Badie and Birnbaum, 1983; Nordlinger, 1981; and Skocpol, 1979: 24–33.
19. This literature is reviewed more extensively in Moore, 1981d: Chapter 1. Among the most prominent contributors to the study of peasant politics from within this paradigm are Alavi, 1973; Hobsbawm, 1973; Barrington Moore, 1967; Shanin, 1971; Scott, 1976; and Wolf, 1971.
20. One might note in particular the creation of *The Journal of Peasant Studies* (London), first published in 1973; and the *Peasant Studies Newsletter*, later *Peasant Studies* (Pittsburgh), first published in 1972.
21. See especially Shanin, 1971.
22. Barrington Moore, 1967.
23. Kothari, 1970: 10, 6.
24. Weiner, 1963: 116.
25. Skocpol, 1979.
26. *Ibid*: xv.
27. *Ibid*: Chapter 1. Also relevant is an earlier review by Somers and Goldfrank (1979) of Paige's (1975) work on the determinants of peasant political action. It is convincingly argued that Paige's failure to explicitly incorporate state-level variables into his formal theoretical structure seriously mars what is otherwise an excellent analysis of how patterns of socio-economic relationships shape the political actions of different peasant groups.
28. For example, Bates (1984) has recently argued that the socio-economic structure of rural Africa, and thus the political pressures which arise from rural society, is in large part the creation of earlier colonial administrations. Stedman Jones (1983: especially Chapter 3), re-analysing English Chartism, a movement so central to the evolution of the Marxian interpretation of social change, suggests that the rise of a militant organised 'working-class' movement in the 1830s and 1840s owes far less than Marx and most historians have assumed to changes in social relations of production and to the emergence of an industrial proletariat. Lower-class reaction against repressive state policies was an important component of Chartism. The alleviation of repression, rather than changes within society, is held to account for Chartism's subsequent decline. Nordlinger's (1981) analysis of the determinants of public policy is also relevant here. He argues that political scientists of both Marxian and 'liberal–pluralist'

persuasions have overestimated the influence on public policy of pressures on the state from civil society. Instead, the state bureaucracy has a great deal of autonomy and capacity both to shape these pressures and to make policy independently of them. See also Bates, 1983: 144–7.

BIBLIOGRAPHY

Apart from the specific references given below, the following Sri Lankan non-official periodicals have been consulted, mainly for the period 1976–83: *Ceylon Daily News* (later *Sri Lanka Daily News*); *Ceylon News* (later *Sri Lanka News*); *The Economic Review* (People's Bank); *Lanka Guardian*; *Sun*; *Tribune*; and *Weekend*.

This bibliography is divided into the following categories:

    Sri Lanka – Official periodical publications
    Sri Lanka – Official non-periodical publications
    Sri Lanka – legislative enactments
    Sri Lanka – Non-official publications
    India
    General

Sri Lanka – Official periodical publications

(Except where otherwise indicated, all official items are published in Colombo)

Agricultural Statistical Information, irregular, Department of Agriculture, Peradeniya.

Annual Report, annual, Central Bank of Ceylon.

Bulletin, monthly, Central Bank of Ceylon.

Coconut Products Annual Review, annual, Coconut Marketing Board.

Economic and Social Statistics of Sri Lanka, biannual, Central Bank of Ceylon.

Review of the Economy, annual, Central Bank of Ceylon.

Statistical Abstract of Sri Lanka, annual, Department of Census and Statistics.

Statistical Pocketbook of Sri Lanka, annual, Department of Census and Statistics.

Sri Lanka – Official non-periodical publications

Budget Speech, 1973, Government Printer.

Budget Speech, 1975, Government Printer.

Budget Speech, 1977, Government Printer.

Central Bank of Ceylon, 1969, *Survey on Cost of Production of Paddy*, Department of Economic Research.

Commissioner of Agrarian Services, 1973, *Administration Report of the Commissioner of Agrarian Services for 1969–70*.

Department of Census and Statistics, 1950, *Census of Ceylon 1946, Volume 1, Part 1: General Report.*

Department of Census and Statistics, 1951, *Census of Ceylon 1946, Volume 1, Part 2: Statistical Digest.*

Department of Census and Statistics, 1960, *Census of Ceylon 1953, Volume 4, Part 1: The Gainfully Employed Population.*

Department of Census and Statistics, 1965, *Census of Agriculture 1962, Volume 1: Agricultural Land, Agricultural Operations and Tenure.*

Department of Census and Statistics, 1966, *Census of Agriculture 1962, Volume 2: Land Utilisation.*

Department of Census and Statistics, 1966, *Census of Agriculture 1962, Volume 3: Asweddumized Paddy Lands.*

Department of Census and Statistics, 1974, *The Population of Sri Lanka.*

Department of Census and Statistics, 1975, *Census of Agriculture 1973, Preliminary Release No. 1: Smallholdings.*

Department of Census and Statistics, 1975, *Census of Population 1971, Volume 2, Part 1: General Characteristics of the Population.*

Department of Census and Statistics, 1976, *Census of Population 1971, Volume 2, Part 2: The Economically Active Population.*

Department of Census and Statistics, 1977, *Census of Agriculture 1973: Smallholdings, Final Tables – Stage 1.*

Department of Census and Statistics, 1978, *Census of Population 1971, General Report.*

Department of Census and Statistics, 1980, *Census of Agriculture 1973, General Report.*

Department of Census and Statistics, 1982, *Labour Force and Socio-Economic Survey, 1980/81, Preliminary Report.*

Department of Census and Statistics, various years, *Census of Population 1971, Volume 1, Parts 1–22.*

Hansard, The Report of the Proceedings of Parliament/The National State Assembly.

Kandyan Peasantry Commission, 1951, *Report of the Kandyan Peasantry Commission,* Sessional Paper No. 18, 1951.

Kandyan Peasantry Rehabilitation Department, 1970, *Administration Report of the Kandyan Peasantry Rehabilitation Commissioner for 1969–70.*

Land Commission, 1929, *Final Report of the Land Commission,* Sessional Paper No. 18, 1929.

Land Commissioner's Department, 1976, *Administration Report of the Land Commissioner for 1969–70.*

Land Settlement Department, 1977, *Administration Report of the Settlement Officer for 1975.*

Land Utilisation Committee, 1968, *Report of the Land Utilisation Committee, August 1967,* Sessional Paper No. 11, 1968.

Ministry of Lands and Land Development, 1979, *Resource Development, Information Service, the Ministry.*

Ministry of Plan Implementation, 1978, *Agricultural Credit: Investigations into Irregularities in Granting of Sugarcane Loans, Amparai District.*

Social Services Department, 1974, *Administration Report of the Director of Social Services for 1971–2.*

Sri Lanka – legislative enactments

Agrarian Services Act, No. 58 of 1979.
Agricultural Lands Law, No. 42 of 1973.
Agricultural Productivity Law, No. 2 of 1972.
Land Development (Amendment) Act, No. 27 of 1981.
Paddy Lands Act, No. 1 of 1958.

Sri Lanka – non-official publications

Abeysekera, D., 1980, 'Urbanisation and the growth of small towns in Sri Lanka', *Paper No. 67 of the East–West Population Institute*, East–West Center, Honolulu.

Abeysinghe, A., 1978, 'Ancient land tenure to modern land reform in Sri Lanka, volume 1', *Quest*, Series No. 51, Centre for Society and Religion, Colombo.

Ameer Ali, A. C. L., 1970/2, 'Changing conditions and persisting problems in the peasant sector under British rule in the period 1833–1893', *Ceylon Studies Seminar, 1970–72 Series, No. 3*, Peradeniya, mimeo.

Amerasinghe, N., 1977, 'The Minipe colonisation scheme', in N. D. A. Hameed, *et al.*, *Rice Revolution*.

Amunugama, S., 1965, 'Chandrikawewa: a recent attempt at colonisation on a peasant framework', *The Ceylon Journal of Historical and Social Studies*, 8(1, 2).

Arasaratnam, S., 1979, 'Nationalism in Sri Lanka and the Tamils', in M. Roberts (ed.), *Collective Identities.*

ARTI (Agrarian Research and Training Institute), 1974a, 'The agrarian situation relating to paddy cultivation in five selected districts of Sri Lanka, part 1, Hambantota district', *Research Study No. 6*, Colombo.

ARTI, 1974b, 'The agrarian situation relating to paddy cultivation in five selected districts of Sri Lanka, part 2, Kandy district', *Research Study No. 7*, Colombo.

ARTI, 1975a, 'The agrarian situation relating to paddy cultivation in five selected districts of Sri Lanka, part 3, Polonnaruwa district', *Research Study No. 8*, Colombo.

ARTI, 1975b, 'The agrarian situation relating to paddy cultivation in five selected districts of Sri Lanka, part 4, Anuradhapura district', *Research Study No. 9*, Colombo.

ARTI, 1975c, 'The agrarian situation relating to paddy cultivation in five selected districts of Sri Lanka, part 5, Colombo district', *Research Study No. 10*, Colombo.

ARTI, 1975d, 'The agrarian situation relating to paddy cultivation in five selected districts of Sri Lanka, part 6, comparative analysis', *Research Study No. 11*, Colombo.

ARTI, 1977, 'Land reform and the development of coconut lands. A case study of selected villages and estates in the class II coconut lands of Colombo district', *Research Study Series No. 14*, Colombo.

ARTI, 1979a, 'A study of five settlement schemes prior to irrigation modernisation, volume 1, Mahawilachchiya', *Research Study No. 28*, Colombo.

ARTI, 1979b, 'A study of five settlement schemes prior to irrigation modernisation, volume 2, Mahakandarawa', *Research Study No. 31*, Colombo.

Balakrishnan, N., 1977, 'Industrial policy and development since independence', in K. M. de Silva (ed.), *Sri Lanka: A Survey*.

Balakrishnan, N. and Gunasekere, H. M., 1977, 'A review of demographic trends', in K. M. de Silva (ed.), *Sri Lanka: A Survey*.

Balasuriya, T., 1977, 'To socialism through the liberation of the village', *Logos* (Colombo) **15**(3, 4) and **16**(1).

Bandaranaike, S. W. R. D., 1961, *Towards a New Era: Selected Speeches of S. W. R. D. Bandaranaike Made in the Legislature of Ceylon, 1931–1959*, Department of Information, Colombo.

Bansil, P. C., 1971, *Ceylon Agriculture: A Perspective*, Dhanpat Rai and Sons, Delhi.

Blackton, C. S., 1978, 'The Europeans in the Ceylon Civil Service in the nineteen twenties: the view from the Kachcheri', *Ceylon Journal of Historical and Social Studies*, NS **8**(1).

Brow, J., 1978, *Vedda Villages of Anuradhapura: The Historical Anthropology of a Community in Sri Lanka*, University of Washington Press.

Burch, D., 1979, 'Overseas Aid and the Transfer of Technology: A Case Study of Agricultural Mechanisation in Sri Lanka', D.Phil. thesis, University of Sussex.

Carrithers, M., 1979, 'The modern ascetics of Lanka and the pattern of change in Buddhism', *Man*, **14**(2).

Collins, C., 1966, 'Ceylon: the imperial heritage', in R. Braibanti (ed.), *Asian Bureaucratic Systems*.

Corea, G., 1975, *The Instability of an Export Economy*, Marga Institute, Colombo.

Dawson, P., 1978, 'Decentralisation in Sri Lanka: the significance of district ministries', in University of London, Institute of Commonwealth Studies, Collected Seminar Papers No. 23, *A Revival of Local Government and Administration?*, Cass, London.

De Mel, B. V. and Fernando, M., 1980, 'Tradition, modernity and value movement: a study of dietary changes in a Sri Lanka village', *Marga*, **6**(1).

De Mel, B. V. and Jogaratnam, T., 1977, 'Population growth, nutrition and food supplies in Sri Lanka', *Marga*, **4**(3).

Denham, E. B., 1912, *Ceylon at the Census of 1911 : Being a Review of the Results of the Census of 1911*, Government Printer, Colombo.

De Silva, C. R., 1972, *The Portuguese in Ceylon 1617–1638*, H. W. Cave and Company, Colombo.

De Silva, C. R., 1977, 'The rise and fall of the kingdom of Sitawaka (1521–1593)', *Ceylon Journal of Historical and Social Studies*, NS 7(1).

De Silva, C. R., 1978, 'The politics of university admissions: a review of some aspects of admissions policy in Sri Lanka, 1971–1978', *Sri Lanka Journal of Social Studies*, 1(2).

De Silva, C. R., 1979, 'The impact of nationalism on education: the schools takeover (1961) and the university admissions crisis, 1970–1975', in M. Roberts (ed.), *Collective Identities*.

De Silva, Colvin R., 1953, *Ceylon Under the British Occupation, 1795–1833, Volume 1*, The Colombo Apothecaries Co. Ltd., Colombo.

De Silva, Colvin R., 1962, *Ceylon Under the British Occupation, 1795–1833, Volume 2*, The Colombo Apothecaries Co. Ltd., Colombo.

De Silva, Colvin R., 1975, 'The class struggle in Sri Lanka and the nationalisation of the plantations', *State* (Colombo), 3(75).

De Silva, Colvin R., n.d. (circa 1978), *The Politics of the Budget*, Lanka Sama Samaj Party, Colombo.

De Silva, G. P. S. H., 1979, *A Statistical Survey of Elections to the Legislatures of Sri Lanka, 1911–1977*, Marga Institute, Colombo.

De Silva, K. M., 1964, 'Studies in land policy in Ceylon – 1', *Ceylon Journal of Historical and Social Studies*, 7(1).

De Silva, K. M. (ed.), 1973, *History of Ceylon, Volume 3 : From the Beginning of the Nineteenth Century to 1948*, University of Ceylon, Peradeniya.

De Silva, K. M., 1973a, 'The reform and nationalist movements in the early twentieth century', in K. M. de Silva (ed.), *History of Ceylon*.

De Silva, K. M., 1973b, 'The history and politics of the transfer of power', in K. M. de Silva (ed.), *History of Ceylon*.

De Silva, K. M., 1973c, 'The development of the administrative system, 1833–c.1910', in K. M. de Silva (ed.), *History of Ceylon*.

De Silva, K. M., 1973d, 'The government and religion: problems and policies c.1832 to c.1910', in K. M. de Silva (ed.), *History of Ceylon*.

De Silva, K. M., 1973e, 'The Kandyan kingdom and the British – the last phase, 1796 to 1818', in K. M. de Silva (ed.), *History of Ceylon*.

De Silva, K. M., 1973f, 'Nineteenth-century origins of nationalism in Ceylon', in K. M. de Silva (ed.), *History of Ceylon*.

De Silva, K. M. (ed.), 1977, *Sri Lanka: A Survey*, Hurst and Co., London.

De Silva, K. M., 1977a, 'Introduction', in K. M. de Silva (ed.), *Sri Lanka: A Survey*.

De Silva, K. M., 1977b, 'Historical survey', in K. M. de Silva (ed.), *Sri Lanka: A Survey*.

De Silva, K. M., 1979, 'The transfer of power in Sri Lanka: a review of British perspectives, 1938–1947', in M. Roberts (ed.), *Collective Identities*.

De Silva, Mervyn, 1979, 'Grand alliance, grander design', *Lanka Guardian*, 2(16).

Dharmadasa, K. N. O., 1979, 'The Sinhala-Buddhist identity and the Nayakkar dynasty in the politics of the Kandyan kingdom, 1739–1815', in M. Roberts (ed.), *Collective Identities*.

Dharmasena, K., 1980, *The Port of Colombo 1860–1939*, Ministry of Higher Education, Colombo.

Dias, H. D. and Wickramanayake, B. W. E., 1977, 'The Gambaraya system in the Hambantota district', in S. W. R. de A. Samarasinghe (ed.), *Agriculture in the Peasant Sector of Sri Lanka*, Ceylon Studies Seminar, Peradeniya.

Edirisinghe, N. and Poleman, T. T., 1976, 'Implications of government intervention in the rice economy of Sri Lanka', *Cornell International Agriculture Mimeograph No. 48*, Department of Agricultural Economics, Cornell University, Ithaca.

Edirisinghe, N. and Poleman, T. T., 1977, 'Rice economy in Sri Lanka: consumption characteristics and production trends', *Marga*, 4(3).

Ellman, A. and Ratnaweera, D. de S., 1973, 'Thannimurrippu Paripalana Sabai case study: the transfer of administration of an irrigated settlement scheme from government officials to a people's organisation', *Occasional Publication Series No. 1*, Agrarian Research and Training Institute, Colombo.

Ellman, A. and Ratnaweera, D. de S., 1974, 'New settlement schemes in Sri Lanka', *Research Study Series No. 5*, Agrarian Research and Training Institute, Colombo.

Ellman, A. *et al.*, 1976, 'Land settlement in Sri Lanka 1840–1975: a review of major writings on the subject', *Research Study Series No. 16*, Agrarian Research and Training Institute, Colombo.

ESCAP (Economic and Social Commission for Asia and the Pacific), 1975, 'Comparative study of population growth and agricultural change. D. Case study of Sri Lanka', *Asian Population Studies Series No. 23*, Bangkok.

Evers, H-D., 1972, *Monks, Priests and Peasants: A Study of Buddhism and Social Structure in Central Ceylon*, E. J. Brill, Leiden.

Farmer, B. H., 1957, *Pioneer Peasant Colonisation in Ceylon*, Oxford University Press.

Farmer, B. H., 1972, 'Ceylon', in O. H. K. Spate *et al.*, *India, Pakistan and Ceylon: The Regions*, Methuen, London (Third Edition).

Farrington, J., 1983, 'Small farm capital in Sri Lanka: the case of draft power', *Development Study No. 25*, Department of Agricultural Economics and Farm Management, University of Reading.

Farrington, J. and Abeyratne, F., 1982, 'Farm power in Sri Lanka', *Development Study No. 22*, Department of Agricultural Economics and Farm Management, University of Reading.

Farrington, J. *et al.*, 1980, 'Farm power and water use in the Dry Zone. Part 1', *Research Study No. 43*, Agrarian Research and Training Institute, Colombo.

Fernando, T., 1973, 'Elite politics in the new states: the case of post-independence Sri Lanka', *Pacific Affairs*, **46**(3).

Fieldson, R. S. and Farrington, J., 1980, 'Labour supply for small farm development in the Dry Zone: recent patterns and future prospects', paper presented to seminar on Research, Development and Rural Workers, Agrarian Research and Training Institute, Colombo, 25 April.

Gavan, J. D. and Chandrasekere, I. S., 1979, 'The impact of public foodgrain distribution on food consumption and welfare in Sri Lanka', *Research Report 13*, International Food Policy Research Institute, Washington DC.

Gold, M. E., 1977, *Law and Social Change: A Study of Land Reform in Sri Lanka*, Nellon Publishing Co., New York.

Gooneratne, W. *et al.*, 1977, 'Kurundakulama dry farming settlement: a socio-economic appraisal', *Research Study Series No. 17*, Agrarian Research and Training Institute, Colombo.

Gooneratne, W. *et al.*, 1978, *Rainfed farming in the Dry Zone of Sri Lanka: a socio-economic study*, mimeo, Agrarian Research and Training Institute, Colombo.

Gunasekere, H. M., 1977, 'Foreign trade of Sri Lanka', in K. M. de Silva (ed.), *Sri Lanka: A Survey*.

Gunasinghe, N., 1984, 'The open economy and its impact on ethnic relations in Sri Lanka', *Lanka Guardian*, **6**(17–19).

Gunatilleke, G., 1973, 'The rural–urban balance and development – the experience in Sri Lanka', *Marga*, **2**(1).

Gunatilleke, G., 1978, 'Participatory development and dependence – the case of Sri Lanka', *Marga*, **5**(3).

Gunawardena, P. J., 1979, 'Agricultural policies, rural workers and rural workers' organisations: the case of wage earners in the rural economy', in *Employment, Resource Mobilisation and Basic Needs Through Local Level Planning*, report on a national seminar held in Colombo, 15–18 May 1979, International Labour Organisation, Bangkok.

Hameed, N. D. A. *et al.*, 1977, *Rice Revolution in Sri Lanka*, United Nations Research Institute for Social Development, Geneva.

Harriss, B., 1978, 'Access and the cooperative: a study of an intermedium in structural change in Sri Lankan Dry Zone paddy cultivation', *Development and Change*, **9**(2).

Harriss, J., 1977a, 'Aspects of rural society in the Dry Zone relating to the problem of intensifying paddy production', in S. W. R. de A. Samarasinghe (ed.), *Agriculture in the Peasant Sector of Sri Lanka*, Ceylon Studies Seminar, Peradeniya.

Harriss, J., 1977b, 'Social implications of changes in agriculture in Hambantota district', in B. Farmer (ed.), *Green Revolution?*, Cambridge University Press.

Herring, R. J., 1972, 'The forgotten 1953 Paddy Lands Act in Ceylon: ideology, capacity and response', *Modern Ceylon Studies*, **3**(2).

Herring, R. J., 1977, 'Policy and ecology in the origins of discontinuities in the land tenure system of the Hambantota district', in S. W. R. de A. Samarasinghe (ed.), *Agriculture in the Peasant Sector of Sri Lanka*, Ceylon Studies Seminar, Peradeniya.

Hussain, S. M., 1977, 'Sectoral analysis of paddy production, marketing and processing in Sri Lanka', *Research Paper No. 6*, Development Planning Unit, Ministry of Planning and Economic Affairs, Colombo.

IBRD, 1975, *Republic of Sri Lanka Agricultural Development Project Report No. 911 CE*, International Bank for Reconstruction and Development, Washington.

International Labour Office, 1971a, *Matching Employment Opportunities and Expectations: A Programme of Action for Ceylon, Report*, Geneva.

International Labour Office, 1971b, *Matching Employment Opportunities and Expectations: A Programme of Action for Ceylon, Technical Papers*, Geneva.

Iriyagolle, G., 1978, *The Truth About the Mahaweli*, private publication, Colombo.

Isenman, P., 1980, 'Basic needs: the case of Sri Lanka', *World Development*, **8**(3).

Izumi, K. and Ranatunga, A. S., 1973, 'Cost of production of paddy: Yala 1972', *Research Study Series No. 1*, Agrarian Research and Training Institute, Colombo.

Izumi, K. and Ranatunga, A. S., 1974, 'Cost of production of paddy: Maha 1972–73', *Research Study No. 12*, Agrarian Research and Training Institute, Colombo.

Jackson, D. W., 1976, 'Polas in central Sri Lanka: some preliminary remarks on the development and functioning of periodic markets', in S. W. R. de A. Samarasinghe (ed.), *Agriculture in the Peasant Sector of Sri Lanka*, Ceylon Studies Seminar, Peradeniya.

Jayanath, G., 1980, 'Some problems connected with the cultivation of other food crops', *Economic Review* (Colombo), **6**(9).

Jayanntha, D., 1983, 'The Economic and Social Bases of Political Allegiance in Sri Lanka, 1947–82', Ph.D. thesis, University of Cambridge.

Jayaraman, R., 1975, *Caste Continuities in Ceylon: A Study of the Social Structure of Three Tea Plantations*, Popular Prakashan, Bombay.

Jayatilleke, S. R. de S., 1980, 'Patterns of Local Leadership: A Case Study of Two Sri Lankan Villages', M.Phil. thesis, University of Sussex.

Jayawardena, V. K., 1972, *The Rise of the Labor Movement in Ceylon*, Duke University Press.

Jiggins, J., 1979, *Caste and Family in the Politics of the Sinhalese, 1947–1976*, Cambridge University Press.

Jupp, J., 1978, *Sri Lanka: Third World Democracy*, Cass, London.

Kannangara, P. D., 1966, *The History of the Ceylon Civil Service, 1802–1833*, Tisara Prakasakayo, Colombo.

Kearney, R. N., 1966, 'Ceylon: the contemporary bureaucracy', in R. Braibanti (ed.), *Asian Bureaucratic Systems*.

Kearney, R. N., 1971, *Trades Unions and Politics in Ceylon*, University of California Press.

Bibliography

Kearney, R. N., 1973, *The Politics of Ceylon (Sri Lanka)*, Cornell University Press.

Keerawella, G. B., 1980, 'The Janatha Vimukthi Peramuna and the 1971 Uprising', *Social Science Review* (Colombo), 2.

Kemp, C. P., 1982, 'Spring Valley: A Social Anthropological and Historical Inquiry into the Impact of the Tea Estates upon a Sinhalese Village in the Uva Highlands of Sri Lanka', D.Phil. thesis, University of Sussex.

Knox, R., 1686, *An Historical Relation of Ceylon*, reprinted as volume 6 of the *Ceylon Historical Journal*, Colombo, July 1956–April 1957.

Kuruppu, C. R., 1979, 'Fertiliser and agricultural productivity', *Sri Lanka Journal of Social Sciences*, **1**(1).

Kuruppu, C. R., n.d., *Role of Regional Fertiliser Warehouse Complexes*, National Fertiliser Secretariat, Ministry of Plan Implementation, Colombo.

Lake House, 1977, *The Ceylon Daily News 8th Parliament of Sri Lanka*, ed. H. B. W. Abeynaike, The Associated Newspapers of Ceylon Ltd., Colombo.

Lanka Sama Samaj Party, 1978, *The Road to a Socialist Sri Lanka*, political resolution adopted by the delegates at a conference of the Lanka Sama Samaj Party on 17 to 19 March 1978, Colombo.

Leach, E., 1961, *Pul Eliya: A Village in Ceylon*, Cambridge University Press.

Lebbe, I. *et al.*, 1977, 'The role of local groups in rural development: a case study', *Research Study No. 22*, Agrarian Research and Training Institute, Colombo.

Lebbe, M. U. I., 1979, 'Chemman: building a new economy in rural Jaffna', in B. M. Morrison *et al.* (eds.), *The Disintegrating Village*.

Lee, E., 1977, 'Development and income distribution: a case study of Sri Lanka and Malaysia', *World Development*, **5**(4).

Leitan, G. R. T., 1979, *Local Government and Decentralised Administration in Sri Lanka*, Lake House Investments, Colombo.

Malalgoda, K., 1976, *Buddhism in Sinhalese Society 1750–1900*, University of California Press.

Manor, J., 1978, 'The youth of a leader in a transitional polity: S. W. R. D. Bandaranaike of Ceylon', *Ceylon Studies Seminar, Series No. 6, Serial No. 73*, Peradeniya.

Manor, J., 1979, 'The failure of political integration in Sri Lanka (Ceylon)', *The Journal of Commonwealth and Comparative Politics*, **17**(1).

Mattis, A. R., 1978, 'An experience of need-oriented development', *Marga*, **5**(3).

Meyer, E., 1978, 'Between village and plantation: Sinhalese estate labour in British Ceylon', paper presented at the 6th European Conference on Modern South Asian Studies, Sèvres, July.

Meyer, E., 1980a, 'The plantation system and the village structure in British Sri Lanka: involution or evolution?', paper presented to the Symposium on the External Dimension in Rural South Asia: Linkages between Localities and the Wider World, Centre of South Asian Studies, School of Oriental and African Studies, University of London, June.

Meyer, E., 1980b, 'Dépression et malaria à Sri Lanka: 1925–1939', thesis, 3ᵉ cycle, Ecole des Hautes Etudes en Sciences Sociales, Paris.

Meyer, E., 1982, 'Bourgeoisie et société rurale à Sri Lanka (1880–1940)', *Purusartha* (Paris), **6**.

Moore, M. P., 1978, 'The state and the cinnamon industry in Sri Lanka', *Occasional Publication No. 15*, Agrarian Research and Training Institute, Colombo.

Moore, M. P., 1979, 'Social structure and institutional performance: local farmers' organisations in Sri Lanka', *Journal of Administration Overseas*, **18**(4).

Moore, M. P., 1980a, 'Farewell to agrarian radicalism', *Lanka Guardian*, **2**(17).

Moore, M. P., 1980b, 'Deficit paddy farming in Sri Lanka', *Sri Lanka Journal of Agrarian Studies*, **1**(2).

Moore, M. P., 1980c, 'Approaches to improving water management on large-scale irrigation schemes in Sri Lanka', *Occasional Publication No. 20*, Agrarian Research and Training Institute, Colombo.

Moore, M. P., 1981a, 'The sociology of irrigation management in Sri Lanka', *Water Supply and Management*, **5**(1).

Moore, M. P., 1981b, 'Politics in Sri Lanka. A review article', *Modern Asian Studies*, **15**(1).

Moore, M. P., 1981c, 'The ideological function of kinship: the Sinhalese and the Merina', *Man*, NS **16**(4).

Moore, M. P., 1981d, 'The State and the Peasantry in Sri Lanka', D.Phil. thesis, University of Sussex.

Moore, M. P., 1984a, 'The 1982 elections and the new Gaullist-Bonapartist state in Sri Lanka', in J. Manor (ed.), *Sri Lanka in Change and Crisis*, Croom Helm, London.

Moore, M. P., 1984b, 'Categorising space: urban–rural and core–periphery in Sri Lanka', in J. Harriss and M. Moore (eds.), *Development and the Rural–Urban Divide*, Cass, London.

Moore, M.P. and Perera, U. L. J., 1978, 'Land policy and village expansion in Sri Lanka', *Marga*, **5**(1).

Moore, M. P. and Wickremesinghe, G., 1978a, 'Managing the village environment', *Occasional Publication No. 16*, Agrarian Research and Training Institute, Colombo.

Moore, M. P. and Wickremesinghe, G., 1978b, 'Thattumaru-kattimaru systems of land tenure', *Research Study No. 26*, Agrarian Research and Training Institute, Colombo.

Moore, M. P. and Wickremesinghe, G., 1980, *Agriculture and Society in the Low Country (Sri Lanka)*, Agrarian Research and Training Institute, Colombo.

Moore, M. P. *et al.*, 1979, 'Weligalogoda: an "internal colony" in the Galle district', in B. M. Morrison *et al.* (eds.), *The Disintegrating Village*.

Morrison, B. M., 1979, 'Meegama: seeking livelihoods in a Kandyan village', in B. M. Morrison *et al.* (eds.), *The Disintegrating Village*.

Morrison, B. M. *et al.* (eds.), 1979, *The Disintegrating Village: Social Change in Rural Sri Lanka*, Lake House Investments, Colombo.

Murray-Rust, H. and Moore, M. P., 1983, 'Formal and informal water management systems: cultivation meetings and water deliveries in two Sri Lankan irrigation schemes', *Cornell Studies in Irrigation No. 2*, Ithaca.

Obeyesekera, J., 1973, 'Revolutionary movements in Ceylon', in K. Gough and H. P. Sharma (eds.), *Imperialism and Revolution in South Asia*, Monthly Review Press, New York and London.

Obeyesekere, G., 1967, *Land Tenure in Village Ceylon*, Cambridge University Press.

Obeyesekere, G., 1970, 'Religious symbolism and political change in Ceylon', *Modern Ceylon Studies*, **1**(1).

Obeyesekere, G., 1974, 'Some comments on the social backgrounds of the April 1971 Insurgency in Sri Lanka (Ceylon)', *Journal of Asian Studies*, **33**(3).

Obeyesekere, G., 1979, 'The vicissitudes of the Sinhala-Buddhist identity through time and change', in M. Roberts (ed.), *Collective Identities*.

Oliver, H. M., 1957, *Economic Opinion and Policy in Ceylon*, Duke University Press.

Panditaratne, B. L., 1960, 'The harbour and port of Colombo: a geographical appraisal of its historical and functional aspects', *The Ceylon Journal of Historical and Social Studies*, **3**(2).

Panditaratne, B. L., 1961, 'A geographical description and analysis of Ceylonese towns', *The Ceylon Journal of Historical and Social Studies*, **4**(1).

Parker, R. N., 1978, *Tank irrigation modernisation project: characteristics of existing tractor operations*, mimeo, n.p.

Peiris, G., 1977a, 'The physical environment', in K. M. de Silva (ed.), *Sri Lanka: A Survey*.

Peiris, G., 1977b, 'Plantation agriculture', in K. M. de Silva (ed.), *Sri Lanka: A Survey*.

Peiris, G. H., 1976, 'Share tenancy and tenurial reform in Sri Lanka', *Ceylon Journal of Historical and Social Studies*, NS **6**(1).

Peiris, G. H., 1978, 'Land reform and agrarian change in Sri Lanka', *Modern Asian Studies*, **12**(4).

Peiris, G. H., 1981a, *Basic Needs and the Provision of Government Services in Sri Lanka: A Case Study of Kandy District*, International Labour Office, Geneva, WEP 2–32/WP 35.

Peiris, G. H., 1981b, 'Agrarian transformations in British Sri Lanka', *Sri Lanka Journal of Agrarian Studies*, **2**(2).

Perera, L. N. *et al.*, 1973, 'The effect of income on food habits in Ceylon. The findings of the socio-economic survey of Ceylon, 1969/70', *Marga*, **2**(1).

Perera, U. L. J., 1979a, 'Nigaruppe: settlement and conflict in the coconut triangle', in B. M. Morrison *et al.* (eds.), *The Disintegrating Village*.

Perera, U. L. J., 1979b, *Change and settlement in Mahaweli: an in-depth study of a purana village*, mimeo, Agrarian Research and Training Institute, Colombo.

Perera, U. L. J., 1982, 'Social Change and Class Relations in Rural Sri Lanka', D.Phil. thesis, University of Sussex.

Perera, U. L. J. and Gunawardena, P. J., 1980, 'Hired labourers in peasant agriculture in Sri Lanka', *Research Study No. 40*, Agrarian Research and Training Institute, Colombo.

Perera, U. L. J. and Kraise, G., 1977, 'The role of local groups in rural development. A case study of a village in the class II coconut area – Colombo District', *Research Study No. 20*, Agrarian Research and Training Institute, Colombo.

Phadnis, U., 1976, *Religion and Politics in Sri Lanka*, Manohar, Delhi.

Pieris, R., 1956, *Sinhalese Social Organisation*, The Ceylon University Press Board, Colombo.

Pieris, R., 1965, 'The effects of technological development on the population of the Gal Oya Valley, Ceylon', *The Ceylon Journal of Historical and Social Studies*, 8(1, 2).

Ponnambalam, G. G., 1980, 'Development Councils Act – 2. Controlled councils', *Lanka Guardian*, 3(11).

Ranatunga, A. S. and Abeysekere, W. A. T., 1977, 'Profitability and resource characteristics of paddy farming', *Research Study No. 23*, Agrarian Research and Training Institute, Colombo.

Ranatunga, A. S. *et al.*, 1981, 'Some issues confronting the rehabilitation of major irrigation schemes in the Dry Zone', *Research Study No. 44*, Agrarian Research and Training Institute, Colombo.

Ranbanda, H. A., 1980, *Economics of Seasonal Migration*, mimeo, Agrarian Research and Training Institute, Colombo.

Richards, P. and Gooneratne, W., 1980, *Basic Needs, Poverty and Government Policies in Sri Lanka*, International Labour Office, Geneva.

Roberts, M., 1966, 'Indian estate labour in Ceylon during the Coffee Period, 1830–1880', *Indian Economic and Social History Review*, 3.

Roberts, M., 1970a, 'Grain taxes in British Ceylon, 1832–1878, theories, prejudices and controversies', *Modern Ceylon Studies*, 1(1).

Roberts, M., 1970b, 'The impact of the waste lands legislation and the growth of plantations on the techniques of paddy cultivation in British Ceylon: a critique', *Modern Ceylon Studies*, 1(2).

Roberts, M., 1970c, 'The political antecedents of the revivialist elite within the MEP coalition of 1956', *Ceylon Studies Seminar, 1969/70 Series No. 11*, Peradeniya, mimeo.

Roberts, M., 1970/2a, 'Variations on the theme of resistance movements: the Kandyan rebellion of 1817–18 and latter-day nationalism in Ceylon', *Ceylon Studies Seminar, 1970/72 Series No. 4*, Peradeniya.

Roberts, M., 1970/2b, 'Some comments on Ameer Ali's paper', *Ceylon Studies Seminar, 1970/72 Series No. 36*, Peradeniya.

Roberts, M., 1972, 'Irrigation policy in British Ceylon during the nineteenth century', *South Asia: Journal of South Asian Studies*, 2.

Roberts, M., 1973a, 'Elite formation and elites, 1832–1931', in K. M. de Silva (ed.), *History of Ceylon*.

Roberts, M., 1973b, 'Land problems and policies, *c*.1832 to *c*.1900', in K. M. de Silva (ed.), *History of Ceylon*.

Roberts, M., 1973c, 'Aspects of Ceylon's agrarian economy in the nineteenth century', in K. M. de Silva (ed.), *History of Ceylon*.

Roberts, M., 1975, 'A new marriage, an old dichotomy: the "middle class" in British Ceylon', in K. Indrapala (ed.), *James Thevathasan Rutnam Felicitation Volume*, Jaffna Archaeological Society, Jaffna.

Roberts, M., 1978, 'Reformism, nationalism and protest in British Ceylon', in P. Robb and D. Taylor (eds.), *Rule, Protest, Identity: Aspects of Modern South Asia*, Curzon Press, London.

Roberts, M. (ed.), 1979, *Collective Identities, Nationalisms and Protest in Modern Sri Lanka*, Marga Institute, Colombo.

Roberts, M., 1979a, 'Meanderings in the pathways of collective identity and nationalism', in M. Roberts (ed.), *Collective Identities*.

Roberts, M., 1979b, 'Elite formation and elites, 1832–1931', in M. Roberts (ed.), *Collective Identities*.

Roberts, M., 1979c, 'Stimulants and ingredients in the awakening of the latter-day nationalisms', in M. Roberts (ed.), *Collective Identities*.

Roberts, M., 1979d, 'Occupational culture of fishing and the emergence of Karava entrepreneurs in colonial times', *Ceylon Studies Seminar, 1979 Series No. 3, Serial No. 80*, Peradeniya.

Roberts, M., 1979e, 'Nationalism in economic and social thought 1915–1945', in M. Roberts (ed.), *Collective Identities*.

Roberts, M., 1982, *Caste Conflict and Elite Formation: The Rise of a Karava Elite in Sri Lanka, 1500–1931*, Cambridge University Press.

Roberts, M. and Wickremeratne, L. A., 1973, 'Export agriculture in the nineteenth century', in K. M. de Silva (ed.), *History of Ceylon*.

Robinson, M. S., 1975, *Political Structure in a Changing Sinhalese Village*, Cambridge University Press.

Rogers, J. D., 1984, *The 'criminal classes' of Sri Lanka at the end of the 19th century: social assumptions and realities*, paper presented to postgraduate seminar, Institute of Commonwealth Studies, London, 17 January, mimeo.

Ryan, B., 1953, *Caste in Modern Ceylon*, Rutgers University Press.

Ryan, B. *et al.*, 1958, *Sinhalese Village*, University of Miami Press.

Samaraweera, V., 1973a, 'The Colebrooke–Cameron reforms', in K. M. de Silva (ed.), *History of Ceylon*.

Samaraweera, V., 1973b, 'Land policy and peasant colonisation, 1914–1948', in K. M. de Silva (ed.), *History of Ceylon*.

Samaraweera, V., 1973c, 'The development of the administrative system from 1802 to 1832', in K. M. de Silva (ed.), *History of Ceylon*.

Samaraweera, V., 1973d, 'Economic and social developments under the British, 1796–1832', in K. M. de Silva (ed.), *History of Ceylon*.

Samaraweera, V., 1977a, 'The evolution of a plural society', in K. M. de Silva (ed.), *Sri Lanka: A Survey*.

Samaraweera, V., 1977b, 'Land as "patrimony": nationalist response to immigrant labour demand for land in early 20th century Sri Lanka', *Indian*

Economic and Social History Review, **14**.

Samaraweera, V., 1978, 'The "village community" and reform in colonial Sri Lanka', *Ceylon Journal of Historical and Social Studies*, NS **8**(1).

Samaraweera, V., 1979a, 'The Muslim revivalist movement, 1880–1915', in M. Roberts (ed.), *Collective Identities*.

Samaraweera, V., 1979b, 'Litigation and legal reform in colonial Sri Lanka', *South Asia*, **2**(1, 2).

Samaraweera, V., 1980, 'Sri Lankan Marxists in electoral politics, 1947–1977', *The Journal of Commonwealth and Comparative Politics*, **18**(3).

Samaraweera, V., 1981, 'Land, labor, capital and sectional interests in the national politics of Sri Lanka', *Modern Asian Studies*, **15**(1).

Samuel, S. N. and Abayaratna, G. M., 1974, 'An analysis of fertiliser marketing in the context of Sri Lanka's paddy subsector development', *Central Bank of Ceylon Staff Studies*, **4**(1), April.

Sanderatne, N., 1972a, 'Tenancy in Ceylon's paddy lands: the 1958 reform', *South Asian Review*, **5**(2).

Sanderatne, N., 1972b, 'Sri Lanka's new land reform', *South Asian Review*, **6**(1).

Sarkar, N. K. and Thambaiyah, S. K., 1957, *The Disintegrating Village, Part 1*, University of Ceylon Press Board, Colombo.

Sathasivampillai, K., 1973, 'Summary report of the study on fertiliser use in paddy production in selected nine districts of Sri Lanka 1971–72', *Agricultural Economic Study No. 5*, Division of Agricultural Economics, Farm Management and Statistics, Department of Agriculture, Peradeniya.

Sathasivampillai, K. and de Silva, G. A. C., 1976a, 'Farm business management in the Dry Zone of Sri Lanka', *Agricultural Economic Study No. 17*, Division of Agricultural Economics, Farm Management and Statistics, Department of Agriculture, Peradeniya.

Sathasivampillai, K. and de Silva, G. A. C., 1976b, 'Farm business management in the Intermediate Zone of Sri Lanka during 1973/4', *Agricultural Economic Study No. 18*, Division of Agricultural Economics, Farm Management and Statistics, Department of Agriculture, Peradeniya.

Sathasivampillai, K. and de Silva, G. A. C., 1976c, 'Farm business management in the Wet Zone of Sri Lanka', *Agricultural Economic Study No. 19*, Division of Agricultural Economics, Farm Management and Statistics, Department of Agriculture, Peradeniya.

Selvanayagam, S., 1977, 'Palamunai village', in N. D. A. Hameed *et al.*, *Rice Revolution*.

Seneratne, S. P. F., 1970, 'Status, Power and Resources: The Study of a Sinhalese Village', Ph.D. thesis, University of London.

Seneviratne, H. L., 1977, 'Politics and pageantry: universalisation of ritual in Sri Lanka', *Man*, **12**(1).

Seneviratne, H. L., 1978, *Rituals of the Kandyan State*, Cambridge University Press.

Shanmugaratnam, N. and Siriwardana, S., 1979, 'Employment generation and resource mobilisation through the integration of plantation and rural sectors', in *Employment, Resource Mobilisation and Basic Needs Through Local Level Planning*, Report of a national seminar held in Colombo, 15–18 May 1979, International Labour Organisation, Bangkok.

Silva, K. T., 1979, 'Welivita: the demise of Kandyan feudalism', in B. M. Morrison *et al.* (eds.), *The Disintegrating Village*.

Singer, M. R., 1964, *The Emerging Elite: A Study of Political Leadership in Ceylon*, MIT Press.

Siriwardena, R., 1979, 'N. M. – a political assessment', *Lanka Guardian*, **2**(9).

Sivathamby, K., 1980, 'The Northern Province', *Lanka Guardian*, **2**(21).

Smith, D. E., 1979, 'Religion, politics and the myth of reconquest', in T. Fernando and R. N. Kearney (eds.), *Modern Sri Lanka: A Society in Transition*, Syracuse University, Maxwell School of Citizenship and Public Affairs, South Asia Series No. 4.

Snodgrass, D. R., 1966, *Ceylon: An Export Economy in Transition*, Richard D. Irwin, Homewood, Illinois.

Snodgrass, D. R., 1974, 'Sri Lanka's economic development during twenty-five years since Independence', *The Ceylon Journal of Historical and Social Studies*, NS **4**(1, 2).

Stirrat, J. 1984, 'The riots and the Roman Catholic Church in historical perspective', in J. Manor (ed.), *Sri Lanka in Change and Crisis*, Croom Helm, London.

Tambaiah, S. J., 1963, 'Ceylon', in R. D. Lambert and B. F. Hoselitz (eds.), *The Role of Savings and Wealth in Southern Asia and the West*, UNESCO, Paris.

United Front, n.d., *Joint Election Manifesto of the United Front, 1970*, Government Printer, Colombo.

Uphoff, N. and Wanigaratne, R., 1982, 'Local organisation and rural development in Sri Lanka', in N. Uphoff (ed.), *Rural Development and Local Organisation in Asia, Volume 1: Introduction and South Asia*, Macmillan, Delhi.

Uswatte-Aratchi, G., 1974, 'University admissions in Ceylon: their economic and social background and employment expectations', *Modern Asian Studies*, **8**(3).

Volz, U., n.d., *Fertiliser Retail Distribution*, National Fertiliser Secretariat, Ministry of Plan Implementation, Colombo.

Wanasinghe, S., 1980a, 'Administrative reforms for decentralised development: the Sri Lankan experience', in A. P. Saxena (ed.), *Administrative Reforms for Decentralised Development*, Asian and Pacific Development Administration Centre, Kuala Lumpur.

Wanasinghe, S., 1980b, 'Formulation and implementation of land reform in Sri Lanka', in Inayatullah (ed.), *Land Reform: Some Asian Experiences*, Asian and Pacific Development Administration Centre, Kuala Lumpur.

Wanigaratne, R. D., 1977, *The Ambana Village*, Agrarian Research and Training Institute and Communications Strategy Project, Ministry of Information and Broadcasting, Colombo.

Wanigaratne, R. D., 1979a, 'Minitalawa: a peasant settlement in the Dry

Zone', in B. M. Morrison *et al.* (eds.), *The Disintegrating Village*.

Wanigaratne, R. D., 1979b, 'The Minipe colonisation scheme – an appraisal', *Research Study No. 29*, Agrarian Research and Training Institute, Colombo.

Wanigaratne, R. D. *et al.*, 1980, *Implementation of Land Reform in Selected Villages of Sri Lanka*, Asian and Pacific Development Administration Centre, Kuala Lumpur.

Warnapala, W. A. W., 1973, 'Bureaucratic transformation *c.*1910–1948', in K. M. de Silva (ed.), *History of Ceylon*.

Warnapala, W. A. W., 1974, *Civil Service Administration in Ceylon: A Study in Bureaucratic Adaptation*, Department of Government Printing, Colombo.

Weerawardena, I. K., 1975, 'Lessons of an experiment: the Paddy Lands Act of 1958', *Evaluation Studies No. 3*, Department of Rural Institutions and Productivity Laws, Colombo.

Weerawardena, I. K. and Collonnege, I., 1971, *Thattumaru-Kattimaru Study*, Department of Rural Institutions and Productivity Laws, Colombo.

Wesumperuma, D., 1967, 'The evictions under the paddy tax, and their impact on the peasantry of Walapane', *The Ceylon Journal of Historical and Social Studies*, **10**(1, 2).

Wickremasekera, P., 1977, 'Aspects of the hired labour situation in rural Sri Lanka: preliminary findings', in S. Hirashima (ed.), *Hired Labor in Rural Asia*, Institute of Developing Economies, Tokyo.

Wickremeratne, L. A., 1973a, 'The development of transportation in Ceylon, *c.*1800–1947', in K. M. de Silva (ed.), *History of Ceylon*.

Wickremeratne, L. A., 1973b, 'Economic development in the plantation sector, *c.*1900–1947', in K. M. de Silva (ed.), *History of Ceylon*.

Wickremeratne, L. A., 1973c, 'The emergence of a welfare policy, 1931–1948', in K. M. de Silva (ed.), *History of Ceylon*.

Wickremeratne, L. A., 1973d, 'Education and social change, 1832 to *c.*1800', in K. M. de Silva (ed.), *History of Ceylon*.

Wickremeratne, L. A., 1973e, 'Grain consumption and famine conditions in late nineteenth-century Ceylon', *The Ceylon Journal of Historical and Social Studies*, NS **3**(2).

Wickremeratne, L. A., 1975, 'Kandyans and nationalism in Sri Lanka: some reflections', *The Ceylon Journal of Historical and Social Studies*, NS **6**(1, 2).

Wickremeratne, L. A., 1977a, 'Planning and economic development', in K. M. de Silva (ed.), *Sri Lanka: A Survey*.

Wickremeratne, L. A., 1977b, 'Peasant agriculture', in K. M. de Silva (ed.), *Sri Lanka: A Survey*.

Wijesinghe, M., 1976, *The Economy of Sri Lanka 1948–1975*, Ranco Printers and Publishers, Colombo.

Wilson, A. J., 1973, 'The development of the constitution, 1910–1947', in K. M. de Silva (ed.), *History of Ceylon*.

Wilson, A. J., 1974, 'The future of parliamentary government', *The Ceylon Journal of Historical and Social Studies*, NS **4**(1, 2).

Wilson, A. J., 1979, *Politics in Sri Lanka, 1947–1979*, Macmillan, London.

Bibliography

Wilson, A. J., 1980, *The Gaullist System in Asia: The Constitution of Sri Lanka (1978)*, Macmillan, London.

Woodward, C. A., 1969, *The Growth of a Party System in Ceylon*, Brown University Press.

Wriggins, W. H., 1960, *Ceylon: Dilemmas of a New Nation*, Princeton University Press.

Wriggins, W. H., 1979, 'Why bureaucracies fall short', *Tribune* (Colombo), 24 November.

Yalman, N., 1967, *Under the Bo Tree: Studies in Caste, Kinship and Marriage in the Interior of Ceylon*, University of California Press.

India

Bailey, F. G., 1957, 'For a sociology of India', *Contributions to Indian Sociology*, 2.

Brass, P., 1974, *Religion, Language and Politics in North India*, Cambridge University Press.

Broomfield, J. H., 1968, 'The regional elites: a theory of modern Indian history', in R. Bendix (ed.), *State and Society: A Reader in Comparative Political Sociology*, University of California Press.

Chaudhuri, K. N., 1978, 'Some reflections on the town and country in Mughal India', *Modern Asian Studies*, 12(1).

Cohn, B., 1968, 'Notes on the history of the study of Indian society and culture', in M. Singer and B. Cohn (eds.), *Structure and Change in Indian History*, Aldine Publishing Co., Chicago.

Dumont, L., 1966, 'The "village community" from Munro to Maine', *Contributions to Indian Sociology*, 9.

Dumont, L. and Pocock, D., 1957a, 'For a sociology of India', *Contributions to Indian Sociology*, 1.

Dumont, L. and Pocock, D., 1957b, 'Village studies', *Contributions to Indian Sociology*, 1.

Duncan, I., 1979, 'The Communication of Programmes and Sectional Strategies in Indian Politics, with reference to the Bharantiya Kranti Dal and the Republican Party of India in Uttar Pradesh State and Aligarh District (U.P.)', D.Phil. thesis, University of Sussex.

Habib, I., 1963, *The Agrarian System of Mughal India*, Asia Publishing House, London.

Harriss, J., 1982, *Capitalism and Peasant Farming: Agrarian Structure and Ideology in Northern Tamil Nadu*, Oxford University Press, Bombay.

Kothari, R., 1970, *Politics in India*, Little, Brown and Co., Boston.

Mandelbaum, D. G., 1970a, *Society in India, Volume One: Continuity and Change*, University of California Press.

Mandelbaum, D. G., 1970b, *Society in India, Volume Two: Change and Continuity*, University of California Press.

Marriott, M., 1965, 'Little communities in an indigenous civilisation', in

M. Marriott (ed.), *Village India: Studies in the Little Community*, University of Chicago Press.

Mason, P., 1967, 'Unity and diversity: an introductory review', in P. Mason (ed.), *India and Ceylon: Unity and Diversity*, Oxford University Press.

Mitra, A., 1977, *Terms of Trade and Class Relations*, Cass, London.

Nadkarni, M. V., 1983, *Farmers' movements in South India: claims of urban bias and their substance*, mimeo, Institute for Social and Economic Change, Bangalore.

Rudolph, L. E., 1968, 'The modernity of tradition: the democratic incarnation of caste in India', in R. Bendix (ed.), *State and Society: A Reader in Comparative Political Sociology*, University of California Press.

Rudolph, L. E. and Rudolph, S. H., 1967, *The Modernity of Tradition: Political Development in India*, University of Chicago Press.

Seal, A., 1973, 'Imperialism and nationalism in India', *Modern Asian Studies*, 7(3).

Shah, A. M., 1974, *The Household Dimension of the Family in India*, University of California Press.

Sharma, B. K., 1979, 'Peasant power', *India Today*, 4(1).

Srinivas, M. N., 1962, *Caste in Modern India and Other Essays*, Asia Publishing House, Bombay.

Srinivas, M. N., 1969, 'The caste system in India', in A. Beteille (ed.), *Social Inequality*, Penguin, London.

Srinivas, M. N. and Shah, A. M., 1960, 'The myth of self-sufficiency of the Indian village', *The Economic Weekly* (later *Economic and Political Weekly*), 12.

Washbrook, D., 1977, *The Emergence of Provincial Politics: The Madras Presidency 1870–1920*, Vikas Publishing House, New Delhi.

Weiner, M., 1963, *Political Change in South Asia*, Firma K. L. Mukhopadhyay, Calcutta.

General

Abercrombie, N. *et al.*, 1980, *The Dominant Ideology Thesis*, Allen and Unwin, London.

Alavi, H., 1973, 'Peasants and revolution', in K. Gough and H. P. Sharma (eds.), *Imperialism and Revolution in South Asia*, Monthly Review Press, New York and London (first published 1964).

Badie, B. and Birnbaum, P., 1983, *The Sociology of the State*, University of Chicago Press.

Bates, R. H., 1983, *Essays on the Political Economy of Rural Africa*, Cambridge University Press.

Bates, R. H., 1984, 'Some conventional orthodoxies in the study of agrarian change', *World Politics*, 36(2).

Berry, R. A. and Cline, W. R., 1979, *Agrarian Structure and Productivity in Developing Countries*, Johns Hopkins University Press.

Birnberg, T. B. and Resnick, S. A., 1975, *Colonial Development: An Econometric Study*, Yale University Press.

Bibliography

Bottomore, T., 1979, *Political Sociology*, Hutchinson, London.

Braibanti, R. (ed.), 1966, *Asian Bureaucratic Systems Emergent from the British Imperial Tradition*, Duke University Press.

Claval, P., 1980, 'Centre–periphery and space: models of political geography', in J. Gottman (ed.), *Centre and Periphery: Spatial Variation in Politics*, Sage Publications, Beverly Hills and London.

Connolly, W. E., 1974, *The Terms of Political Discourse*, D. C. Heath and Co., Lexington, Mass.

Dore, R., 1976, *The Diploma Disease: Education, Qualifications and Development*, Unwin, London.

FAO, 1958, *Agricultural Price Policies in Asia and the Far East*, UN/CN11/484, Food and Agriculture Organisation, Rome.

Frank, A. G., 1969, *Capitalism and Underdevelopment in Latin America*, Monthly Review Press, New York and London.

Gottman, J., 1980, 'Confronting centre and periphery', in J. Gottman (ed.), *Centre and Periphery: Spatial Variation in Politics*, Sage Publications, Beverly Hills and London.

Herring, R. J., 1980a, 'Abolition of landlordism in Kerala: a redistribution of privilege', *Economic and Political Weekly*, **15**(26).

Herring, R. J., 1980b, 'Zulfikar Ali Bhutto and the "eradication of feudalism" in Pakistan', *Comparative Studies in Society and History*, **21**(4).

Hobsbawm, E., 1973, 'Peasants and politics', *The Journal of Peasant Studies*, **1**(1).

Huntington, S. P., 1968, *Political Order in Changing Societies*, Yale University Press, New Haven and London.

Leys, C., 1971, 'Politics in Kenya: the development of peasant society', *British Journal of Political Science*, **1**(3).

Ling, T., 1976, *The Buddha*, Penguin, London.

Linz, J. J., 1976, 'Patterns of land tenure, division of labor and voting behaviour in Europe', *Comparative Politics*, **8**(3).

Lipton, M., 1977, *Why Poor People Stay Poor: Urban Bias in World Development*, Temple Smith, London.

Lukes, S., 1974, *Power: A Radical View*, Macmillan, London.

Mills, D. R., 1980, *Land and Peasant in Nineteenth-Century Britain*, Croom Helm, London.

Moore, Barrington Jr, 1967, *Social Origins of Dictatorship and Democracy: Lord and Peasant in the Making of the Modern World*, Allen Lane, The Penguin Press, London.

Newby, H., 1978, 'The rural sociology of advanced capitalist societies', in H. Newby (ed.), *International Perspectives*.

Newby, H. (ed.), 1978, *International Perspectives in Rural Sociology*, John Wiley and Sons, Chichester.

Newby, H. et. al., 1978, *Property, Paternalism and Power: Class and Control in Rural England*, Hutchinson, London.

Nordlinger, E., 1981, *On the Autonomy of the Democratic State*, Harvard University Press.

Paige, J. M., 1975, *Agrarian Revolution: Social Movements and Export*

Bibliography

Agriculture in the Underdeveloped World, The Free Press, New York.

Parsons, T., 1951, *The Social System*, The Free Press, Glencoe.

Pipes, R., 1977, *Russia under the Old Regime*, Penguin, London.

Poggi, G., 1978, *The Development of the Modern State: A Sociological Introduction*, Hutchinson, London.

Radwan, S. and Lee, E., 1979, 'The State and agrarian change: a case study of Egypt, 1952–77', in D. Ghai *et al.* (eds.), *Agrarian Systems and Rural Development*, Macmillan, London.

Roxborough, I., 1979, *Theories of Underdevelopment*, Macmillan, London.

Scott, J. C., 1976, *The Moral Economy of the Peasant: Rebellion and Subsistence in Southeast Asia*, Yale University Press, New Haven and London.

Shanin, T., 1971, 'The peasantry as a political factor', in T. Shanin (ed.), *Peasants and Peasant Societies*, Penguin, London.

Skocpol, T., 1979, *States and Social Revolutions*, Cambridge University Press.

Skocpol, T. and Somers, M., 1980, 'The uses of comparative history in macrosocial inquiry', *Comparative Studies in Society and History*, **22**(2).

Somers, M. R. and Goldfrank, W. L., 1979, 'The limits of agronomic determinism: a critique of Paige's "Agrarian Revolution"', *Comparative Studies in Society and History*, **21**(3).

Stedman Jones, G., 1983, *Languages of Class: Studies in English Working-Class History, 1832–1982*, Cambridge University Press.

Stenson, M., 1980, *Race, Class and Colonialism in West Malaysia*, University of Queensland Press.

Stinchcombe, A. L., 1971, 'Agricultural enterprise and rural class relations', *American Journal of Sociology*, **67**(2).

Timmer, C. P. and Falcon, W. P., 1975, 'The political economy of rice production and trade in Asia', in L. G. Reynolds (ed.), *Agriculture in Development Theory*, Yale University Press.

Verba, S. *et al.*, 1978, *Participation and Political Equality: A Seven Nation Comparison*, Cambridge University Press.

Westergaard, J., 1974, 'Some aspects of the study of modern British society', in J. Rex (ed.), *Approaches to Sociology*, Routledge and Kegan Paul, London.

Wiener, M., 1981, *English Culture and the Decline of the Industrial Spirit, 1850–1980*, Cambridge University Press.

Wilson, G., 1978, 'Farmers' organizations in advanced societies', in H. Newby (ed.), *International Perspectives*.

Wolf, E., 1971, *Peasant Wars in the Twentieth Century*, Faber and Faber, London.

INDEX

Agrarian Services Act 1979, 57–8, 63–5, 111–12
agricultural credit, 93–4, 198
agricultural labourers, 42, 46–7, 62–3, 186–8; seasonal migration of, 46, 62, 187–8
Agricultural Lands Law 1973, 57, 63
agricultural prices and policy, 2–3, 5, 8–10, 27–8, 34–5, 85–120, 149–66, 190
Agricultural Productivity Law 1972, 57, 63
Amparai, 96, 132, 139, 157, 193
Anuradhapura, 45, 96, 109, 193

Badulla, 25, 74, 109
banana production, *see* minor crops
Bandaranaike, S. W. R. D., 20, 25, 54, 60–1, 75, 77, 86, 117, 207, 217, 218, 220, 229
Bandaranaike, Sirimavo, 1, 56, 75, 79, 199, 217, 218, 235
Batticaloa, 51–3, 96, 123, 133–4, 139, 154, 157, 183, 193, 196, 197
Bhoomidari, 39
Borahs, 15, 28, 129, 130
Brayne, C. V., 38
Buddhism, 18, 29, 45, 83, 128, 132, 173–5, 179, 213
Burghers, 15–16, 28, 129, 130

'capitalists', 38–9, 48, 113
caste, Sinhalese: structure, 47, 59, 89, 129, 172–3, 179, 207; and politics, 14, 59, 181–2, 210–11, 214, 221, 235
Central Province, *see* Kandyan areas
Ceylon Civil Service, *see* public administration
chena, 32, 159
Chetties, 28, 129, 130
chillie production, *see* minor crops
cinnamon production and economy, 163
class structure and consciousness, 5–6, 7, 42, 53–4, 83, 167–90, 193–201, 205–13, 221–4
coconut production and economy, 6, 69–

71, 101–2, 115, 129, 158–61; *see also* plantation sector and export crop production
Colombo, city and district, 10, 25, 115, 129–31, 207–9, 215
colonial rule: British, 17–20, 35, 128–31; Dutch, 18, 28, 128; Portuguese, 18, 28, 128
Communist Party, 1, 20, 214, 235; *see also* Marxist political movements
constitutional change, 20, 24, 174, 236
cooperatives, 91–2, 99, 105, 120, 155–6, 229
Cooray, E. J., 206
crop insurance scheme, 90, 95
cultivation committees, 57–60, 64, 228
CWC (Ceylon Workers Congress), 233–4

De Silva, C. P., 60, 115, 199
De Silva, Colvin R., 20, 62, 79
De Souza, Doric, 79
Department for Kandyan Peasantry Rehabilitation, 76–7
Department of Agrarian Services, 58, 64–5
Department of Agriculture, 90, 132, 163
Department of Minor Export Crops, 163
District Development Councils, 236
District Ministers, 229
Donoughmore Commission, 19
dual economy, 72

education, 128–32, 135–9, 196, 226
electoral system, 24–5, 236
elite, 3, 19, 35–9, 54, 130, 181, 204–13, 218, 228, 229
employment patterns, 22–4, 61, 124, 135–7, 186–8, 223–4
ethnic identity and conflict, 7, 15–16, 29, 45–6, 48, 73–5, 128–34, 191–201, 217, 232
export crop production, *see* plantation sector

United Front, 1, 20
United Left Front, 61
United National Party, 19–20, 24–5, 29, 39, 45, 51–5, 81, 114–16, 196, 215, 222
Uva Province, 32, 77, 109, 193

Vavuniya, 133, 157, 196
vegetable production, *see* minor crops

Vel Vidanes, 59–60
Village Expansion Schemes, 40–2, 97, 125
VLSSP (Revolutionary Lanka Sama Samaj Party), 55; *see also* Marxist political movements

Waste Lands Ordinance 1840, 32
Western Province, *see* Low Country

CAMBRIDGE SOUTH ASIAN STUDIES

These monographs are published by the Syndics of Cambridge University Press in association with the Cambridge University Centre for South Asian Studies. The following books have been published in this series:

1 S. Gopal: *British Policy in India, 1858–1905*
2 J. A. B. Palmer: *The Mutiny Outbreak at Meerut in 1857*
3 A. Das Gupta: *Malabar in Asian Trade, 1740–1800*
4 G. Obeyesekere: *Land Tenure in Village Ceylon*
5 H. L. Erdman: *The Swatantra Party and Indian Conservatism*
6 S. N. Mukherjee: *Sir William Jones: A Study in Eighteenth-Century British Attitudes to India*
7 Abdul Majed Khan: *The Transition in Bengal, 1756–1775: A Study of Saiyid Muhammad Reza Khan*
8 Radhe Shyam Rungta: *The Rise of Business Corporations in India, 1851–1900*
9 Pamela Nightingale: *Trade and Empire in Western India, 1784–1806*
10 Amiya Kumar Bagchi: *Private Investment in India, 1900–1939*
11 Judith M. Brown: *Gandhi's Rise to Power: Indian Politics, 1915–1922*
12 Mary C. Carras: *The Dynamics of Indian Political Factions*
13 P. Hardy: *The Muslims of British India*
14 Gordon Johnson: *Provincial Politics and Indian Nationalism*
15 Marguerite S. Robinson: *Political Structure in a Changing Sinhalese Village*
16 Francis Robinson: *Separation among Indian Muslims: The Politics of the United Provinces' Muslims, 1860–1923*
17 Christopher John Baker: *The Politics of South India, 1920–1936*
18 David Washbrook: *The Emergence of Provincial Politics: The Madras Presidency, 1870–1920*
19 Deepak Nayyar: *India's Exports and Export Policies in the 1960s*
20 Mark Holmström: *South Indian Factory Workers: Their Life and Their World*
21 S. Ambirajan: *Classical Political Economy and British Policy in India*
22 M. M. Islam: *Bengal Agriculture 1920–1946: A Quantitative Study*
23 Eric Stokes: *The Peasant and the Raj: Studies in Agrarian Society and Peasant Rebellion in Colonial India*
24 Michael Roberts: *Caste Conflict and Elite Formation: The Rise of a Karāva Elite in Sri Lanka, 1500–1931*
25 J. F. J. Toye: *Public Expenditure and Indian Development Policy, 1960–70*
26 Rashid Amjad: *Private Industrial Development in Pakistan, 1960–70*